# HISTORICAL DICTIONARIES OF AFRICA
## Edited by Jon Woronoff

1. *Cameroon,* by Victor T. Le Vine and Roger P. Nye. 1974. *Out of print. See No. 48.*
2. *The Congo,* 2nd ed., by Virginia Thompson and Richard Adloff. 1984. *Out of print. See No. 69.*
3. *Swaziland,* by John J. Grotpeter. 1975.
4. *The Gambia,* 2nd ed., by Harry A. Gailey. 1987. *Out of print. See No. 79.*
5. *Botswana,* by Richard P. Stevens. 1975. *Out of print. See No. 70.*
6. *Somalia,* by Margaret F. Castagno. 1975. *Out of print. See No. 87.*
7. *Benin (Dahomey),* 2nd ed., by Samuel Decalo. 1987. *Out of print. See No. 61.*
8. *Burundi,* by Warren Weinstein. 1976. *Out of print. See No. 73.*
9. *Togo,* 3rd ed., by Samuel Decalo. 1996.
10. *Lesotho,* by Gordon Haliburton. 1977. *Out of print. See No. 90.*
11. *Mali,* 3rd ed., by Pascal James Imperato. 1996.
12. *Sierra Leone,* by Cyril Patrick Foray. 1977.
13. *Chad,* 3rd ed., by Samuel Decalo. 1997.
14. *Upper Volta,* by Daniel Miles McFarland. 1978.
15. *Tanzania,* by Laura S. Kurtz. 1978.
16. *Guinea,* 3rd ed., by Thomas O'Toole with Ibrahima Bah-Lalya. 1995.
17. *Sudan,* by John Voll. 1978. *Out of print. See No. 53.*
18. *Rhodesia/Zimbabwe,* by R. Kent Rasmussen. 1979. *Out of print. See No. 46.*
19. *Zambia,* 2nd ed., by John J. Grotpeter, Brian V. Siegel, and James R. Pletcher. 1998.
20. *Niger,* 3rd ed., by Samuel Decalo. 1997.
21. *Equatorial Guinea,* 3rd ed., by Max Liniger-Goumaz. 2000.
22. *Guinea-Bissau,* 3rd ed., by Richard Lobban and Peter Mendy. 1997.
23. *Senegal,* by Lucie G. Colvin. 1981. *Out of print. See No. 65.*
24. *Morocco,* by William Spencer. 1980. *Out of print. See No. 71.*
25. *Malawi,* by Cynthia A. Crosby. 1980. *Out of print. See No. 84.*
26. *Angola,* by Phyllis Martin. 1980. *Out of print. See No. 92.*
27. *The Central African Republic,* by Pierre Kalck. 1980. *Out of print. See No. 51.*
28. *Algeria,* by Alf Andrew Heggoy. 1981. *Out of print. See No. 66.*
29. *Kenya,* by Bethwell A. Ogot. 1981. *Out of print. See No. 77.*
30. *Gabon,* by David E. Gardinier. 1981. *Out of print. See No. 58.*
31. *Mauritania,* by Alfred G. Gerteiny. 1981. *Out of print. See No. 68.*

32. *Ethiopia,* by Chris Prouty and Eugene Rosenfeld. 1981. *Out of print. See No. 91.*

33. *Libya,* 3rd ed., by Ronald Bruce St John. 1998.

34. *Mauritius,* by Lindsay Riviere. 1982. *Out of print. See No. 49.*

35. *Western Sahara,* by Tony Hodges. 1982. *Out of print. See No. 55.*

36. *Egypt,* by Joan Wucher King. 1984. *Out of print. See No. 89.*

37. *South Africa,* by Christopher Saunders. 1983. *Out of print. See No. 78.*

38. *Liberia,* by D. Elwood Dunn and Svend E. Holsoe. 1985. *Out of print. See No. 83.*

39. *Ghana,* by Daniel Miles McFarland. 1985. *Out of print. See No. 63.*

40. *Nigeria,* 2nd ed., by Anthony Oyewole and John Lucas. 2000.

41. *Côte d'Ivoire (The Ivory Coast),* 2nd ed., by Robert J. Mundt. 1995.

42. *Cape Verde,* 2nd ed., by Richard Lobban and Marilyn Halter. 1988. *Out of print. See No. 62.*

43. *Zaire,* by F. Scott Bobb. 1988. *Out of print. See No. 76.*

44. *Botswana,* 2nd ed., by Fred Morton, Andrew Murray, and Jeff Ramsay. 1989. *Out of print. See No. 70.*

45. *Tunisia,* 2nd ed., by Kenneth J. Perkins. 1997.

46. *Zimbabwe,* 2nd ed., by Steven C. Rubert and R. Kent Rasmussen. 1990. *Out of print. See No. 86.*

47. *Mozambique,* by Mario Azevedo. 1991. *Out of print. See No. 88.*

48. *Cameroon,* 2nd ed., by Mark W. DeLancey and H. Mbella Mokeba. 1990.

49. *Mauritius,* 2nd ed., by Sydney Selvon. 1991.

50. *Madagascar,* by Maureen Covell. 1995.

51. *The Central African Republic,* 2nd ed., by Pierre Kalck; translated by Thomas O'Toole. 1992. *Out of print. See No. 93.*

52. *Angola,* 2nd ed., by Susan H. Broadhead. 1992. *Out of print. See No. 92.*

53. *Sudan,* 2nd ed., by Carolyn Fluehr-Lobban, Richard A. Lobban Jr., and John Obert Voll. 1992. *Out of print. See No. 85.*

54. *Malawi,* 2nd ed., by Cynthia A. Crosby. 1993. *Out of print. See No. 84.*

55. *Western Sahara,* 2nd ed., by Anthony Pazzanita and Tony Hodges. 1994.

56. *Ethiopia and Eritrea,* 2nd ed., by Chris Prouty and Eugene Rosenfeld. 1994. *Out of print. See No. 91.*

57. *Namibia,* by John J. Grotpeter. 1994.

58. *Gabon,* 2nd ed., by David E. Gardinier. 1994.

59. *Comoro Islands,* by Martin Ottenheimer and Harriet Ottenheimer. 1994.

60. *Rwanda,* by Learthen Dorsey. 1994.

61. *Benin,* 3rd ed., by Samuel Decalo. 1995.
62. *Republic of Cape Verde,* 3rd ed., by Richard Lobban and Marlene Lopes. 1995.
63. *Ghana,* 2nd ed., by David Owusu-Ansah and Daniel Miles McFarland. 1995.
64. *Uganda,* by M. Louise Pirouet. 1995.
65. *Senegal,* 2nd ed., by Andrew F. Clark and Lucie Colvin Phillips. 1994.
66. *Algeria,* 2nd ed., by Phillip Chiviges Naylor and Alf Andrew Heggoy. 1994.
67. *Egypt,* 2nd ed., by Arthur Goldschmidt Jr. 1994. *Out of print. See No. 89.*
68. *Mauritania,* 2nd ed., by Anthony G. Pazzanita. 1996.
69. *Congo,* 3rd ed., by Samuel Decalo, Virginia Thompson, and Richard Adloff. 1996.
70. *Botswana,* 3rd ed., by Jeff Ramsay, Barry Morton, and Fred Morton. 1996.
71. *Morocco,* 2nd ed., by Thomas K. Park. 1996.
72. *Tanzania,* 2nd ed., by Thomas P. Ofcansky and Rodger Yeager. 1997.
73. *Burundi,* 2nd ed., by Ellen K. Eggers. 1997.
74. *Burkina Faso,* 2nd ed., by Daniel Miles McFarland and Lawrence Rupley. 1998.
75. *Eritrea,* by Tom Killion. 1998.
76. *Democratic Republic of the Congo (Zaire),* by F. Scott Bobb. 1999. (Revised edition of *Historical Dictionary of Zaire*, No. 43)
77. *Kenya,* 2nd ed., by Robert M. Maxon and Thomas P. Ofcansky. 2000.
78. *South Africa,* 2nd ed., by Christopher Saunders and Nicholas Southey. 2000.
79. *The Gambia,* 3rd ed., by Arnold Hughes and Harry A. Gailey. 2000.
80. *Swaziland,* 2nd ed., by Alan R. Booth. 2000.
81. *Republic of Cameroon,* 3rd ed., by Mark W. DeLancey and Mark Dike DeLancey. 2000.
82. *Djibouti,* by Daoud A. Alwan and Yohanis Mibrathu. 2000.
83. *Liberia,* 2nd ed., by D. Elwood Dunn, Amos J. Beyan, and Carl Patrick Burrowes. 2001.
84. *Malawi,* 3rd ed., by Owen J. Kalinga and Cynthia A. Crosby. 2001.
85. *Sudan,* 3rd ed., by Richard A. Lobban Jr., Robert S. Kramer, and Carolyn Fluehr-Lobban. 2002.
86. *Zimbabwe,* 3rd ed., by Steven C. Rubert and R. Kent Rasmussen. 2001.
87. *Somalia,* 2nd ed., by Mohamed Haji Mukhtar. 2002.
88. *Mozambique,* 2nd ed., by Mario Azevedo, Emmanuel Nnadozie, and Tomé Mbuia João. 2003.

# Historical Dictionary of the Central African Republic

Pierre Kalck
Translated by Xavier-Samuel Kalck

*Historical Dictionaries of Africa, No. 93*

The Scarecrow Press, Inc.
Lanham, Maryland • Toronto • Oxford
2005

# SCARECROW PRESS, INC.

Published in the United States of America
by Scarecrow Press, Inc.
A wholly owned subsidiary of The Rowman & Littlefield Publishing Group, Inc.
4501 Forbes Boulevard, Suite 200
Lanham, Maryland 20706
www.scarecrowpress.com

PO Box 317
Oxford
OX2 9RU, UK

British Library Cataloguing in Publication Information Available

**Library of Congress Cataloging-in-Publication Data**

Kalck, Pierre.
  Historical dictionary of the Central African Republic / Pierre Kalck ;
translated by Xavier-Samuel Kalck.— 3rd ed.
      p. cm. — (Historical dictionaries of Africa ; 93)
  Includes bibliographical references.
  ISBN 0-8108-4913-5 (hardcover : alk. paper)
  1. Central African Republic—History—Dictionaries. I. Title. II. African
historical dictionaries ; no. 93.
DT546.35.K353 2005
967.41'003—dc22

2004012177

♾️<sup>TM</sup> The paper used in this publication meets the minimum requirements of
American National Standard for Information Sciences—Permanence of Paper
for Printed Library Materials, ANSI/NISO Z39.48-1992.
Manufactured in the United States of America.

*This book is dedicated to the late President Barthélémy Boganda, founder of the Central African Republic, and to all those who have given the best of their lives to the building of this country.*

—Pierre Kalck

The translator also wishes to acknowledge how enduring was Pierre Kalck's commitment to the completion of this book, which more than his last work represented his life's work.

# Contents

# Editor's Foreword

One of the principal goals of this series of African Historical Dictionaries is to provide information on those countries that are least known. The Central African Republic (CAR) is certainly one of them. It is poorly researched even in French, and precious little exists in English. So the publication of this third edition is definitely a welcome event. It fills gaps in our knowledge of what has been happening, and sheds more light on a country that was only widely covered—and then sensationally—under the reign of the self-appointed and ill-fated Emperor Bokassa. Things have definitely taken a turn for the better, but not always that much better, and there is no doubt that the CAR remains one of the continent's poorest countries, faced with innumerable problems, not the least of which is forming a satisfactory government that can lead it forward instead of dragging it down.

This new edition of the *Historical Dictionary of the Central African Republic* appears more than a decade after the previous edition, so there is a lot of ground to cover, especially since there have been so many twists and turns in the intervening period. Perhaps the easiest way to follow them is through the chronology, which plots the trajectory month by month and sometimes even day by day. But the situation is usually sufficiently confusing that dictionary entries are essential to learn more about the specific events, institutions and parties, and especially persons. The cast of characters is large and varied, and some of the old ones keep coming back, while new ones often have just a fleeting career. Moreover, the present situation only really makes sense when seen on the panorama of the past, a rather "tragic" one as the author shows. The bibliography may be a bit disappointing, since it has not changed that much, which only confirms the above comment that the Central African Republic remains sadly underresearched.

This third edition, like the previous two, was written by the leading authority on the country, Pierre Kalck. He has known the region since well before independence, having served as a French administrator in the then Ubangui-Shari from 1949 to 1959. He continued on in various capacities in the young state, where he was a friend of President Barthélémy Boganda, who soon passed away tragically, and adviser to the first head of government, Dr. Abel Goumba, who has repeatedly resurfaced. Until 1967, he acted as economic adviser and then the CAR's permanent representative to GATT and ECOSOC. During that period, and until recently, he continued writing historical, political, and economic studies as well as one of the two major works in English, *Central African Republic: A Failure in Decolonization*. He passed away recently while this book was being completed and will be sorely missed by many in the country and by others who only know the CAR from his writing.

We are thus very grateful that Jacques Serre, a former graduate of the French Overseas Academy who has long known the Central African Republic and the author of several books on this country, was so helpful as to update the introduction and expand the recent chronology for this edition. This has greatly contributed to producing a more timely study. It should also be mentioned that the first and second editions of this volume were translated by Thomas O'Toole, a specialist in African studies at St. Cloud State University in Minnesota and the author of another major work, *The Central African Republic: The Continent's Hidden Heart*. The third edition was translated by Xavier-Samuel Kalck, the author's grandson.

Jon Woronoff  
Series Editor

# Acknowledgments

The publication of the third edition of the dictionary gives the author the opportunity to thank all those who have helped and assisted him in this research, especially

- Professor Abel Goumba, now vice president of the Central African Republic, and a friend of the author of this book since becoming the first Ubanguian president in 1958.
- Professor Thomas O'Toole, presently a professor of African Studies at St. Cloud University in Minnesota, and earlier a history teacher at the Boganda High School in Bangui, who translated the first two editions of this historical dictionary and whose work has helped make Central Africa known in America.
- Yves Boulvert, Jean Cantournet, and Jacques Serre, members of the French Overseas Academy, who thanks to their perfect knowledge of Central African history have allowed me to fill in the gaps and correct any errors in the previous editions.
- All the friends whose contributions have been highly valuable to me over the years, especially the Father in charge of the archives of the Holy-Ghost Fathers and Pastor Jean-Arnold de Clermont, president of the French Protestant Church Consistory, and Jean-Bosco Peleket, joint director of the intercommunal hospital in Montreuil-sous-Bois.

# Acronyms and Abbreviations

| | |
|---|---|
| ACDA | Agence Centrafricaine de Développement Agricole |
| ADECAF | Agence de Développement de la Caféiculture |
| ADP | Alliance Démocratique pour le Progrès |
| AEF | Afrique équatoriale française |
| ANDE | Agence Nationale pour le Développement et l'Elevage |
| ANECA | Association Nationale des Etudiants Centrafricains |
| ASOM | Académie des Sciences d'Outre-Mer |
| ATOC | Assemblée Territoriale de l'Oubangui-Chari |
| BADEA | Banque Arabe pour le Développement de l'Afrique |
| BDPA | Bureau pour le Développement de la Production Agricole |
| BEAC | Banque des Etats d'Afrique Central |
| BEPC | Brevet d'Etudes du Premier Cycle |
| BM1/BM2 | Bataillon de Marche 1 et 2 de 1'AEF |
| BONUCA | Bureau d'Observation des Nations Unies en Centrafrique |
| CATADIAM | Centrafricaine de Taillerie de Diamants |
| CBC | Commercial Bank Centrafrique |
| CCCE | Caisse Centrale de Coopération Economique |
| CEM | Compagnie Equatoriale des Mines |
| CEMAC | Communauté Economique et Monétaire d'Afrique Centrale |
| CEMI | Commission Electorale Mixte Indépendante |
| CENTRAMINES | Société Centrafricaine des Mines |
| CFA | Colonies Françaises d'Afrique, *then* Communauté financière africaine |

| | |
|---|---|
| CFD | Caisse Française pour le Développement |
| CFD | Concertation des Forces Démocratiques |
| CFDT | Compagnie Française pour le Développement des fibres Textiles |
| CHEAM | Centre des Hautes Etudes sur l'Afrique et l'Asie Modernes |
| CMOO | Compagnie Minière de l'Oubangui Oriental |
| CMRN | Comité Militaire de Redressement National |
| CN | Convention Nationale |
| CNR | Conférence Nationale de Réconciliation |
| CNRI | Centre National de Recherches et d'Investigations |
| COMESSA | Communauté des Etats Sahélo-Sahariens |
| COTONFRAN | Société Cotonnière Française |
| COTOUBANGUI | Société Cotonnière du Haut-Oubangui |
| COTOUNA | Compagnie Cotonnière de l'Ouham-Nana |
| CPO | Concertation des Partis d'Opposition |
| CTP-PAS | Comité Technique Permanent du suivi des Programmes d'Ajustement Structurel |
| CTRO | Compagnie de Transport Routier de l'Oubangui |
| CURDHACA | Centre Universitaire de Recherche et de Documentation en Histoire et Archéologie Centrafricaines |
| DDI | Diamond Distributors Incorporated |
| ECA | Empire Centrafricain |
| ECOSOC | Economic and Social Council (of the United Nations) |
| E(E)C | European (Economic) Community |
| EFAO | Eléments Français d'Assistance Opérationnelle |
| EMPROCAF | Entente Professionnelle des Producteurs de café |
| ENERCA | Energie Centrafricaine |
| EU | European Union |
| FAC | Fonds d'Aide et de Coopération |
| FACA | Forces Armées Centrafricaines |
| FASR | Facilité d'Ajustement Structurel Renforcé |
| FC | Forum Civique |
| FED | Fonds Européens de Développement |
| FIDES | Fonds d'investissement pour le Développement Economique et Social |

| | |
|---|---|
| FIDH | Fédération Internationale des Droits de l'Homme |
| FLN | Front de Libération Nationale |
| FLO | Front de Libération des Oubanguiens |
| FLPC | Front de Libération du Peuple Centrafricain |
| FNEC | Fédération Nationale des Eleveurs Centrafricains |
| FODEM | Forum Démocratique pour la Modernité |
| FORSUIR | Forces de Sûreté des Institutions de la République |
| FPO | Front Patriotique Oubanguien |
| FPO-PT | Front Patriotique Oubanguien—Parti du Travail |
| FPP | Front Patriotique pour le Progrès |
| FRUD | Front Uni pour la restauration de l'Unité nationale et de la Démocratie |
| GADD | Gouvernement d'Action pour la Défense de la Démocratie |
| GATT | General Agreement on Tariffs and Trade |
| GDP | Gross domestic product |
| GIR | Groupement d'Intérêts Ruraux |
| GIRA | Groupement Indépendant de Réflexion et d'Action |
| GUN | Gouvernement d'Union Nationale |
| ICAT | Industrie Centrafricaine du Textile |
| ICCA | Industrie Cotonnière Centrafricaine |
| ICOT | Industrie Cotonnière (de l'Oubangui) |
| ILO | Intergroupe Libéral Oubanguien |
| ILO | International Labour Organisation |
| IMF | International Monetary Fund |
| IPHOM | Institut d'Histoire des Pays d'Outre-Mer |
| IRD | Institut de Recherches pour le Développement; formerly, Overseas Science and Technique Studies Center (ORSTOM) |
| JOC | Jeunesse Oubanguienne Catholique |
| MCLN | Mouvement Centrafricain de Libération Nationale |
| MDD | Mouvement pour la Démocratie et le Développement |
| MDI | Mouvement pour la Démocratie et l'Indépendance |
| MDI-PS | Mouvement pour la Démocratie, l'Indépendance et le Progrès Social |

| | |
|---|---|
| MDREC | Mouvement Démocratique pour la Renaissance et l'Evolution du Centrafrique |
| MEDAC | Mouvement pour l'Evolution Démocratique de l'Afrique Centrale |
| MESAN | Mouvement pour l'Evolution sociale de l'Afrique Noire |
| MINURCA | Mission des Nations Unies pour la République Centrafricaine |
| MISAB | Mission d'Interposition et de Surveillance des accords de Bangui |
| MLNC | Mouvement de Libération Nationale Centrafricaine |
| MLPC | Mouvement de Libération du Peuple Centrafricain |
| MSA | Mouvement Socialiste Africain |
| NEPAP | Nouveau Partenariat pour le Développement de l'Afrique |
| OAS | Organisation de l'Armée Secrète |
| OAU | Organization of African Unity |
| PETROCA | Pétrole de Centrafrique |
| PLD | Parti Libéral Démocrate |
| PRA | Parti du Regroupement Africain |
| PRC | Parti Républicain Centrafricain |
| PRP | Parti Républicain du Progrès |
| PSD | Parti Social Démocrate |
| PST | Projet Sectoriel des Transports |
| PUN | Parti de l'Unité Nationale |
| RCA | République Centrafricaine |
| RDA | Rassemblement Démocratique Africain |
| RDC | Rassemblement Démocratique Centrafricain |
| RDC | République Démocratique du Congo |
| REP | Régiment Etranger de Parachutistes |
| RGR | Rassemblement des Gauches Républicaines |
| RMI | Régiment Mixte d'Intervention |
| RPF | Rassemblement du Peuple Français |
| SAB | Société Anonyme Belge du Haut-Congo |
| SAFA | Société Agricole et Forestière Africaine |
| SAM | Société Africaine des Mines |

| | |
|---|---|
| SAP | Société Africaine de Prévoyance |
| SCED | Société Centrafricaine d'Exploitation Diamantifère |
| SEITA | Société d'Exploitation Industrielle du Tabac et des Allumettes |
| SERD | Section Enquêtes, Recherches et Documentation |
| SIP | Société Indigène de Prévoyance |
| SMDR | Société Mutuelle de Développement Rural |
| SMEO | Société Minière d'Est Oubangui |
| SNEA | Société Nationale d'Exploitation Agricole |
| SOCADA | Société Centrafricaine de Développement Agricole |
| SOCOCA | Société Cotonnière Centrafricaine |
| SOCOULOLE | Société Coopérative de l'Oubangui-Lobaye Lesse |
| TOCAGES | Total Centrafrique Gestion |
| UBAC | Union Bancaire de l'Afrique Centrale |
| UCCA | Union Commerciale Cotonnière Centrafricaine |
| UDC | Union Démocratique Centrafricaine |
| UDEAC | Union Douanière des Etats de l'Afrique Centrale |
| UFAPC | Union des Forces Acquises à la Paix et au Changement |
| UGTCA | Union Générale des Travailleurs Centrafricains |
| UN | United Nations |
| UNDP | United Nations Development Program |
| UNELCO | Union des Sociétés Electriques Coloniales |
| UPR | Union Pour la République |
| URAC | Union des Républiques d'Afrique Centrale |
| USCA | Union des Scolaires Centrafricains |
| USP | Unité de Sécurité Présidentielle |
| USTC | Union Syndicale des Travailleurs Centrafricains |
| WHO | World Health Organization |
| WTO | World Trade Organization (ex-GATT) |

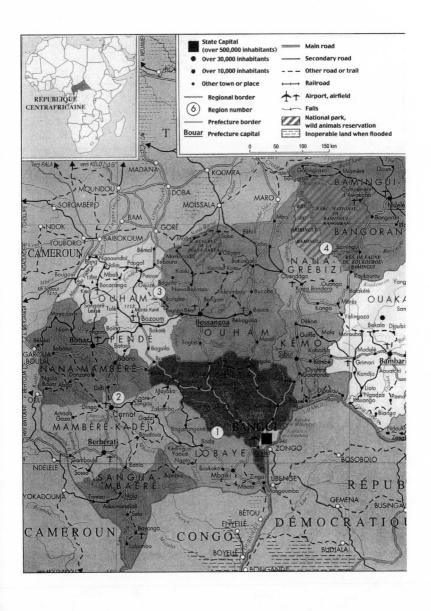

RÉPUBLIQUE
CENTRAFRICAINE

State Capital
(over 500,000 inhabitants)

● Over 30,000 inhabitants

● Over 10,000 inhabitants

• Other town or place

—— Regional border

⑥ Region number

---------- Prefecture border

**Bouar** Prefecture capital

═══ Main road

—— Secondary road

– – – Other road or trail

＋—＋ Railroad

✈ Airport, airfield

✕ Falls

▨ National park,
wild animals reservation

▤ Inoperable land when flooded

0    50    100    150 km

# CENTRAL AFRICAN REPUBLIC

# A Note on Spelling

Problems always occur when writing Arabic and African words in the Latin alphabet. This is especially true when very different spellings of the same words in English and French have become standard. In most cases the variations are easy to recognize, as with Ubangui-Oubangui, Oudaï-Wadaï, and Darfur-Darfour, and have been thus indicated. Any decision as to which form of spelling to use in this book would be arbitrary, especially since authors in the English language often opt for the French spelling. The translator of this book simply sought to find a middle ground and has used the usual French spellings except when a reasonably common English usage was available. As a matter of principle, spelling has most often followed that used by the U.S. scholar Dennis D. Cordell, whose works on the Central African Republic are standard references on the country's history.

An issue that must be brought to the reader's attention is the important change in usage regarding names, such as Ndélé or Mbaïki, which were until recently written *N'délé* and *M'baïki*. The use of an apostrophe after the first capital letter is now considered wrong, and this edition has been amended accordingly.

# Chronology

**ca. 1800**  Ngoura, Kogobili leader, founds the Zandé nation. Ndounga founds the Bandia kingdom of the Nzakara.

**ca. 1820**  The Baya people establish themselves on Central African soil due to attacks by the Fulbé of Adamawa.

**ca. 1825**  The Mandjia people settle north of the Ubangui.

**ca. 1830**  Beginning of the migration of the Banda people from Ferra toward the south and west. In the northeast part of the Central African territory the Banguirmian prince, Omar, called Djougoultoum, founds the Wadian province of Dar-Alkuti.

**ca. 1850**  Zenith of the Zandé nation with the Angoura dynasty. Zenith of the Bandia nation with the Abaya dynasty.

**1854–1864**  The commercial brotherhood of "merchant lords" of the Upper Nile (Bahara) multiply their slaving operations in the eastern part of the Central African territory.

**1867–1872**  Zubayr (Ziber) makes himself master of a vast territory from Darfur to Mbomou, then recognizes the authority of Egypt over his domain.

**1877**  Suleyman ben Zubayr—successor of his father, who is arrested in Cairo—revolts against Egypt. The Zandé sultans disassociate themselves from him.

**1879**  Rabih quits Suleyman ben Zubayr, who submits to the Sudanese authorities. Rabih installs himself in Dar Fertit.

**1882**  Rabih establishes his capital at Gribindji at the headwaters of the Gribingui.

**1883**   Nzakara Sultan Bali defeats Rabih at Fode.

**1884   20 February:** "Discovery" of the Ubangui River by the English pastor George Grenfell from Kinshasa.

**1885**   Mandjia defeat of Rabih at Kaga Kazomba.

**1887   29 April:** Franco-Leopoldian convention recognizes the French rights to the north bank of the Ubangui.

**1889   25 June:** Foundation of the French post at Bangui.

**1890**   Coup d'etat in Dar al-Kuti. Rabih removes Sultan Kober and replaces him with Kober's nephew, Muhamm ad as-Sanusi. **24 September:** Paul Crampel, head of the exploration mission of the Committee of French Africa, arrives at Bangui, designated by Brazza as "delegate of the Commission General in Ubangui."

**1891   8 April:** Paul Crampel, marching toward Chad, is killed not far from Aoul by Muhamm ad as-Sanusi's men.

**1891–1894**   French exploration missions in Central African territory led by Dybowski, Maistre, Fourneau, Brazza, and Clozel. Protectorate treaties with the leaders of central Ubangui and the Upper Sangha. Leopoldian mission in Mbomou and Upper Kotto in defiance of the 19 April 1887 convention. Protectorate treaties with the Bandia Sultans Bangassou and Rafaï, and the Zandé sultan, Zemio.

**1894   15 March:** The Franco-German convention fixes the limits between the French Congo and the German Cameroons. **28 August:** The Franco-Leopoldian convention recognizes French rights to the regions situated north of the Mbomou. Evacuation of this zone by Leopold's agents and French movement toward the Nile. **October**: Invasion of Dar-al-Kuti by Wadian army of Cherfeddine. As-Sanusi flees.

**1896   17 April:** Occupation of Dem Ziber in Bahr-el Ghazal by Victor Liotard, government commissioner in Upper Ubangui. **30 June:** Victory at Bouare, won by the Baya and the Banda-Yaguere, commanded by the French administrator Alphonse Goujon, against the army of the Fulbé's lamido of Ngaounderé.

**1897   6 April:** Arrival at Bangui of the French Congo Nile mission led by Captain Jean-Baptiste Marchand. **1 November:** After signing an agreement with the Sultan of Baguirmi, Emile Gentil comes to the shores of Lake Chad in Rabih's empire. **12 December:** As-Sanusi accepts a French protectorate over Dar-al-Kuti and undertakes the devastation of Upper Kotto.

**1898  10 July:** Arrival of the Marchand mission at Fashoda on the Nile. **16 July:** Establishment in Paris of a commission of high officials in charge of the partition of the French possessions in the Congo and Ubangui among 39 concessionary companies endowed with regal rights.

**1899  21 March:** A Franco-British convention attributes Bahr-el-Ghazal, occupied by the French of Ubangui, to the Anglo-Egyptian Sudan. This convention places Wadaï in the French zone of influence. **24 May:** A circular of the minister of the colonies orders the French colonial administration to completely support the actions of concessionary companies. The concession decrees are put into effect gradually from May to December. **17 July:** Rabih's troops, after reoccupying Kouno, inflict a severe defeat on the Sultan of the Baguirmi, Gaourang, and the French administrator Bretonnet at Togbuo.

**1900  22 April:** Defeat of Rabih's army by three French missions coming from Algiers, St. Louis in Senegal, and Bangui. Rabih is killed in the combat. His empire breaks up in the following months. **13 August:** The French parliament votes a law confirming the abandonment of government subsidies to the colonies and placing the costs of all equipment and upkeep on the colonial budgets.

**1900–1904** Wars of the Upper Ubangui sultans against neighboring ethnic groups, wars of as-Sanusi against the Kreich and the Banda of Upper Kotto.

**1903  18 February:** New protectorate treaty between France and as-Sanusi. **29 December:** Decree creating a new colony made up of the region of Upper Ubangui and of the Shari under the name of *Ubangui-Shari*.

**1902–1904** Mandjia insurrection against the tax and portage demands.

**1904–1905** Insurrection of the population against the concessionary companies. Military occupation of Lobaye and of Ibenga.

**1905  16 May:** Pierre Savorgnan de Brazza's arrival in the Congo and Ubangui on an inspection mission.

**1906  19–21 February:** French parliament debates the extortions ascertained by Brazza.

**1906–1908**  New military interventions into the western forest zone.

**1907**  The Mpoko affair. Discovery of numerous crimes committed by the agents of this company.

**1908–1911**  Military reconquest operations throughout the territory.

**1909  July:** Surrender of Baram-Bakie, leader of the Banda insurgents.

**1910**  The French Congo and its dependencies take the name of *French Equatorial Africa (Afrique Equatoriale Française).* **July:** As-Sanusi's army takes Ouanda-Djallé, Youlou exodus.

**1911  11 January:** As-Sanusi is killed during his arrest by Lieutenant Gründfelder. **November 4:** France cedes to Germany an important part of French Equatorial Africa, notably all of the western part of the territory of present-day Central Africa.

**1912  17 December 17:** Captain Souclier takes Ouanda Djallé, defended by Kamoun, son of as-Sanusi.

**1914**  Discovery of the first Central African diamond near Ippy.

**1914  August–December:** Reoccupation by the French military of the regions ceded to Germany on 4 November 1911.

**1915**  Dji and Bangana insurrections.

**1916  17 May:** Belgian, French, and British operation against the insurrection of Mopoi Inguizimo, heir of the Zandé sultans.

**1918**  Bougbou and Mobaye insurrection.

**1925**  Arrival in Bangui of André Gide, who later reveals the Lobaye and Upper Sangha scandals. Denunciation by the leader Samba-Ngotto of the Botembélé massacre.

**1926  February:** The village of the Bougbou leader Ajou is taken and shot.

**1928–1931**  So-called Kongo-Wara War, also known as the "Baya War." A general uprising of the Baya and numerous other groups in French Equatorial Africa against the colonizers.

**1928   11 December:** Karinou (Karnou), prophet of the Baya insurrection, is discovered. He is allowed to be murdered.

**1929**   Scandals in the construction of the Congo-Ocean rail route, on which numerous Central African laborers died, are revealed by Albert Londres and Robert Poulaine. **24 June:** Berandjoko, in rebellion since 1906 against the colonial authorities, is, in his turn, captured and killed in the Lobaye forests.

**1931**   Operations against the Karre, insurgents for 20 years, who have taken refuge in the Pana mountains.

**1934   15 November:** Administrative reorganization of the French Equatorial Africa colony. The Ubangui-Shari region, including the Sara country, represents more than half of the French Equatorial Africa population.

**1936   29 April and 28 December:** New administrative reorganization of French Equatorial Africa. Detached from Ubangui-Shari, the Sara country is reunited with Chad.

**1938   27 March:** Ordination of the first Ubanguian Catholic priest, Barthélémy Boganda.

**1940   20 July:** Defeat of a Gaullist putsch at Bangui. **28 August:** Gaullist coup d'etat at Brazzaville. Colonel de Larminat takes power. **29–30 August:** Armed French civilians, claiming allegiance to the Gaullist movement, take control of the town of Bangui. **3 September:** Having maintained their position in the military camp and remaining loyal to the Vichy regime, Commander of Arms Henri Cammas and his officers surrender to Captain Robert de Roux. **21 October:** General Charles de Gaulle arrives in Bangui. **28 December:** The infantry battalions, BM1 and BM2, with many Ubanguians, leave for the Free French theaters of operation.

**1941   27 February:** Decree on the administration reorganization of French Equatorial Africa, which changes it from a unitary colony and defines it as a group of four territories.

**1942   May–June:** The Ubanguian rifles become famous in the battle of Bir-Hakeim on Libyan front.

**1944   30 January:** Opening at Brazzaville (with De Gaulle present) of the conference on the French African Empire.

**1945   19 December:** Governor General Bayardelle envisages the division of French Equatorial Africa into three territories: the Gabon-Middle Congo, the Islamic Area of Chad, the Upper-River Country, with Bangui as its headquarters. The Chambers of Commerce oppose this project.

**1946   11 April:** A law bans all forms of forced labor still remaining in the French overseas possessions. **7 June:** A Bangui Chamber of Commerce motion holds that the measures adopted by the Parliament can only be applied where populations are less backward than in French Equatorial Africa. **July:** Paris meeting of the States General of Colonization. The colonists' representatives criticize the accession to French citizenship of native Africans as well as the ban on forced labor. **19–29 October:** A new administrative reorganization of French Equatorial Africa confirms its division into four territories.

**1947   19 December:** Adoption by the Grand Council of French Equatorial Africa, at the proposal of the Ubanguian Antoine Darlan, of the motion that French Equatorial Africa henceforth take the name Equatorial France.

**1949   28 September:** Constitutive meeting at Bangui of the Mouvement pour l'évolution sociale de l'Afrique noire (MESAN; Movement for the Social Evolution of Black Africa), founded by Deputy Boganda.

**1950** Constitution in Ubangui of 27 sections of the RPF opposed to MESAN.

**1951   10 January:** Bokanga incident in Lobaye in a local products market. Deputy Boganda and his wife are arrested. **17 June:** Reelection of Barthélémy Boganda, in spite of strong opposition by the administration, colonists, and the missions.

**1952   30 March:** MESAN is assured of control of the new Ubangui-Shari Territorial Assembly.

**1953   17 March:** Trip to Bangui of General de Gaulle, who disavows the negative action of the Rassemblement du Peuple Français (RPF; French People Party) sections.

**1954   30 April–1 May:** Berberati riot. Calm is restored by Deputy Boganda's arrival on the scene.

**1956   2 January:** Reelection of Boganda. **23 June:** Loi-Cadre (Enabling Act) called the Defferre Law gives way to domestic autonomy for the overseas territories. **18 November:** Deputy Boganda is elected mayor of Bangui.

**1957   February:** Last administrative reorganization of French Equatorial Africa. Each of the four territories receives its own legal status and financial autonomy. **31 March:** MESAN wins all of the seats in the Ubangui-Shari Territorial Assembly. A little later, Boganda is elected president of the Grand Council of French Equatorial Africa. **17 May:** Constitution of the first Ubanguian government presided over by Dr. Abel Goumba.

**1958   28 September:** At Boganda's call, the Ubanguian electors respond "yes" to the constitutional referendum instituting a French Community composed of France and its overseas territories. **24–25 November:** Conference at Brazzaville of the political leaders of the four territories of French Equatorial Africa. Failure of Boganda's project to create a large Central African Republic made up of, in the first stage, French Equatorial Africa, and destined to be the core of the future United States of Latin Africa, from Douala to Rwanda and from Chad to Angola. **1 December:** Since Congo, Gabon, and Chad have opted for membership in the French Community as separate states on 28 November, Ubangui-Shari proclaims a Central African Republic limited to its own territory. Boganda takes charge of the government, seconded by Goumba.

**1959   16 February:** The Assembly adopts the democratic constitution presented to Boganda. **29 March:** Boganda disappears in an airplane crash. **30 March:** Dr. Goumba takes charge of an interim government. **5 May:** David Dacko is elected president of the government by the Assembly. **July:** Goumba is excluded from the government. **7 October:** Threatened by a censure motion filed against him, Dacko has the Assembly surrounded by his partisans. The Assembly rejects the censure motion.

**1960   9 May:** Pierre Maleombho is rejected as the Assembly's president and replaced by Michel Adama-Tamboux, a Dacko partisan. **30 June–14 July:** Chaos reigns in the neighboring Belgian Congo. **13 August:** The Central African Republic gains independence. Cooperative agreements are signed with France. **14 August:** Dacko provisional chief of state. **25 September:** Dr. Goumba's opposition party Mouvement pour l'évolution démocratique de l'Afrique centrale (MEDAC; Movement for the Democratic Evolution of Central Africa) achieves relative success in the partial elections for the National Assembly. **25 November:** The Assembly agrees to adopt the restrictions of public liberties proposed by Dacko, who guarantees their mandate to the deputies until 1964. MEDAC demonstration against the laws. **24 December:** Arrest of Dr. Goumba and other MEDAC personalities.

**1961  1 January:** Central Africanization of the territorial administration. Nomination of prefects and subprefects. **26 June:** Dacko dissolves the youth committees formed in his own party.

**1962** Creation of a Central African national army. **January–June:** Trial, before the criminal court in Bangui, of Goumba and of his friends. **28 July–1 August:** MESAN congress at Bambari. Creation of a MESAN direction committee constituted by Dacko. **November:** Dissolution of all political parties other than MESAN. Creation of a single union.

**1963  15 November:** A constitutional law installs a presidential regime.

**1964  5 January:** Election of the single candidate, Dacko, as president of the Republic for seven years. **19 March:** Election of a new National Assembly. The single national MESAN slate is elected. **20 November:** Adoption by the Assembly of a new constitution proposed by Dacko. Hardening of the presidential regime and the state-party system. **1 December:** Colonel Jean-Bedel Bokassa is appointed chief of staff of the Central African army. **8 December:** Brazzaville Treaty creating and organizing the Union douanière des états de l'Afrique centrale (UDEAC; Economic and Customs Union of the Central African States) comprising Cameroon, Gabon, Chad, and the Central African Republic.

**1965  13 May:** Dacko announces measures against widespread corruption. **31 December:** Flight of Dacko. The Commander of the Gendarmerie Jean Izamo, ready to take power, is lured into an ambush by Chief of Staff Jean-Bedel Bokassa and assassinated.

**1966  1 January:** Under the direction of Captain Alexandre Banza, the Central African military takes control of the administrative center of Bangui. Dacko is arrested and turns his power over to Colonel Bokassa.

**4–8 January:** Constitutional acts, based on Vichy regime models, install a dictatorship. Abolition of the 20 November 1964 Constitution. **6 January:** People's Republic of China diplomats are expelled from Bangui.

**1967 10 November:** At Bokassa's request, a French paratroop detachment of the 11th Intervention Division is sent to Bangui for a "tropical country acclimatization exercise."

**1968 9 December:** The Central African Republic returns to UDEAC.

**1969 February:** General de Gaulle receives Bokassa on an official visit to Paris. **11–12 April:** Arrest and execution of Lieutenant Colonel Banza, accused of conspiracy. **24 December:** Following the sending of an important delegation to Moscow by Bokassa, the French government assures the Central African head of state of its "fraternal esteem."

**1970 June:** Expulsion of the director of the French Cultural Center. **July:** Cooperative agreements with the USSR and Romania. **September:** Expulsion of 70 French agricultural technicians. **December:** Missions in Bangui of Jacques Foccart, French Secretary-General for African and Malagasy Affairs, and Yvon Bourges, Secretary of State for Foreign Affairs.

**1971 29 September:** At Bokassa's instigation, the French ambassador to Bangui is assailed by demonstrators who burn the French flag. **December:** The French Minister of Justice asks that proceedings be sought for offending a foreign head of state against a weekly that had lampooned Bokassa.

**1972 4 March:** Bokassa, who has granted himself all the grades of general, is proclaimed President for Life of the Central African Republic and of his party by the MESAN Congress. **1 August:** Beatings at the Bangui prison directed in person by Bokassa. Central Africans are called to march before the cadavers. **15 August:** Bokassa speaks abusively with regard to Kurt Waldheim, Secretary-General of the United Nations.

**1973 18 October:** Diplomatic relations with Israel are broken. **8 November:** Ordinance making the diamond trade a free market.

**1974 2 January:** Madame Elisabeth Domitien, vice president of MESAN, is appointed Prime Minister. **10 April:** Attempted plot against

Bokassa. **11 May:** The Union commerciale cotonnière centrafricaine (UCCA; Central African Cotton Trade Union, of which the Central African state already possessed 44.8 percent of the capital) is nationalized. **16 May:** The Central African government closes the French consulate general at Bangui. **20 May:** Bokassa names himself marshal. **27 May:** Bokassa accuses France, and notably the military *cooperants*, of having been the instigators of the 10 April plot.

**1975    23 January:** The Equatorial Guinean dictator Francisco Macias Nguema is officially received in Bangui. A friendship and cooperation agreement between the two nations is signed. **6–7 March:** The president of the French Republic, Valéry Giscard d'Estaing, makes an official visit to the Central African Republic during a Franco-African conference at Bangui.

**1976    3 February:** At the Bangui airport Bokassa's son-in-law, squadron leader Fidèle Obrou, leader of the Central African air force, his brother Martin Meya, and another officer attempt to assassinate Bokassa. They are slaughtered during a six-hour fusillade. Some days later, the military tribunal pronounces eight death sentences and heavy penalties against military personnel accused of having participated in this conspiracy. **30 March:** Withdrawal of the Canadian-American Central African mixed private-public company Sociéte centrafricaine d'exploitation diamantifère (SCED; Central African Diamond Company) of all its bonds and permits and the expulsion of its agents. **22 May:** Grant of a diamond purchasing, selling, and mining monopoly to the Société centrafricaine arabe des mines (Arabic Central African Mining Company). **5 September:** Constitution of a new government, called the Council of the Revolution. Ange Patassé is Prime Minister. **17 September:** Ex-President Dacko is appointed Bokassa's personal adviser. **17 October:** Official visit of Colonel Mouammar Kadhafi, Libyan head of state. **20 October:** Bokassa announces his conversion to Islam, takes the name Salah Eddine Ahmed Bou-Kassa, and invites the Central African people to follow his example. **Late November:** A new attempt on Bokassa's life, of military origin. **4 December:** The extraordinary session of the MESAN congress, renewed, adopts a new constitution, establishing Central Africa as an empire of hereditary monarchical parliamentary type. Marshal Bokassa, President for Life of the Central African Republic, becomes emperor under the name Bokassa the First.

He abandons the Muslim religion. **14 December:** Constitution of the first imperial government directed by Ange Patassé, Prime Minister. Bokassa no longer assumes direct government responsibility. An imperial court is constituted at Berengo, the location of Bokassa's residence.

**1977 August:** The ambassador of the United States to Bangui is recalled following the imprisonment of journalists. **4 December:** Ostentatious coronation ceremony at Bangui of Emperor Bokassa I and Empress Catherine. None of the heads of state invited by Bokassa bother to come. **6 December:** Suspension of American aid to the Central African Empire.

**1978 17 March:** Bokassa attempts to regain control of the army. **14 July:** Emperor Bokassa I dissolves the government of Ange Patassé. **17 July:** Formation of a new government under the direction of Henri Maïdou, appointed Prime Minister. **22 August:** Meeting at Bangui of the heads of state from Central Africa in the presence of the president of the French Republic. **6 October:** Bokassa expels his oldest son, Prince Georges, and takes away his Central African citizenship.

**1979 19–22 January:** Demonstrations in Bangui of students who refuse to wear the obligatory uniforms sold in Bokassa's stores. A bloody repression is carried out by the emperor with the aid of a division of Zairian paratroopers. Mortar fire hits the Malimaka, Boy-Rabe, Fou, and Balabadja sections of Bangui. Several hundred dead. The population strikes back by firing poisoned arrows at the soldiers. **29 January:** Teachers' strike, which is joined by several high officials. **1 March:** Arrest of Minister Barthelemy Yangongo and several high officials after the discovery of pamphlets calling for insurrection. **April:** Bokassa escapes another attempt on his life. **17 April:** Bokassa organizes a counterdemonstration in the municipal stadium. He is greeted by rock throwing. **18–19 April:** A roundup of young children between eight and 16 years of age by the police force. Bokassa participates in the massacre of about 100 of them. **14 May:** Amnesty International reveals the Bangui Children's Massacre to the world. **21–22 May:** Sixth Franco-African summit at Kigali (Rwanda) with the participation of the president of the French Republic. Bokassa accepts the sending of a commission of five African jurists, in charge of looking into the events in Bangui. **22 May:** Resignation of the Central African ambassador to Paris, General Sylvestre Bangui, who confirms the children's massacre and calls for the constitution of a "Ubanguian Liberation Front" against Bokassa's tyranny. **7 June:** Former Prime Minister Ange Patassé, moving force of the Front de libération du peuple centrafricain (FLPC; Liberation Front of the Central African People), calls for the constitution of a national union committee to overthrow Bokassa. **13 June:** Arrival in Bangui of the inquiry commission presided over by the Senegalese jurist Youssoupha Ndiaye. **14 June:** Agreement in Paris of the four opposition movements: Dr. Goumba's Front patriotique oubanguien (FPO; Ubanguian Patriotic Front), Ange Patassé's Front de libération du peuple centrafricain (FLPC; Central African People's Liberation Front), Sylvestre Bangui's Front de libération des oubanguiens (FLO; Ubangui People's Liberation Front), and the Association nationale des étudiants centrafricains (ANECA; National Central African Students Association). **7–9 July:** The representatives of the four Central African movements meet with former President Goumba at Cotonou to form a common front. **22 July:** Municipal elections with single slates in eight urban centers. **16 August:** The African inquiry commission's report published in Dakar contains conclusions that are damning for Emperor Bokassa. **17 August:** The French Minister of Cooperation announces the suspension of aid to the Central African Empire with the exception of health, education, and food that directly affect the lives of the population. **18 August:** The Commission of the European Economic Community joins in the indignation manifested by public opinion everywhere. **11 September:** Sylvestre Bangui proclaims a Republic of Ubangui in Paris and forms a government in exile. **14 September:** The Ubanguian Patriotic Front (FPO) of Dr. Goumba denounces the new massacres in Bangui. **21 September:** During the night of 20 September, 21 French soldiers occupy, with no resistance, the airport and city of Bangui while Bokassa is absent on a mission to Tripoli. **24 September:** Turned down by France, Bokassa finds asylum in the Côte d'Ivoire. **27 September:** Dacko constitutes a government in which General Bangui agrees to participate. Former Prime Minister Maïdou, who had called on the French government for help in a 4 September letter, is appointed vice president of the Republic. Bernard-Christian Ayandho is appointed prime minister. Alphonse Koyamba, minister of finance under Bokassa, is placed in charge of the Economy and Finance Ministry. François Gueret is appointed deputy minister. Goumba's Ubanguian Patriotic Front demands the organization within six months of presidential and legislative elections. **28 September:** Former Prime Minister Patassé demands Dacko's resignation and the organization of a round table conference of the various political forces. **10 October:** In Paris the *Canard Enchaîné* weekly reveals that President Giscard d'Estaing had received a gift of diamonds from Bokassa. **15 October:** A "round table" of political parties opens in Bangui. **24 October:** Returning from Tripoli, Patassé is arrested in Bangui. **26 October:** The free creation of political parties is allowed by ordinance with the reservation that their statutes must be approved by decree.

**1980  4 January:** David Dacko announces the abolition of the right to strike for 1980. **8 January:** The 4 January order is retracted when faced by the threat of a general strike. **February:** A single party, the Union démocratique centrafricaine (UDC; Central African Democratic Union), is created. Several of Bokassa's accomplices are sentenced to death. **10 March:** Congress of the UDC. **22 March:** François Gueret, Minister of Justice, is dismissed. **March and April:** Active members of the Front patriotique oubanguien/Parti du travail (FPO-PT; Ubangui Patriotic Front/Labor Party) are arrested. **10 May:** Delpey, Bokassa's adviser, is arrested at the exit of the Libyan embassy in Paris. **May:** Strikers are arrested in Bangui. **June:** Demonstrations by school and university students in Bangui and disorder in Batangalo. **9 July:** The Government of Public Safety, set up after Bokassa's overthrow, is dissolved. Maïdou reveals that he had asked for French military intervention on 4 September 1979. **17 July:** Formation of a new government with Ayandho as Prime Minister and General Bangui as Vice Prime Minister. **1 August:** Martin Kirsch, President Giscard d'Estaing's adviser, arrives in Bangui on an official visit. **22 August:** Vice President Maïdou and Prime Minister Ayandho are dismissed from their positions and placed under house arrest. **15–19 September:** Dr. Dedeavode, Bokassa's son in-law, and a number of officials of Ngaragba Prison are sentenced to death. **21 September:** In Paris, Dacko announces the framing of a new constitution, the promulgation of which will be followed by presidential elections. **October:** Strike movements in the civil service. **31 October:** Financial aid is requested from Gabon. **19 November:** Jean-Pierre Lebouder is appointed Prime Minister. **26 November:** The plea for pardon for the death sentences of five people is rejected. **28 November:** Roger Delpey is released in Paris, and Patassé is released in Bangui. **8–14 December:**

Dacko organizes a seminar of national reflection. **19–24 December:** Bokassa is condemned to death in absentia by the Bangui Criminal Court, and his arrest is ordered. The ex-emperor requests that France intervene on his behalf at the United Nations and calls for an international commission of inquiry. **27 December:** Dacko recognizes the FPO-PT, the FLPC, and the FLO as opposition parties. Henri Maïdou founds the Parti républicain du progrès (PRP; Republican Party of Progress).

**1981 7 January:** Colonel Kadhafi announces the merger of Libya and Chad. **9 January:** Some 320 French military reinforcements are sent to Bangui. Colonel Kadhafi receives Rodolphe Iddi-Lala, the founder of the Mouvement centrafricain de libération nationale (MCLN; Central African National Liberation Movement). In Bangui, former minister François Gueret creates the Mouvement pour la démocratie et l'indépendance (MDI; Democracy and Independence Movement). **24 January:** Six of Bokassa's accomplices condemned to death in September and February are shot: Dr. Dedeavode, Bokassa's son-in-law, General Josephat Mayamokala, Minister Robert Boukende, Captain Joseph Mokoa, and the soldiers Koba and Baïssa. **1 February:** The new constitution is adopted with 837,410 out of 859,447 votes cast. The former Israeli general, Samuel Gonen, a mining speculator, is placed under house arrest. **March:** Goumba returns from exile to run for president. **15 March:** Dacko wins the presidential elections by a very slim majority (50.23 percent). Patassé follows with 38.11 percent of the votes while the other candidates, Maïdou, François Pehoua, and Goumba, receive a total of 9.9 percent. Due to widespread fraud, violence erupts in Bangui, resulting in five deaths and approximately 100 people injured. **21 March:** Troubles in Bossangoa cause a number of Europeans to take refuge in Bangui. **2 April:** The five defeated candidates join to form a Provisional Political Council. **3 April:** Simon Bozanga is appointed Prime Minister. **13 April:** Giscard d'Estaing's adviser, Martin Kirsch, arrives in Bangui on official business. **4 July:** Bozanga's official visit to Paris receives a cool welcome from the socialist government. **14 July:** An explosion at *Le Club* cinema in Bangui results in four deaths and 32 injured. Shortly afterward in Lagos, Iddi Lala claims responsibility. **18 July:** Dacko blames the opposition for the 14 July bombing. The FPO-PT and the MCLN are dissolved, and the FLPC is suspended. An international arrest order is issued against Goumba, who flees to Paris. **21 July:** Proclamation of martial law. **10**

**August:** Dacko lifts the interdiction against the opposition. **31 August:** Demonstrators greet Patassé on his return from Brazzaville. **1 September:** Dacko advises the French embassy that he has resigned and turned power over to General André Kolingba, head of the army chiefs of staff. **2 September:** General Kolingba suspends the constitution and forbids all political parties. He forms the Comité militaire de redressement national (CMRN; Military Committee of National Recovery) composed solely of military personnel, among which is General Mbaikoua, a supporter of Patassé. **3 November:** Libyan troops retreat from Chad. **3–4 November:** General Kolingba participates in a Franco-African summit meeting in Paris. **12 November:** The High Court in Paris rules that Bokassa is no longer a French citizen. **December:** General Bozizé, another of Patassé's assistants, is appointed Minister.

**1982  4 January:** Dr. Goumba is appointed rector of the University of Bangui. **6–10 January:** First meetings of the Central African Church. **8 February:** Guy Penne, François Mitterrand's adviser, visits Bangui. General Kolingba is invited to Paris for an official visit. **27 February:** Patassé is greeted by a crowd of 5,000 people upon his return to Bangui after a five-month absence. **3 March:** Around 11 p.m., *Radio Bangui* broadcasts a message from General François Bozizé, Minister of Information, accusing General Kolingba of treason and announces the takeover of power by Patassé. Demonstrations by Patassé's supporters break out in several places in Bangui. The Presidential Guard under the command of French Colonel Mantion intervenes, and three demonstrators are killed and 30 injured. **4 March:** Early in the morning, Colonel Diallo and then General Kolingba announce over *Radio Bangui* that the "coup" has been checked. **6 March:** The FLPC is dissolved and outlawed. **8 March:** Patassé asks for and receives asylum at the French embassy in Bangui through the intervention of French Prime Minister Lionel Jospin and the Socialist Party. **9 March:** The Central African government issues an ultimatum to the French government demanding the extradition of Patassé. Central African police search the house of the French military attaché, Colonel Faure. **10 April:** The French government continues to refuse to turn Patassé over to the Central African government. **13 April:** Agreement is reached between the Central African and French governments. A French military plane takes Ange Patassé to Lome in Togo, where he is granted political asylum along with three of his supporters. More than 130 men, women, and children, relatives of the conspirators, are arrested in the Central African Republic. General Mbaikoua reaches Cotonou, while General Bozizé finds refuge in France. A number of judges and civil servants are arrested in Bangui. **June:** Between 16 and 21 June, *baccalauréat* examination results are announced amidst questions about cheating among those with high grades. **12 June:** The French embassy makes it known that its budgetary aid must cease and that the Central African Republic (CAR) government will have to seek help from the International Monetary Fund. This causes the laying off of 3,000 civil servants. **9–12 July:** During an official visit to Bangui, Jean-Pierre Cot, French Minister of Cooperation, irritates General Kolingba by giving too much consideration to Dr. Goumba, the first Ubanguian head of government. **17 August:** Patrice Enjimoungou, secretary general of both the University and the FPO-PT, is arrested at the airport. He is found to be carrying letters from Goumba to his French friends. **22 August:** Goumba is arrested in his office for giving information to foreign persons of potential harm to the diplomatic interests of the CAR. **24 September:** Jean-Christophe Mitterrand, adviser to his father, visits Bangui. French budgetary aid is resumed. **22 October:** Sixty-two Libyan military advisers arrive to take charge of four TG2 Soviet tanks, eight light armored vehicles, and some transport vehicles. **25–28 October:** General Kolingba makes an official visit to Paris. **28 October:** Returning from Paris, General Kolingba stops off in Tripoli. **7 December:** Hissene Habre's troops enter Ndjamena. **10 December:** A committee of support for all political prisoners in the Central African Republic is established in Paris. **15 December:** Jean-Pierre Cot, the French Minister of Cooperation, leaves the government and refuses the position of ambassador to Spain.

**1983  15 January:** François Pehoua, director of the Union bancaire de l'Afrique Centrale (UBAC; Central African Banking Union), is dismissed for inciting demonstrations against the extension of a supertax on the private sector in order to balance the budget. **2 February:** Colonel Gaston Wedane, Minister of the Interior and Public Works in the CMRN, is dismissed, accused of preparing a coup d'etat. **10 February:** In a cabinet reshuffle, Christophe Grelombe becomes minister of the interior; François Diallo, minister of public works; and Sylvestre Bangui, minister of economy and finance. **28 February:** The wives of Mbaikoua, Fayanga, and Patassé are released after being imprisoned since 2 March 1982 after the failed coup. **21 April:** Dr. Goumba is condemned to five years in prison and given a large fine. Patrice Endji-moungou is given the same sentence. **20 May:** The Libyan military advisers are asked to leave the country. **27 May:** In another cabinet shuffle, Colonel Gervil Yambala, creator of the Libyan connection, is forced to give up the foreign affairs position. **August:** Dialogue with the International Monetary Fund (IMF) breaks off, and the $18 million standby credit is left hanging. **1 September:** Dr. Goumba and 64 other political prisoners are released. **1 October:** Ruth Rolland, president of the Central African Red Cross, and her collaborator, François Pehoua, former candidate for president of the Republic, are arrested. **27 October:** A "coup" organized by Joseph Songomali, director of General Kolingba's military cabinet, and by Parachute Commander Gregoire Miango fails. **27 October:** The trial of 18 persons implicated in the 3 March 1982 attempted coup opens. **21 November:** Bokassa attempts to regain power. Chartered by friends of the ex-emperor, notably his adviser Roger Delpey, an airplane leaves Paris for Abidjan to pick up Bokassa and take him to Bangui. This plane carries pamphlets inviting all Central Africans to go to the Bangui airport to help return Bokassa to his throne. The Ivorian army surrounds the airplane at the Abidjan airport and forces it to return to France without Bokassa. **24 November:** A number of Patassé's supporters, arrested in March 1982, are given limited prison sentences; some are acquitted. **29 November:** Joseph Potolot, Bokassa's former Minister of Foreign Affairs, is arrested for participation in the attempt to restore ex-Emperor Bokassa. **4 December:** Bokassa makes a surprise return to France. He goes to live with part of his family in his Château de Hardricourt, not far from Paris.

**1984 16 January:** Following the 9 December publication of an ordinance instituting examinations for student scholarships and civil service positions, a general strike is held in all schools. **17 January:** A budget conforming to IMF recommendations is adopted. **26 January:** Goumba, Simon Bozanga, Henri Maïdou, Cyriaque Bomba-Bengabo, and Aristide Sokambi are arrested for breaking the political truce, incitation, and offenses against the head of state. They are deported to different villages in the east and northeast by nonappealable administrative measures. The leaders of the Association nationale des étudiants centrafricains (ANECA; National Association of Central African students) and the Union des scolaires centrafricains (USCA; Union of Central African Pupils) are also arrested. **31 January:** All schools in Bangui are closed. **3 February:** Revisions of scholarship regulations are promised, and the leaders of the ANECA and the USCA are released. **15 April:** A collective of Central Africans in France is formed to restore the 1981 constitution and to promote liberties and the right to democracy. **10 June:** Donatien Ndamokodjiade is arrested under suspicion of planning a coup against the head of state. **28 July:** Colonel Gaston Wedane and Commandant Jerome Alloum, former CMRN ministers, are condemned to 10 years in prison for attacks against state security. **8 August:** Patrice Endjimoungou is arrested and deported to the east for breaking the political truce. **15 August:** At Hardricourt, Bokassa declares to the French press that he is a prisoner of imposed hospitality. **17 September:** The people arrested on 26 January and 8 August, and subsequently administratively interned, are adopted by Amnesty International as political prisoners. **8 October:** A band of young Central Africans attempts to enter the French military camp in Bangui. Three are shot, and demonstrators surround the camp. Two French officers are molested, and five soldiers are injured. **9–10 November:** The Markounda post at the Chad border is attacked by commandos calling themselves Mbakaras and calling for Patassé. Four people are killed. The locality is retaken by a Central African army detachment, which burns several villages including General Mbaikoua's home village. **10 December:** The FLPC executive council announces a government in exile. **12–13 December:** François Mitterrand, president of the French Republic, visits Bangui. **31 December:** After his end-of-the-year speech, General Kolingba announces the liberation of people under house arrest and 43 political prisoners. He also drops the punishment for 14 other condemned persons, including the former Ministers Wedane and Alloum.

**1985   8 January:** A list of opposition personalities who participated in the government in exile formed under the presidency of General Mbaikoua is published. Most people cited disclaim any such participation. **Early January:** 24 poachers are arrested and elephant hunting is forbidden. Between 1972 and 1983 more than 20,000 elephants were slaughtered in the Central African Republic. **18 January:** General Kolingba lays the cornerstone for a new National Assembly building. He announces a forthcoming constitutional referendum and denounces an externally based secessionist movement with the goal of creating a Logone Republic. **13 February:** François Gueret, former Minister, is arrested upon his return from Paris. **1–4 April:** Madame Danielle Mitterrand travels to Bangui. **5 April:** At Poubati near Paoua, there are lively encounters between peasants and the Central African army over cotton prices. Five villages are burned. **14 May:** The seizure of the book *Ma Verité* (My Truth), written by Bokassa with the help of Roger Holeindre, deputy of the *Front National*, is declared in Paris. **11 July:** A loan of $4 million is granted to the CAR by the Banque Arabe pour le Développement de l'Afrique (BADEA; Arab Bank for African Development). **18 July:** The European Economic Community (EEC) agrees to finance a rural development plan. **31 July:** François Gueret is condemned to 10 years in prison for attacks on state security and offenses against the head of state. **16 August:** Pope John Paul II visits Bangui. **21 February:** President Kolingba visits Paris to discuss Chad with President Mitterrand. **14 March:** Fourteen students are arrested in Bangui for attacks against state security. **8 April:** Proceedings are held against 10 students arrested on 14 March. The ANECA is listed as a nonrecognized organization. **16 April:** Two Libyan diplomats are implicated in the 1 April bombing. **24 April:** Schools reopen. **May:** School and university strikes are forbidden. A national arbitration council is formed to give rulings. **5 May:** Yasser Arafat makes an official visit to Bangui. **7 May:** A new single party, the Rassemblement démocratique centrafricain (RDC; Central African Democratic Party), is formed. **15–16 May:** The French Minister for Cooperation, Michel Aurillac, visits Bangui. **21 July:** A common front of the FPO/PT and the FLPC is created. **1 September:** Nine students and Gaston Wedane, former Minister of the Interior, are set free. **19 September:** Jacques Foccart, adviser to the French Prime Minister Jacques Chirac, visits Bangui. **23 October:** Fleeing France, Bokassa arrives at the Bangui airport by way of Brussels and Rome. He and two French people accompanying him are arrested immediately. **13 November:** Jacques Foccart announces to the press that unscrupulous persons, with the backing of Belgian diamond-exploiting firms, gave Bokassa the funds to leave France. **21 November:** An 80 percent vote in favor of the referendum on the new constitution is recorded and the single party is firmly seated in office. Kolingba is elected for a six-year term as president. **26 November:** Proceedings against Bokassa open and a stay is granted him until 15 December to gather evidence. **29 November:** Another ministerial reshuffle takes place.

**1987** **6–7 February:** A meeting officially inaugurating the RDC is held. Jean-Paul Ngoupandé is appointed executive secretary. President

Kolingba announces the next legislative elections. **Late March:** Noting a number of incidents between people in Bangui and the French garrison, President Kolingba asks for the recall to France of Colonel Jacques Genest, commander of the EFAO. **4 June:** Gabriel Faustin Mbodou, the chief justice, asks for the death penalty against former Emperor Bokassa. **12 June:** After a 90-day trial, former Emperor Bokassa is condemned to death. Bokassa appeals the verdict. **15 July:** The FPO-PT and the FLPC call for a boycott of the 31 July legislative elections. **31 July:** In the first legislative elections in 20 years, 52 deputies are elected out of 142 candidates. **1 August:** The first session of the National Assembly opens. Maurice Methot, deputy from the Lower Kotto, is elected president. He denounces the corruption that reigns in the higher governmental and administrative spheres. **17 August:** Journalist Thomas Koazo is condemned to three years in prison. **27 October:** A presidential decree ratifies the election of Maurice Methot to the presidency of the National Assembly. **14 November:** The Supreme Court of Appeal rejects former Emperor Bokassa's appeal. **30 November:** The National Assembly meets with the Economic and Social Council. **3 December:** Another ministerial reshuffle takes place.

**1988   15 January:** André Giraud, the French Army Minister, visits Bangui. **28 January:** Iddi Lala is placed under armed guard in Cotonou. He will not be released until 17 February. **2 February:** Edouard Franck is appointed president of the High Court of Justice as called for by the constitution. **15 February:** Kolingba begins a three-day official visit to France. **29 February:** Former Emperor Bokassa is granted a presidential pardon. His death penalty is reduced to life imprisonment at hard labor. **17 March:** Diplomatic relations with the USSR, broken since 1980, are reestablished. **May:** The budget is readjusted following an agreement with the World Bank. **28 May:** Municipal elections are held. Some 3,000 candidates run for 1,085 positions, and all of those elected are members of the RDC. **30 June:** Jacques Pelletier, the French Minister of Cooperation, visits Bangui. **June:** President Kolingba says that Central African prisons hold no political prisoners except some soldiers who are accused of illegal possession of weapons. **7 July:** A ministerial reshuffle makes diplomat Michel Gbezera-Bria the minister of foreign affairs in place of Jean Louis Psimbis. Joseph Malingui, vice rector of the University of Bangui, is appointed executive secretary of the RDC. **9 July:** Danielle Mitterrand inaugurates a pediatric clinic. **July:**

A five-year program against AIDS is initiated. International assistance of $2.2 million is released for the first year. **9 November:** President Kolingba takes an official trip to the Federal Republic of Germany. **12 December:** The Administrative Council of the IMF approves the economic and financial program presented by the Central African Republic. **16 December:** Repayment of the public debt is rescheduled with Paris Club conforming to the Toronto Plan for the poorest countries.

**1989 5 January:** Another cabinet shuffle with Edouard Franck appointed minister. **16 January:** Diplomatic ties with Israel, broken since 1973, are resumed. **20 January:** USAID agrees to finance a hydroelectric program (that of a dam on the Mbali). **25 April:** Madame Balenguélé is appointed mayor of Bangui. She is the 25th mayor of the capital since Boganda. **28 May:** Sudanese authorities forbid President Kolingba's plane the right to fly over Sudanese territory, making his visit to Israel very difficult. **29 May:** Diplomatic ties with Sudan are broken. Michel Docko, deputy from Bangui, replaces Maurice Mehot as president of the National Assembly. **13 September:** A women's demonstration in Bangui is repressed by the police. **25 September:** Bernard Kowasa, private consel to General Kolingba, is assassinated following the arrest of several Mbaka civil servants. **9 October:** Lawsuit against Nicolas Tiangaye, lawyer, who is accused of insulting the army. This affair led to the dismissal of the Minister of Justice Hugues Dobozendi and to his temporary replacement by Colonel Christophe Grelombe. The government also brought sanctions against civil servants who had come out in favor of a multiparty system.

**1990 12 September:** Goumba and 22 other opposition members in charge of the Coordinating Committee for the Calling of a National Conference (CCCCN) are arrested. **13–15 October:** Demonstrations in Bangui with 40 wounded, 100 automobiles burned, and numerous arrests including that of Timothee Malendoma, a former minister. **18–23 October:** Congress at Berberati of the Rassemblement Democratique Centrafricain (RDC; Central African Democratic Party), now the country's single party.

**1991 1 January:** General Kolingba announces the creation of a post of Prime Minister. **3 January:** Agreement signed with Germany for the financing of various infrastructures and agricultural projects. **4 March:** General Kolingba frees the persons arrested on 12 September 1990.

General Timothee Malendoma, who had offered his support to the committee founded on 15 May, remains in detention in the Kassaï military base. **6 March:** The National Assembly and Economic and Social Council adopt constitutional reform. **15 March:** Edouard Franck becomes prime minister. **20 March:** Important cabinet changes. **22 April:** Kolingba declares the multiparty system is now official; political prisoners are released. **5 May:** Goumba's Ubangi Patriotic Front or Labor Party becomes the *Front Patriotique pour le Progrès* (FPP; Patriotic Front for Progress). **7 May:** Riots in Bangui. Demonstrators build barricades and loot the stores. **30 May:** The civil servants who had gone on unlimited strike since 29 April choose to remain on strike in spite of the government's paying their back wages for March and April. **11 June:** Private sector strike in its third week. Government requisitions the bank personnel. **14 June:** The government blames the unions. **20 June:** In a pastoral letter, the Central African Episcopal Conference asks for a national plan for recovery. **3 June:** The army occupies the Labor Exchange in Bangui. **2–5 July:** Union leaders are arrested. **5 August:** The strike continues only in the education and health sectors. **17 August:** Kolingba leaves the head of the RDC to stand above parties. **20 August:** The RDC Congress calls for a National Conference. **14 September:** Representatives from the eight opposition parties are met by Kolingba. **16 September:** Call for a general strike throughout the public sector. **31 October:** The opposition meeting in Bangui assembles over 10,000 people. **7 November:** Constitution of a technical government composed of 13 ministers and six secretaries of state. **1 December:** General Bozizé released after acquittal on 24 September.

**1992    13 February:** Twenty opposition parties call for an independent national conference. **27 April:** Kolingba refuses such a conference. **Mid-June:** Teachers and public servants go on strike. **1 August:** Kolingba opens the Great National Debate. Political parties and trade unions refuse to take part. Disturbances break out in Bangui during which Doctor Jean-Claude Conjugo, one of the leaders of the Alliance pour la Démocratie et le Progrès (ADP; Alliance for Democracy and Progress), is killed by police. **7 September:** A decree sets the date of the legislative and presidential elections for 25 October. **24 September:** Goumba, president of the Patriotic Front for Progress, is chosen to be the only opposition candidate for the presidential election of 25 October. **25 October:** First round of the legislative and presidential elections. Badly organized, the ballot was suspended in Bangui. Results from the provinces show Kolingba badly outrun. **29 October:** The Supreme Court cancels election results. **27 November:** Presidential and legislative elections rescheduled for February 1993. **28 November:** Despite the fact that his mandate has expired, Kolingba chooses to remain in power. **4 December:** General Malendoma, who had been kept out of the opposition rallies for his participation in the Great National Debate of August, becomes prime minister and forms a government that includes moderate opposition representatives.

**1993   3 February:** General Kolingba sets up an interim organization called the Conseil National Politique de la République (CNPPR; Provisional National Political Council of the Republic). It also includes three of the other candidates in the presidential elections: David Dacko, Ange Patassé, and Enoch Lakoué. The elections are postponed to 18 April and 2 May. **26 February:** General Malendoma is sacked and replaced as prime minister by Enoch Lakoué. **28 February:** Goumba, leader of the Concertation des Forces Démocratiques (CFD; Democratic Forces Concertation), who refused to be involved in the provisional government, proclaims Kolingba was no longer president as of 28 February. **26 April:** Demonstrations in Bangui of students and civil servants against the government. Police intervention causes two dead and 45 injured. **29 April:** Elections postponed again. The government announces they will take place on 17 and 31 October. The opposition strongly protests. **15 May:** A meeting of the Presidential Guard. **20 May:** Creation of the Union des Forces acquises à la Paix et au Changement (UFAC; Union of the Forces for Peace and Change), which unites almost all of the opposition parties. Meeting of the Régiment pour la Défense Opérationnelle du Territoire (RDOT; Regiment for the Operational Defense of the Territory) and part of the police force who threaten to go on strike. This is caused by an eight months' lack of wages; they are given two months of salary on account. **2 June:** Kolingba requisitions civil servants on strike since April. **4 June:** Five thousand women hold a demonstration in Bangui. The gathering is dispersed when shots are fired. **5 June:** Michel Roussin, the French Minister for Cooperation, makes a quick visit to Bangui. Colonel Jean-Claude Mantion, Kolingba's special adviser, and Ambassador Alain Pallu de Beaupuy are recalled to France. Roussin asks Kolingba to advance to July the elections scheduled for October. **6 June:** Kolingba and Mobutu meet in Gbadolité in Zaire. **10 June:** Elections advanced to August. **24 June:** Political crisis. The prime minister opposes Kolingba's decision to offer a position as minister to one of his close friends. **22 August:** First round of the elections, organized by France. High participation rates. **29 August:** Presidential decrees modifying certain provisions of the electoral code and the Constitutional Court's composition. Publication of the results is delayed. France withholds cooperation and insists on an immediate return to the democratic process. Kolingba withdraws his controversial decrees. **1 September:** Kolingba signs a decree releasing ex-Emperor Bokassa. The same decree also frees prisoners, convicted and accused. Results for the first round of the presidential election are made public. Kolingba is defeated. He holds third position with 12 percent of the votes, behind Patassé with 37 percent and Goumba with 33 percent. The participation rate is of 68 percent of registered voters. **19 September:** Second round of the presidential elections and legislative elections in the presence of 80 international observers. Participation is much lower. **27 September:** Former Prime Minister Patassé wins the second round of the presidential elections with 53 percent of the votes against Goumba with 46 percent. **10 October:** The MLPC is the largest group within the National Assembly but does not have an absolute majority (34 members of parliament out of 85). **25 October:** The vice president of the political bureau of the MLPC, Doctor Jean-Luc Mandaba, becomes prime minister. **5 November:** Hughes Dobozandi is elected president of the National Assembly. **26 November:** France offers financial aid (9 billion CFA francs), allowing the CAR to deal with the international community, especially the IMF. **12 December:** Civil servants slowly resume work after over seven months of strike. **15 December:** Former President Dacko founds a new party, the Mouvement pour la Démocratie et le Progrès (MDD; Movement for Democracy and Progress). **25 December:** Creation of a commission of audit.

**1994   4 January:** The government announces the end of the individual tax (3,500 CFA francs) according to the campaign promise of Patassé. **12 January:** The CFA Franc is devaluated throughout the franc zone. This devaluation doubles the amount of the Central African debt. **16–18 January:** Michel Roussin, French Minister for Cooperation, visits Bangui. Two financial agreements are signed. **20–21 April:** Student demonstrations in Bangui turn violent. **21 April:** Gathering of the Rassemblement

Démocratique Centrafricain (RDC; Central African Democratic Party). **5–8 May:** Meeting in Bangui of the representatives of various states (Germany, United States, France, Italy, Japan, Morocco, Nigeria) backing and sponsoring the CAR. **29 May:** President Patassé pardons five students who are convicted during the April demonstrations. **19–21 July:** Official visit to Paris of President Patassé. **12 September:** The Permanent Military Tribunal condemns former Minister Christophe Grelombe to one year imprisonment for fraud and misappropriation of confiscated funds. The sentence is reduced to half by a presidential pardon on 30 November. **1 October:** After three years, school begins for 300,000 pupils. **27 November:** Legislative by-elections take place in five districts. **28 December:** Constitutional referendum. IMF suspends loans since six measures it had recommended have not been implemented. The debt reaches 165 billion CFA francs.

**1995   8 January:** Results of the constitutional referendum of 28 December are announced. The new constitution proposed by the government is adopted by 82 percent of voters against 18 percent; abstentions reach 55 percent. The text of the new constitution states that the head of state is elected for a six-year mandate once renewable. Regional assemblies to be elected by universal suffrage. **10 April:** No confidence motion against the government filed by 34 members of parliament belonging to the MLPC and backed by over half of the 83 members of parliament. **12 April:** Even before the motion, filed by his own party, is put to a vote, Prime Minister Jean-Luc Manbada resigns. **20 April:** Gabriel Koyambonou, a member of the executive committee of the MLPC, becomes prime minister and forms a new government including nine members of the former in a total of 26, all belonging to the presidential majority. **22 April:** 7,000 refugees return to Chad. **13–15 September:** President Patassé visits France. **17 November:** The World Bank notices a visible improvement in the Central African economy. **13 December:** France and the CAR sign three financing agreements for about 25 billion CFA francs. The CAR debt of 230 billion French francs toward the French development fund is canceled.

**1996   18 April:** A dozen soldiers, who came from Kassaï base, stop several vehicles, take them, and reach Bangui's center shooting rounds in the air. Panic spreads to lower-class districts. **19 April:** French military are in position in the streets of Bangui. Armed vehicles surround the presidential palace. The archbishop and the president of the Human Rights League offer to arbitrate the conflict between the rebels and the authorities. The rebellion ends on 22 April. **18 May:** Government transfers the weapons at Kassaï base to the base at Roux, where the presidential guard is stationed and thus causes a second rebellion. Soldiers of the Régiment mixte d'intervention (RMI; Mixed Intervention Regiment or Strike Force) control the center of Bangui. Rebels take several persons hostage, among which is Hugues Dobozendi, president of the National Assembly. They present 10 demands, including payment of back wages and sacking of the head of the presidential guard. Expatriate families are evacuated. **22 May:** Rebels capture the radio headquarters building. Crowds begin to loot businesses and shops. One of the banks is set on fire. Private residences are attacked and ransacked. The French embassy evacuates expatriates. The political disarray is complete. General Thorette, commander of the French regiment, and Ambassador Paul Angelier convince President Patassé to form a new government. **5 June:** A draft of agreement necessary for the forming of a government of national unity is signed by 22 political parties, some of which are down to a few members and whose official existence is mainly theoretical. The CAR ambassador in Paris, Jean-Paul Ngoupandé, becomes prime minister. **11 June:** Ngoupandé arrives in Bangui. **July:** Ngoupandé addresses the police and begins to crack down on crime that has spread to all of Bangui. **August:** In agreement with the rebels, the prime minister sets up general hearings regarding the army and its duties, organization, pacification, equipment, recruiting, development, and renewal of its command. French General Thorette and General Niang of the Senegalese army assist the effort. Representatives from political parties, unions, the church, and various NGOs take part in the debate. The disbanding of the Centre national de recherches et d'investigations (CNRI; National Investigation and Research Center) and of the Section d'enquêtes, de recherches et de documentation (SERD; Investigation, Research and Documentation Section, which answers to the presidency) is advised, but turned down by the president. All back wages are paid. The operation lasts until 15 November. **3 November:** Death in Bangui of former Emperor Bokassa. **13 November:** President Patassé leaves for Athens and Rome, after ordering the arrest of Captain Anicet Saulet, leader of the rebels. **15 November:** Attempted rearrest of one of the prisoners that was released and did not go back to the Ngaragba Prison fails and causes the death of one police officer. Rebelling for the third time, the soldiers at Kassaï base attack the arms depot. **16 November:** Instead of going to the city center as in April and May, the rebels take hold of two specific districts: the Ouango area and its surroundings, in the southeast of the capital, and the Brussels and Bimbo urban areas, by way of the Petevo area. Access to the harbor is closed. **24 November:** Meeting in Paris of Presidents Chirac and Patassé. Well established, the rebels free two hostages. After a meeting with the French ambassador, the prime minister, backed by the political parties, the unions and the church, agrees to a cease-fire. **25 November:** Back in Bangui President Patassé calls for appeasement, seeking negotiations and reconciliation. **30 November:** A manhunt is initiated by the aggressive wing of the MLPC seeking to lynch Yakomas. Four parliamentary groups file a request for the indictment of President Patassé. **4 December:** Heads of states of French-speaking African countries meet for the second Frenco-African summit in Ouagadougou. Presidents Omar Bongo (Gabon), Blaise Campaoré (Burkina-Fasso), Alpha Oumar Konaré (Mali), and Idriss Deby (Chad) are given a mandate for a mission of mediation in the Bangui crisis. Troops from several African countries including Burkina Faso, Ghana, Gabon, Mali, Senegal, and Togo are sent to the CAR. **5 December:** Christophe Grelombe, former minister under Kolingba, and his son Martin are kidnapped by the presidential guard and then tortured and murdered. Prime Minister Jean-Paul Ngoupandé strongly reacts against this double murder. **6 December:** The four heads of states designated at the Ouagadougou summit arrive in Bangui to offer their help. **7–8 December:** They meet at the French ambassador's house with a delegation of rebel soldiers, under the authority of Captain Anicet Saulet. With Captain Saulet, they sign a statement that includes a cease-fire agreement and the creation of a control committee under the leadership of the former Mali head of state, General Amadou Toumani Touré. **14 December:** At the request of General Amadou Toumani Touré, the truce is prolonged until 22 December. The motion against President Patassé fails to rally enough of a majority at the National Assembly.

**1997  4 January:** Tensions mount in Bangui following the death of a young national. A French officer and a noncommissioned officer come to investigate this incident are attacked and murdered in the Kouanga district. **5 January:** Violent reply from the Fench military. The districts in southeast Bangui held by the rebels are bombed. Crowds demonstrate against French presence. **12 January:** The Archbishop attempts conciliation. The bishops of the CAR publish a pastoral letter pleading, "Let us not let our country die. Let us begin the reconciliation." Operation "Méné Oko" (One Blood) begins with a view to ending ethnic rivalries. A gathering of representatives from political parties and society members takes place. **19 January:** General Amadou Toumani Touré recommends reaching new agreements and reinforcing the powers of the prime minister by a modification of article 37 of the constitution. The presidential guard arrests Jean-Paul Ngoupandé's cabinet director Karim Meckassoua as he leaves the presidential palace after talks with General Touré. **25 January:** The Bangui agreements signed during an official ceremony at the French ambassador's house in the presence of the Gabon and Chad leaders. It is countersigned by representatives from 24 political parties and associations that agree not to resort to violence to solve their problems. The agreement includes the forming of an African Multinational Force (MISAB) including soldiers from Burkina Faso, Gabon, Mali, Senegal, Chad, and Togo. Equipment and logistics for the MISAB are to be provided by France. Its mission will be to enforce the democratic process leading to legislative and presidential elections and to ensure peace and security in the capital. **31 January:** The MISAB is set up and implemented as agreed until 9 February. These forces are joined by French troops. Bangui is patrolled by mixed units from the MISAB and the Forces armées centrafricaines (FACA; Central African Armed Forces). **18 February:** Michel Gbézara-Bria, former minister under Bokassa and Kolingba, appointed as prime minister by a presidential decree, forms a Gouvernement d'Action pour la Démocratie et le Développement (GADD; Government of Action for Democracy and Development), in which the opposition agrees to participate. On 4 February and again on 25 February, the police prevent former Prime Minister Jean-Paul Ngoupandé from flying to Paris. **22 February:** Stormy altercation between the two emissaries sent by President Chirac, Vice-Admiral Delaunay and Michel Dupuch, and President Patassé. The latter is immediately deprived of the 23 technical advisers in charge of his personal security. The president must accept an agenda disarming the rebels, and agrees to call a national conference of reconciliation. **15 March:** The National Assembly votes an amnesty law regarding the army's third rebellion. **18 March:** The prime minister introduces his new government, which states it has not the means to pay for the five months back wages due to civil servants, nor to disarm the rebels or the population. **Early April:** For the first time, the government begins talks with the rebels. President Patassé agrees to meet with their leader, Captain Anicet Saulet. **7 May:** The nine ministers from the opposition resign and leave the government. **11 May:** Civil servants begin a new strike. **18 May:** New army rebellion. **20 June:** The policing of the capital by mixed patrols does not succeed in preventing combat. The fighting spreads to several districts. Districts supposed to be friendly to the rebels are searched and civilians are executed randomly. A third of the capital's inhabitants flee. Kassaï base, over which Mirage fighter jets and helicopters have been flying, retaliates with heavy artillery. Mortar shells reach the French embassy. A cease-fire, agreed to on 21 June upon a French intervention, is immediately broken. Bangui city is left to looting. **22 June:** President Chirac decides to send French troops to back the MISAB units. President Omar Bongo intervenes through the Gabonese general in charge of the MISAB. **23 June:** Fighting stops after French intervention. Over 100,000 civilians have fled Bangui. Over 100 people are reported dead, and many are wounded. The rebels agree to lay down their arms, beginning with the heavy ones. Colonel Evariste Konzallé is appointed coordinator for disarming of the rebels and the population. **2 July:** Cease-fire agreed on by the MISAB and the rebels. **18 July:** Over 400 rebel soldiers join the FACA units. **4 August:** French Defense Minister Alain Richard decides to close down Bouar military base. **1 October:** Teachers and health personnel go on strike. **5 October:** Over 85 percent of heavy weapons and 56 percent of light weapons have been reclaimed by the MISAB.

**1998  January:** The IMF demands that the CAR government claim the export taxes owed by the diamonds sales offices in the amount of 5.6 billion CFA francs. **25 February:** Because of the position taken by Bangui in favor of the Republic of China, the Taiwan embassy closes. **26 February:** Opening of a Conference for National Reconciliation, which gathers the MLPC and a united 11 opposition parties. The conference ends on 4 March. General Touré presents the participants with his evaluation report of the agreements reached in Bangui. **5 March:** Official signature of the national reconciliation pledge, amended the day before by the 400 participants to the conference. Present at the ceremony are

Presidents Omar Bongo from Gabon, Idriss Déby from Chad, Oumar Alpha Konaré from Mali, Laurent-Désiré Kabila from the République démocratique du Congo (RDC; Democratic Republic of Congo, or Congo), and Omar Bechia from Sudan, as well as the foreign ministers from Togo and Cameroon. **7 March:** Operation *Cigogne* (Stork) begins. Bréal base camp in the center of Bangui is returned by the French military to the CAR army. The conference is presided over by General Touré. **27 March:** The UN Security Council adopts resolution 1,159, which designates an international peace force of 1,350 men, the Mission des Nations Unies en République Centrafricaine (MINURCA; United Nations Mission in the CAR). **4 April:** Meeting at Pointe-Noire of the Congo, CAR and Chad presidents. **6 April:** The last French soldiers leave the CAR. **17 April:** The first troops from the MINURCA arrive in Bangui. It is composed of units from the Côte d'Ivoire, Ghana, Canada, and France. The 252 French soldiers in the MINURCA are in charge of logistics. The MINURCA has a mission to gather unreturned weapons, to ensure safety in Bangui, and to monitor the legislative and presidential elections. Its mission is initially set to last three months but is then extended to 28 February 1999. **1 May:** The bishop at Bambari protests against repeated attacks on the clergy of his diocese. **7 June:** Bilateral treaty signed with Germany for over 8.4 billion CFA francs worth of projects. President Patassé leaves for China. **10–13 September:** Presidents Patassé and Kabila meet. **18 September:** The National Assembly passes a law on liberalizing the oil sector. **1 October:** The MINURCA has recovered nearly all of the heavy weapons and most light ones. **15 October:** The Paris Club announces an important reconsideration of the CAR's debt. **4 November:** President Biya of Cameroon and President Patassé sign an agreement regarding the use of the Cameroon transportation axis for Central African exports. **7 November:** The campaign for the legislative elections begins. **22 November:** Monitored by the MINURCA deployed in Bangui and in five of the 17 jurisdictions of the country, the legislative elections proceed without any serious trouble. The MLPC wins 22 seats in the first round, the opposition wins 15. **3 December:** Before the second round, the opposition parties regroup into the Union des Forces Aquises à la Paix et au Changement (UFAPC; Union of Forces for Peace and Change). **23 December:** The second round of the legislative elections allows the opposition to narrow the presidential majority. Out of 109 seats, the MLPC wins a total of 47 and its ally, the Democratic Party, wins two. The UFAPC gets 53 seats to which are added two seats won by independent members of parliament. The UFAPC deems that with 55 seats, it should form the new government. One elected member of the opposition nevertheless joins the MLPC. The majority shifts. Ten ministers within the government join the opposition and resign, taking the prime minister with them. The UN representative in Bangui suggests the leader of the opposition party, Abel Goumba, to preside over the National Assembly. None the less the Assembly elects Luc-Appolinaire Don Konamabay, a member of the majority, to this office. Upon the CAR president's request, the UN agrees to extend until 31 December 1999 the MINURCA mandate. It insists that the additional time must be used for implementation of necessary reforms in the economic and social sectors.

**1999   4 January:** Anicet-George Dologuélé, finance minister in the previous government, becomes prime minister. **6 January:** Strikes in Bangui. Several union leaders are arrested. **15 January:** The government is formed with 22 ministers and three secretaries of state. Three ministers belong to the MDD, the opposition party. **28 February:** Departure of the remaining French soldiers belonging to the MINURCA, whose mandate is extended to the year 2000. **14 February:** Meeting in Syrtis of Libyan President Kadhafi and President Patassé. The CAR joins the Communauté des Etats Sahélo-Sahariens (COMESSA; Community of the Sahel and Sahara States), which includes ten other African countries. **24 April:** The Nigerian and Central African presidents sign a commercial agreement. **30 August:** Start of the presidential campaign. **31 August:** An opposition party meeting in Bangui gathers 10,000 people. The electoral campaign shows the blatant discrepancy between the resources of the candidates. Opposition candidates renew their promise of stepping down in the second round for the one best in place. **12 September:** Two hours before the ballot starts, the first round is postponed due to "technical difficulties." **19 September:** Contrary to predictions, Patassé is reelected in the first round with 51.68 percent of votes. After Patassé follow A. Kolingba (19.38 percent), D. Dacko (11.50 percent), A. Goumba (6.6 percent), H. Pouzébe (4.19 percent), and J. C. Ngoupandé (3.16 percent). **26 October:** Anicet-George Dologuélé is reinstated as prime minister. **1 November:** A new government is formed with 22 ministers and three delegate ministers, one of which is in charge of "relations with the Arab world." **24 December:** IMF financial mission in Bangui calling for a rise in tax revenues through the recovery of funds coming from the canceling of fiscal advantages given to various groups and NGOs.

**2000    5 February:** Near Grimari, a nun is murdered by *zaraguinas* (hijackers). With the help of France, two mobile units are set up at Bria and Bouar to put a stop to these crimes. **14 February:** Extraordinary session at the National Assembly to examine the new laws concerning the 2000 financial budget and to ratify the CAR's joining of COMESSA. The prime minister speaks out against corruption and embezzlement, which remain "unpunished, and even covered up." **22 February:** Deadline for the MINURCA's mandate. Bureau d'observation des Nations Unies en Centrafrique (BONUCA; United Nations' Monitoring Bureau in Central Africa) created for an initial period of one year, and the political presence of the UN is maintained. **27 February:** The 2000 budget is adopted by the National Assembly. The budget innovates by introducing a value-added tax (VAT). **28 February:** Payment of the back wages for February 1999 owed to over 17,000 civil servants. **3 July:** Electricity rationed in Bangui because of the fuel shortage. **7 July:** The UN Security Council expresses its concern for the human rights violations. **1 October:** Civil servant unions announce that "unless at least 12 months of back wages are paid" they will take large-scale actions. The start of the new school year is delayed at both primary and secondary levels. **14 October:** The Centralafrican Union of Workers decides on a warning strike of four days starting 17 October in order to protest against the nonpayment of back wages. **23 October:** President Patassé promises to take $10 million out of his personal accounts to pay the back wages. In fact, it was merely to come from a financial deal on the basis of a mining permit granted by the president to a German corporation. **25 October:** The heads of six unions declare that the president's promise will not alter their position. **2 November:** The strike grows and extends among civil servants. **14 November:** Demonstrations in Bangui are organized by a youth movement, unknown until then, calling itself Le Flambeau Centrafricain (FLAC; Central African Torch), which protests the "mass suicide" imposed upon the country by the Patassé regime. The police and the presidential guard scatter the demonstrators. **24 November:** In spite of the minister of the interior's last minute ban, a march of several thousand civil servants takes place in the streets of Bangui. A large number of students join the protest, which has also won the support of the leading police union. President Patassé accuses former Prime Minister Ngoupandé of wanting to come to power by force. **11 December:** The operation Centrafrique, pays mort (Central Africa dead silent), organized by the unions, paralyzes the country. **15 December:** Fifteen opposition parties ask President Patassé to resign. They form a coordinating committee in charge of "preparing for non-violent political change." The president replaces Minister of the Interior Maurice Regonessa. The office of Secretary of State, in charge of public security, is entrusted to a former high-ranking member of the Bokassa regime, Robert Zana. General Regonessa, Director General of Customs, is replaced by Théodore Bikoo. **30 December:** The UN Security Council adopts the report presented by Secretary-General Kofi Annan in which he states his concern about the persistence of the civil servants strikes in the CAR and about the consequences of the war in the Congo.

**2001   8 January:** Following a vigorous closing speech of the president of the High Court of Appeal in Bangui, Louis-Pierre Gamba, Jacob Béti, and Marguerite Balinguélé—all three elected members of the RDC—are finally released after being imprisoned since 19 December. **11 January:** After intense discussions, the IMF and CAR reach a final agreement. The IMF allows $10 million to be transferred to Bangui; the unions accept a truce against the paying of back wages due to civil servants. **27 February:** The Cameroon authorities decide, for the needs of a construction site on the road from Yaoundé to Bangui, to move their customs post into the Garoua-Boulaï area, thus disregarding the limits of the buffer zone implemented in 1974. **4 March:** Some 200 CAR soldiers cross the border into the disputed zone to protest Cameroon's decision. **7 March:** Following the CAR's request, the UN Secretary-General sends a mediating team of two high-ranking officers from France and Benin to the Garoua-Boulai zone. The mission succeeds in maintaining the status quo, and the troops from both parties withdraw. The road construction is delayed. **1 April:** President Patassé removes Prime Minister Aniat-Georges Doléguélé by a decree replacing him with his own nephew Martin Ziguélé. **5 May:** Meeting for a general assembly, the civil servant unions allow the March truce to last 10 more days. A warning strike is scheduled between 14 and 18 May if the government does not offer a "positive response." **28 May:** President Patassé's residence is attacked: the president and his family, defended by the presidential security company of Colonel Bombayaké, face the assault of heavily armed rebels 500 men strong. Some of them are officers who had taken part in the 1997 rebellion and been reinstated: Lieutenant Guy-Serge Kolingba, Commander Saulet, and Captain Gailloty. The push has resulted in over 20 deaths, and many more bodies litter the streets of the capital. The attack is repelled at dawn. The assailants fall back on the south and southeast districts of the capital and to Kassaï base. On their way, they attack the national radio station and camp Roux, freeing General Ndjengbot, serving a 10-year sentence for having ordered his men to fire on the crowd during the 1992 presidential campaign. The UN Secretary-General Kofi Annan comdemns the attempted coup. **29 May:** Under Army Chief of Staff General François Bozizé, the counteroffensive begins. Kassaï base is taken, then lost again. The population flees massively. **30 May:** Coming from Zongo, about 100 soldiers from the Congo Liberation Front of Jean-Pierre Bemba arrive to help the loyalists. Two Libyan *Tupolevs* land at Bangui-Mpoko airport providing light armored vehicles and 100 men destined to be President Patassé's close guard. **31 May:** Former head of state André Kolingba, who on 29 May asked the French ambassador to help put him back in power, is reduced to the rank of private second class. He escapes after having asked the rebels to surrender. **1 June:** Calm returns to Bangui. A hunt for Yakomas is organized. A member of the opposition, Théophile Touba, is decapitated. President Patassé urges the population to remain calm and promises that the rebels will receive exemplary punishment. **7 June:** Minister of Defense Jean-Jacques Demafouth announces that the whole capital is back under army control. **8 June:** President Patassé accuses France of sending arms to the rebels through the French embassy in Bangui. **11 June:** A combined national commission of inquiry is created to investigate the attempted coup of 28 May. Consisting of 11 members, it is presided over by Chief Prosecutor Joseph Bindoumi and must within three months submit a report to the Court of the Permanent Military Tribunal in charge of judging the hundred people imprisoned since the creation of the commission. It must also judge the escaped plotters, namely former President Kolingba. **12 June:** A temporary count of the victims of the coup is made: 39 dead (25 military and 14 civilians) and 89 wounded. The toll is really much higher, a great number of victims having been buried and incinerated by the population. The Paris-Bangui air connection reopens. **5–22 July:** A mission of the International Human Rights Federation visits Bangui to investigate the numerous human rights violations during and after the attempted coup, particularly the violence against members of the Yakoma ethnic group. The mission's report is highly damning regarding the authorities. **5 July:** UN Secretary-General Kofi Annan, in a report to the Security Council, asks for emergency financial support for the CAR. Referring to the attempted coup of 28 May, the UN states that "international support may only take place in a context of national reconciliation and political dialogue." **17 July:** The border is closed between the Congo and the CAR. **8 July:** Six opposition political parties—Parti de l'Unité Nationale (Party for National Unity, of former Prime Minister Jean-Paul Ngoupandé), Parti du Forum Civique (Civil Forum Party), Parti de l'Union pour la République (Union for the Republic), Association pour la Solidarité et le développement de la Centrafrique (Association for Solidarity and the Development of the CAR), Perspectives Nouvelles (New Perspectives), and the Parti du Mouvement pour la Démocratie et l'Indépendance (Movement for Democracy and Independence)—ask for the resignation of President Patassé. **25 August:** The presidential guard arrests Defense Minister Jean-Jacques Demafouth. A telephone conversation of the latter on 26 July with the Congo rebel chief Jean-Pierre Bemba is intercepted in which Demafouth asked Bemba to send him 60 men to "help him take power." **30 August:** A terrorist attack in Bangui kills the Libyan ambassador. This attack takes place only hours before a scheduled visit of President Patassé to Libya. **13 September:** An order from Minister of Justice Marcel Métifera extends the combined national inquiry commission's mandate until 11 December. **10 October:** Signature in Washington of a six-month interim agreement preparing for a three-year program. The CAR agrees to respect the objectives of its budget, which marked a 31 percent decrease on the 2001 budget. In exchange, the World Bank will pay $15 million under the conditions of the public finance agreement. Besides, $2.4 million are put at the CAR's disposal as postconflict support. Also, the Banque des Etats de l'Afrique Centrale (BEAC; Central African States Bank) will grant the CAR an advance of 3.5 billion CFA francs on the sums due to its lending the airbase of Bangui-Mpoko to the UN's mission in Congo. **18 October:** President Patassé breaks up the National Coordination of the MLPC board members, some of whom have been compromised in the attempted coup. **27**

**October:** Army Chief of Staff General François Bozizé is sacked and replaced by his Assistant Colonel Ernest Bété.

**2002   January:** The Organization of African Unity (OAU) decides to send peacekeeping troops to the Central African Republic. General François Bozizé, living in Chad after escaping arrest in December 2001, begins to launch an attack from the border. **19 February:** Sudanese soldiers arrive in Bangui, as part of the military aid sent by the Communauté des Etats Sahélo-Sahariens (COMESSA; Community of the Sahel and Sahara States), headed by Libya. **8 May:** Abel Goumba withdraws his party, the Front Patriotique Oubanguien (FPO; Ubanguian Patriotic Front), from the coalition of opposition parties struggling against President Ange Patassé. Enoch-Dérant Lakoué's party, the Parti Social Démocrate (PSD; Socialist Democratic Party) has also done the same. **26 July:** The Mouvement pour la démocratie et le développement (MDD; Movement for Democracy and Development) of former President David Dacko follows. **6 August:** A violent clash occurs between General Bozizé's troops, some 200 men strong, and President Ange Patassé's forces. General François Bozizé's troops enter the Central African Republic. **26 August:** André Kolingba and 20 other officers are sentenced to death in absentia for the attempted coup in May 2001. **26 September:** Libya announces that the 200 men sent in June 2001 to serve as President Patassé's close guard will be recalled. **October:** Teachers go on strike again. After difficult negotiations between Chad and the Central African Republic, and due to pressure on the part of the OAU, it is decided that General Bozizé is to be extradited from Chad to Togo, but this decision is never implemented. Bozizé continues his operations in the Central African Republic, using Chad as his rear base. **2–30 October:** Bozizé's men try to take Bangui but are repelled by the Central African Armed Forces and Jean-Pierre Bemba's militia. Still, Bozizé's troops occupy a large part in the north and west of the country, and are less than 50 miles from Bangui. **Late October:** Civil servants are promised their back wages for the last three to five months due to credits from the International Monetary Fund (IMF). **28 November:** The European Union (EU) helps the Central African Republic pay for its civil servants' pensions, and to help reduce its debt worldwide. **21 December:** Libyan troops begin to withdraw, along with the troops sent by the COMESSA.

**2003   1 January:** President Patassé declares that his country is in a virtual state of war and that the population must henceforth unite at all costs. **6 January:** The president of the Episcopal conference Monsignor Paulin Pomodimo and his assistant the former Prime Minister Maïdou are appointed as negotiators and begin talks with political and diplomatic figures, namely the Coordination des Partis Politiques d'Opposition (CPPO; Coordination of the Political Parties of the Opposition). **11 January:** The radio calls attention to the population fleeing the areas under rebel control. Among those leaving are prefects and subprefects. The opposition parties call for a cease-fire and a general amnesty. A delegation of the International Committee of the Red Cross (CICR) is stationed in Bangui. **23 January:** General François Bozizé declares he is trying to regroup all the opposition tendencies in close collaboration with the *Coordination des Patriotes Centraficains* (CPC; Central African Patriots Coordination) run by Karim Meckassoua, former director of the Jean-Paul Ngoupandé cabinet. The CPC urges a new Central Africa and asks for negotiations with the president and a general amnesty for the rebels. **3 February:** The government's spokesman, Gabriel Koyambounoun, declares that a national debate to end the crisis will take place in March. **4 February:** Henri Maïdou and Paulin Pomodimo go to Libreville to meet with President Bongo before going to Brazzaville to meet with President Sassou-Nguesso. **13 February:** Counteroffensive of the Central African forces against the rebels in the cities of Sibut, Buzoum, Kaga, Banduro, and Bossangoa. The International Human Rights Federation files a complaint for crimes against humanity against Patassé, Bemba, and Miskine. **14 February:** The American government closes its embassy in Bangui and asks its citizen to leave the country. **15 February:** At the request of Paris, Chad President Idriss Deby makes a visit to Bangui that is called one of friendship and support. **16 February:** After a visit to Bangui, French Minister for Cooperation P. A. Wiltzer says he trusts the national debate will be a success. **21 February:** President Deby accuses President Patassé of wanting to exterminate Chad citizens living in the CAR. **7 March:** The CAR's armed forces assert that they control all of the territories held by Bozizé's rebels. They say they have taken possession of the cities of Buzoum, Kabo, Bossangoa, Sibut, Kaga-Bandoro, and Damara. **13 March:** President Patassé arrives in Niamey to take part in the 5th session of the Communauté Economique des Etats Sub-Sahariens (CENSAD; Economic Community of the Sahel-Sahara states). **15 March:**

While reconciliation is attempted at Niamey between Presidents Patassé and Deby, rebel forces move toward Bangui. Several rounds fired over the Bangui-Mpoko airport prevent the president's plane coming from Libya to land. It turns around and goes toward Yaoundé. Within a few hours, Bangui falls into the hands of the rebels. The Forces Armées Centrafricaines (FACA, Central African Armed Forces) that have been rejected in favor of forces from Libya and the Congo refuse to defend President Patassé's residence, which is looted. The FACA and the presidential guard as well join the rebels; militicians and Bemba cross the Ubangui River and take refuge in Zongo. **16 March:** In a speech to the nation, General Bozizé explains the action of the rebels by the situation of "extreme poverty," which has spread throughout the land. He makes a catastrophic assessment of the previous regime. He announces the return of "peace and true democracy," but wishes to go by steps and therefore the need for "emergency measures and a recovery program." The self-proclaimed head of state, President Bozizé, dissolves the National Assembly while maintaining the existing political parties and meeting with them to agree on a minimal program to implement at once. He calls for the creation of a National Transition Council including former presidents. The looting is worse in the capital. Chad soldiers arrive in Bangui to reinforce the CEMAC forces. France maintains its 300 men there in charge of the safety and evacuation of foreigners. **18 March:** The Congo and Gabon ministers, in the name of the CEMAC, go to Bangui to pay their respects to the "new President." The French ambassador also meets the new man in power. Set up in camp Bréal, General Bozizé receives the allegiance of the highest military leaders who are kept in place. **20 March:** Professor Abel Goumba, president of the CFPO, says that General Bozizé's taking power cannot be assimilated to a classic coup d'etat because it had "rid the country of a dictator who had made his people live miserably." French Minister for Cooperation P. A. Witzler deems the coup "absolutely unacceptable" and demands a return to civil power. **21 March:** General Bozizé attends Friday prayers at a mosque, then goes to the cathedral and to the small Protestant temple of which he is the founder. **22 March:** The Congolese foreign minister goes to Bangui. President Kabila asks the CAR to put an end to the "ambiguous relationship" former President Patassé had with Jean-Pierre Bemba's rebels. **23 March:** Radio Centrafrique resumes its normal activities. General Bozizé chooses Abel Goumba as prime minister to set up a united government including members of all the different segments of civil society. The Ministries of the Interior and the Defense are entrusted on military men, the Defense Ministry being under the responsibility of General Bozizé himself. Prime Minister Goumba controls the Economy, Finance, Budget and International Cooperation Ministries. **2 April:** President Bozizé meets with the two negotiators chosen by his predecessor. The prime minister asks all members of the government to make a declaration of wealth before they begin their office. **4 April:** The presidential guard is disbanded and replaced with the Presidential Security Unit, about 800 men strong. Its former leader, General Ferdinand Bombayaké, takes refuge in a foreign embassy. **10 April:** A Conseil National de Transition (CNT; National Transition Council) is created by presidential decree. Its mission is "to assist the president in his legislative functions by examining the bills that are presented him" and "to offer to the president or the government all the recommendations it esteems will benefit the nation" as well as "to assist the government in its task of drawing up a new constitution and regarding the preparation of the coming regional elections." The president announces that thanks to the support of the People's Republic of China the civil servants' back wages will be paid within a week. **18 April:** Creation of an interdepartmental committee in charge of preparing an emergency program of economic and social recovery. **6 May:** Prime Minister Goumba begins an international tour. In Paris he meets with the foreign minister and the Minister for Cooperation, which means in fact that General Bozizé's regime is officially recognized. **12 May:** Prime Minister Goumba visits Brussels. **15 June:** Nicolas Tiangaye, a lawyer, is elected president of the CNT (which counts 90 members). **1 July:** In order to prevent any future accusations of corruption, Prime Minister Goumba makes public the amount of his personal wealth and asks all his ministers to do the same. President Bozizé invites every important state officials to act likewise. **11 August:** The CNT votes against the participation of former President Patassé in the "national debate." Isaac Zokoué, a clergyman who had in 1998 directed the Conference for National Reconciliation, becomes president of the Preliminary Committee for the National Debate (11 members). **27 August:** The dates for the "national debate" are set from 11 September to 20 September 2003. This debate must gather 350 delegates from all walks of life: political parties, military, representatives of different religions, businessmen, students, women's associations, and so on. **2 September:** Former

President Patassé, who has escaped to Togo, files a lawsuit against General Bozizé for crimes of war before the International Penal Court. The lawsuit, dated 5 April, is addressed to the Bangui tribunals by Prosper Ndouba, spokesman of the defeated president. **20 November:** Teachers at Bangui University go on strike. It lasts until 30 December. Former President David Dacko dies in Yaoundé—on his way to France to be hospitalized—after his reconciliation with Abel Goumba. The government gives him a national funeral. **27–28 November:** André Wiltzer, French Minister for Cooperation, visits Bangui. **11 December:** Prime Minister Goumba protests against the execution without trial of two outcasts and is obliged to resign by General Bozizé. Immediately replaced by the retired insurance businessman Célestin Gaombalet, who is seconded by Jean-Pierre Lebouder (who worked for the World Bank) and by economist Daniel Nditifei-Boysembé, the Delegate Minister for Planning and International Cooperation. The main concern of the new government is to induce the European Union to resume its cooperation with the CAR. Since June, Bangui has been negotiating with Brussels the terms of a 70 billion CFA franc funding credit. **12 December:** General Bozizé entrusts Abel Goumba with the newly instated function of vice president. **15 December:** Working in Bangui, Enoch Dérant-Lakoué joins the staff of the Banque des Etats d'Afrique Centrale (BEAC; Central African States' Bank) **30 December:** French Minister of Defense Michèle Alliot-Marie makes a trip to Bangui. **31 December:** "As Jesus has overcome Satan, so shall we, children of Christ, overcome the sons of the rebellion," declares in Lomé former President Ange Patassé in his New Year's address to the Central African Republic.

# Introduction

The present-day Central African Republic (former French colony of Ubangui-Shari) is a vast quadrilateral having the form of an ax head stretching over a 618,130-square kilometer area between 2°13' and 11°01' north latitude and 14°25' and 27°27' east longitude, which means it is almost twice as big in longitude (1,450 km) as it is in latitude (870 km). The center of the Upper Mbomou region is 1,750 km away from any shore.

The current Central African boundaries, like those of other states on the African continent, are a colonial inheritance and can be characterized as arbitrary. They were, nonetheless, like other frontiers, made permanent by the Addis Ababa Conference of 1963.

In the area of the Central African Republic lives a small and widely dispersed population, but one that is rapidly growing. The official population on 31 December 1975 was 2,088,000 people. By 2000 the population was estimated around 3,485,000 inhabitants, on the basis of the last official population census of 1989 (2,611,000 inhabitants). This results in a density of less than six inhabitants per square kilometer, ranging from 20 in Lower Kotto to less than 0.5 on the border with Sudan. Half of the inhabitants are under 20 years old, and more than 60 percent of the population lives in rural areas. In Bangui live 590,000 people, in Berberati and in Bouar around 40,000 each, in Bambari 39,000, and in Bussagoa 32,000. The life expectancy at birth is of 44.3 years; the fertility rate is 5.3 children per woman. The combined schooling rate (from primary school to university) is 24 percent, and the adult literacy rate (people over 15) is 45 percent. Around half the population is considered to have access to basic medical treatment. Some 41 percent of the inhabitants suffer from malnutrition. The population (between 15 and 49 years of age) suffering from HIV-AIDS is approximately 14 percent (official percentage).

The history of Central Africa, little known and little studied, is one of the world's most tragic. Contrary to what has been written, the region has been settled for a very long time. Diamond digs in the river flats of Central African rivers have permitted the discovery of innumerable chipped and polished stone implements. The oldest of these date to the late Paleolithic era.

The so-called Pygmies (named *Tvides* by French Africanists), secluded in the forest of Lobaye and Upper-Sangha, in all likelihood constitute the relic of prehistoric or protohistoric populations. These people were already known to the Egyptians of the third millennium before Christ, and were rediscovered by the West at the end of the 19th century.

It has been very hard to uncover the precolonial history of Central Africa. The region remained unexplored for a long time, and in 1890 it constituted the last blank space on the maps of the continent. The work of Africanists is only beginning to allow a real exploration of Central Africa of earlier times.

Historians of Africa attribute Central Africa's backwardness to the three worst centuries of the slave trade from the 16th through 18th centuries. More precisely, one can speak of a regression into which all Central African civilizations must have fallen. Among these centers of civilization was Kush, the prestigious kingdom on the Upper Nile, right next to Central Africa.

Sixteenth-century Central Africa was made up of numerous nations divided among many prestigious states, most of which were condemned to disappear. A few traces can be found of the ancient kingdom of Gaoga cited by Leo Africanus. Its center was at the very door of Central Africa, in the mountains of Darfur. The large confederation of Anzica peoples that caused the Christian kingdom of the Congo to tremble in the 16th century also seems to have included Central Africa.

The Atlantic slave trade in the 17th century and certainly its intensification in the 18th century provoked a great displacement of peoples in the interior. The Central African crossroads was most harmed by these displacements. At the beginning of the 19th century the Sabanga, Kreich, Banda, Baya, and Zandé peoples were notable holders of Central African land. Slave hunters, first from the north then the west and east, struck deadly blows among these groups. The fortunes of the Baguirmi, Wadaï, and Darfur states were based on trade in the men and women of the country—its major "raw material."

From the middle of the 19th century, the Fulbé states of Adamawa, then the well-armed merchant lords of the Upper Nile, in their turn, joined in the hunt for Central African slaves. Rabih built his power at the end of the century at the price of the extermination of whole groups. As-Sanusi followed him.

After 1890 Europeans began to intervene in this ravaged country. Central African territory became a stake in the European powers' "scramble for Africa." With limited means, France was able to ensure its possession of Central Africa through the audacity of its young explorers. The most remarkable of these explorers was Paul Crampel, who died on the present-day Chad–Central African border in 1891. The Crampel plan for a single united French Africa from Algiers to Dakar to Brazzaville became a national program. A little later, France thrilled to the audacious raid by the Marchand column at Fashoda on the Nile. In 1900, the Crampel plan was fulfilled by three military columns from Algeria, Senegal, and Bangui after combat with Rabih near Lake Chad.

Even before Rabih's fall, while the military conquest of Chad was proving to be long and costly, the French government decided to activate the exploitation of the Congo and Ubangui regions. Even before they had been fully explored, extensive parts of present-day Congolese and Central African territories were divided among 27 concessionary companies. These companies, without financial standing, were endowed, in return for fees, with legal rights over the conceded regions.

Despite the scandals denounced by Pierre Brazza and the French anticolonists, little serious effort was undertaken to reform the system. The population succumbed to the constraints of forced labor as porters, paddlers, and others. The local population was also forced to pay taxes. From 1910 to 1912, the French had to conquer the country valley by valley.

In 1911 France accepted the cession to Germany of a large portion of its Congolese and Ubanguian possessions in exchange for freedom of action in Morocco. From 1913 to 1939, a period during which the French empire was shaken first by World War I and its aftermath, then by the world economic depression, French Equatorial Africa, and more particularly Ubangui-Shari, deserved the nickname "Cinderella of the French Empire." After more years of excessive exploitation much of the population revolted (the Kongo-Wara War of 1928–1930).

Like the other French Equatorial African colonies, Ubangui-Shari joined forces with General Charles de Gaulle and participated in the war effort with the Allies. In 1946 the liberal measures of the French government ran up against the private sector in France, which held all real power in the colony.

Barthélémy Boganda, the first Ubanguian priest, elected a deputy on 10 November 1946, took charge of the battle for equal rights in the heart of an "Equatorial France." In 1958 he called for independence but, considering that Ubangui-Shari, heavily afflicted by history, could not constitute a viable state, he pleaded for a large Central African Republic made up of French Equatorial Africa, Cameroon, the Belgian Congo, Angola, Rwanda, and Burundi. Boganda termed this proposed entity the "United States of Latin Africa" in his speeches.

This ambitious project rapidly ran up against the internal state of affairs in the three other colonies of French Equatorial Africa. Boganda's plan was blocked. Thus Balkanized, French Equatorial Africa announced its independence in disastrous conditions. On 1 December 1958, a heartsick Boganda proclaimed a Central African Republic, closely tied to the French community but limited to only Ubangui-Shari. The 29 March death (and perhaps assassination) of Boganda was a very hard blow for the Central African people.

In 1960 David Dacko established a single-party regime and struck the first blows against freedom. In spite of a letter of appeal addressed to General de Gaulle, Dr. Abel Goumba was dismissed from power and imprisoned. Later, during the night from 31 December 1965 to 1 January 1966, a burned-out Dacko prepared to abandon his post to the head of the gendarmerie, Jean Izamo. However, the Army Chief of Staff Jean-Bedel Bokassa, a relative of Boganda, after having assassinated Izamo, took over the administrative center and had Dacko turn all power over to him. The Central African people were informed of this at dawn. For 13 years this people, reduced to greater pauperism than it had suffered during the colonial period, became the unhappy victims of this alcoholic and psychotic former colonial troop sergeant. In 1969 Bokassa had his military rival, Colonel Alexander Banza, shot. Banza had been the actual organizer of the Saint-Sylvestre coup.

While running the most sinister of dictatorships inside the country, Bokassa used all sorts of blackmail against France and the West. The greatest share of foreign aid was turned toward his personal ends. Central African officials, of necessity, and foreigners, for their own ends, accepted all his fantasies. He proclaimed himself a partisan of scientific Marxism, converted to Islam, and returned to the Catholic faith; then in 1976, having miraculously escaped an attempt on his life, he decided to proclaim himself emperor. He then imposed on the world, and most particularly on the Central African and French taxpayers, the burlesque and expensive comedy of a coronation, the smallest details of which were copied from that of Napoleon I. Under the pretext of respect for the principles of states' sovereignty and the noninterference in their internal affairs, the international community seemed to accommodate itself to this tragicomedy.

The 14 May 1979 revelation by Amnesty International of a massacre of children at the Ngaragba Prison, with the personal participation of the mad emperor, finally, in the middle of the International Year of the Child, troubled world opinion. On 16 August 1979, confirmation that these atrocities had taken place, following the publication of the report by a commission of experts established by the African heads of state, equaled a condemnation of the tyrant. At the beginning of September, new massacres in the Bangui prison and Bokassa's project to cede a base to the Libyan army finally incited the French government to intervene. In the night of 20–21 September, French troops took over, with no resistance, the airport and city of Bangui. Dacko announced that he was reassuming the post that he had abandoned during the night of 31 December 1965.

On 1 February 1981, after numerous lapses, Dacko succeeded in having a constitution that seemed to satisfy the opposition adopted by the Central African people. The fraud involved in the 15 March 1981 presidential elections once again called everything into question. On 1 September 1981, as he had already done on 1 January 1966, Dacko turned over his power to his military chief of staff. Distancing himself from civilians, General André Kolingba suspended the constitution and created a Comité Militaire de Redressement National (CMRN; Military Committee of National Recovery). On 3 March 1982 two generals, members of the CMRN, attempted a coup on behalf of Ange Patassé, the former prime minister under Emperor Bokassa. After the failure of this attempt, Patassé took refuge in the French embassy, from which he left for exile in Togo. During the years 1982 to 1985, the principal opponents of the regime were imprisoned.

On 21 November 1986, a new constitution was adopted by referendum and General Kolingba was elected President of the Republic for six years. He continued the single party system and created the Rassemblement démocratique centrafricain (RDC; Central African Democratic Party). On 31 July 1987, for the first time in 20 years, legislative elections were held.

Bokassa, who took refuge in Abidjan in 1979, was condemned to death in absentia on 24 December 1980. On 21 November 1983, his first attempt to return to Bangui failed. On 4 December 1983, he set himself up in one of his châteaux near Paris. On 23 October 1986 he succeeded in returning to Bangui by way of Brussels and Rome. Arrested at the Bangui-Mpoko airport, Bokassa appeared before the Criminal Court to be judged once again on 26 November 1986. His trial lasted more than six months. He was again condemned to death on 12 June 1987. The death penalty was commuted by presidential decree to a life sentence at hard labor on 29 February 1988. In 1989—the centennial of the French foundation of Bangui, 30 years since the death of Barthélémy Boganda, and 10 years since the fall of Jean-Bedel Bokassa—the Central African people, who had suffered through colonization and decolonization, hoped for a better future.

In 1990, President André Kolingba restored the multiparty system and appointed a prime minister as the head of the government. When in 1980 President David Dacko had restored political plurality, many political parties emerged. About eight of these often ethnic-based parties, usually with relatively few members, were elected to the Assembly. In 1990 and 1991 civil servants and teachers particularly went on long strikes in order to protest the delay in payment of their back-wages. Soon these strikes spread to the private sector as well. The legislative and presidential elections took place in 1992, but the results were invalidated. President Kolingba decided to remain in power though his mandate had expired. He was assisted by a Conseil National Politique Provisoire de la République (CNPPR; Provisional National Political Council of the Republic), which included the candidates in the presidential campaign. In fact, only David Dacko, Enoch-Dérant Lakoué, and a close acquaintance of Kolingba took part in this Council. It was meant to replace the National Assembly and to present advice on legislative measures. In May the presidential guard demonstrated along with the army's special units, protesting the eight-month delay in the payment of their wages. During the August 1993 presidential election, Kolingba was defeated. Ange Patassé won over Abel Goumba, the opposition parties' candidate. In December 1993, the civil servants' strike that had begun six months earlier finally ended due to France's help in paying their back wages.

In January 1995 a new constitution was adopted: it installed a six-year presidential mandate and the election of regional assemblies by universal suffrage. But in 1996 the military rebellions of April, May, and November caused many deaths both civilian and military, and the destruction of industrial infrastructure and housing in the south and southeast of Bangui. These rebellions were due to lack of pay but were also based on ethnic conflicts: during his 14 years in power General Kolingba had massively recruited within his own ethnic group, the Yakoma living along the Ubangui River, whereas the new government was now related to other ethnic groups, living in the center and west of the Central African Republic. The conflict ended in December 1996 due to the mediation of the heads of other African states. General Amadou Toumani Touré, former Mali president, led the troops from Ghana, Gabon, Mali, Senegal, and Togo in charge of keeping the peace, and he successfully directed the arbitration of this entangled and lasting crisis.

In January 1997 the assassination of a French officer provoked violent retaliation from the French forces there that bombed the southwest of Bangui, and on 18 May a new military rebellion began. A third of Bangui, in rebel hands, was bombed. In June France sent troops to protect its nationals, and the fighting stopped in July. In October a new teachers' strike started.

The year 1998 proved more peaceful. In February Patassé's party joined with 11 opposition parties for a national reconciliation conference. An agreement was reached on 5 March, and in April the French forces withdrew. The United Nations decided on sending a peacekeeping mission, the Mission des Nations Unies en République Centrafricaine (MINURCA; United Nations Mission in the Central African Republic). In December the legislative elections renewed the National Assembly: Ange Patassé's party won the majority by 11 votes.

In 1999, a new strike began and the last French troops of the MINURCA left the country. Patassé attempted to draw closer to Libya by joining the Communauté des Etats Sahélo-Sahariens (COMESSA; Community of the Sahel and Sahara States), headed by Colonel

Mouammar Khadafy, and in November of that year he created a Ministry in Charge of Relations with the Arab World. In September Patassé won the presidential elections. In February 2000 civil servants were paid their wages for February 1999. In November they threatened the government with a new strike if their last 12 months' wages were not paid. Patassé offered to pay them $10 million from his personal accounts, which did not prevent a new strike. The same problem occurred the next year, and another strike started in February 2001.

On 25 May 2001 about 500 soldiers and former military, often reinstated rebels from 1997, attacked Ange Patassé's presidential palace. The presidential guard succeeded in defending the palace, but the rebels took camp Kasaï and the southwest of Bangui. Army Chief of Staff General François Bozizé led a successful counterattack on camp Kasaï. The Yakoma, General Bozizé's ethnic group, threatened by Patassé's men, massively fled the area. President Patassé asked for the help of the head of the northern Congo-Kinshasa region, Jean-Pierre Bemba, who sent him a hundred men. Libya flew in about another hundred military to be Ange Patassé's close guard. General André Kolingba claimed responsibility for the failed coup and had to leave the country.

On 1 June 2001, the fighting had stopped but members of Kolingba's ethnic group, the Yakoma, were still hunted and killed throughout Bangui. Jean-Pierre Bemba's men tightened their hold on Bangui, looting, raping, and murdering their way through the city. In July the opposition parties asked for President Patassé's resignation. In October General Bozizé was dismissed and on 3 November, after he and his men had resisted his arrest, he fled to Chad.

In January 2002, the Organization of African Unity (OAU) decided to send troops to Bangui to maintain peace. But in February, General Bozizé and some 200 men launched an attack from the Chad border. Gradually, Bozizé's troops occupied the north and the west of the Central African Republic, and soon they were within 50 miles of Bangui. On 26 October they attempted to take Bangui, but Libyan troops, Bemba's men, and the Central African Army succeeded in repelling the onslaught. In spite of this, the Libyan soldiers and the COMESSA troops left the country in December.

A new strike began, with civil servants asking for their back wages for the last two years. The help of the International Monetary Fund (IMF) then allowed the Central African Republic to pay its civil servants, and the European Union's increased credits somewhat improved the situation.

Yet in 2003 decisive changes occurred. In January, General Bozizé announced that he wished to regroup all opponents to the Patassé regime. In February the Central African Army failed in its repeated attacks to gain back Bozum, Bossangoa, Fort Sibut, and Kaga Bandoro. On 13 March, President Patassé left Bangui to go to Niamey in Niger to attend a COMESSA conference. But as early as 15 March, Bozizé's troops took Bangui and prevented President Patassé's returning plane from landing. The Central African Armed Forces joined General Bozizé, while Bemba's militia left to the Congo: General Bozizé appointed himself President of the Republic and dissolved the National Assembly. Soon the world recognized his "legitimacy."

On 23 March a government was created, presided over by Abel Goumba, which gathered all the opposition ministers, members of Ange Patassé's party, and even a son of former President David Dacko and a son of General André Kolingba. Ange Patassé's presidential guard was dismissed.

On 10 April, a National Transition Council was created: its 10 members were of different ethnic origins and political affiliations, and their task was to assist President François Bozizé in his legislative work. Chinese help allowed for the payment of back wages. Some 350 people representing the whole country then took part in a great "national debate" in order to achieve national reconciliation and to study what measures should be taken for the future. On 11 December, Abel Goumba resigned from his office of prime minister and became Vice President of the Republic. When, on 20 November 2003, former President David Dacko died at Youndé Hospital, a page was turned. But a lack of a solution to the budget crisis, which was long overdue, impeded the new government's efforts, and civil servants soon protested against the situation. Teachers went on strike again from 20 November to 30 December 2003.

After the violence and the inequities of Jean-Bedel Bokassa's 1966 to 1979 regime, followed by David Dacko's short-lived attempts at rebuilding the country, and after André Kolingba's 1981 to 1994 mismanagement of the Republic, the rule of Ange Patassé from 1994 to 2003 prolonged the corruption and pilfering of the country's riches. Such long-lasting policies plunged the country into a chronic financial crisis, aggravated by the absence of foreign support due to a lack of democracy and blatant state fraud.

As a result of this, civil servants were frequently paid their wages with a growing delay—sometimes years, with a few temporary compromises. The repeated strikes disorganized all the administrations (schools were, in fact, closed for three years), and corruption reached unprecedented proportions. The military rebellions and the riots that ensued destroyed all of Bangui's industrial facilities (textile, tobacco, brewery, small workshops, and so on). The population, fleeing the villages to reach the capital, endured widespread unemployment and misery: the city of Bangui swelled from 25,000 inhabitants in 1966 to about 600,000 in 2003. The roads were in a terrible condition, and very unsafe for travel. Transportation was at a standstill, and farmers could not market their meager production. Every level of the country's economy and all of its social classes were deeply disrupted.

There is some hope that General François Bozizé's new government, formed in the context of a widely acknowledged need for change and rebuilding of the nation, will be up to the task. But already in 2004 the financial difficulties worsened, and foreign aid was insufficient and unsuccessful in restoring an efficient civil service. The future of the Central African Republic therefore remains very uncertain.

# The Dictionary

## – A –

**ABATCHOU, RAOUL (?–28 April 1968).** Head of the **Banda** Vidri canton at **Yalinga** in 1950. Member of the Mouvement pour l'Evolution Sociale de l'Afrique Noire (**MESAN**, Movement for the Social Evolution of Black Africa) governing committee (1962–1966). During the **Saint-Sylvestre coup d'etat** of 1965, he was one of the few dignitaries of the regime who resisted, weapons in hand, the rebellious soldiers. Imprisoned at **Ngaragba**, chained and tortured, he lost his mind and died in his cell.

**ABAZA.** Noble family claiming descent from Bakia (or Baza), the mythical head of the **Sabanga** in the 16th century. In the 19th century, under the name of Abandia, this family founded three states: one on the Mbari River under the leadership of **Ndounga**, an ancestor of **Bangassou**; another under **Kassanga**, an ancestor of **Rafaï** on the **Chinko** River; and the third under Louzian, an ancestor of **Djabir**, on the **Ouellé**.

**ABDALLAH.** Head of a commercial agency (**zeriba**) in Lower **Ouellé**. In 1878 he worked for **Gnawi-Bey**.

**ABD EL MENTALIB.** Youngest son of **Kobur**, the Sultan of **Dar-al-Kuti** (deposed in 1890 by **Rabih**). In March 1900 he led an attempted coup against **as-Sanusi** with the aid of Moungasche, a **Wadaï** official posted at **Ndélé**.

**ABEILLE DE LA COLLE, DR. ELZEAR.** Chief medical officer and head of the **Bangui** region in 1900, he was accused by **Emile Gentil** of negligence in directing the supply of the Chad army.

1

**ABIRAS (presently KEMBA).** First French post in Upper **Ubangui**, founded in September 1890 on the north bank of the river, by the administrator **Gaston Gaillard**, just opposite **Yakoma**, a post established by officials of King **Leopold** of Belgium.

**ABO BEN AÏSSA. Lamido** of **Ngaoundéré**. He followed his father, Aïssa, who had been killed in a war against the **Baya**. He helped the French explorer **Louis Mizon** in his journey to the **Sangha** and entered into relations with Pierre **Brazza** in 1892. His troops were defeated on 30 June 1896 by a combined Baya and **Banda** Yanguéré army commanded by the administrator **Alphonse Goujon**.

**ABOUGOUROUN (or ABD ER RAHMAN).** One of the principal merchant lords of the Upper Nile, he exchanged livestock from **Kreich** for **Zandé slaves**. He was allied with the Zandé Sultan Ndorouma.

**ABOUKA, PAUL.** Paul Abouka was **Barthélémy Boganda**'s representative among the Bougbou (Alindao) and member of the **MESAN** governing committee (1962–1966). Arrested during the 1965 coup d'etat, he was imprisoned at **Ngaragba**. He was released with other political prisoners on 1 January 1970.

**ADAMA.** Learned person (**modibo**) of the Vallerbé, a **Fulbé** group, Adama was chosen by the conqueror **Usman dan Fodio** to administer the old Hausa province of **Fombina** in the early 19th century. He took the name **Adamawa**. He conducted a number of **slave** wars against the **Baya** and the **Mboum**.

**ADAMAOUA (or ADAMAWA).** Cameroonian province, base of the **Fulbé slaving** expeditions into the present-day **Central African Republic** (1820–1900).

**ADAMA-TAMBOUX, MAURICE.** Instructor, then councilor of the **Territorial Assembly of Ubangui-Shari** (ATOC), he was elected president of this Assembly on 9 May 1960, replacing **Pierre Maleombho**. He kept this post until the **Saint-Sylvestre coup d'etat** in 1965. Arrested on 4 February 1966 he was not released until 1 January 1970. Retired from public life he agreed, in 1993, to preside over the commission in charge of supervising the elections.

**ADMINISTRATIVE POSTS.** Between 1900 and 1914 administrative posts were created to maintain order and collect taxes, and also to watch over the activities of the **concessionary companies**. Depending on the case, these posts were assigned to a military officer or a colonial administrator. Administrative posts became commercial centers, and gradually **schools**, dispensaries, and **missions** were built. The most important posts eventually developed a diversification of administrative activities. All the necessary conditions united to create a population influx in the surrounding areas and thus the growth of urban agglomerations. The modest **Bangui** administrative post created in 1889 gave birth to the present-day capital of Bangui. *See also* TAXATION.

**AFRIQUE ET CONGO. Concessionary company** founded in 1900 by William Guynet, on the concession of the Upper-Sangha company. **Alphonse Fondere**, former head of the **Bangui** post in 1889, became its president director general.

**AGRICULTURE.** Agricultural production was stationary at the beginning of the 20th century and represented 34 percent of the GDP. In 2001 it was estimated at 115,900 tons of peanut oil, 101,000 tons of corn, 47,600 tons of millet (sorghum), 24,500 tons of **cotton**-seeds, 24,300 tons of squash, 23,100 tons of rice (paddy), and 11,500 tons of **coffee**. **Manioc**, after the retting of its roots, is the basic food for Central Africans—it often replaces millet. The price of the manioc "bowl" serves in **Bangui** as the economy's barometer— the manioc bowl being the basic day-to-day food. *See also* LIVE-STOCK RAISING.

**AJOU.** Leader of the Bougbou insurgents, he submitted to Captain **Jules Jacquier** in 1912. He led another uprising in 1925. Captured in 1926, he was instantly executed.

**AL TOUNSY (EL TOUNSY), SHEIK (CHEIK) MUHAMMAD.** A Tunisian, Al Tounsy traveled throughout **Wadaï** and **Darfur** in the first years of the 19th century. His accounts are very important for Central African history, describing the metallurgy of the **Banda** country and the **slave** raids conducted by Darfur throughout **Dar Fertit** to **Mbomou**. His accounts, originally written in Arabic and published in Cairo, were translated into French by Dr. Perron.

**ALAZOULA, LOUIS (1935–).** Born at Mongoumba (Lobaye), he completed the minor seminary in Brazzaville and then worked as a government agent in **agriculture**. He was appointed Minister of the Interior by his cousin, Emperor **Bokassa**. On 14 July 1981 he was condemned by the Criminal Court at **Bangui** to 10 years of hard labor.

**ALEXAKIS, VASSILIS.** At the age of 52, this French-speaking Greek citizen felt the need to learn yet a new language. He chose **Sango**, the second Central African language after French. After a trip to **Bangui** at the end of last century, he published the very successful book *Les Mots Etrangers* (Foreign Words).

**ALI.** Ethnic group constituted in Lobaye by the merger of **Baya** elements and various Bantu-speaking groups.

**ALI, ABOU MOURI.** One of the three principal merchant lords, called the "Triumvirate of Bahr-el-Ghazal." He sat in judgment over a vast territory of the **Kreich** people on the headwaters of the Kosanga River around 1860. He was **Zubayr (Ziber) Pasha**'s patron.

**ALI FENTAMI.** Bornu trader, he served as an informant to Gustav **Nachtigal** during his travels in **Wadaï** in the areas populated by the **Rounga** and **Banda** (1873).

**ALIKOBO.** Head of a commercial company in Lower **Ouellé**, he conducted a war against the **Bandia**, with his colleague Abdullah. The explorer **Wilhelm Junker** visited his **zeriba** on 24 February 1883.

**ALIMA.** The name of the Alima River was given to a steamboat of the **Daumas** trading house. It was used by Administrator **Albert Dolisie** during his travels in the bend of the **Ubangui** in December 1887.

**ALIS, HARRY (1857–1895).** Pseudonym of Hyppolite Perchet, born in Moulins, and a journalist with the *Journal des Débats*. A friend of the explorer **Paul Crampel**, he encouraged the **Comité de l'Afrique** (French Africa Committee) between 1890 and 1895, which stimulated French exploration. He was killed by Captain Le Châtelier in a duel on 1 March 1895.

**ALLAH DJABOU.** A **Banda** Marba, first a **slave**, then the principal war leader of as-**Sanusi**, Sultan of **Daral-Kuti** (1890). In December 1910 he seized the **Ouanda-Djallé** heights, defended by the Youlou leader, **Djellab**. Allah Djabou was defeated by Captain **Jean Modat**'s troops on 7 February 1911, near **Ndélé**.

**AMADOU TOUMANI TOURE.** Former head of state of Mali, a general, he was chosen by the French-speaking leaders as negotiator and head of the international force appointed by the United Nations in the Central African Republic. He performed his duty remarkably well and his arbitration ended the **army** rebellion.

**AMITY, JEAN.** Director of **David Dacko**'s cabinet, after the coup d'etat of 1 January 1966; he was retained by then-Colonel **Jean-Bedel Bokassa**. He later became state minister under Bokassa. *See also* SAINT-SYLVESTRE, COUP D'ETAT OF.

**ANCIENS COMBATTANTS (VETERANS).** After World War II, the veterans constituted a group that proved to be politically useful for white territorial advisers against Bogandist elements in the first college.

**ANGER.** Vice President of the **Chamber of Commerce of Bangui**, he was one of the first elected to the first college of the **Territorial Assembly of Ubangui-Shari** on 30 March 1952.

**ANTONETTI, GOVERNOR GENERAL RAPHAEL (1872–1938).** Appointed governor general of French Equatorial Africa on 8 July 1924. He directed the work on the **Congo-Ocean** railway with an iron hand. This railway cost the lives of numerous Ubanguian workers. In October 1928, Antonetti ordered a severe repression of the **Baya** revolt.

**AOUK.** Right tributary of the **Shari** River, it now constitutes the border between the Republic of Chad and the Central African Republic.

**ARA.** Locality that no longer exists today. Ara was situated to the east of **Ndélé**. It was the capital of **Gono**, the **Banda Ngao** leader who was one of the principal adversaries of as-**Sanusi**.

**ARMY.** The Central African army was created in 1962 by President **David Dacko** with the assistance of French advisers under the command of Colonel Marcel Bigeard. A relative of **Barthélémy Boganda**, **Jean-Bedel Bokassa**, who had reached the rank of lieutenant in the French army was appointed chief of staff in the new army, with the rank of Colonel. At the end of 1965 Bokassa was irritated by the preference given to the gendarmerie budget by the head of state and blamed President Dacko for assigning the army to nonmilitary tasks. On New Year's Eve 1965 (the night of the **Saint-Sylvestre** in French), a coup d'etat organized by Commander **Alexandre Banza** allowed the military to seize the public buildings in **Bangui**. Dacko, along with his ministers and the leaders of the single party—the **MESAN**—were arrested and thrown in jail. Commander **Jean-Henri Izamo**, Chief of the gendarmerie, then **Jean Mounoumbaye**, Chief of Security to the President, were arrested attempting to escape and then tortured and put to death. The population remained much indifferent to these events. France and the international community let a military dictatorship take power in Bangui. Subsequently the Central African army underwent a series of serious dramas. In 1969 Bokassa had his assistant Colonel Banza arrested under suspicion of plotting. Arrested and tortured even during the Ministerial Council, Banza was sentenced to death by the military tribunal and executed right away. By a nationwide decree issued on 25 April 1969, Bokassa cited the Central African National army for honoring the nation and made 10 April of each year "a memorial day and day of rest and rejoicing for all the Central African armed forces."

Colonel Bokassa, who appointed himself general, President for Life and then marshal, made many decisions revealing his megalomania. He inducted many of his own family into the army, including babies, as simple second class privates who were promoted corporals at the age of four and paid as such. He created a personal guard nicknamed "les abeilles" ("the bees"). He decided to have a Central African air force and navy, which remained wishful thinking due to the lack of planes and ships. Before declaring himself Emperor of Central Africa in 1976, obsessed with plots against him, be they fictitious or real, he purged the army several times, eliminating any possible rivals. Thus, on 12 April 1973 he had his close collaborator General **Auguste Mbongo**, Minister of Civil Engineering, arrested. The latter, chained to a block of concrete, died in **Mbaïki** in March 1974. General **Jean-Claude Mandaba** became ambassador in Romania before he was himself arrested and executed. The same happened to the head of the gendarmerie **Martin Lingoupou**, presented for show to a court martial and executed on 27 December 1974. That same year Bokassa had his former schoolmates at Saint-Cyr, Colonels **Mandé** and **Basile Kolegnako**, arrested and executed. Many heads of departments in the army were arrested, causing unrest among the officers.

On 13 February 1976, a very real plot almost cost the dictator his life. As Bokassa arrived at Bangui airport Chief Warrant Officer Zoukango threw a grenade at him. With its pin only half-pulled, this Soviet grenade failed to explode and Zoukango killed himself. Arrested while fleeing, Lieutenant **Fidèle Obrou**, Bokassa's own nephew and leader of the conspiracy, as well as his companions, were arrested and executed shortly after. Bokassa kept taking revenge on the family and close friends of any conspirators for a long time.

Early in 1979 the Central African army was implicated in the bloody repression of youths protesting and asking for their unpaid scholarships and their parents' back wages. On 19 January the army surrounded the university and the crossroads of the capital. Under the authority of Generals **François Bozizé** and **Josyhat Mayomokala** the military attacked the barricades. Demonstrations began again on 17 April. The fighting caused many deaths. On 19 April many young demonstrators were thrown in jail. The army swept the districts that were known to favor the demonstrators.

On 20 September 1979 neither the army nor the presidential guard offered any resistance to the French military of operation **Barracuda**. On 19 September 1980 several military leaders were arrested on charges of violence upon their prisoners. They were sentenced to death and executed. On 2 September 1981, with the help of the French Colonel **Jean-Claude Mantion**, General **André Kolingba**, the army chief of staff, took power. He began a new military dictatorship and created a Comité Militaire de Redressement National (CMRN; Military Committee for National Recovery). Kolingba favored his ethnic minority, the **Yakomas**, for recruiting and promotions. The French military schools were asked to provide training for the new leading class. Some were also sent from neighboring countries such as Zaire.

On 3 March 1982 the presidential guard under the authority of Colonel Mantion prevented a new coup d'etat from succeeding: the plot involved Generals Bozizé and Mbaikoua, both close to **Ange Patassé**, Bokassa's former prime minister. As the latter managed to escape abroad, the former prime minister took refuge in the French embassy. Following negotiations led by Guy Penne, an adviser to President François Mittérand, a French plane took Patassé to Togo, where he lived for 10 years. Kolingba, unhindered by the French, remained in power until September 1993, when the elections—under international scrutiny—resulted in the victory of Patassé. Kolingba, during his stay in power, privileged members of his ethnic minority the Yakomas. Patassé now favored ethnic minorities from the northwest.

Delays in paying the army and **civil servants** caused a great deal of serious disorder among the army and the population. Part of the Central African army rebelled in 1996 and 1997 and fighting occurred between the army and members of the presidential guard that had remained faithful to Patassé. In August 1996 the new Prime Minister **Jean-Paul Ngoupandé** organized, with the rebels' assent, the Etats Généraux de l'Armée Centrafricaine (Central African Army States General) in order to define "its new mission which means it's becoming peaceful, its reorganization, a new recruitment policy, perfecting its capabilities and a new promotion for its officers." But in November 1996 a new mutiny allowed the rebels to take control of certain districts of the capital as they blocked the oil imports and demanded the resignation of President Patassé. The president, after meeting in Paris with Jacques Chirac, called for negotiations and national reconciliation. The leaders of French-speaking African states, meeting at Ouagadocigou, offered to serve as go-betweens and decided on sending an inter-African armed force under the authority of the former president of Mali, General **Amadou Toumani Touré**. Violent fighting still took place until early 1997, in spite of cease-fire agreements. Peace was not restored until late June after the intervention of the Mission d'Interposition et de Surveillance des Accords de Bangui (**MISAB**; Peacekeeping and Supervision Mission of the **Bangui Agreement**) and the French military. In July 1997, 400 rebel soldiers were reinstated in the army. But it was only after the meeting in March 1998 of a vast Conférence de Réconciliation Nationale (CNR; National Reconciliation Conference) that the military and population finally abandoned their weapons on the steps of the French embassy. The weapons, heavy and light, were gathered under the supervision of the Mission des Nations Unies en République Centrafricaine (**MINURCA**; United Nations Mission in the Central African Republic), the new international force implemented by the UN Security Council early that year. The bases in Bangui (camp Bréal) and Bouar, held by the French, were turned over to the Forces Armées Centrafricaine (**FACA**; Central African Armed Forces). The mandate of the International Force, renewed several times, ended on 22 February 2000. An International Observation Bureau was maintained in the Central African capital.

**ASSEMBLY, LEGISLATIVE and NATIONAL.** The **constitution** of 6 February 1959 provided for the election of a Legislative Assembly elected for five years under universal suffrage. The elections were held on 5 April 1959, a few days after the death of the founder of the Central African Republic, **Barthélémy Boganda**, who had himself chosen the Mouvement pour l'évolution sociale de l'Afrique Noire (**MESAN**; Movement for the Social Evolution of Black Africa) candidates. These candidates obtained all the seats in the three administrative divisions where their list was the only one presented, the other candidates having been disqualified by the verification commission. More than 45 percent of the registered electors abstained. In the fourth administrative division the elections could not be held until 25 April because all the candidates had been disqualified. Five seats out of 60 were reserved for French citizens of the Intergroup Libéral Oubanguien (ILO; Ubanguian Liberal Intergroup).

This new assembly was obliged to elect **Pierre Maleombho** as its president. In May 1959 the Assembly refused full powers to

President **David Dacko**. On 3 October 1959, following dissension in the MESAN, a motion of censure that received votes from two-thirds of the active assembly was submitted for 7 October. Partisans of Dacko surrounded the Assembly Palace, and this motion was more or less overcome. On 9 May 1960 Maleombho was turned out of the presidency, which returned to **Maurice Adama-Tamboux**. On 7 July 1960, the minority faction of the MESAN formed an opposition group, attaching itself to a new party, the Mouvement pour l'évolution démocratique de l'Afrique Centrale (**MEDAC**; Movement for Democratic Evolution of Central Africa), founded by Dr. **Abel Goumba**. In the course of an extraordinary session (18–21 July 1960) the Assembly ratified the cooperative agreements with France that had existed since before **independence**. On 14 August the Assembly granted the president of the government the right to exercise the functions of head of state.

After the partial poll of 24 September 1960, which revealed a strong advance by the opposition, the head of state, with the support of France, decided to liquidate the opposition. On 25 September, the Deputies confirmed President Dacko in his functions as head of state until the end of the legislature. On 24 December, Dr. Goumba's parliamentary immunity was withdrawn and the Council of Ministers declared the dissolution of the opposition party. The Legislative Assembly, becoming National, was given only a rubber-stamp role, the real power residing entirely in the head of state. In December 1962, the Assembly adopted a constitutional law that, on installing an all-powerful governing committee of the single party, could annul the mandate of the deputies and the functions of the ministers, practically ending the Assembly's powers. In November 1963 the Assembly adopted a new constitutional amendment that permitted the direct election of the president for seven years.

After the 5 January 1964 plebiscite, David Dacko had a single list of 60 candidates elected on 15 March 1964, destined to make up the new National Assembly. This second legislature was cut short by Colonel **Jean-Bedel Bokassa**'s coup d'etat. Constitutional Act number 2 of 8 January 1966 suppressed the National Assembly. The proclamation of the empire in 1976 was not followed by the establishment of a parliament, even though this was called for in the Imperial Constitution. However, in 1979 Bokassa scheduled elections from a single list of candidates for September. These elections were never held since Bokassa was deposed.

After David Dacko's presidential election in 1981 he promised legislative elections following the new constitution. These were never held either. Finally, in July 1987 Dacko's successor General **André Kolingba**, under yet another constitution, held legislative elections from a single list of candidates.

Elections took place again in October 1993 but the results were declared null and void. The mandate of the National Assembly having expired, President André Kolingba set up the Conseil National Politique Provisoire de la République (CNPPR; Provisional National Political Council of the Republic), but it only consisted of former President David Dacko, **Enoch Dérant-Lakoué** and a protégé of Kolingba's. It was meant to replace the parliament and supply a legislative backbone to the presidency.

New legislative elections took place in September 1994, along with presidential elections. The new assembly consisted of 34 representatives of President **Ange Patassé**'s party out of 85 members, which required the formation of coalition governments that grouped several small opposition parties. Patassé was reelected on December 1999 and the National Assembly, following the concurrent legislative elections, was then composed of 54 members of his own party and 55 members of the opposition. Because one elected opposton member in the assembly was co-opted by Ange Patassé, the new government was completely favorable to him.

As soon as he had seized power on 15 March 2003, General **François Bozizé** decided to dissolve the existing National Assembly and promised that new legislative elections would be held as early as possible.

**AUBE, ROBERT (1906–?).** Born on 10 June 1906, he became director of the **Compagnie Equatoriale des Mines** (CEM; Equatorial Mine Company) and was elected councilor of the Republic of **Ubangui-Shari** on 14 November 1948, on the *Rassemblement des Gauches Républicaines* (RGR, Left-Wing Republican Party) ticket. He was reelected until 1958, when he left Ubangui. In 1959 Senator Aubé, now a member of the French Economic and Social Council, was assigned to the Ministry for Cooperation.

**AUGAGNEUR, VICTOR (1855–1931).** Born on 16 May 1855 in Lyon, he died in Vésinet (Yvelines) on 3 April 1931. A professor of medicine, Minister of Civil Engineering, of Education, of the Navy, and Governor General of Madagascar, in 1920 Augagneur was appointed Governor General of French Western Africa, a post he occupied until 1924. In his circular of 1 October he condemned the "active politics" conducted by his predecessor, **Martial Merlin**, and he forbade the violent methods employed during "police tours," notably in **Ubangui-Shari**.

**AUGOUARD, MONSIGNOR PROSPER (1852–1921).** Born on 15 September 1852 in Poitiers, he died on 3 October 1921 in Paris. He was a missionary sent to Gabon in 1878, then to Boma in 1881 and to Brazzaville in 1883. Appointed Apostolic Vicar of **Ubangui** in 1890, he founded, with **Father Remy**, the **Saint Paul Mission** of **Bangui** on 13 February 1893 at the village of the local leader Souguebiou. In 1902 Monsignor Augouard, taking the side of **concessionary companies**, criticized in the *Dépêche Colonial* (Colonial Dispatch) the methods of the colonial administration, which he judged "too liberal."

**AUTOMOBILE.** The first automobiles appeared in **Ubangui-Shari** in May 1923, when Governor **Auguste Lamblin** motored from **Bangui** to Fouroumbala. The first roads useable by automobile were built in 1923–1924. On 1 March 1924 Administrator Chaumel left France by automobile, reached Bangui, and returned in only 132 days.

**AVIATION.** In 1931 Bangui was chosen as the base for the French Equatorial African Flight. Regular ties between North Africa and French Equatorial Africa were ensured by the planes of the Algiers-Congo region. In 1935 Governor General **Edouard Renard**, returning from **Brazzaville** to **Bangui**, died in an air accident. World War II allowed the establishment of several airports in the Central African Territory. At the end of the war weekly connections with France were established. In 1965 the international airport of Bangui-Mpoko was constructed. The Central African government participates in the Air Afrique Company and has developed some domestic lines.

**AVOUNGARA.** A name that appears to have been given to his family by Ngoura at the beginning of the 19th century, during the conquest of present-day **Zandé** by his fighting men. According to Father Van-den Plas, the word can be broken up as follows: "*A* (plural), *vo* (present participle of the verb *vo*—to bind), and *ngara* (force), that is to say 'binding the forces,' or 'the dominators.'"

**AYANDHO, BERNARD-CHRISTIAN (1930–1993).** Born in Bangassar on 15 December 1930, he died in Paris on 18 December 1993. A former student at the **Brazzaville** Staff School (Ecole des Cadres), he was an adviser to the administration, was the national **economy** minister from 1961 to 1965, financial auditor from 1966 to 1970, a minister in the economic sector in both the **David Dacko** and the Emperor **Bokassa** governments, then Air Afrique delegate to Gabon and Air Afriquedirector general. On 25 September 1979, he was appointed prime minister by David Dacko. He served as president of the **Chamber of Commerce (of Bangui)**, Agriculture and Industry in 1987 until his death.

**AZREG.** A **slaver**, he was a companion of as-**Sanusi**, and his delegate in December 1897 to **Emile Gentil** with the mission of concluding a protectorate treaty. He attended a troop review with the president of the French Republic at Moulins on 14 July 1898.

**– B –**

**BABINGA.** In the Central African **forests**, one still finds a number of "Pygmy" groups called Babinga. They may number about 10,000, localized in the sub**prefectures** of Nola, Boda (**Ngotto** and Bambio), Mbaïki, and Mongoumba.

**BACPAYO.** *See* DJABIR.

**BADA.** Initiation camp among the **Mandjia**, a veritable traditional **school**. Such institutions exist, under other names, in various Central African regions.

**BAFATORO.** Representative councilor of **Ubangui-Shari**, elected on the independent ticket in 1947. Appointed head of the **Baya** ethnic group by the colonial administration, Bafatoro died in 1955.

**BAFIO.** Head of the Boupane clan of the **Baya**. Born on the Mambéré River in 1890, Bafio gathered together several thousand Baya and Yanguéré fighters against the **Fulbé**. On 12 May 1891, he attacked the **Fourneau mission** at Zaourou-Koussio near **Carnot** and forced it to fall back toward **Sangha**.

**BAGO (or BAGOU).** Heir of **Ganda**, this Nzakara leader was a cousin of Bangassou. He became a protégé of the French, and was vested with power by **Victor Liotard**. Bago counted on French support in his military efforts against the Bougbou. He contributed to Liotard's reprisal operation against this group in February 1893.

**BAGUIRMI.** Founded during the 16th century, this strong Chadian state was never able to overpower the Sara people. In the 19th century, the Baguirmians increased their **slave** raids into the country just north of the present-day Central African Republic. Defeated by **Rabih** in 1893, the **mbang** of Baguirmi, Gaourang, solicited and obtained in 1897 French Protectorate status while continuing his ravages on the Sara.

**BAMINGUI.** One of the tributaries of the **Shari** River, this river rises in the center of **Banda** country, in the **Kaga** region, ravaged by as-**Sanusi** and **Rabih**. It is today deserted.

**BAMINGUI-BANGORAN.** Name given in 1962 to the **Ndélé** prefecture, the former autonomous district of Ndélé, which closely corresponded to the territory of the Sultanate of **Dar-al-Kuti** at the time of as-**Sanusi**.

**BANDA.** Apparently originating in the mountains of **Darfur**, then established in Upper Kotto, this great people was involved in a migration in the 19th century that carried some groups deep into the equatorial **forest**. Between 1840 and 1850 some Banda laid seige to **Sabanga** country; others attacked the **Mandjia**. About 1860 the Yanguéré took the west. Others settled not far from the **Ubangui** valley. The Banda refused to submit to the slaving Sultans of **Wadaï** and **Darfur**, as well as to the conquerors, **Zubayr** and **Rabih**. They resisted as-**Sanusi**'s activities until the Belgians (1892) and then the French (early 20th century) penetrated into Upper Ubangui. Today they are the most numerous ethnic group in the Central African Republic, spilling over into Zaire and Cameroon. *See also* ERE.

**BANDERO (KAGA).** Celebrated mountain fortress of the **Mandjia**, at the foot of which was founded, in 1897, the French post of Fort **Crampel** (today a Central African sub**prefecture**).

**BANDIA.** Before the arrival on the **Mbomou** of the Azandé (**Zandé**) early in the 19th century, the Bandia caste (not to be confused with the **Banda** ethnic group) of the **Ubangui** had formed kingdoms there that joined several ethnic groups. Two Bandia kingdoms were established in **Nzakara** country and on the **Chinko**. These became the Sultanates of **Bangassou** and **Rafaï** over which King **Leopold**'s forces and then the French established protectorates at the end of the 19th century. *See also* BANGASSOU and RAFAÏ.

**BANDIO, JEAN-ARTHUR (1923–1992).** Born in **Brazzaville** on 6 June 1923, he died in Blois (Loire et Cher) on 16 November 1992. Bandio was a former Central African instructor who became a French overseas administrator in 1958. He was Minister of the Interior in 1962 but opposed President **Dacko** in 1965. Named foreign minister in 1967 he then served as an ambassador in Rome, Cairo, and to the United Nations before becoming mayor of **Bangui** in 1980.

**BANGANA REVOLT.** A rebellion against the forced labor imposed by the **concessionary companies** in 1914 in the basin of this small **Dji** River tributary in Upper Kotto. An actual military operation had to be mounted by the Curault battalion to put it down. Those not killed fled into the Anglo-Egyptian Sudan.

**BANGASSOU.** Post under King **Leopold**'s regime, then the French, which became the headquarters of the region and the **prefecture**. It was established at the residence of **Bandia** Sultan Bangassou, not far from the juncture of the **Mbari** and the **Mbomou** Rivers. It is the seat of the bishopric.

**BANGASSOU, SULTAN (?–1907).** The **Nzakara** Sultan Bali, a former adversary of **Rabih**, died in 1890 in a war against the Bougbou. His oldest son, Bangassou, succeeded him in the face of serious dynastic quarrels. On 14 June 1890, Bangassou appeared at **Yakoma**, a post held by King **Leopold**'s officers, and signed a treaty with Captain **Alphonse Vangele**, ceding his kingdom completely to the Congo Free State. Bangassou facilitated the Belgian advance and delivered enormous quantities of ivory to them. He was thus able to acquire 1,500 guns and reinforce his army. After 1894 Bangassou became a French protégé, but with the arrival of **concessionary companies** in 1900 he rapidly lost his power. His army continued to conduct skirmishes in middle **Ubangui** all the way to **Mobaye** for some years. Injured in an elephant hunt, Sultan Bangassou passed away on 8 June 1907, in the presence of Captain **Jules Jacquier**. His designated heir, Mbari, had died in 1904, and the Chiefs' Council designated Labassou, a half-blind leper, as Bangassou's successor.

**BANGASSOU INCIDENT.** One of the culminating points in the French rivalry with King **Leopold**'s forces in Central Africa. **Victor Liotard**, appointed director of Upper **Ubangui** by **Pierre Brazza** in 1892, had as his mission penetration toward the east. This region was already occupied by Leopold's agents, in violation of the 29 April 1887 convention that recognized France's claim to the north bank of the Ubangui. Leaving Bangassou on 16 March 1893, Liotard's small group of Senegalese and Algerian rangers bumped into a Zanzibari platoon commanded by the Belgian Lieutenant **Emile Mathieu**. An armed confrontation was avoided thanks to Liotard's self-control. **Sultan Bangassou**, who had a treaty with Leopold's agents, fled. Upon his return on 23 April, Bangassou reaffirmed his fidelity to the Belgians. The incident provoked the sending of French reinforcements into the Upper Ubangui while the Belgians increased their missions to the traders of **Wadaï** and **Dar-al-Kuti**, even soliciting an alliance with **Rabih**. On 12 May 1894 Leopold obtained a lease transfer from Bahr-el-Ghazal, but German pressure led to the annulment of the treaty on 27 June. On 14 August 1894 Leopold recognized the French possession of the north bank of the **Mbomou** River and agreed to evacuate his posts, including Bangassou.

**BANGUI.** The first French post at Bangui was founded on 25 June 1889 by **Michel Dolisie** not far from the juncture of the **Ubangui** and **Mpoko** Rivers. Transferred further upstream to the rapids in 1891, the post became the base for French penetration toward the north (into Chad) as well as the east (toward the Nile). The beginnings of the post were difficult. Two post chiefs were killed in combat with neighboring populations (Maurice Musy, 3 January 1890, and Paul Comte, 13 July 1890). On 11 December 1906, as the headquarters of the central cercle, called Mpoko, Bangui was detached from the Middle Congo and became the capital of the **Ubangui-Shari** territory created in 1903. The cluster around the **administrative post** and the river post grew rapidly. Today greater Bangui has a population of about 280,000. It is the capital of the Central African Republic and one of the largest towns in Central Africa. In 1963 Kwamme Nkrumah proposed that it become the headquarters of the Organization of African Unity (OAU). The town has hosted a number of inter-African meetings. It has also been chosen as the seat of the secretariat of the Union Douanière des Etats de l'Afrique Centrale (UDEAC; Central African States Customs Union).

**BANGUI, CEASE-FIRE AGREEMENT OF.** On 8 December 1996 the four heads of states, Camponé of Burkina-Faso, Bongo from Gabon, Konaré of Mali, and Déby of Chad signed a cease-fire agreement in Bangui with President **Ange Patassé** and Captain Anicet Saulet, the rebel leader. The agreement included a cease-fire within two weeks and the creation of a "supervision committee," including representatives from the four African countries and presided over by General **Amadou Toumani Touré** of Mali.

**BANGUI, CHILDREN'S MASSACRE OF.** When youths in Bangui stoned his car on 17 April 1979, Emperor **Bokassa I** ordered a huge round-up of children and young people. Arrests were carried out in the northern districts of the capital, which had already suffered a mortar shelling during the course of the 21 January events. During the nights of 18–19 April, about 100 children were killed in an atrocious manner at the **Ngaragba** Prison. Bokassa personally participated in this massacre. The facts were established by a commission composed of five African judicial officers established on 22 May during the Kigali African Conference. The commission's report was made public on 16 August 1979 at Dakar.

**BANGUI, GENERAL SYLVESTRE.** Appointed ambassador to Canada in 1973, he was ambassador to France in 1979 when the African Inquiry Commission confirmed Emperor **Bokassa**'s massacre of the children in **Bangui**. He spectacularly resigned on 22 May 1979 and announced the formation of the Front de Liberation Oubanguien (FLO; Ubangui Liberation Front). On 11 September 1979, he proclaimed a **Ubangui** Republic in Paris. He returned to Bangui to work for **David Dacko** and was appointed minister a number of times. He was appointed vice prime minister on 6 July 1980.

**BANGUI, GEORGES.** Commander George Bangui, head of the military cabinet of President **David Dacko**, trained in France. He was arrested by **Jean-Bedel Bokassa** during the **Saint-Sylvester coup d'etat**. He died of his wounds and of hunger at **Ngaragba** Prison on 30 January 1966.

**BANGUI, HOSTAGE AFFAIR OF.** In May 1904 French **Dr. Fulconis** discovered at **Bangui** about 50 women and children hostages, dead and dying, captured by the **tax** collectors in the Mongoumba region. **Pierre Brazza** held an inquest into the affair in 1905.

**BANGUI-CHAD RAILWAY.** Railroad project promoted between 1956 and 1960 at the initiative of the **Chamber of Commerce (of Bangui)**. It was abandoned in 1961 to the profit of the Transcameroon project.

**BANIA.** Village in Upper Sangha in which **Pierre Brazza** founded a post named Banca, then Sangha, on 4 January 1892. It was the starting point for the French advance into the western part of Central Africa.

**BANVILLE, REVEREND FATHER GHISLAIN DE (1938–1998).** Born in Frênes (Orne) on 29 January 1938, he died at the Kremelin-

Bicêtre hospital on 14 July 1998. After having done his military service in **Bangui** in 1965, he began his preaching as a **missionary** attached to the Holy Ghost Congregation in Bangui and in Bambari. A history teacher at the Bangui Seminary, Father Banville studied history himself. He wrote several books on the history of Central Africa and more particularly on the Catholic missionaries there. In 1993 he organized the ceremonies for the celebration of the centenary of the Central African Church. He was elected to the French Overseas Science Academy in Paris. In 1998 Banville became the director of the general archives of the Holy Ghost Congregation at Chevilly-Larue before he was caught by ill health.

**BANZA, LIEUTENANT COLONEL ALEXANDRE (1932–1969).** Born in **Carnot** in Gbaya country in 1932, Captain Banza, a veteran of the Indochina War, was the principal agent of the military **coup d'etat** on the night of 31 December 1965–1 January 1966. Minister of Finance until 12 January 1967, he undertook a campaign against dishonesty. Eased out of this post, he was placed in charge of public health by Colonel **Jean-Bedel Bokassa**. Relations between him and the head of state continued to deteriorate. Accused of a plot, he was arrested on 11 April 1969, tortured, and shot the next day. Within a few days Bokassa had his wife and nine children arrested and deported to **Berbérati**, then to **Birao**. They were released on 6 May 1971 during Mother's Day. Bokassa hunted down Banza's close relations, which included **Joseph Kallot** and **Polycarpe Gbaguili**. Kallot died around 30 June 1969, and Faustin Marigot, another relation, on 30 April 1971. The others were released several weeks after their arrest. Gbaguili remained in prison until Bokassa's fall on 20 September 1979. He then proved to be an implacable witness, describing very accurately the multiple crimes of the former dictator. Gbaguili, of remarkable moral strength, assisted in their agony many of the prisoners sentenced to death by Bokassa.

**BANZIRI.** Ethnic group of the so-called **Ubanguian** family established in the region where the Kouango and Ubangui Rivers join. Their leaders signed a protectorate treaty with the French explorer **Paul Crampel** in 1890. They were reputed to be excellent canoe fishermen and traders.

**BARAM-BAKIE.** Leader of the **Banda Vidri** to the north of Bria, Baram-Bakie involved many of the **Banda** ethnic groups in the resistance against the French. Entrenched in a solid fortification at the juncture of the Ndahaye and Baidou Rivers, he was attacked on 10 May 1909 by the troops of Captain **Jules Jacquier**, who took possession of the camp. The fleeing Vidri leader submitted in July to Lieutenant Arnould, head of the Bria post.

**BARAM-BARIA (?–1913).** **Baram-Bakie**'s principal assistant in the Bria region. Accused of murder, he was condemned to life imprisonment on 15 June 1912, and died in **Mobaye** Prison on 9 February 1913.

**BARBEROT, ROGER.** A ship's ensign, he rallied in July 1940 to **Free France**. A friend of **General Charles de Gaulle**, Colonel Barberot was the French ambassador to the Central African Republic from 1960 to 1963. He helped President **David Dacko** establish the structure of the new state.

**BARRACUDA.** This word for a type of carnivorous tropical fish is the code name of the military operation carried out by France in September 1979 to bring down Emperor **Bokassa** and establish a democratic regime in Central Africa. Two C160 Tronsall freight-planes carrying 130 men and an airborne division from the 1st navy infantry regiment landed at **Bangui**-Mpoko airport at 11:45 p.m., after the men had jumped. On board one of the planes was former President **David Dacko**, formerly Bokassa's special adviser, who had been living in Paris since July for health reasons. The French military quickly and safely took all the key sectors of the capital. At 11:55 p.m., Dacko announced through a national radio broadcast that Emperor Bokassa, then on an official visit in Libya, ruled no more and that the Republic was reinstated. A few minutes before a fictitious press agency had released the information that Dacko was asking for the help and protection of France. As early as 21 September the airborne division was back in France. A few Libyan soldiers who were captured were sent back to **Mouammar Kadhafi**. Told during the night about the operation, the fallen emperor decided to leave Libya for France. His plane was grounded for four days at the military base of Evreux with all its passengers. His stay on French soil being refused him in spite of his claiming French citizenship, Bokassa was sent to Abidjan where, upon French request, the Côte d'Ivoire President Houphouët-Boigny granted him political asylum. Former Secretary-General of the Community and of African and Malagasy Affairs Jacques Foccart rejected in his memoirs the "neo-colonialist" aspect of the Barracuda operation and instead called it only France's last colonial operation.

**BARRIL, CAPTAIN PAUL.** An Officer in the Gendarmerie's special unit the Groupement d'Intervention de la Gendarmerie Nationale (GIGN; National Gendarmerie's Intervention Group), Barril is famous for reconquering Islam's holy ground for the benefit of the King of Arabia. Forced to leave the Gendarmerie after dubious dealings, he specialized in assistance to the police of Third World countries. In December 1995, after a mission he had been assigned to fight illegal hunting in the Sudan, Barril and his men were decorated by President **David Dacko**. In the following years, Barril supplied President **Ange Patassé** with mercenaries attached to his personal guard.

**BASSAMONGOU, FERDINAND.** Former teaching supervisor, he was one of the first of **Barthélémy Boganda**'s companions. He belonged to the family of the **Bandia** Sultan of **Rafaï**. He was president of the Conseil économique et social (Economic and Social Council) of the Central African Republic from 1962 to 1966 and led a Central African mission to Moscow and Peking in August 1964.

**BASSO, BATTLE OF.** Battle that took place in 1883 between the troops of **Rabih** and those of the **Nzakara** King, Bali, on the banks of the Mbari. Defeated, Rabih renounced his push toward the south. Uneasy about Mahdist penetration into **Ubangui**, Rabih decided to look for a route toward the west.

**BAYA.** After the **Banda**, the Baya are the second largest ethnic group in the Central African Republic. They occupy most of the western part of the country and part of Cameroon. The **Mandjia** and different Lobaye groups with closely related languages and customs are often grouped with them. Tradition fixes the date of their arrival on Central African soil about 1820. According to Tessmann, they can be divided into six principal groups: Bokoto, **Kara**, Bouli, Bodomo, Lai, and **Kaka**. During the 19th century, the Baya were in conflict with numerous Bantu-speaking groups established between the Sangha and the **Ubangui** (Bakota and Boubangui families). Allied with the Banda Yanguéré, they victoriously resisted attacks by the **Fulbé** of **Adamawa**. From 1928 to 1931, almost the entire Baya population rose up against French colonialism. Baya is the administration spelling, while ethnologists spell the group's name Gbaya or Gbeya.

**BAZINGUER.** This is the name given to the armed militias of the merchant lords of the Upper Nile (1860–1875). The term continued to be used by the population in the eastern part of Central Africa to designate certain auxiliaries or messengers of African leaders and both colonial and postcolonial administrations.

**BAZONGA.** Son of Labassou and grandson of **Bangassou**, Bazonga protested in 1918, a little after the death of his father, against the French administration's decision to suppress the sultanate. Accused of murder, he was arrested, but escaped with complicity of the local population. Retaken on 6 August 1918, he was transferred to **Bangui**.

**BDPA.** The Bureau pour le Développement de la Production Agricole (BDPA; Agricultural Development Bureau) was a French state cooperative society that proposed a rural development plan to **David Dacko** in 1963. Based upon its proposal, the head of state created a vast Ministry of Rural Development under the direction of **Albert Payao**.

**BEDOUE.** Grandson of the **Zandé** Sultan **Tikima**, Bedoue was taken into **slavery** in 1872 by **Zubayr**.

**BEGO.** A **Yakoma** leader implicated in the attack on the French **administrative post** of Setema in September 1893. He was arrested and shot at **Mobaye** in 1894.

**BEHAGLE, FERDINAND DE (?–1895).** Explorer sent by the commercial committee called the "Syndicate of Chad and the **Ubangui**." In 1898 Behagle identified the sources of the Tomi and **Gribingui** Rivers.

Having obtained the loan of the steamer *Léon Blot*, he made his way in July of the same year to the Sultan of Banguirmi, Gaourang. Persuaded that a French alliance with **Rabih** would be more profitable, Behagle, equipped with orders for his mission from the administrator Rousset, decided in February 1899 to go to Dikoa in Bornu to meet the conqueror. Combat between Rabih's troups and the French forces sent against them ended with Behagle being taken hostage. He was hung after Rabih's defeat at Kouno on 29 October 1895.

**BELLA.** Central African nurse who was the Rassemblement du Peuple Français (**RPF**; French People's Party) candidate against **Barthélémy Boganda** in the legislative elections of 17 June 1951.

**BELLO.** He commanded the **Fulbé** troops of **Ngaoundéré** engaged against the **Baya** (1875–1880).

**BERANDJOKO.** A religious and political leader, he was well known through the **forest** region from Nola to **Bangui**, Berandjoko headed the 1904 revolt. He was defeated in September 1909. Discovered on 24 June 1929 by a rifle patrol, he made himself known to the patrol leader and, refusing to give up, let them kill him.

**BERBERATI.** Berberati is today one of the principal towns of the Central African Republic with an approximate population of 23,000. It is the headquarters of the Upper Sangha **prefecture**.

**BERBERATI, CONGRESS OF.** The third **MESAN** congress was convened by President **David Dacko** in the principal town of Upper Sangha from 30 March to 14 April 1964. Delegates from the whole region, substituting for the **National Assembly**, adopted decisions prepared by the head of state and his close collaborators. These decisions "were to be applied strictly and scrupulously by the administrative authorities."

**BERBERATI RIOT.** On 30 April 1954, following the death of a domestic servant and his wife in the service of a French official known for his brutal treatment of Africans, the population of Berberati stoned the administrative buildings. A passing Frenchman was killed, and the regional "Chief" and the Justice of the Peace were injured. French military reinforcements were sent from **Bouar** and **Brazzaville**. The agitation spread to the **Baya** area. On 1 May, Deputy **Barthélémy Boganda**, at the demand of Governor **Louis Sanmarco**, arrived and obtained a demobilization of the rioters. The Criminal Court of French Equatorial Africa, however, imposed severe sentences on 4 September 1954.

**BERENGO (COURT OF).** An imperial decree on 21 December 1976 created an Imperial Court at the village of Berengo in Lobaye. This text anticipated that Emperor **Bokassa** would no longer appear in public and that all public meetings and manifestations would be supervised by the prime minister. This appears to have been a maneuver by **Ange Patassé** to attempt to isolate Bokassa who was showing signs of increasing dementia. The Imperial Court was simply superimposed on the government, which became the fearful executor of the orders and whims of the Emperor. Bokassa appointed to his court, besides former President **David Dacko**, Europeans such as **Oliver Robert**, **Jacques Duchemin**, and **Roger Delpey**. Equipped with an airport, Berengo was defended by the imperial guard comprised exclusively of members of Bokassa's own ethnic group the **Mbaka**.

**BERROT, GABRIEL (1915–?).** Born on 13 April 1915, he was a Central African nurse from **Mbaïki**. Berrot became a **MESAN** councilor, then deputy of the Lobaye. A member of the MESAN Governing Committee (1964–1966), he was arrested after the **coup d'etat** of 1 January 1966.

**BILINGA.** Son of Dounga, the founder of the **Bandia** Kingdom of **Nzakara**, Bilinga led wars in the middle of the 19th century against the Bougbou and Togbo **Banda**.

**BIRAO.** The most northerly **administrative post** in the former colony of **Ubangui-Shari**, Birao, not far from the borders of Sudan and Chad, is today the sub**prefecture** seat and a center of big game tourism.

**BIR-HAKEIM.** In May 1942, the BM2 of **Ubangui** participated in the defense of Bir-Hakeim on the Libyan front under the orders of General Koenig. Their losses were heavy: 177 Central African infantry-men and 39 French noncommissioned officers and officers from Ubangui were killed. The battalion was cited for the Order of the Nation by **General Charles de Gaulle**. Seriously injured in this combat, Lieutenant **Georges-Albert Koudoukou**, the first Ubanguian officer in the French army, died in an Alexandria hospital. Rifleman First Class Koudoussaraigne was made a Companion of the Liberation for his conduct during this battle.

**BISELLI.** Merchant lord of the borders of **Ubangui** and Bahrel-Ghazal, Biselli was one of a "triumvirate" who had taken control of the country between 1860 and 1865.

**BLAGUE, ALPHONSE.** Headmaster of Lycée Boganda. He was condemned on 25 August 1977 to 10 years in prison. Released on 28 October, he continued his resistance to Emperor **Bokassa**'s regime. He was appointed minister in **David Dacko**'s second government and represented the Central African Republic at the United Nations Educational, Scientific and Cultural Organization (UNESCO). A professor of sociology in Dakar, he then became President Dacko's cabinet director, then Youth and Sports Minister, and later ambassador to Canada.

**BLAUD, ANDRE (1882–1954).** Born in Beaucaire (Gard) on 15 November 1882, he died in Beaucaire (Gard) on 11 May 1954. Administrator of the **Carnot** subdivision in 1925, Blaud was passed over for being opposed to the strong **forestry** company of **Sangha-Ubangui**. He was then head of the **Dar-Kouti (Ndélé)** subdivision in 1930.

**BLOM.** A companion of **Brazza**, he was injured during the **Baya** attack on the **Fourneau Mission** on 12 May 1891. He participated as head explorer with the Administrator **Gaston Gaillard** in the foundation of **Mobaye** on 14 August 1891. On 7 September 1896, he replaced **Alphonse Goujon** as administrator of Sangha.

**BLOT, LÉON.** Former sergeant of engineers, with one arm amputated, he was **Pierre Brazza**'s secretary during his stay in Upper Sangha in 1892–1894. Blot died without ever fulfilling his dream of going to

Chad. **Emile Gentil** honored him by naming the steamboat that he brought to Lake Chad in 1897 the *Léon Blot*.

**BOALI.** Locality situated to the northeast of **Bangui**, celebrated for its falls, which drive the **hydroelectric** plant.

**BOBANGUI (or BOUGANGUI).** 1. Great merchant people established in the former Anzica, between Stanley Pool and Central **Ubangui**. About 1830 the **Bouaka** drove them toward the Ubangui bend. When the French arrived, the Bobangui were still trading with the populations of Upper Sangha and Middle Ubangui.

2. **Mbaka** village of Lobaye that suffered greatly during the colonial period. Both President **Barthélémy Boganda** and Emperor **Bokassa** were born in this village, in 1910 and 1921 respectively.

**BOBICHON, CHARLES.** Administrator in 1904 of the subdivision of Fort **Crampel**, Bobichon called the attention of the governor general to the drain on the **Mandjia**, who refused further **portage** duty en masse.

**BOBICHON, HENRI (1866–1939).** Transport organizer for the **Marchand mission** on the **Ubangui** in 1897–1898, he took command of Upper Ubangui in 1900. In July 1900 he aided **Sultan Hetman of Rafaï** in putting down a coup d'etat fomented by the Waldaïans. Under suspicion of having poisoned Sultan Rafaï, Henri Bobichon quit his command on 13 April 1931. His career continued with various colonial companies.

**BOFFI.** Ethnic group of Boda sub**prefecture**.

**BOGANDA, BARTHÉLÉMY.** Born on 4 April 1910 in **Bobangui** in the Lobaye basin, the young Barthélémy Boganda attended the school opened at **Mbaïki** by the post's founder, Lieutenant Mayer. He was sent by **Father Gabriel Herriau** to the Catholic School of Betou and then to the school of the **Saint Paul Mission** at **Bangui**. These missionaries helped him continue his studies at seminaries in **Brazzaville**, Yaounde, and Kisantu. On 17 March 1938, he became the first **Ubanguian** Catholic priest. On 10 November 1946, he was the first deputy elected by his fellow citizens to the French **National Assembly**. From 1947 on he conducted a lively campaign against racism and the colonial regime. On 29 March 1951 he was condemned to two months in prison following a market incident. On 17 June 1951 Boganda was reelected in spite of the obstacles placed in his way by the administration. Boganda gave his assistance, to say the least, to the beginning of internal autonomy (1956–1958). The elections of 1956 were for him an uncontested speaker's platform with which the colonial administration had to come to terms. Boganda advocated in 1958 the accession to independence of all of French Equatorial Africa and its integration into a United States of Latin Africa constituted by the former French, Belgian, and Portuguese colonies of Central Africa. On 29 March 1959 he died in an airplane accident for which no clear cause has ever been ascertained. Boganda had married a Frenchwoman, Michelle Jourdain, in 1950, and they had three children. Boganda's movement that he founded in 1949 under the name Mouvement pour l'évolution sociale de l'Afrique noire (**MESAN**; Movement for the Social Evolution of Black Africa) became after his death the single party of the Central African Republic. This name, which Boganda destined for the vast nation he dreamed of creating in Central Africa, was applied after 1 December 1958 to the single territory of **Ubangui-Shari**, the present Central African Republic. Boganda is considered not only the father of the Central African nation but also one of the great leaders of Black African emancipation. He was considered at his death "the most prestigious and the most capable of Equatorial political men" (Georges Chaffard).

**BOGANDA, BERTRAND.** Son of **Barthélémy Boganda**, Battalion Chief of Bertrand Boganda, a former student at Saint-Cyr, died tragically at Villeneuve Saint Georges on 19 September 1989.

**BOHNDORFF, FREDERICK.** Mecklembourg goldsmith and a passionate traveler, he was interpreter for General Charles Gordon in the Sudan in 1874. In 1876 he left Kordofan and penetrated southward. Passing through the **Chinko** valley, he was the first European to reach the **Mbomou**. He was also the first to meet **Rabih**, then leader of a Sudanese **zeriba** between the Chinko and the Mbari.

**BOISSON, PIERRE.** An old Breton schoolteacher, and badly disabled in the war in 1918, he succeeded **Joseph Reste** as governor general of French Equatorial Africa. On 13 July 1940, Marshal Philippe Petain appointed him High Commissioner for all of Black Africa, with residence at Dakar. Some French in Bangui plotted to seize him during a stop that he made there on 20 July. The plot failed.

**BOISSOUDY, COLONEL GUY BACHERON DE.** Born in Toul on 18 July 1908, he was a colonel in the **Free French** Forces and represented **Ubangui-Shari** at the Constitutional Assembly. A brigadier general, he became an administrator in several large companies.

**BOKASSA THE FIRST (1921–1996).** Born on 22 February 1921 at Bobangui (Lobaye), Jean-Bedel Bokassa claimed to be a relative of **Barthélémy Boganda**, the founder of the Central African Republic. A son of Mindogon Mgboundoulou, an African leader killed during the colonial period, he was a member of the **Mbaka** ethnic group. Bokassa joined the French army in 1939 and participated in the Indochina War. He was promoted to lieutenant in 1958, then captain in 1961, and participated in the creation of the Central African **army**. He was appointed colonel of the Central African army in 1964. President **David Dacko** chose him the same year as army chief of staff. Originator of the coup d'etat called the **Saint-Sylvestre coup** (the night of 31 December 1965 and 1 January 1966), he forced Dacko to transfer the Republic's presidential powers to him.

Bokassa soon had himself appointed President for Life, general, then marshal. Desiring to establish absolute power over the country, he had his principal collaborator, Lieutenant Colonel **Alexandre Banza**, arrested on 11 April 1969 on charges of plotting. Tortured, Banza was executed by a firing squad on 12 April. A number of tentative plots were crushed by the marshal-president. For example, on 3 February 1976, Bokassa escaped an attack at the **Bangui**-Mpoko airport. The Permanent Military Tribunal condemned to death eight officers involved in this plot. One of these officers was the Marshal's son-in-law, Battalion Leader **Fidèle Obrou**. Obrou was executed a few hours after the sentence. A new plot was foiled at the end of November 1976.

On 4 December 1976 Bokassa had the Congress of the Mouvement pour l'évolution sociale de l'Afrique noire (**MESAN**; Movement for the Social Evolution of Black Africa) adopt a new constitution that transformed the country into an empire. He himself became the emperor under the name of Bokassa the First. His son, Prince Georges, Minister of Defense, was accused of plotting on 14 December 1976, and had to take refuge in France. In an interview accorded the *Daily Mail*, Bokassa claimed the right to the atomic bomb for his country. On 4 December 1977, Bokassa I, an admirer of Napoleon, crowned himself during a fantastic and costly ceremony. No invited foreign heads of state deigned to attend. Bokassa crowned as empress his latest wife, Catherine Dangueade, and ennobled his family. Emperor Bokassa, who had converted to Islam (under the name Salah Eddine Ahmed Bou-Kassa) in October 1976 during a visit to Bangui of Colonel **Mouammar Kadhafi** in order to benefit from Libyan aid, used the occasion of his crowning to declare his return to the Catholic faith. Violent riots took place in Bangui in 1979 because of a rule obliging students and pupils to buy uniforms made in a sewing shop belonging to Emperor Bokassa. Further unrest followed, which led to international sanctions against his regime.

The repression, with the aid of Zairian paratroopers, was pitiless and caused approximately 100 deaths. Strikes by teachers, students, lycée students, and even civil servants followed. On 17 April 1979, Bokassa's car was stoned by the crowd. The next day the emperor had hundreds of children from eight to 16 years old arrested during the course of a mass round-up. About 100 of them were massacred during the nights of 18 and 19 April with Bokassa's personal participation (see Bangui, children's massacre of). Coming right in the middle of the International Year of the Child, these atrocities, confirmed by the report of the judicial commission constituted by the Kigali Conference of African Heads of State, unleashed an international and notably African movement of reprobation.

During a mission of Bokassa to Tripoli, French troops took over the airport and then the city of Bangui, and David Dacko proclaimed the downfall of the emperor. The emperor, refused asylum by France, found asylum in the Côte d'Ivoire on 24 September 1979. Discoveries made in Bangui and at **Berengo** evidenced the extent and horror of the crimes perpetrated by Bokassa.

Bokassa was condemned to death in absentia on 24 December 1980 by the Criminal Court of Bangui. An international arrest warrant was issued against him, but the Côte d'Ivoire refused his extradition. Bokassa reasserted his French nationality and asked for entry into France. The High Court in Paris denied him French citizenship on 12 December 1981. On 24 December 1983, Bokassa's attempted return to Bangui, arranged by **Roger Delpey**, failed. The Caravelle airplane chartered in Paris was surrounded at the Abidjan airport and sent back to France. Bokassa arrived back in Paris that same day to establish himself at his Chateau de Hardricourt with some of his children and his Ivorian concubine. Escaping surveillance, he made his way to Brussels and Rome on his way to Bangui, where he was arrested at the airport upon arrival on 23 October 1986. Imprisoned at the Roux military camp, he was condemned to death on 12 June 1987, after a 90-day trial. On 14 November 1987 the Court of Appeal rejected Bokassa's appeal. On 29 February 1988, General **André Kolingba** pardoned the former emperor and his death sentence was commuted to a life sentence. Bokassa remained incarcerated at the Roux military camp. In September 1991 his sentence was reduced to twenty years imprisonment. On 1 September 1993 Kolingba granted him a new pardon. He was released from prison and set up, under police surveillance, in the Nasser villa in the center of Bangui. The villa is owned by his wife, who has escaped the court's seizure of property sentence.

The mind of the former ruler was still unhinged. Thinking he was "Christ's last apostle" he wore a white robe, read the Bible constantly, and attended mass. Shaken by detention and alcohol abuse, his health deteriorated. When on 9 October 1995 he learned that his favorite son Saint-Cyr had died, Bokassa suffered a stroke. On 5 April 1996, he was called before the Bangui Tribunal to answer the accusations made against him concerning his use of a 3 billion CFA franc loan destined to the building of a great hotel in Bangui. In September of that same year, evacuation to a Paris hospital for health reasons was refused him. His family had him transferred to a private clinic in Abidjan. Back in Bangui, in serious condition, Bokassa died on 3 November 1996 of heart failure. He had been married 17 times and claimed 53 children. His life has been the subject of many books.

**BONDJO.** Term by which the colonizers designated the **Bouaka** of the north bank of the **Ubangui** bend. This term is just the corruption of a **Sango** word, *mboundjou* (whites), cried out by locals on the riverbank at the approach of French boats. The Bondjo fought the French in a number of battles and were said to practice a rather spectacular form of cannibalism.

**BONE.** Village of Upper Sangha with about 2,000 inhabitants and that, a few days after the passage of the explorer **Louis Mizon** in March 1892, was completely destroyed by the troops of the **Fulbé** amido of **Ngaoundéré**.

**BONNEL DE MEZIERES.** Born in Cambrai on 9 February 1870, he was a member of the **Maistre Mission** in 1892. He was the head of a commercial mission sent in 1895 by the Chad and Ubangui Syndicate to the **Bandia** and **Zandé**, which had to be evacuated by the Belgians. Upon his return Bonnel de Mezieres completed a very solid economic document on these regions before their exploitation by the **concessionary companies**.

**BORDIER, PAUL (1921–).** Born in Saint-Nazaire-sur-Charente (Charente Maritime) 16 January 1921. Head of the **Ubangui-Shari** territory from 1958 to 1960, Governor Paul Bordier, former director of Economic Affairs for French West Africa, received the mission of carrying out the legal transfer from the French Republic to the new Central African state. He became the first high-level French representative to the Central African Republic. In November 1960, in order to show his independence, President **David Dacko** called for and obtained Bordier's immediate recall by the French government. He becomes the general financial auditor, then president of the French employer's federation for mineral water.

**BORNOU, CHARLES (1914–?).** Born in 1914 in the village of Bamingui in **Dar-al-Kuti**, the son of a **Banda** soldier in service to as-**Sanusi**, Charles Bornou became an official in the French administration and president of the cultural circle of Bangui. Prefect of **Ouaka** in December 1960, he became Minister of Agriculture, then of Finance. He was elected deputy in 1964, and then mayor of **Bangui**. President **Dacko** appointed him a member of the governing committee of the Mouvement pour l'évolution sociale de l'Afrique noire (**MESAN**; Movement for the Social Evolution of Black Africa) that same year.

**BORORO.** Groups of pastoral **Fulbé** coming from Cameroon and settling with their herds between 1920 and 1935 in the prefectures of **Bouar**-Bakoua, **Ouaka**, and Lower Kotto.

**BOS, LIEUTENANT.** Determined to know more about the Upper Kotto region in which as-**Sanusi** carried on his **slave**-raiding activities, Administrator **Charles Bobichon** sent Lieutenant Bos on an inspection tour of the area. This tour was not immediately followed by the creation of **administrative posts**. Disturbed, Sultan as-Sanusi stepped up his expeditions and toward the end of 1902 set in motion a veritable war of extermination against the **Kreich** and **Banda** ethnic groups.

**BOSSANGOA.** Main town of the Ouham **prefecture** in the north of the country, an agglomeration of about 22,000 people.

**BOTEMBÉLÉ MASSACRE.** Georges Pacha, head of the Boda subdivision, forced some **Boffi** villages to relocate on the new route from Boda to Lobaye. At the village of Botembélé, Sergeant Yambe and Guard Bonjo massacred 20 women and children, locked up and burned alive in their houses. These facts were revealed by the leader **Samba-Ngotto** to the writer **André Gide**, who arrived in **Ngotto** in Governor **Auguste Lamblin**'s automobile.

**BOUAKA.** Ethnic group related to the **Baya** that settled in the bend of the **Ubangui** River about 1830.

**BOUAR.** French military post at the Cameroon border; today it is the **Nana**-Mambéré's **prefect** headquarters.

**BOUL.** Head of the French **administrative post** at **Nana**, Boul was killed on 17 December 1901 by some **Ngao** prisoners. His death resulted in the reinforcement of military groups in Upper **Shari**.

**BOURAKA.** Ethnic group belonging to the so-called **Ubanguian** group.

**BOURDARIE, PAUL.** One of the principal movers in the French colonial party. In 1906 he founded the *Revue Indigène* and launched an energetic campaign to safeguard the interests of **concessionary companies**.

**BOURGEOISIE.** In the Central African political vocabulary, this word means the administrative caste put in place by the colonizers and to whom independence brought considerable advantages. It also includes the local elected officials. On 1 January 1966, Colonel **Jean-Bedel Bokassa** announced "the abolition of the bourgeoisie," that is, the privileges of which this caste is the beneficiary. This announcement remained purely verbal.

**BOURGES, YVON (1921–).** Born in Pau (Pyrénées Atlantiques) on 29 June 1921. He was the last High Commissioner General of the French Republic in French Equatorial Africa in 1958. Elected Member of Parliament for Ille et Vilaine, then a Senator, he was a minister and secretary of state from 1968 to 1980 in several French governments.

**BOZANGA, SIMON NARCISSE (1942–).** Born 26 December 1942, he was the Central African ambassador to Gabon in 1978 and 1979. He was appointed secretary general of the government and then Minister of Justice by **David Dacko**. He was prime minister from 3 April until 1 September 1981.

**BOZIZÉ, GENERAL.** A noncommissioned officer in Emperor **Bokassa**'s Air Force, Emperor Bokassa then made him a frontline general for having slapped a French noncommissioned officer. While Minister of Information in **André Kolingba**'s government, he was one of the authors of the failed coup of 1982 that planned to put **Ange Patassé** in power—he went into exile after this. In July 1989 Kolingba had Bozizé kidnapped from his Cotonou residence in Bénin, where he had escaped, in order to bring him to justice along with 11 of his accomplices. He spent many months in prison without a trial, was then released, and sought refuge in Paris. Patassé's election changed all this, and Bozizé became the latter's **army** chief of staff. Bozizé was also active in **Bangui** as the leader of a sectarian Church called the Chrétiens Célestes (Celestial Christians). He took an active part in the repression of the 1996–1997 army rebellions, as well as that of the 28 May 2001 rebellion. Accused of conspiring against the president, he was sacked.

With the help of 100 men, Bozizé resisted the warrant for his arrest. With his followers, he fled into southern Chad on 18 November. The Chad government refused to extradite him to the CAR. While he was in Paris, the 2002 rebellion spread to nearly two-thirds of the country. Helped by the Congolese troops of Jean-Pierre Bemba, the Forces armées centrafricaines (**FACA**; Central African Armed Forces) regained control of several towns in February 2003. But in March, while Patassé was in Niamey, Bozizé's troops counterattacked and took Bangui. Thereupon, Bozizé proclaimed himself president of the Republic and entrusted **Abel Goumba** with forming a new transitional united government.

**BRAZZA, PIERRE SAVORGNAN DE** (?–1905). Brazza, the commissioner general of the French Republic of the Congo, occupies an important place in the history of Central Africa. In 1886 he took an active part in the negotiations with the Congo Free State to try to maintain within the French sphere of influence the still unknown **Ubangui** basin. In 1889 his collaborator, **Albert Dolisie**, decided to set up the **Bangui administrative** post. Brazza charged his former personal secretary, the explorer **Paul Crampel**—whom he appointed acting commissioner general in Ubangui—to restore order around the Bangui post before continuing his advance north in 1890. In 1891 he sent the **Alfred Fourneau** expedition into **Baya** country. It had to strike a retreat. In 1891 he appointed **Victor Liotard** director of Upper Ubangui with a mission of penetrating east toward Bahr-el-Ghazal. In 1892, taking the head of an expedition to Upper Sangha himself, he established the Sangha territory.

Brazza remained in Central Africa until 1894. As commissioner general, he had to withstand military interests that were forcibly pressing at the Nile and Chad. He also had to resist commercial interests that wished to divide the as-yet-unexplored territories among the large speculating **concessionary companies**. In 1896 these forces were able to have Brazza removed. Asked by the government in 1905 to direct the Commission of Inquiry into the Crimes committed in the Congo and Upper Shari, Brazza was surprised by the extent of these crimes. From Bangui, he asked for his recall and died in Dakar on the way home. The results of the Brazza Mission provoked the great debate of February 1906 in the French Parliament over Congolese affairs.

**BRAZZAVILLE CONFERENCES.** Three Brazzaville Conferences are important in Central African history.

1. The imperial conference of Brazzaville opened on 30 January 1944 by **General Charles de Gaulle**, head of the **Free French**, set aside the constitutional question of "even distant" self-government in the colonies, but introduced a political personalization and greater economic and political freedom. This conference adopted the "indigenous politics" advocated by Governor General **Félix Eboué**, formed during his 25 years of experience as territorial commander in **Ubangui-Shari**.

2. In November 1958, President **Barthélémy Boganda**, faced with the reluctance of the Chadians and Gabonese to constitute an Equatorial African state, called together Ubanguian and Congolese leaders at Brazzaville. They adopted a motion inviting the assemblies of these two territories to proclaim their merger. On 24 and 25 September, the High Commissioner in turn called a meeting of the leaders of the four territories, who, while affirming the necessity of a union, refused Boganda's unitary proposal.

3. In December 1960, Dr. **Abel Goumba** submitted the internal problems of the Central African Republic to the heads of state of French-speaking Africa meeting in Brazzaville. The memorandum he submitted was regarded by **David Dacko** as a threat to the external security of the state. This qualification brought about the arrest and indictment of the memorandum's author on 26 December 1960.

**BRETONNET, HENRI-ETIENNE (?–1899).** Administrator Bretonnet, a former naval officer, arrived at **Gribingui** on 30 March 1899, in order to reach **Baguirmi** overland. He passed through **Ndélé**, where he rested 20 days, receiving the finest welcome of Sultan as-**Sanusi**. Arriving at Sultan Gaourang's headquarters at Kouno, he had to evacuate the post on 14 July 1899, and it was immediately occupied by **Rabih**'s army. Taking refuge in the rocks of Togbao, Bretonnet was killed three days later with his men by supporters of Rabih, Gaourang having fled.

**BROWNE, WALTER GEORGE (1768–1813).** Born in London on 25 July 1768, and assassinated in Iran in 1813, he arrived in **Darfur** in May 1793. He was the author of the first English document on what is today the Central African Republic. He named it **Dar Koula** and affirmed that it was traversed by a grand river flowing from east to west (the **Ubangui**).

**BRUEL, GEORGES (1871–1944).** Born in Moulins (Allier) on 23 May 1871, he died in Neuilly le Réal (Allier) on 31 October 1944. The French administrator Georges Bruel, in charge of the Upper **Shari** region, was sent to conclude a new protectorate with as-**Sanusi** in 1903. He then held several commands, notably at **Mobaye**. He is the author of several works on French Equatorial Africa and over 350 brochures, geographical, historical, and ethnographical articles on Equatorial Africa and also on the Bourbonnais. His archives have been given to the Académie des Sciences d'Outre-Mer (Academy for Overseas Sciences)—Bruel archives, where they have been studied by Jean Cantournet.

**BUTEL, JOSEPH (?–1929).** Born in Pointe-Noire (Guadeloupe), he died in Trois-Rivière (Gouadeloupe) on 12 January 1929. Assistant administrator of Colonies in 1907, Butel, head of inspection of the companies, carried out an inquiry in the northern zone of the Kotto **concessionary company**. Receiving his overwhelming report of the wrongdoings committed by the company's agents, **Emile Gentil** demanded in vain the immediate disqualification of the concession on 1 October 1907. For his part, the Minister of Colonies transmitted Butel's report to the president of the Republic and the president of the Council. An inquiry carried out in the southern zone proved to be even more damning. He then became mayor-administrator of **Brazzaville**.

– **C** –

**CADRES, SCHOOL OF.** Founded in 1935 by Governor General **Edouard Renard**, this school became the Ecole des Cadres. It was destined to give an administrative formation to young Africans who held the Brevet d'Etudes du Premier Cycle (BEPC; Secondary School Certificate).

**CAILLAUX, JOSEPH (1863–1944).** President of the French Council, Caillaux in 1911 took into his own hands the problems growing out of the operations of French **concessionary companies** in Equatorial Africa. Negotiations between French and German companies had resulted in the establishment of a German railroad project between Douala and the **Ubangui** River. Caillaux yielded to German pressure and accepted the amputation of French colonial territory in Central Africa. In exchange he received from the Germans a free hand to intervene in Moroccan affairs.

**CALLOCH, MONSIGNOR JEAN-RENE (1876–1928).** Born in Prat-Maria in Armel (Finistère), he died in Batangafo 16 June 1928. A Holy Ghost missionary, Monsignor Calloch arrived at **Brazzaville** in 1901 and was immediately sent to **Bangui**. He was Apostolic Vicar of **Ubangui** from 1914 until 1928 and created a number of **Catholic missions** in the country. He directed the studies of the young **Barthélémy Boganda** at the Saint Paul of Bangui Mission and directed him toward the priesthood. President Boganda affirmed that Monsignor Calloch was his spiritual father. Calloch was an expert in Central African **languages** and was the author of numerous publications in **Sango**, Ngbaka, Gbanziri, Mondjombo, and Nghaya.

**CAMMAS, HENRI.** Commander of the **Bangui** Fort, this officer was occupied as early as 1939 in putting together several **Ubangui** rifle units destined for the front. After the **Gaullist** putsch in **Brazzaville**, Commander Cammas refused to give allegiance to Colonel **René Edgar de Larminat** when he arrived in Bangui. Cammas entrenched himself with his officers in the military camp from 30 August to 30 September 1940, and yielded only to avoid armed confrontation between French people. After a five-month imprisonment in Brazzaville, he was repatriated, with his officers, to Vichy France via Portugal.

**CAPSUL.** One of the principal banner chiefs in **Rabih**'s army, Capsul died heroically during the capture of Kousseri in 1900. He was of **Banda** origin.

**CARNOT. Administrative post** founded on the Mambéré in 1894 near the village of Tendira by **François Clozel**. It was named Carnot in honor of French President Sadi Carnot, who was assassinated that same year. Today it is a sub**prefecture**.

**CARRIERS.** *See* PORTAGE.

**CATHOLICISM.** *See* MISSIONS, CATHOLIC.

**CEMAC (COMMUNAUTE ECONOMIQUE ET MONETAIRE DE L'AFRIQUE CENTRALE: CENTRAL AFRICAN ECONOMIC AND MONETARY COMMUNITY).** This customs union joins the six states from Central Africa that belong to the franc zone. Created in 1998, it replaced the Union Douanière et Economique de l'Afrique Central (UDEAC; Union of Central African Customs and Economy). For the Central African Republic, the new union means a simplification of the Tarif Extérieur Commun (TEC; common external tariff) and the Taxe sur le Chiffre d'Affaire (TCA; turnover tax). The Tarif Préférentiel Généralisé (TPG; general preferential tariff) was brought down to zero in January 1998 in the hope of favoring the region's integration and in view of a later arrival of a Taxe sur la valeur ajoutée (TVA; value-added tax) based on the French model.

**CENTRAL AFRICAN REPUBLIC (CAR).** Name proposed to **Barthélémy Boganda** in 1958 by the author of this dictionary to designate the new state, which was to encompass French Equatorial Africa and the neighboring foreign colonies. The **Ubanguian** leader, after the failure of his plan, had to proclaim on 1 December 1958, under this name, a Republic reduced to only the **Ubangui-Shari** territory. In 1977, President for Life and Emperor **Jean-Bedel Bokassa** transformed the Central African Republic into the **Central African Empire**. The Republic was restored on 21 September 1979 by **David Dacko**.

**CHA.** Capital of **Dar-al-Kuti**, founded about 1830 by **Omar Djougoultoum** not far from the Diangara, a tributary of the **Aouk**. Cha was destroyed in 1894 by a **Wadaïan** army. The capital of Dar-al-Kuti was transferred in 1895 by as-**Sanusi** to **Ndélé** on the **Banda** plateau.

**CHALLA (or CAALA).** A population related to the Youlou, long settled at the headwaters of the Kotto (from which comes the name Dar-challa for this mountainous region). Practically exterminated in the **slave** wars, in 1950 they numbered fewer than 200 persons living as refugees in Bahr el-Ghazal.

**CHALLAYE, FELICIEN.** After advanced study in philosophy, he served as **Pierre Brazza**'s secretary during the inspection mission of 1905 and wrote a work presenting the findings made during this trip. He was also the founder of the Indigenous Defense League of the Congo Basin.

**CHALVET, JEAN (1893–1975).** Born in Tours (Indre et Loire) on 15 June 1893, he died in Vincennes (Val de Marne) on 28 July 1975. Governor Jean Chalvet was in charge of the **Ubangui-Shari** territory from 1946 to 1948.

**CHAMBELLANT, RENE.** French dental surgeon favorable to **MESAN**, Chambellant was elected representative councilor, then deputy to the **Territorial and Legislative Assemblies**. In 1952 he was one of the founders of the Intergroupe Libéral Oubanguien (ILO; Ubangian Liberal Association).

**CHAMBER OF COMMERCE (OF BANGUI).** This consular assembly played the role of a pressure group in opposition to the reforms passed by the French government and parliament from 1946 to 1958, and applied by the territorial administration. On 7 June the chamber rose up against the suppression of forced labor. On 30 November 1956 it called a general strike to protest **taxes** resulting from the application of the Loi-Cadre (Enabling Act). During the first years after independence, the chamber sought to ensure control of the economic affairs of the new state.

**CHARI (or SHARI).** The Chari River flows toward Lake Chad and is fed by three large streams that irrigate the whole northern part of the country: the Ouham or Bara Sara, the **Bamingui**, and the **Aouk**. Geographer Yves Boulvert has shown that the Ouham or Bara Sara was the actual upper stream of the Chari River, and that the Bamingui and the Aouk were only its tributaries on the right.

**CHARI (or SHARI), REGION OF.** The administrative region of Chari was created in the heart of the French Congo in 1897 and placed in the hands of a director, **Emile Gentil**. It was dissolved on 5 September 1900 by a decree organizing a "Military Territory and Protectorate of Chad." Upper Chari, still without a civil **administration**, became an autonomous region. The headquarters were successively Fort **Sibut**, Fort **Crampel**, and Fort Archambault. In 1903, with the creation of the **Ubangui-Shari** territory, the southern part of this region became the Kemo-**Gribingui** region.

**CHAUVET, PAUL (1904–?).** Born in Ruffec (Charente) on 13 January 1904. Director of Political Affairs at the France d'Outre-Mer (French Overseas Ministry), Paul Chauvet found himself placed in charge of the French Equatorial African High Commission in November 1951. He stopped the pressure exerted against **Barthélémy Boganda** and his supporters in **Ubangui**.

**CHERFEDDINE.** *Aguid* of the **Wadaï**, he attacked **Dar-al-Kuti** in October 1894. **Cha** was taken by assault and destroyed. As-**Sanusi** fled into **Banda** country. The *aguid* stayed four months in Dar-al-Kuti, forcing leaders as far as **Dji** to swear allegiance to the Sultan of Wadaï.

**CHERRY.** An American adventurer and mechanic on a river steamer, Cherry became an elephant hunter and trader in Upper **Ubangui**. In 1900 he became private adviser to the **Bandia** Chief Sate-Rato, who was directing a war against Sultan **Rafaï**. Cherry then set himself up on the Kotto with the **Banda** Chief **Baram-Baria**, at a spot that became a French military post (Bria) in 1909.

**CHEVALIER, AUGUSTE (1873–1956).** The botanist and explorer Auguste Chevalier visited **Dar-al-Kuti** as the guest of as-**Sanusi** in 1903. Chevalier took a stand against the destruction of villages and the requisition of populations practiced by **concessionary companies** and the administration in the Congo, Sangha, and **Ubangui** regions. He wrote an account of his journey, *French Central Africa*, which was published in Paris in 1908. Chevalier recommended the introduction of commercial **agricultural** products, notably **coffee**. He made his last trip to **Ubangui-Shari** in 1951.

**CHIEFS, CHIEFDOMS.** The traditional rulers, *chefs*, in Central Africa combined political, economic, and religious powers. They were disempowered by the colonizers and replaced with administrative "chiefs" (village chiefs, canton chiefs, and so on). Their role was limited to **tax** gathering and transmitting, and executing the colonial administration's orders. In the circular on indigenous politics in 1931, Governor General **Félix Eboué** recommended that traditional "chiefs" be sought out if they still existed. These orders were not effectively carried out. In 1955 Governor General **Paul Chauvet** maintained that the chiefs "had lost almost all their authority, and were also incapable of carrying out the orders that the administration wished to place in their hands." In 1958 the **Ubanguian** government substituted municipalities for the cantons into which rural communities had been organized. The village "chiefs" were maintained. A law of 20 November 1964 decided the respective administrative roles of **MESAN** representatives and village "chiefs" or mayors.

**CHILDREN. School** is in principle mandatory until the age of five, but the lack of means given to the **education** system and the repeated strikes of unpaid teachers have caused an important decrease in the number of teachers and the proliferation of "street children" in the urban areas, many of them becoming delinquents (*godobé* in **Sango**).

**CHINA.** On 5 Febraury 1964, President **David Dacko** announced his intention to recognize the People's Republic of China. At the same time Chou En-Lai was making a large-scale tour of Africa. Diplomatic relations were not established, though, until November when the Nationalist Chinese ambassador left. In 1965 the People's Republic of China assigned a full ambassador in Bangui. After the **Saint-Sylvestre coup**, **Jean-Bedel Bokassa** spectacularly broke off ties with Beijing and renewed relations with Taipei. Then, in August 1976, he closed the Nationalist Chinese embassy and renewed ties with Beijing. In 1987 China financed the building of a new hospital in **Bangui**. In 2003 China stated it was willing to help the CAR pay its civil servants their back wages. On occasion, the CAR government broke off relations with Beijing and recognized Taiwan, then vice versa. Each time, the Central African government negotiated its position for substantial financial benefits.

**CHINKO (or SHINKO).** Large northern tributary of the **Mbomou** River, it is also known under the **Kreich** name of Kpakpa. Today the Chinko flows through an uninhabited region.

**CIRQUE D'HIVER (CONFERENCES).** On 21 April 1886, **Pierre Brazza** announced to the public the French rights to the **Ubangui** basin recently discovered and claimed by King **Leopold II** at a conference held at the *Cirque d'hiver* in Paris.

**CIVIL SERVANTS.** *See* BOURGEOISIE; FONCTIONNAIRES.

**CLEMENTEL, ETIENNE.** Colonial minister during the great 1906 debate on the Congo affairs, Clementel favored maintaining the **concessionary companies** in spite of the heavy burden they imposed on the African populations.

**CLIMATE.** As with many African countries located on the equator or in the tropics, the cycle of Central African climate, which does not have a regular change from the rainy season to the dry one, conditions all **agricultural** activity. It can be said that the rainy season in Central Africa stretches roughly from the end of April to November. Its length varies, however, from north to south. It lasts, in fact, from February–March until November–December south of a line that goes from Bouar to Bambari to Babubakouma, and to the north of this line it lasts from April-May to September. The climate and the plant life in the CAR are divided into three horizontal zones: in the south, the **forest** is dense due to the equatorial weather with a short dry season; in the center, the savannah contains scattered small woods due to the tropical weather, humid from June to October and dry from November to May, blown over by the Harmattan wind.

**CLOZEL, FRANÇOIS.** Explorer in charge of the last expedition of the *Comité de l'Afrique Française*, Clozel was to leave Sangha for Chad and return to France by way of Dahomey. At Brazzaville he learned of the 15 March 1894 Franco-German convention, which granted Germany access to Chad through Cameroon. He therefore limited himself to the exploration of Upper Sangha and returned to France in 1895. He then continued a brilliant career in the colonial administration.

**COFFEE.** Many species of coffee grow wild in the **Ubanguian** countryside. Until 1927 wild coffee was simply gathered. The first plantations using the more resistant and productive excelsa were promising. Visions of extending such plantations throughout the territory grew only to be met by a tracheomycose outbreak, which ruined most of the plantations in 1934. New plantations were begun by European colonists in the west and in the Ubangui valley with robusta plants. Of excellent quality, Central African coffee production was nevertheless limited to 9,000 metric tons by the International Coffee agreement signed in 1963. This quota was later increased. A project begun in 1958 by Minister of Economics **Roger Guerillot** to grow tracheomycose-resistant excelsa plants throughout the country was therefore abandoned. Since 1976 commercial coffee production in Central Africa has been given over to the Egyptian society, Elmas. The maximum production of robusta coffee in Central Africa reached 12,427 metric tons in 1976–1977. Since 1979 Central African coffee production has been considerably more than 10,000 metric tons each season. It has even been more than 15,000 metric tons three times (1981–1982: 15,430 tons; 1982–1993: 16,773 tons; and in 1984–1985: 18,246 tons).

During the last 15 years of the 20th century, after the last European plantation owners had left, Central African coffee production stabilized at around its quota as determined by the International Coffee Organization in 1963. The Central African state tried to support this sector through an Agence de Développement de la Caféiculture (ADECAF; Agency for the Development of Coffee Production), which grouped the planters in rural collective units. Those nevertheless failed in their efforts as many planters abandoned their crops to look for **diamonds**. Part of the crops was lost as the plantations had been deserted. In the year 2000, the price paid to the producer fell to less than 115 CFA francs per kilo (of coffee still in its shell).

Today coffee family plantations cover 53,000 hectares in the west and 26,500 hectares in the east. The industrial plantations only concern 2,300 hectares in the west and 2,400 in the east. Coffee production is presently in a very critical situation. Production remains around 11,000 or 12,000 tons a year and the exports to the Sudan have ceased.

**COLOMBANI, IGNACE (1908–1989).** Born in Montreal, Canada, on 18 August 1908, he died in Bastia, Corsica, on 19 August 1989. He was the head governor of the **Ubangui Territory** in 1950–1951. He was then appointed governor of Chad. Living subsequently in Corsica he wrote several books on the Corsican language and poetry.

**COMITE CONSTITUTIONNEL (CONSTITUTIONAL COMMITTEE).** Purely consultative committee constituted by **David Dacko** in October 1960 to give opinion on government institutions. **Abel Goumba**, leader of the opposition, participated in it.

**COMITE DE L'AFRIQUE FRANCAISE (FRENCH AFRICA COMMITTEE).** On 1 December 1890, the group that had sponsored the **Paul Crampel** mission founded the French Africa Committee, which until 1895 was in charge of the organizing and financing exploration in Central Africa.

**COMMITTEE OF ECONOMIC SAFETY (COMITE DE SALUT ECONOMIQUE).** This committee was constituted with local leaders in 1957 by Roger Guerillot, French territorial councilor who had rallied to **Boganda**. Its object was to replace traditional administrative activity with regard to **Ubanguian agriculture** with a committee, subdivided into regional committees, composed of French colonials and **MESAN** territorial councilors. On 30 December 1957, **Barthélémy Boganda** celebrated before the **Assembly** "the union of capital and Ubanguian labor." He soon sang a different tune. However, no French colonials wished to invest money in such a risky project, and the Ubanguian villagers refused to participate in what they considered a return to the **concessionary** regime. Moreover, the banks and the French aid organization abstained from supporting the project.

**COMPAGNIE EQUATORIALE DES MINES (CEM; EQUATORIAL MINING COMPANY).** This was the first mining company established in **Ubangui** in 1927 under the auspices of the Bernard Brothers Bank.

**COMPAGNIE FRANCAISE POUR LE DEVELOPPEMENT DES FIBRES TEXTILES (CFDT; FRENCH COMPANY FOR THE**

**DEVELOPMENT OF TEXTILE FIBERS).** A French state company that helped President **David Dacko** in the reform of the **cotton** industry in 1964.

**COMPAGNIE MINIERE DE L'OUBANGUI ORIENTAL (CMOO; MINING COMPANY OF WESTERN UBANGUI).** Founded in 1928 by the geologist Lombard for the mining of **diamonds** in the northeastern part of the country, this company was especially active in Upper Sangha. Its activity was stimulated by World War II. In May 1950, it accepted Marshall Plan aid and a few years later came under American control as part of Centramines.

**COMPANIES.** Between 1994 and 1997, nine national or mixed-capital companies found private owners. This includes the HUSECA (vegetable oil and soap factory), the SCET-SOFITEL, the SOCOCA (cotton marketing), the SNE-SODECA (water supply), the SOCATEL (telecommunications), and the SOCATRAF-ACCT (river transportation). At the end of 1996, this restructuring of the economy was interrupted by the political uprisings.

**COMPTOIR NATIONAL DU DIAMANT (CND; NATIONAL DIAMOND TRADING POST).** A mixed company formed in 1964 with equal shares belonging to the Central African government and Diamond Distributors, Inc. in order to establish a diamond-cutting shop in **Bangui**. This company was to become completely private as would other national or mixed companies.

**COMTE, PAUL (1866–1897).** Born in Bar le Duc (Meuse) on 25 January 1866. A French administrator and author of a study on the **Nzakara**, he was killed on 13 July 1897 on the **Ubangui** River during a reprisals operation against the Ngbaka.

**CONCESSIONARY COMPANIES.** In 1897, dazzled by the profits made by Belgian firms in King **Leopold**'s Congo, the French business community wanted to transpose this system to the French Congo. From 1898 to 1900 limited companies were created to divide up 90 percent of the Congo and Ubangui. The concessionary system soon resulted in the most extreme exploitation of the population. In spite of scandals the companies preserved their privileges. When the **rubber** crisis ended the wild rubber–gathering activities, the companies received special commercial privileges in compensation. Concessionary companies simply became **trading** and transportation companies, which allowed them to hold on to their monopoly positions until independence.

**CONGO FRANÇAIS (AND DEPENDENCIES).** The French possessions in Equatorial Africa carried this name until 1910.

**CONGO-OCEAN.** The decision to begin a railroad between Brazzaville and the ocean was not really made until after World War I. The first pickax blow was struck on 6 February 1921, and the work went on for some 10 years and cost the lives of numerous forced laborers. A great number of these were **Ubanguians**. The writer **Albert Londres** in 1928 denounced the treatment inflicted on men working on the Congo-Ocean railways in *Terre d'Ebène* (Ebony Land). The effect this tragedy caused was best defined with the formula "a black life for each cross tie."

**CONSEIL REPRESENTATIF (REPRESENTATIVE COUNCIL).** It was under this name that the **Territorial Assembly** was created in 1947, as called for in the 7 October 1946 law and the decree of 25 October 1946.

**CONSEIL REVOLUTIONNAIRE (REVOLUTIONARY COUNCIL).** On 3 January 1966, **Jean-Bedel Bokassa** formed a government that he called the "Revolutionary Council," a name abandoned a few weeks later. *See also* SAINT-SYLVESTRE, COUP D'ETAT OF.

**CONSEILS DE DISTRICT (DISTRICT COUNCILS).** Created at the late date of 1956, these elected councils assisted French administrators in the distribution of a modest district **tax** for local work projects.

**CONSTITUTIONS.** The constitutional situation of the Central African Republic and then the Central African Empire was as follows. The first Central African constitution was adopted on 9 February 1959 by the **Territorial Assembly**, which became a constitutional assembly.

**Barthélémy Boganda** had affirmed, in a handwritten preamble, "the rights and fundamental liberties of democracy, notably the sacred character of the human person, the existence of human rights as the basis for all communities, the right of each person to free development of his (or her) personality, the inviolability of the law, the right of defense at all degrees of procedure." It was proclaimed that there were "neither subject, nor privilege of birthplace, person or family." This preamble enumerated completely all the public liberties that made the new state a well-defined democracy. The constitution called for a parliamentary-type government with a legislative assembly elected for five years and holding two sessions annually; a president of the government invested by the assembly; and ministers appointed by the president, who were to be placed at the head of the respective departments and remain in their post during the term of the legislature. The president of the government could dissolve the assembly, which, for its part, could turn out the government by a motion of censure, including the naming of the successor as adopted by a two-thirds majority of the deputies.

With a goal of achieving African unity, it was held that the Central African Republic could conclude agreements allowing partial or total abandonment of sovereignty with other states. No revision procedures that infringed on the republican form and democratic principles governing the Republic were allowed. After Boganda's death and the country's independence, a simple law passed by the Assembly on 14 August 1960 gave **David Dacko**, head of government, the rank and prerogatives of president of the Republic.

Four amendments (12 December 1960, 4 May 1961, 28 September 1962, and 19 November 1963) modified this constitution, suppressed some public freedoms, set up a single party and a presidential regime. Law Number 64/37 of 26 November 1964 promulgated a new constitution dated 20 November that retained only a few appearances of democracy. After the **Saint-Sylvestre coup d'etat** (31 December 1965–1 January 1966), a first constitutional act enabled President **Jean-Bedel Bokassa** to take "all necessary measures under the circumstances." He proclaimed "a new constitution which was to be submitted for the approval of the people," but this was never done. A second constitutional act, dated 8 January 1966, inspired by the acts taken in 1940 in France by Marshal Philippe Petain, laid down "the provisional organization of the powers of the Republic." The Central African Republic became a dictatorship directed by a soldier and self-declared President for Life, who placed himself above the law.

On 4 December 1976, the Marshal-President-for-Life decided to transform the Republic into an Empire. A charter was granted, under the name of "Imperial Constitution." The charter made the new regime a parliamentary monarchy. The preamble reinstated the enumeration of public liberties proclaimed by the Constitution of 1959. The principle of a single party was maintained. A national assembly, with legislative power, was foreseen. An independent judiciary was affirmed. The imperial dignity was proclaimed hereditary by order of primogeniture, unless the emperor, while living, designated another member of the imperial family as his successor.

None of the institutions provided for were even put into place and all the democratic principles proclaimed were blatantly flouted. The constitutional text written, as were the preceding ones, by a French law professor was only accepted by the emperor so he could continue to benefit from the aid of western democracies that were troubled by the totalitarian character of his regime.

On 21 September 1979, a provisional constitutional act for the Central African Republic was signed by President Dacko. Dacko refused to reinstate the constitution of 26 November 1964, suspended in 1966 by Bokassa and then replaced by the imperial constitution. On 1 February 1981 the Central African people accepted, almost unanimously, a new democratic constitution. Article 14 of the constitution unequivocally maintained the principle of checks and balances. The two posts of prime minister and president as head of state were proposed. Violating his own constitution, Dacko placed all power in the hands of his chief of staff, General **André Kolingba**, on 1 September 1981. Kolingba hurried to suspend this constitution. Two constitutional acts, not passed until two years later on 21 September 1985, instituted the position of president of the Republic endorsing the omnipotence of the head of state.

On 21 November 1986, as usual written by a French law professor, a new constitution was adopted by referendum. This constitution invested the president of the Republic with full executive power, which he could exercise without control or sharing. It reestablished a single party regime. Article 3 clearly stated that this party, the Rassemblement Démocratique Centrafricain (RDC; Central African Democratic Party), includes the entire population and represents all the people and gives them their full voting expression.

On 22 April 1990 the constitution was modified to allow for the return of a multiparty system. In December 1995 a new constitution, with an emphasis on decentralization, was adopted in a referendum by less than 10 percent of registered voters and put into force on 28 January 1995. This constitution was suspended by General **François Bozizé** on March 2003.

**CONUS, CAPTAIN.** French **coffee** planter and transporter from **Ubangui**, who distinguished himself as part of the second military battalion in the **Free French** battles of World War II.

**COOPERANTS.** This French term has been used since independence for technical, civil, and military assistants whom the French government sends to Africa to carry out cooperative aid. The number of such French *coopérants* in the Central African Republic has been gradually declining and is below 500 now.

**CORNUT-GENTILE, BERNARD.** Sub**prefect** appointed Governor General, High Commissioner of the Republic in French Equatorial Africa in February 1948. He replaced the former prefect of police, Charles Luizet, who had died a few months after having begun his duties. In August 1958 Cornut-Gentile, as Minister of Overseas France, accompanied **General Charles de Gaulle** on his trip to Brazzaville.

**COTTON.** After World War I, the collapse of the **rubber** market led the colonial authorities to search for another export product. Their choice was cotton, already cultivated on large areas in the neighboring Belgian Congo. The growing of this crop was made compulsory by the administration. Each man and woman was obliged to produce enough to satisfy a head **tax**. Faced with the reluctance of private companies, prices were underwritten in case the world market declined. After World War II, a price-support fund was formed. Prices were fixed for cotton harvests and maintained at a very low rate. In spite of considerable efforts for technical assistance, because of the mandatory nature of the production, and also because of climatic and soil problems, the results were not too good. Cotton production, which was 39,211 metric tons in 1939–1940, was only 37,614 metric tons at the eve of independence in 1957–1958. The maximum was recorded in 1969–1970 (57,743 metric tons).

During the past two decades, cotton production has remained rather weak. Only during two seasons did the crop exceed 40,000 metric tons (1974–1975, 47,517 tons; and 1984–1985, 45,514 tons). The 1981–1982 crop was catastrophic: only 17,256 metric tons. Annual crops have tended to stabilize at about 25,000 to 30,000 metric tons. The 1987–1988 crop marked a new drop with less than 20,000 metric tons produced.

In spite of foreign aid and of the quality of its cotton, the Central African production kept dropping though cotton production in other African countries was rising to 2,270,000 tons, thanks to favorable world rates. In 1990 Central African production fell to 12,000 tons. It increased thanks to the CFA franc's devaluation and exceeded 30,000 tons in 1995–1996, then 42,400 tons in 1997–1998. It must be noted that since 1984 the price paid to the Central African producer has never been more than half of the world market price.

During the last decade of the 20th century, a new decline of the cotton production occurred, and it was largely outdistanced by **diamond** and **wood** production. The yield per hectare is less than 300 kilos a hectare. The Compagnie française pour le développement des fibres textiles (CFDT; French Textile Development Company) ended its support. The deterioration of the cotton production in Central Africa is in sharp contrast with that of the neighbouring Cameroon and Chad. *See also* COTTON COMPANIES.

**COTTON COMPANIES (SOCIETÉS COTONNIERES).** In 1926 and 1930, four companies were created for the purchase, ginning, and export of cotton harvested by **Ubanguian** peasants: the Société Cotonnière Française (Cotonfran), the Compagnie Coloniale Cotonniere Ouham-Nana (Cotouna), the Societé de la Kotto, and, a little later, the Societé Cotonnière du haut Oubangui (Cotonbangui). The first three were linked to Belgian and Dutch companies.

The conventions between the government of French Equatorial Africa and these companies were renewed in 1949, and the Central

African government followed with another renewal in 1960. In 1964 **David Dacko** reformed the cotton economy. He obtained these companies' giving up these conventions and their integration into a new body, the Union Cotonnière Centrafricaine (UCCA; Central African Cotton Association). The Central African state; the Bureau pour le developpement de la production agricole (BDPA; Agricultural Production Development Office) a French government enterprise for agricultural cooperation; and the Compagnie française pour le développement des fibres textiles (CFDT; French Textile Development Company) obtained 48.8 percent of the shares. The cotton-growing zone was reduced to only those areas that were sufficiently productive.

In 1965 the UCCA decided to take over its own transportation, which noticeably lowered its production costs. It focused on the use and export of cottonseed, even using it as a fuel in gins. On 11 May 1974, Emperor **Bokassa** decided to nationalize the UCCA.

**CRAFTS (ARTISANAT).** The explorers **Georg Schweinfurth**, **Wilhelm Junker**, and **Auguste Chevalier** have left interesting notes on the existence of handmade textiles in the eastern **Ubangui** at the end of the 19th century. At the same time, the **Banda** operated many indigenous smelters that fed an important cottage metal industry. **Muhammad al Tounsy** noted that in 1813 this region furnished numerous "white man's" weapons to **Wadaï** and **Darfur**. The making of pottery, woven mats, leather articles, and musical instruments was also well developed throughout the area. This craft industry, endangered by the **slave** wars, almost completely disappeared during the early years of colonization.

**CRAMPEL, PAUL (1864–1891).** Born in Nancy on 17 November 1864, Crampel became **Pierre Brazza**'s private secretary in November 1885. In 1888 he engaged in exploration of the area of Gabon and Cameroon, in the course of which he was severely wounded. Hospitalized in 1889 in Paris, he outlined a plan that was to bear his name and consisted of linking the Congo to the Mediterranean by Lake Chad and the Tuareg country. Thanks to his friend Harry Alis, on the staff of the *Journal des Débats*, he found private funds to finance the project, to which the colonial undersecretary of state, **Eugène Etienne**, granted his agreement. In **Bangui**, on 25 September 1890, he was given the delegated functions of commissioner general in **Ubangui**. The post, the officer of which, **Maurice Musy**, had been killed in January, was in a pitiful state. Crampel restored peace in the region before taking up his own explorations. At the end of 1890, he concluded a number of treaties with the Bangui leaders, then headed for the unexplored country to the north.

Crampel reached **Cha**, the capital of **Dar-al-Kuti**, in March just after **Rabih** had left, leaving his vassal, Sultan **Muhammad as-Sanusi**, in a weak position. As-Sanusi decided to take Crampel's arms and ammunition, since the explorer had spread his mission thin and lost several of his European companions. Crampel, on his part, refused to grant his African riflemen the right to looting even though this was the usual practice in colonial expeditions. A large part of his riflemen deserted. On 9 April 1891, Crampel was assassinated in an ambush by as-Sanusi's men on the banks of the Diangara, a tributary of the **Aouk**, just as he decided to make his way to Rabih. Crampel's assistant, Albert Nebout, on learning of his death, retraced the route and brought the last unit of the mission back to Brazzaville. Crampel's death triggered a lively debate in France between those who wished to abandon and those who wished to continue the colonial expeditions.

**CUCHEROUSSET, MONSIGNOR JOSEPH (1907–1970).** Born in Laviron (Doubs), he died in Chevilly-Larue (94) on 16 July 1970. Arriving in **Ubangui** in 1945, Father Cucherousset was consecrated Bishop of **Bangui** on 26 July 1948. Under his impetus, **missions** and **schools** multiplied. As bishop of Bangui, he became the archbishop on 14 September 1955. In 1962 Monsignor Cucherousset came into conflict with **David Dacko** who had nationalized private schools. In 1969 he allowed Monsignor **Joachim Ndayen** to replace him and retired to become Bishop of the newly created diocese of Bambari.

**CULARD.** Head of the Mongoumba **administrative post** incriminated by **Dr. Fulconis** in the **Hostages of Bangui affair**, which had been discovered in May 1904. The Brazzaville judges granted him an acquittal in spite of the charges against him.

**CUREAU, DR. ALDOLPHE.** Chief colonial administrator and **Victor Liotard**'s successor in Upper Ubangui, on 4 May 1904 he was appointed Permanent Delegate of the Commissioner General in charge of the administration of the **Ubangui-Shari** territory.

## – D –

**DABAGO.** The **Banda**-Wassa leader, Dabago resisted the troops of Sultan **Rafaï** with **Yangou-Mbili** in 1900. Defeated, he withdrew to the Upper **Dji**.

**DACKO, DAVID (1930–2003).** Born on 24 March 1930 in Bouchia (Lobaye), he died in Yaounde. David Dacko attended primary **school** in **Mbaïki**, where his father was a night watchman. After having attended the upper primary school of Bambari, he was admitted to the teachers' school of Mouyoundzi in the neighboring territory of Middle-Congo. In 1951, as an instructor in **Bangui**, he took part in a basic-**education** experiment conducted by the colonial administration. Appointed school director in 1955, he became close to Deputy **Barthélémy Boganda** and was elected a member of the **Territorial Assembly**. When forming the first Government Council of **Ubangui-Shari**, Boganda chose him as Minister of Agriculture. On 1 December 1958 Boganda selected him for the post of Minister of the Interior and Administrative Affairs.

After the death of the founder of the Central African Republic, Dacko, laying claim to his alleged kinship with Boganda, was able to brush aside the succession of the vice president of the government, **Abel Goumba**. He was elected president and a little later he substituted himself for Senator Etienne Gounio as the head of the Mouvement pour l'évolution sociale de l'Afrique Noire (**MESAN**; Movement for the Social Evolution of Black Africa). Goumba and his friends founded an opposition party, the Mouvement pour l'Evolution Démocratique de l'Afrique Centrale (**MEDAC**; Movement for the Democratic Evolution of Central Africa). Independence was granted the Central African Republic on 13 August 1960. With the help of French authorities Dacko suppressed the opposition party and arrested Goumba and his friends. From then on the regime was strengthened. In internal affairs Dacko, like Boganda, relied on a group of notables from various ethnic groups, joined together in the governing committee of MESAN. In external affairs he followed the French lead, but sought friendly relations with the other great powers as well.

In 1964 the events of Stanleyville in the Belgian Congo upset him. Fearing that he would be overtaken by younger party members, he tried to improve relations with the People's Republic of China. Deciding to profoundly modify the **economic** structure of the country, Dacko was able to set up a number of industries, control the **diamond** market, and reorganize village **agriculture**. But he collided with the large European import-export companies, which continued to occupy a dominant position. Poorly served by a corrupt administration, betrayed by a number of his ministers and close collaborators, Dacko was overthrown during the night of 1 January 1965 by a military coup d'etat organized by his Army Chief of Staff Colonel **Jean-Bedel Bokassa**, with the help of Commander **Alexandre Banza**. After a long detention in Bangui, then in his hometown Lobaye, in September 1976 Dacko was appointed by Bokassa as his private adviser.

During the night of 20–21 September 1979, Dacko arrived with French troops, who occupied the airport terminal and the town of Bangui. He then proclaimed Bokassa's overthrow and the restoration of the Republic. Dacko resumed the presidential office he had abandoned 13 years before and made Bokassa's prime minister, **Henri Maïdou**, vice president of the Republic. On 27 September he formed a government.

On 15 October 1979 Dacko convened a round table conference of political organizations and unions, but in February 1980 Dacko founded a single party, the Union Démocratique Centrafricaine (UDC; Central African Democratic Union). During a visit to Paris from 21 to 24 December 1980, he announced the beginning of work on a constitution to be followed by presidential elections. After the adoption of this constitution by referendum, Dacko organized elections, which he won. The results of these elections were contested by his opponents. Dacko, expecting **Valéry Giscard d'Estaing** to win the French presidency, was shaken up by François Mitterrand's success.

After the explosion of a bomb in a Bangui movie theater on 14 July 1981, Dacko outlawed the two principal opposition parties. On 1

September 1981, under considerable pressure, he transferred power to his chief of staff, General **André Kolingba**.

Retired on his plantation at Mokinda, then living in Bangui, Dacko still wanted, despite his ill health, to take part in his country's politics. He created a new party, the Mouvement pour la Démocratie et le Développement (MDD; Movement for Democracy and Development), but failed in the presidential elections.

**DAIGRE, REVEREND FATHER JOSEPH (1881–1952).** Born in Belle-ile-en-mer on 23 May 1881, he died in Langonnet on 24 September 1952. He was a Holy Ghost **missionary** who lived many years in Bambari. Father Daigre wrote a book on his stay in **Ubangui-Shari** that was an overwhelming condemnation of the excesses of the colonial regime.

**DALLOT-BEFIOT, AUGUSTIN.** A minister under President **David Dacko**, he was mistreated by the military during the 1965 coup d'etat. Under the regime of Emperor **Bokassa I**, he became governor of the imperial domain of **Berengo**. He helped the French airborne division that attacked the presidential palace and took part in a commission assigned by President Dacko to do an inventory of the former emperor's possessions.

**DAMPIERRE, ERIC DE (1928–1998).** Born in Paris on 4 July 1928, he died on 9 March 1998. Eric de Dampièrre was assigned in 1954 by a French government organization to go to **Bangui** and examine the causes of the decline in birth rate of the **Nzakara** people. From 1955 to 1967, he wrote a monumental thesis about the **Bangassou** kingdom, the former **Bandia** kingdom, in Upper **Ubangui**. Presented at the Sorbonne in 1967, this thesis remains the best work about the history of the eastern regions of the Central African Republic. A sociology professor at the Paris-X University of Nanterre, he led an ethnology and comparative sociology team that publishes a special collection, *Recherches Oubanguiennes* (Ubanguian Research). He directed many theses and master's degrees of Central African students.

**DAR-AL-KUTI (DAR-EL-KOUTI).** **Wadaïan** frontier area founded south of the **Aouk** by **Omar Djougoultoum**, an exiled member of the

**Baguirmiam** royal family. His descendant, **Kobur**, was attacked by **Rabih**, who substituted for him his own nephew, **Muhammad as-Sanusi**, whom he forced to break with Wadaï. In 1891 as-Sanusi exterminated the **Paul Crampel** expedition. In 1897 he sent his emissaries to **Emile Gentil** to ask for a French protectorate. Dar-al-Kuti remained little more than a **slaving** state, and the armies of as-Sanusi ravaged all of northern **Ubangui**. The protectorate, revised on several occasions, ended with the sultan's death on 12 January 1911. The name of Dar-al-Kuti was used for a while for a colonial administrative division that corresponded to the former sultanate.

**DAR FERTIT.** Still called Fertit by Arab caravaners, Dar Fertit designated the northeast part of the Central African Republic that was emptied of its inhabitants by the **slaving** expeditions of the 19th and early 20th centuries.

**DARFUR (DARFOUR).** The **Banda** and other Central African ethnic groups originated in this mountainous area, in which a strong kingdom continued until 1916.

**DAR KOULA (DAR KULLA).** According to **Walter George Browne**'s account at the end of the 18th century, this term designated a "strong and organized Negro state situated to the southwest of **Darfur**."

**DARLAN, ANTOINE.** Elected on 19 October 1947 as councilor of French West Africa by the **Territorial Assembly** of **Ubangui-Shari**, Antoine Darlan was elected vice president of the Grand Council of French West Africa. At first a member of the Rassemblement Démocratique Africain (**RDA**; African Democratic Rally) he later allied with **Barthélémy Boganda** and the Mouvement pour l'évolution sociale de l'Afrique Noire (**MESAN**; Movement for the Social Evolution of Black Africa). He was reelected councilor of the French Union in November 1953. Excluded in 1957 from MESAN by Boganda at the instigation of the French colonists **René Naud** and **Roger Guerillot**, who blamed him for his sympathies with the French Left, Darlan founded a small opposition group. In 1962 **David Dacko** appointed him Director of Finance.

**DARLAN, GEORGES.** The brother of **Antoine Darlan** and, like him, of Franco-African ancestry, Georges Darlan was elected president of the **Ubangui-Shari** Representative Council in 1949. As president of Cotoncoop, he had received subsidies from the territorial budget. Deputy **René Malbrant** and the **Chamber of Commerce (of Bangui)** accused him of squandering public funds. They then succeeded in hindering the development of the cooperative movement.

**DATO.** A cotton grower in the Alindao district, he died after having been struck by an agricultural labor driver in 1953. **Barthélémy Boganda** regarded Dato to be a national hero.

**DAUMAS.** Daumas was, in 1891, the first French commercial firm to be established in **Bangui**. In 1892 King **Leopold** gave the order to the Société Anonyme Belge du Haut-Congo (**SAB**; Belgian Companie of Upper Congo) to take control of this company, thus creating the first merger of French and Belgian commercial interests in the region.

**DAYO.** The **Yakoma** leader Dayo, who had participated in the combat of 5 January 1888 during which King **Leopold**'s Captain **Alphonse Vangele** had been beaten and forced to retreat, signed a treaty with the same officer in the following year to avoid the destruction of his country.

**DECAZES, CAPTAIN.** One of the first companions of **Pierre Brazza**, Captain Decazes arrived in **Bangui** on 5 December 1893, at the head of the first unit of a French expeditionary corps sent into Upper **Ubangui** following France's dispute with King **Leopold**.

**DECORSE, LIEUTENANT.** A member of Professor **Auguste Chevalier**'s expedition in 1903, this French officer gave an account of the destruction that was taking place in Sara country at the hands of **as-Sanusi**'s troops during that period.

**DEDEAVODE, JEAN-BRUNO (?–1981).** A Central African doctor, Jean-Bruno Dedeavode became Emperor **Bokassa**'s son-in-law when on 30 January 1973 he married his daughter **Martine**, who had arrived in **Bangui** from Vietnam on 10 January 1971 and been recognized as the dictator's actual daughter. On 23 February 1976 Dr.

Dedeavode, using a deadly injection, killed the five-day-old baby of Martine Nguyen-Thi-Ba'i and Captain **Fidèle Obrou**, who was sentenced to death for conspiring against Bokassa. Arrested after the fall of Bokassa, the doctor was sentenced to death for this crime and was executed along with five close relatives of the former emperor on 24 January 1981. *See also* MARTINES (THE TWO "MARTINES").

**DEGENNE, BERNARD.** Colonel Degenne, the chief of staff of an airborne division, the Groupement parachutiste (GAP) at Albi, was asked to come to Paris on 7 August 1973 for a mission in Africa. On 8 August he arrived in Ndjamena along with Lieutenant Colonel Massa, the military attaché to the French embassy in **Bangui**, and with Guy Georgy, the French Foreign Office's African Affairs Director. They staged operation **Barracuda**, launched on 20 September.

**DEGRAIN, JOSEPH.** One of the most active French businessmen in **Ubangui** after World War II, Joseph Degrain directed two semistate companies, the CTRO (**road** transportation) as well as the CO-TOUNAC (**cotton** marketing). His realism made possible, in 1964, the creation of an important mixed company, the UCCA, which was placed in charge of all cotton production.

**DEITTE, GOVERNOR ALPHONSE.** Deitte succeeded Governor **Auguste Lamblin** as the head of the **Ubangui-Shari** colony in 1931.

**DEJEAN, MAURICE (?–1966).** Minister of Foreign Affairs in the **David Dacko** government, Maurice Dejean set up the first Central African diplomatic missions in 1960. He was killed during the **Saint-Sylvestre coup** against Dacko the night of 31 December 1965 and 1 January 1966.

**DELPEY, ROGER.** A former colonial infantry sergeant in Indochina and author of a book on the Vietnam War called *Soldats de boue* (Soldiers of Mud), Delpey served with the OAS in Algeria. In May 1979 he offered his services to Emperor **Bokassa**, who employed Delpey as his liaison after his overthrow. Following the revelation of the **diamond** affair in the French press, he was arrested 10 May 1980 in front of the Libyan embassy in Paris and implicated in relations with international powers in a manner detrimental to France's diplomatic situation. He was released 28 November 1980. The press presented his jailing as a "royal order" from President **Giscard d'Estaing**. Delpey organized Bokassa's failed attempt to regain the throne in November 1983. He is the author of several books on his adventures.

**DEM ZIBER.** Founded by **Zubayr** Pasha, who set it up as his main center (the *dem* of Zubayr), this settlement became the headquarters of the province (*mouderira*) of Bahr-el-Ghazal during the Egyptian occupation. **Victor Liotard** took possession for France on 17 April 1897, more than a year before the Fashoda incident. The French evacuated the post in 1900 after the cession of Bahr-el-Ghazal to the Anglo-Egyptian Sudan by the Franco-British convention of 8 September 1899.

**DEMAFOUTH, JEAN-JACQUES.** A student in France, close to **Ange Patassé**, he was recognized as a political refugee and chosen as the legal adviser to the CIMADE, thus becoming a lawyer. He returned to **Bangui** after the election of Patassé and became his legal adviser. As such he also advised former Emperor **Bokassa I** on 4 November 1993 to leave the Renaissance Palace appartements where General **André Kolingba** had put him up after granting him a pardon. Demafouth was then appointed National Defense Minister.

**DEMBAO.** Leader of a **Banda Vidri** group of **Lesse**, he was arrested in 1913 by the French for "complicity with the unconquered northerners," and was killed during an attempted escape.

**DENGUIADE, CATHERINE-MARTINE.** Born at Fort-Archambault (now Sarh) in Chad on 7 August 1949. In 1963 she became the wife of **Jean-Bedel Bokassa** who, once emperor, made her the empress.

**DEPARTEMENTS.** On 30 June 1934 a decree made French Equatorial Africa a unitary colony divided into departements, which were in turn grouped into four regions. The region of **Ubangui-Shari**, which also included southern Chad, was divided into six departements: Haute-Sangha-Mpoko, with **Bangui** as its administrative center; Ubangui-Ouaka, with Bambari; Mbomou, with **Bangassou**; Shari-Bangoran, with Fort-Archambault; Ouham-Pende, with Bozoum; and Logone, with Moundou as its administrative center. In 1936, following the modification of the frontiers with Chad and Middle-Congo, new departements were created in Ubangui-Shari. As of 1 January 1937 the region became a territory made up of 10 departements: Ombella Mpoko, with Bangui as its administrative center; Lobaye, with Mabiki; Ouham-Pende, with Bozoum; Ouham, with Bossangoa; Kemo-Gribingui, with Fort Sibut; Ouaka, with Bambari; Basse-Kotto, with **Mobaye**; **Dar-al-Kuti**, with **Ndélé**; Bas-Mbomou, with Bangassou; and Haut-Mbomou, with Zemio as its administrative center.

**DEPUTIES.** The term designates both the representatives of **Ubangui-Shari** to the Constituent Assembly and those to the French National Assembly from 1945 to 1958. These were, for the First College, from 1945 to 1946, General de Boissoudy and from 1946 to 1958 **Barthélémy Boganda**, and for the Second College (representing both Chad and Ubangui) **René Malbrant**. Malbrant served from 1945 to 1958. The term deputy was also used to designate the members of the **National Assembly** of the Central African Republic, which sat from 1958 to 31 December 1965.

**DÉRANT-LAKOUÉ, ENOCH.** Born in 1944, he became minister on 26 February 1993. After having run for the presidency, he was also defeated in the 1998 legislative elections.

**DERVAUX, CAPTAIN.** Head of the Upper **Ubangui** region, this French officer refused to execute the order given to him on 13 August 1910 by Governor Lucien Fourneau to arrest the African leader **Ajou** Alindao and deport him to Chad. Renouncing the use of force for **tax** collecting, this officer could only transfer to the treasury a third of the tax sum required for the region he commanded. On 3 October 1910 a decree did away with the Upper Ubangui region and Dervaux was dismissed. In 1911 the former Upper Ubangui area revolted against the French.

**DESCLAUX, CAPTAIN.** Captain Desclaux directed the repression operations against the uprising in the Bodengue and Lobaye valleys in 1906.

**DESRETOUR, DR.** A French veterinarian kept on as the head of the livestock service by the **Abel Goumba** and **David Dacko** governments, Desrotour successfully carried out the transplantation in Central Africa of trypano-resistant Baoule cattle from the Côte d'Ivoire.

**DESTENAVE, LIEUTENANT-COLONEL GEORGES.** Destenave received **Muhammad as-Sanusi**, the Sultan of **Dar-al-Kuti**, with an escort of 1,500 men at Fort **Crampel** on 19 May 1901. Following this interview, as-Sanusi signed an alliance. As commander of the **Shari** region, Destenave's name was attached to a collection of particularly repressive and expeditious rulings, which rapidly became known throughout the colony under the name of "Code Destenave."

**DIAMONDS.** The first Central African diamond was discovered in 1913 near Ippy by an amateur geologist named Brustier. It was not until 1930 that the Compagnie Equatoriale des Mines (CEM) opened its first works in the **Mouka** sandstone near Bria. Then in 1936 the Compagnie Minière de l'Oubangui Oriental (CMOO; Mining Company of Western Ubangui), passing from east to west, opened other works near **Berberati**, followed in the same region in 1938 by the Société Minière Intercoloniale (SMI; Inter-Colonial Mining Company). World War II stimulated production, which in 1945 attained 82,891 carats. In July 1944, a diamond of 391 carats was extracted near **Carnot**. Thanks to Marshall Plan aid, production grew between 1946 and 1956. In 1947 it was 104,277 carats and in 1956 reached 143,061 carats. All the production came from these fields as private prospecting was not allowed. Possession of diamonds was forbidden, and export was strictly controlled. Production in the east proved full of promise. New companies such as the Société Africaine des Mines (SAM; African Mining Company) and the Société Minière de l'est Oubangui (SMEO; Eastern Ubangui Mining Company) opened fields there. But labor difficulties and fraud caused production to drop to 69,662 carats in 1960.

In 1961 **David Dacko** took the initiative. He abolished the colonial regulations and authorized diamond prospecting by villagers who could sell the diamonds they collected at government-approved purchasing offices. The principal one was set up by Diamond Distributors, Inc. of New York (DDI), which became the major owner of

CMOO and SMI and regrouped the old fields into a Société centrafricaine des mines (Centramines; Central African Mining Company) the same year. Production increased rapidly. In 1965 it was 91,794 carats and by 1969 it reached a peak of 535,316 carats. Diamonds took first place in all Central African **economic** plans. In 1965 the DDI set up the first diamond-cutting workshop in **Bangui** (Comptoir national du diamant, a mixed company). But difficulties with the directors increased. In 1971 Emperor **Bokassa** threw out the Centramines technicians who had refused to pay arbitrary assessments. The head of state himself held interests in the diamond trade, bringing in little by little a series of doubtful brokers. From 1973 production fell below 400,000 carats (380,466 carats), then in 1976 below 300,000 carats (286,007 carats). In 1973 the Sociéte Centrafricaine d'exploitation diamantifère (SCED; Central African Diamond Prospecting Company) was created between the state (20 percent), COMINCO Limited of Vancouver (6 percent), and Diamond Distributors, Inc. (20 percent). That same year, Bokassa granted a prospecting permit to a Romanian company (Geomin-Bangui). In 1976 he withdrew the SCED's mining permit, and in 1978 he issued a 30,000 square-kilometer permit to an Israeli, General **Samuel Gonen**, who had been dismissed after the Yom Kippur War.

At the start of the 21st century, diamond production remains mainly a craft and amounts to about 500,000 carats (about $700 millions). Quite certainly these numbers only concern the official production—illegal exports being at least of the same amount. Unfortunately, the search for diamonds meant that many **cotton** and **coffee** plantations were soon deserted. The quick money made by the lucky prospectors is just as rapidly spent, those earnings soon being called "devil's money." Today, the Central African Republic ranks 11th for diamond production.

The Central African Republic exported about 449,000 carats in 2001, against 461,000 in 2000, and 431,000 in 1999. The value of these exports is roughly 41 billion CFA francs for the year 2001, 44 billion in 2000, and 38 billion in 1999. In 2001 diamonds represented 45.8 percent of Central African exports (in terms of value). In 2002 these exports declined because of the low sales rates and the accumulation of stored diamonds at Anvers. Fraud remains a widespread practice. In 2001 the British group GEMKIN established, in partnership with the government, the International Diamond Bureau of Bangui (BIDB). The Diamonds and Gold Assessment and Control Bureau (BEDCOR) is in charge of evaluating the stones and of receiving the export taxes for the state.

**DIFFRE, THADDEE (1912–1971).** Born in Cambrai (Nord) on 24 October 1912, he died in Orleix (Hautes Pyrénnées) on 30 December 1971. Colonel Diffre, commander of the French commandos in Palestine, became the Director of Economic Affairs in 1950 for **Ubangui-Shari** and organizer in 1950 of a production conference with the aim of stimulating the territory's exports.

**DIMBRI, GABRIELLA (A.K.A. "LA MARECHALE").** A Romanian dancer noticed by Emperor **Bokassa** in 1975 during an official visit to Romania, she was offered as a wife to him by his peer Nicolae Ceaucescu. In 1977 Bokassa had three alleged lovers of hers arrested and beaten to death with chains. Gabriella was imprisoned on an island on the **Ubangui** River but sent back to Romania shortly after Bokassa's imperial coronation.

**DITTE, CAPTAIN LEONCE.** Commander of the 11th Company of Senegalese Rifles, Ditte took possession on 22 February 1895 of the **Bangassou administrative post**, evacuated by King **Leopold**'s forces in keeping with the agreement of 28 August 1894.

**DIVISIONS ADMINISTRATIVES (ADMINISTRATIVE DIVISIONS).** The Central African state is very centralized in spite of an attempt to decentralize it in 1993. No elections are held at a local level, although the constitution states there must be. Indeed, there have not been any for many years, officially for financial reasons. In April 1995 the country was divided into 16 districts grouped into seven regions. The **prefects** and subprefects are appointed from the top.

**DJABIR (called SULTAN BACPAYO).** A relative of the **Bandia** Sultan **Rafaï** and, like him, a one-time companion of **Zubayr** Pasha. Djabir was born about 1835 in the Ouellé (Uéllé). A prisoner of Rafaï from 1886 to 1888, he was able to escape and form an alliance with the Arab **slave** trader, **Panga-Panga**. He was eager to sign a treaty with the Belgian Captain **Alphonse Vangele** shortly after.

**DJAMBALA.** The Upper Sangha leader who accepted the protection of the **Fulbé** of **Ngaoundéré** and then that of the French (1891).

**DJEBEL MELA.** This rocky mountain peak in Upper Kotto on the Sudanese border guarded the ancient trans-African trail that went from the Adda Valley in the Nile basin to the Kotto Valley, giving access along the **Ubangui** to the Congo region. Djebel Mela served as a fortress for the area's populations. The last occupants were defeated by the French in 1925.

**DJELLAB.** This high ruler of the Youlou refused to submit to as-**Sanusi**, sultan of **Dar-al-Kuti**, during the first decade of the 20th century. He then heroically resisted the assaults of as-Sanusi's lieutenant, **Allah-Djabou**, who laid siege to his fortress at **Ouanda-Djallé**. This fortress was nevertheless taken by Allah-Djabou in December 1910. Djellab and a great many Youlou took refuge in the Sudan. This conquest by as-Sanusi's troops caused French Captain **Jean Modat**, resident to the sultan, to use force to end the sultan's **slaving** activities.

**DJEMA.** A French **administrative post** to the north of Zemio, this locality constituted the main stop on the Zemio-Dem Ziber route.

**DJEMBRE (or DEMBE).** Leader of the **Pande** ethnic group, Djembe authorized **Pierre Brazza** to found the first French post in Upper Sangha near the **Bania** rapids on 4 January 1892.

**DJERBARI.** After having attacked the **Goula** on the Ouandjia, **Rabih** set up his first camp in July 1874 at Djerbari, an elevated site dominating the Tété-Monovo. This camp was a day's march east of **Cha**, then the capital of **Dar-al-Kuti**.

**DJI.** This south tributary of the Kotto in the very center of Dar **Banda** was the theater of numerous **slaving** expeditions throughout the 19th century. This river was claimed by as-**Sanusi** as the southern limit of his states. **Rafaï** and **Bangassou**, in turn, saw it as the northern limits of their possessions.

**DJONGOLI.** Djongofi, the *ouarnak* of **Wadaï** (reputed for his gigantic size), commanded, with Emir Moungache, the army sent by the Sultan of this country against as-**Sanusi** in 1896. The Wadaïan force surprised the **slave** caravan sent by as-Sanusi and his ally Abou Riche, Sultan of Sila, after the destruction of **Mbelle**. Djongofi and Moungache were killed in this engagement by as-Sanusi's men. It was essentially the fear of Wadaïan reprisals that incited as-Sanusi to ask for a French protectorate from **Emile Gentil**.

**DJOUGOULTOUM (or OMAR).** Ousman, or Omar, otherwise known as *Djougoultoum*, was the son of the *mbang* of Banguirmi, Aden Bangoumanda el Kebir, who died in 1826. He was forced to flee into **Wadaï** to avoid having his eyes put out by his older brother, Abd el Kader, the new sultan. The *kalak* of Wadaï sent him to the **Rounga** in the military border area founded between the Azoum and the **Aouk**. Djougoultoum married Fatme, daughter of Boker, the Sultan of Dar Rounga. In 1830 he created an even more southerly border zone called Belad-el-Kouti as a **slaving** area south of the Aouk. **Cha**, on the Diangara, became the capital of this province.

**DJOUKOUDOU (A.K.A. KOKO).** Djoukoudou was the head leader of the **Kara** in the 18th century before his people were dispersed by the attacks of the Forians.

**DOBOZENDI, HUGHES.** Leader of the Mouvement de libération du peuple centrafricain (MLPC; Movement for the Central African People's Liberation), Dobozendi was imprisoned by **André Kolingba**. After the rise to power of **Ange Patassé** he became president of the **National Assembly**. He was taken hostage by the **rebels** in 1997.

**DOLISIE, ALBERT.** As administrator of Brazzaville, Albert Dolisie decided to forestall King **Leopold**'s forces and on 16 May 1885 he founded the **Nkoundjia** post on the **Ubangui** River not far from its juncture with the Congo. This possession was the point of departure for French claims to the whole Ubangui basin and set loose a furor by King Leopold.

**DOLISIE, MICHEL. Albert Dolisie** ordered his brother, Michel, and Albert Uzac, head of the Madzaka post, to create a post at the bend of the **Ubangui** River on 10 May 1889. Michel Dolisie founded the post on 26 June 1889, and he called it **Bangui** (rapids). He proceeded to exchange blood with the leader, Bembe, and symbolically buried war by burying a shell and an iron lance at the foot of his flagpole. On 23 September 1890, a sick Michel Dolisie left the post under the command of **Maurice Musy**.

**DOLOGUELE, ANICET (1957–).** Born in Bozoum in 1957, Dologuélé belongs to the **Mboum** ethnic group, many of whom live in Ouham-**Pendé**. The son of a schoolteacher and of a **Yakoma** brother, he studied at the **Berbérati** Catholic secondary school. In 1982 he passed the Banque des Etats d'Afrique centrale (BEAC; Central African States Bank) exam. He was assigned several missions by the BEAC in Paris and to the World Bank. In 1994 he was the Director of Financial Relations at the BEAC headquarters in Yaoundé, then became Director of Management and Computing for that bank. Close to President **Ange Patassé** without belonging to the Mouvement de libération du peuple centrafricain (MLPC; Movement for the Central African People's Liberation), he became Finance Minister in 1992 in the **Michel Gbezara-Bria** government. He was appointed Prime Minister on 4 January 1998.

**DOMITIEN, ELISABETH.** Appointed Emperor **Bokassa**'s prime minister on 9 June 1976, she was sacked for having criticized his desire to accede to the imperial dignity. After Bokassa's fall, she was imprisoned for two years. Now retired, she lives in **Bangui**.

**DOUMERGUE, GASTON.** As Minister of Colonies, Doumergue sent **Emile Gentil** to Brazzaville with the following instructions: "Do what you can to cause the disappearance of the atrocities of porter recruitment."

**DOUZIMA, MARCEL (1926–).** Born on 20 December 1926 at Bafi in the Batangafo district. From 1960 on, he was **David Dacko**'s Minister of Justice. He was arrested by **Jean-Bedel Bokassa** on 13 January 1966, and deported to **Birao**. Then he was incarcerated in **Ngaragba** Prison about 25 January 1966. He was released on 13 October 1969.

**DUCHEMIN, JACQUES.** Secretary for a number of African parties from 1951 to 1960. He was secretary of state under Moïse Tshombe from October 1960 to September 1961 in the Katanga separatist state. This journalist led a secret agent career in a number of Third World countries. He is the author of a secret history of the Front de Libération Nationale (FLN; National Liberation Front), which appeared in 1963. He arrived at the Imperial Court of **Berengo** in June 1979 and was appointed minister by the emperor. He is the author of a book about Emperor **Jean-Bedel Bokassa** that is as phantasmagoric as Bokassa himself.

**DUCQ, ERNEST.** Head of the **Bangassou** post in 1902, Ducq attacked a caravan of Arabized traders from **Dar-al-Kuti**. Injured, he was extricated by Sultan **Bangassou**'s men and the Compagnie des Sultanats du Haut-Oubangui.

**DUMONT, RENE.** At the demand of **David Dacko**, the author of *False Start in Africa* arrived in **Bangui** in July 1965. The report he wrote was an indictment of the political, economic, and social administration since independence. Dacko forbade its distribution.

**DYBOWSKI, JEAN.** Sent by the **Comité de l'Afrique Française** (French Africa Committee) to reinforce the **Paul Crampel** mission, Jean Dybowski heard of the mission's massacre on 14 July 1891, after his arrival in Brazzaville. He went into **Banda** country, among the Ngapou, and wiped out a camp of Muslim caravanners. He gave up trying to reach as-**Sanusi** and looked for a more westerly route toward the Chad basin. In March 1893, going up the Kemo and then the Tomi, he found the Kemo post among the **Banda**-Togbo. Taken ill, he was repatriated to Brazzaville. His place was taken by **Casimir Maistre**.

– E –

**EBOUÉ, FÉLIX (1883–1944).** Born in Cayenne (French Guyana) in December 1883, he died in Cairo on 17 May 1944. As a colonial administrator, Eboué spent most of his career in **Ubangui-Shari**, where he successfully commanded the Kwango, Bambari, **Bangassou**, and Bozoum districts. He was the governor of Guadeloupe in 1936, then of Chad in 1940. He joined forces with **General Charles de Gaulle** and the **Free French** on 26 August 1940. He was appointed governor general of French Equatorial Africa on 12 November 1940. On 8 November 1941, he sent his famous circular on the indigenous policy of French Equatorial Africa to all subdivision heads. This circular was one of the principal working documents for the **Brazzaville Conference** in February 1944, which marked the point of departure for the French African colonies toward a new rule. He was the author of several books of ethnographic research on Ubangui-Shari published in Paris between 1918 and 1937. He created the first **school** for local higher education in French Equatorial Africa.

**ECONOMIC AND SOCIAL COUNCIL (CONSEIL ECONOMIQUE ET SOCIAL).** A Socioprofessional consultative organization created by **David Dacko** and suppressed by Emperor **Bokassa**. It was presided over by **Clément Hassen** and later by **Ferdinand Bassamongou**.

**ECONOMY.** Thanks to its large network of rivers and streams, the Central African Republic is good agricultural land and has considerable mineral resources (**diamond**, gold, uranium, and iron). While Chad and Sudan oil fields stretch north and east of the CAR, it is not so fortunate. Export revenues are mainly derived from **agriculture** (**coffee**, **cotton**, **wood**, and **tobacco**) and diamonds. The country's many steep hills and the poor quality of the means of transportation are serious obstacles to its economic development. The civil wars in the two Congos have greatly damaged the country's links with the exterior as it uses, since colonial time, the **Congo-Ocean** railroad, extended by the Congo and Ubangui Rivers.

**EDUCATION.** From the early years of the 20th century, subdivision heads created the first vocational and special schools for sons of indigenous rulers. The first vocational school was opened by Captain **Jules Jacquier** at **Mobaye** in 1910. The Holy Ghost Fathers also founded primary schools in their **missions**. Nonetheless, schooling grew very slowly. In 1935 Governor General **Edouard Renard** set as an objective a school for each **departement**. By 1950, each district was provided with a school. In 1953 the first secondary school, Collège **Emile Gentil**, was established in **Bangui**. The first baccalaureate students did not graduate until 1956. From 1956 to 1962 Presidents **Barthélémy Boganda**, **Abel Goumba**, and **David Dacko** gave absolute priority to educational development but unfortunately neglected the training of teachers. A 9 May 1962 law carrying out the unification of instruction integrated private (essentially Catholic) schools with public schools. By 1963, the actual number of students was more than 100,000. A university was created in Bangui in 1967.

During the next 20 years, the number of lower school pupils and high school students continued to rise. There were 286,422 primary pupils in the fall of 1987 in 1,024 schools. There were 40,370 secondary students in 65 establishments and 2,351 students in four faculties (social science, law and economics, medicine, and science) of the university. There were also 347 students in other postsecondary schools. The number of teachers has increased in the same proportion, with 4,563 primary teachers and 821 secondary teachers.

Since then, the repeated strikes led by unpaid teachers lasting several months, along with the troubles that arose with the **army rebellions**, have seriously damaged the educational system.

**EFAO (ELEMENTS FRANCAIS D'ASSISTANCE OPERATIONELLE: FRENCH OPERATIONAL SUPPORT UNITS).** After the so-called **barracuda** operation of September 1979, the French military established a center in the Central African Republic to serve as a rear base for French operations in Chad during the invasions instigated by Colonel **Mouammar Kadhafi**.

**EMIN PASHA (DR. EDUARD SCHNITZER).** Of Prussian origin, Emin Pasha exercised the functions of Egyptian governor in the equatorial province of the Sudan. Under this title, he organized Upper **Ouellé**. It was at his demand that **Wilhelm Junker** sent **Frederik Bohndorff** to establish the Lacrima government post not far from the residence of the **Zandé** sultan, Ndorouma, on 9 June 1880.

**EMPROCAF (ENTENTE PROFESSIONNELLE DES PRODUCTEURS DE CAFÉ; COFFEE PRODUCERS' PROFESSIONAL ARRANGEMENT).** A professional group of European **coffee** exporters who, even after independence, manipulated the Coffee-price Stabilization Board. This pressure group obtained from **David Dacko** the control of coffee exporting.

**ENERGY.** Created in 1967, the Energie Centrafricaine (ENERCA; Central African Energy) company is state owned and deals in the supply and distribution of electricity throughout the country. It has replaced the Union des Sociétés Electriques Coloniales (UNELCO; Colonial Electricity Companies Union), which operated in colonial times. The city of **Bangui** and 13 provincial towns receive electricity. Bangui is supplied for by the electrical plant of the **Boali** Falls. This plant must urgently be renovated—the necessary investment is of about 11 million euros. A thermo-diesel plant of 15MW can provide a relay. In the provinces electricity is provided for by small thermal power stations. Many streams and rivers could be used to develop micropower stations almost everywhere if suitable efforts and investments were made.

**ENYELLE.** Small locality on the Ibanga River where some European companies' agents were massacred in 1904. The insurrection spread throughout the forest zones of Ibanga, Lobaye, and Bodengue. This insurrection provoked a military expedition and then the establishment of a series of permanent **administrative** military **posts** in this region.

**ERE (or ELE).** Name of the Supreme Being in the **Banda** religion.

**ERIO, PAUL.** Author of a report published in the *Journal de Paris* on 19 July 1912, entitled, "How Porters Are Recruited on the Route to Chad." Paul Erio especially denounced the systematic taking of women as hostages in order to obtain men as porters and the forwarding of these conscripts toward Fort de Possel by armed militia. He also denounced the slaughter of animals by European hunters.

**ESPINASSE, MAURICE.** This French technical assistant met with Lieutenant **Jean-Bedel Bokassa** in Brazzaville. With the rise of the latter to power, he became his close adviser and headed the National Administration School in Central Africa. He was the main source of information for Jacques Foccart. He witnessed the agony of **Alexandre Banza** as well as the execution of several of the dictator's victims. On 23 May 1974, returning from an assignment in France, he was forbidden access to **Bangui** and labeled "undesirable." Maurice Espinasse was then appointed secretary general to the International Center for Students and Trainees in Paris. In October 1979 it was he who gave journalist Pierre Péan the document revealing that Bokassa did offer **diamonds** to French President **Valéry Giscard d'Estaing**. Published by the *Canard Enchaîné* weekly of 10 October 1979, this document played an important role in the 1981 presidential elections in France that brought the defeat of President Giscard d'Estaing.

**ETATS GENERAUX DE LA COLONISATION (STATES GENERAL OF COLONIZATION).** A congress of colonists held in Paris in July 1946 at the prompting of **René Malbrant**, Deputy of the First College of **Ubangui-Shari**-Chad. The colonists spoke out against the collective accession to French citizenship of the inhabitants of what they persisted in calling "The Empire." Malbrant concluded these meetings with a disillusioned proposal on "the feudalism of the past" and the "tyrannies of tomorrow."

**ETIENNE, EUGÈNE.** Prompted by journalist Harry Alis, Secretary of State Eugène Etienne, although the French exploration movement in Africa had come to an end, agreed to support the expedition of **Paul Crampel**, who projected a link between **Bangui** and Algiers.

**EVOLUÉS.** The French colonial administration used the term *evolué* (evolved) for educated Africans having adopted a Western lifestyle. **Barthélémy Boganda** called them by the pejorative *mboundjouvoko*, meaning "white blacks."

## – F –

**FACA.** Acronym for Forces Armées Centrafricaines (Central African Armed Forces), it is around 6,000 men strong, 2,000 of which belong to the presidential guard.

**FAD AL ALLAH.** Eldest son of **Rabih**, Fad al Allah married **Hadia**, daughter of **Muhammad** as-**Sanusi**, Sultan of **Dar-al-Kuti** in 1891.

**FAD AL MOLA.** One of **Rabih**'s banner chiefs, of **Banda** origin.

**FAMINES.** Each **slave** raid, intergroup war, or colonial police operation brought about the systematic destruction of plantations. The famines that resulted were as deadly as the operations that had provoked them. The famines would last several years, while the inhabitants lived on roots, honey, wild fruit, and snared animals, taking care not to clear and start new plantations, which would reveal their presence.

**FANG (or PAHOUIN).** A people established in Gabon in the 19th century. Fang tradition tells of a former homeland, *mvogh et angha* (misty land), which could be the mountains of **Yadé** north of the Central African Republic.

**FAURE, MARCEL-HENRI (1906–1998).** Born in Montpellier on 30 January 1906, he died on 22 May 1998. Colonial Administrator Faure commanded the subdivisions of **Carnot** and Boda. He was the author of several studies on the Gbaya people. In 1939 he was drafted at **Bouar** and the next year played a key role in rallying **Ubangui-Shari** to **General Charles de Gaulle**. He took part in all the fighting by the **Free French** forces, namely in **Bir-Hakeim**, in Syria, Tunisia, Italy, and France. Wounded several times, Captain Faure was made a Companion of the Liberation and commander of the Legion of Honour as well as being awarded the Distinguished Service Cross. After the war he became secretary-general in Niger, an assignment he had to abandon because of his position in favor of a rapid decolonization process. Written off as an official then reinstated after he won his appeal to the State Court, he left the administration of his own accord and went into banking in 1952. He was a financial adviser in Mali.

He corresponded with **Barthélémy Boganda** who relied on his testimony to condemn the crimes of the colonists in Ubangui-Shari. In 1982, in the pages of the French daily *Le Monde*, Faure insisted that the Third World received tragically insufficient support.

**FAYAMA, ALBERT.** Civil servant of **Mbaka** origin, Albert Fayama was already active in youth movements in 1950. He made his way to the United States for the World Assembly of Youth Congress in 1951. He was later elected territorial councilor of **Ubangui-Shari** and high councilor of French Equatorial Africa. Fayama died in the same air crash that cost the life of President **Barthélémy Boganda** on 29 March 1959.

**FAYET, REVEREND FATHER AUGUSTE (?–1952).** Born in Sauxillanges on 10 September (year unknown), he died in Molsheim on 24 April 1952. After the baptism of young **Barthélémy Boganda** in **Bangui** on 24 December 1922, Father Fayet, a missionary of the Holy Ghost Fathers who had developed Boganda's priestly vocation, solicited the help of several French families to pay his seminary costs. In 1929 Father Fayet created the **Bangassou mission**.

**FELIX, ANDRE (1902–1953).** Born in Appaigny (Yonne) on 23 April 1902, he died in Bangui on 19 February 1955. Administrator of Overseas France and head of the **Birao** district, André Felix died in a hunting accident in 1956. He initiated big game hunting tourism in the northeastern part of the Central African Republic. His name was given to a vast natural reserve, the Parc National André Felix.

**FERRY, JULES (1832–1893).** Father of French colonialism, Jules Ferry nonetheless exposed to the Chamber of Deputies on July 1885 the fundamental contradiction that existed between the French colonial enterprise just beginning in the Congo and **Ubangui** and the interests of the populations of these areas. He exclaimed to the deputies: "If the declaration of the rights of man had been written for Black Equatorial Africa, then by what right will you impose commercial exchange?"

**FIDES (FONDS D'INVESTISSEMENT POUR LE DÉVELOPPEMENT ECONOMIQUE ET SOCIAL).** Paralleling the political and administrative reforms of 1946 the French Parliament created the Fonds d'Investissement pour le Développement Economique et Social (FIDES; Investment Funds for Economic and Social Development). In 1947 a five-year plan was launched to stimulate local commerce. In **Ubangui-Shari** more than 3 billion CFA francs out of more than 4 billon in the first plan (1947–1951) were granted for infrastructure (**roads**, bridges, waterways, air transport, and **communications**). The second plan reduced this share in order to place more importance on the production sector and social development. Of 4.6 billion CFA francs given to Ubangui-Shari, 1 billion was reserved for social development. **Schooling**, almost nonexistent in 1939, was promoted and rose from a rate of 1.6 percent in 1939 to 8 percent by 1953. By 1958 it had reached 28 percent. The old **Bangui** colonial hospital was replaced by a modern, 350-bed hospital. However, these efforts remained very modest in comparison to the immense needs of this ill-favored territory.

**FIEVEZ, LIEUTENANT.** This Belgian officer, head of Zemio post under King **Leopold**'s regime, accompanied by Sultan Zemio went up the **Dem Ziber** trail to bring help to two Muslim leaders of Bar-al-Arab under attack by Mahdist troops. He had to retreat in order to defend Leopold's endangered forces in Upper **Ouellé**.

**FLAG.** The Central African Republic's flag has four horizontal stripes (blue, white, green, and yellow), one red vertical stripe in the middle, and a yellow star in the top left corner on the blue stripe. This flag was initially designed by **Barthélémy Boganda** for the Great Central African Republic he wished to create from the territories making up French Equatorial Africa. The four stripes symbolized the four independent states born from the former colonial federation. The red stripe across the flag symbolized the blood shed by those populations to gain their freedom. The yellow star was the symbol for the Mouvement pour l'évolution sociale de l'Afrique noire (**MESAN**; Social Evolution Movement for Black Africa) of Boganda, who had used the insignia of the independent Congo state.

**FLANDRE, PAUL.** A French industrialist in Gabon, Paul Flandre was president of the Grand Council of French Equatorial Africa in 1953. He called for the suppression of the general government of French

Equatorial Africa and showed his hostility to the merger of Gabon and Middle Congo into a single territory as was advocated by the high commissioner of the Republic in French Equatorial Africa.

**FOMBINA.** Former Hausa name of the **Adamawa** plateau, which was conquered around 1835 by the **Fulbé** under **Adama**, principal lieutenant (*modibo*) of **Usman dan Fodio**. Adama set up Emirates (*lamidates*) in **Fombina** (Banuya, Garoua, Tibati, and **Ngaoundéré**). The last two constituted bases for **slaving** expeditions among the western populations of Central Africa.

**FONCTIONNAIRES.** The French colonizers began to create a corps of **Ubanguian civil servants** in 1907. A decree of 7 September 1907 established the organization of an "auxiliary personnel" of administrative clerks. Until 1914 the subdivision officers used these auxiliaries only as interpreters. The nursing aides recruited for the campaign against **sleeping sickness** were also used as clerks. In 1935 Governor General **Edouard Renard** created a staff school (Ecole des Cadres) in Brazzaville. Its first objective was to provide, in less than 10 years, indigenous monitors for each of the 135 subdivision headquarters in French Equatorial Africa. These monitors would also serve as clerks for their district.

The creation of a corps of clerks for the *Services administratifs et Financiers* (SAF, Administrative and Financial Services) put some indigenous workers at the disposal of the French administrators, even if at an insufficient level. The first Ubanguian special agent was appointed in 1950. After the 1956 Loi-Cadre (Enabling Act) a very small number of SAF clerks were chosen to occupy positions previously reserved for the French. After 1958 many of them became ministers in the various governments of the territory and then in the government of the Central African Republic. After 1962 President **David Dacko** proceeded with the Africanization of the posts of district head (from then on called sub**prefect**) and regional head (which became **prefect**). The Central African Civil Service was organized on the French model, and an Ecole Nationale d'Administration (ENA; National Administration School) opened in 1963.

Between 1973 and 1979, the number of civil servants rose from 14,700 to 25,500. The World Bank and the International Monetary

Fund (IMF) have demanded a reduction in the number of civil servants. Their number today is supposedly only 1,700. However, due to financial troubles and political unrest civil service wages are often delayed—by as much as 35 months. This explains the repeated strikes and mounting corruption.

**FONDERE, ALPHONSE.** Former head of the **Bangui** post, Fondere went to work for the Sangha-Ubangui **concessionary company** in 1890. There he rapidly became director general. In May 1911 he was sent by the president of the council, **Joseph Caillaux**, to Berlin to study the proposed Franco-German railroad from Douala to the Ubangui.

**FONDS D'AIDE ET DE COOPERATION (FAC; COOPERATIVE AND AID FUND).** The FAC replaced the **FIDES** in 1959. From 1959 to 1970 these funds provided the Central African Republic a sum of 8.6 million CFA francs, to which must be added 1.9 million as a budget underwrite and 100 million in loans. This aid was divided as follows: 3.2 million for production, 2.5 million for infrastructure, 1.5 million for social equipment, 1.1 million for scientific research, and 0.3 million for general studies. Since 1970 this aid has been increased. The FAC support was raised for the single year 1976 to 9.1 million CFA francs. The FAC support represents only part of French aid, which in 1978 included 400 *coopérants* in the country and budget-balancing support.

**FONDS EUROPÉEN DE DÉVELOPPEMENT (FED; EUROPEAN DEVELOPMENT FUND).** At the end of 1988, the balance sheet of this European aid to the Central African Republic was as follows: first FED—33 projects with 16.2 million ecus (European currency units); second FED—39 projects with 25.6 million ecus; third FED—20 projects with 30 million ecus; fourth FED—34 projects with 35.5 million ecus; fifth FED—30 projects with 45.2 million ecus, and sixth FED—5 projects with 15.3 million ecus.

**FORCE NOIRE (BLACK FORCE).** The colonial **army** recruited in Africa went under this title. This force was begun at the instigation of Lieutenant-Colonel **Charles Mangin**, companion of Captain **Jean-**

**Baptiste Marchand** at Fashoda. He presented his ideas in several articles and in a book entitled *La force noire* (The Black Force, 1909). **Paul Bourdarie**, a spokesperson for the **concessionary companies**, saw in this mercenary army the possibility of ensuring the security of the French colonists, notably in North Africa. "The myth of the black soldier, auxiliaries in future combats, mercenaries in pacification campaigns, gave birth and reassured all who had interests in Africa," he wrote as early as 1909. After having used mainly Senegalese, the French army in French Equatorial Africa ran a number of recruiting campaigns. Already in World War I, a number of **Ubanguian** and Chadian riflemen engaged in combat on all fronts. From 1940 to 1945, the Ubanguian Rifles again took an active part in the operations of **Free France**.

**FORESTRY.** The surface of actual virgin forest is small in the Central African Republic, most of it being secondary growth. In the southeast, forests stretch over 37,500 square kilometers, 27,000 of which are economically exploitable. To this must be added 10,000 square kilometers in the southeast in the Mbomar region. Including the dense semihumid forests the Central African forest can be estimated at 92,500 square kilometers, that is 15 percent of the country.

From 1948 to 1965 the exploitation of this forest had attracted only nine companies because of the great distance from the sea. The production of undressed timber was less than 10,000 cubic meters per year. A considerable inventory effort had been carried out by the Centre technique forestier tropical (Tropical Forestry Technical Center), thanks largely to the continual service at its head of the French technician Colonel **Georges Guigonis**. After 1965 larger companies began to operate. By the end of 1975, permits had been granted for 1.5 million hectares, of which 300,000 were placed in reserve. About 15 companies had been allocated these permits. The production of undressed wood reached a maximum of 154,900 cubic meters in 1973, and fell to 49,600 cubic meters in 1975. A dozen companies with a total capacity of 150,000 cubic meters were in operation. New legislation, designed to ensure the protection of the country's forest heritage, limited the total cutting permit area to 1.2 million hectares a year, and the cutting volume to one cubic meter per hectare per year. Furthermore, by government decree, half of the undressed wood had to be processed in the country.

The wood production has gradually progressed since 1994. At present it is around 700,000-800,000 square meters per year, essentially of undressed timber, plus 15 percent of sawn wood and plywood. The very selective cutting is of about one tree per hectare. Two-thirds of the cutting concerns Sapelli, Ayous, Sipo, and Aningré. Wood exports are now bigger than **diamond** and are the country's top export.

Today, forestry is a booming sector in the Central African Republic. Its contribution to the national economy is constantly growing. Only a handful of producers is present in this sector (as against several hundreds in Gabon and Chad). Out of a total surface of 3.2 million hectares, there are only 10 foresters: IFB, SCAD, SESAM, SEFCA, THANRY, COLOMBE-FORET, SOFORAD, SBB, NDOUNGA-MEUBLES, and SEPFC. There remains an untouched high region 7 million hectares wide in the east of the country. The limited number of permits allows for vast forestry operations, the average concession being around 200,000 hectares wide. The Plan d'Exploitation et d'Aménagement (PEA; Plan for Development and Operation) for the Ngotto forest is presented as a model of forest development. Former President **Ange Patassé** owned the largest concession (over 650,000 hectares). His company was associated with a Chinese group. The woods that are marketed are the Sapelli, Sipo, Kossipo, Iroko, Ilomba, Acajou, Mulu Kulungou, Eyong, Simba, and Dimba Dibettou.

In March 2003, **Abel Goumba**'s government ordered a basic reassessment of all the forestry concessions that were granted by Patassé.

**FORO.** A village in Upper Kotto near Bria, Foro was reached in 1883 by the Englishman **Frank Lupton**, governor of Bahr-el-Ghazal for the Khedive of Egypt.

**FOURNEAU, ALFRED.** Fourneau imposed a new protectorate on **as-Sanusi**, the Sultan of **Dar-al-Kuti**, on 18 February 1903. This administrator organized a police operation against the **Mandjia** revolt against forced **portage** at about the same time.

**FOURNEAU (MISSION).** The Fourneau French Mission into Upper Sangha sent by **Pierre Brazza** in 1891 had for its objective the opening of the route to **Ngaoundéré**. It penetrated into the territory of the **Baya** and Yanguéré, who were rebelling against the **Fulbé**. During the night of 12–13 May 1891, as the expedition reached Kuisso, a village between **Berberati** and **Carnot**, it was attacked by a group of warriors serving the Baya Bonhan leader **Bafio**. Some 30 were killed, as well as 19 riflemen and **porters**. **Alfred Fourneau** and **Blom**, injured, turned back to the **Bania** with the rest of the column. This disaster, followed just a little later by the massacre of the **Crampel** Mission at **Dar-al-Kuti**, shocked France.

**FRANCE-CENTRAFRIQUE.** A Franco-Central African parliamentary group directed by William Jacson, deputy from Meurthe-et-Moselle.

**FRANCE EQUATORIALE.** On 19 December 1957, **Antoine Darlan** proposed to the Grand Council of French Equatorial Africa to change that name to Franco-Equatorial Africa. Although this suggestion was taken up by President **Barthélémy Boganda** and unanimously adopted by the Grand Council, the name was not accepted by the French Government. In 1957 Boganda, then president of the Grand Council of French Equatorial Africa, and **Antoine Darlan**, vice president of the Council, proposed giving this name to French Equatorial Africa.

**FRANCE LIBRE (FREE FRANCE).** In August 1940, the French garrisons of **Bouar**, Bambari, and **Bria** rallied to Free France. On the night of 29 to 30 August, armed French civilians occupied **Bangui** and the banks of the **Ubangui** River. On the 30 August, Governor **Pierre de Saint-Mart** announced that the **Ubangui-Shari** territory was joining the Free French.

Nevertheless, Commander **Henri Cammas** and a group of officers hostile to Free France held out in the military camp. On 3 September Cammas surrendered to Captain **Robert de Roux**, who took command. On 4 September Colonel **René Edgar de Larminat**, who had taken power in Brazzaville in the name of **General Charles de Gaulle** on 28 August arrived in Bangui. On 21 October 1940 the European and African population welcomed the leader of Free France, a little sobered by the news of the fratricidal battle raging in Gabon. On 12 November 1940 General de Gaulle issued an order creating a high commission of Free French Africa and put now General de Larminat in charge. Governor **Félix Eboué**, who had served many years as the administrator of Ubangui-Shari, was appointed governor general of French Equatorial Africa. The BM1 and BM2 infantry battalions, which had many Ubanguians of origin or adoption, were rapidly taken to the various East, West and North African fronts. They prefigured the future Central African **army**.

**FRANCK, ANTONIO.** A steward at the **Berengo** imperial palace, he helped the French airborne division of operation **Barracuda** take possession of the estate in September 1975.

**FRANCK, EDOUARD.** Magistrate, prime minister in 1991 and legal adviser to President **André Kolingba**, he presided over the Criminal Court that sat in judgment on ex-Emperor **Bokassa** in 1986.

**FREE FRANCE.** *See* FRANCE LIBRE.

**FULBÉ (FOULBE, FULANI).** The Fulbé settlement of the **Adamawa** plateau as of 1835 was the cause of 70 years of **slave** wars carried on against Central African populations, especially against the **Baya**. Part of the Baya were overcome by the *lamibé* of **Ngaoundéré**. *Lamido* Zody deported many Baya-**Kaka**, but he was placed in difficulty by the great Baya insurrection of 1837. His successor, Haman, occupied the commercial valley of the Kadef about 1845. The fortified post of **Koundé** assured the Fulbé control of trade south of the **Sangha**. After 1860 Issa attempted to overcome all of the Baya country. The Baya of Upper Sangha, reinforced by the Baya who had been forced to flee by the *lamido* of Tibati, victoriously resisted Issa. The war between the Fulbé of Tibati and those of Ngaoundéré saved Baya independence. In 1892 **Pierre Brazza** tried to make a treaty with the Fulbé of Ngaoundéré, who had warmly welcomed **Louis Mizon**. But in 1894, when France had to recognize German "rights" over the Fulbé-ruled Ngaoundéré, the military and civilian administration played their Baya card. In 1896 the administrator, **Alphonse Goujon**, called the King of Sangha, definitively abandoned Brazza's pro-Fulbé policies and took the leadership of a popular army uniting all Baya groups, including the Baya

Yanguéré. This war of liberation, disavowed by Paris, led to a spectacular defeat of the Fulbé troops (the Battle of **Bouar**, 30 June 1896). The *lamido* of Ngaoundéré recognized the Lom as the frontier between Fulbé possessions, into which the Germans had not yet penetrated, and French Upper Sangha.

**FULCONIS, DR.** In May 1904, the French colonial doctor Fulconis discovered the bodies of 45 women and two children in a house in **Bangui**. These people had been locked up by an *affaires indigènes* ("native" affairs) clerk, **Culard**, in order to force some villages of the Mongoumba region to pay their back **taxes**. High Commissioner **Emile Gentil** arrived on the scene and transferred the administrator in charge to Bangui. The judges in Brazzaville acquitted the clerk. An attempt was made to hush up the affair. **Pierre Brazza**, sent by the French government on an inspection mission with instructions to compare procedures used in the French colony and those of agents of King **Leopold** in the Congo Free State, only became aware of the affair when he arrived in Bangui. On 14 August 1905 he telegraphed the president of the Council that events such as the one uncovered by Dr. Fulconis made such a comparison difficult and dangerous.

– G –

**GABA-CHAMBE.** The **Roulet Mission**, leaving from the **Ubangui**, reached the Sudanese post of Gaba-Chambe on the Nile on 20 March 1899. The occupation of Bahr-el-Ghazal by the French lasted until 18 February 1900.

**GAILLARD, GASTON.** The delegate of the principal administrator at Brazzaville to **Ubangui**, Gaston Gaillard made a protectorate treaty with the **Sango** leaders in the **Mobaye** region on 15 October 1891 and founded the Mobaye post. He also obtained a grant of land from the **Yakoma** leader Inkesse at the juncture of the **Mbomou** and the **Ouellé** Rivers just opposite King **Leopold**'s Yakoma post. On 5 October 1891 he turned this post, named Abiras, over to the young agent **Léon de Poumeyrac de Masredon** before returning to France.

**GALINGUI, MICHEL (called GALLIN-DOUATHE) (1920–1989).** Born in Limassa (**Ubangui-Shari**) on 4 June 1920, he died in **Bangui** on 7 March 1989. He was candidate against **Barthélémy Boganda** in the legislative elections of 1951. The first Ubanguian graduate of the Ecole Nationale de la France d'Outre-Mer (National French Overseas School) he became the first Central African ambassador to the United Nations in 1960. Having distanced himself from the **Jean-Bedel Bokassa** regime, he obtained a job in the Foreign Office in Paris. He was appointed Minister of the Interior by **David Dacko** on 27 September 1979; then, on 24 March 1980, Minister of Justice. He retired in 1988.

**GAMANA-LEGGOS, MAURICE (1925–).** Born on 2 December 1925 at Bamoungue in the Kembe district. He was a clerk in the administrative and financial services and the head of the Kembe district in 1960. He was the **prefect** of Umbella-Mpoko in 1963, the Upper Sangha in December 1965. He became Minister of Civil Engineering in the **Jean-Bedel Bokassa** government in 1966.

**GAMBU, ETIENNE (1904–).** Born on 14 November 1904 in Rouen, as president of the **Chamber of Commerce (of Bangui)**, Gambu was elected territorial councilor in 1952.

**GANDA.** The **Nzakara** leader, Ganda, became a "blood brother" with King **Leopold**'s officer **Alphonse Vangele** in December 1889. When **Bangassou** succeeded **Bafi**, Ganda joined with **Pakourou**, who had been deprived of power. In 1892 he entered into treaties with the French. Ganda then involved **Victor Liotard** in his conflicts with the **Banda**-Bougbou. The Nzakara leader lost five of his sons in combat. Ganda, allied to Pakourou and Bakouma, still continued to plot against Bangassou. On 27 October 1892 he died, most likely poisoned by Bangassou. **Bagou**, Ganda's heir, remained loyal to the French and refused to enter into treaties with Leopold's forces.

**GAOGA.** Probably a deformation of the word *kouka*, the term Gaoga designates a vast Central African kingdom that at the beginning of the 16th century covered, according to the traveler **Leo Africanus**, the center of Chad, **Wadaï**, **Darfur**, the eastern part of the present-day Central

African Republic, and part of Bahr-el-Ghazal. Homara, King of Gaoga, was thus strong enough to threaten the Bornu Empire. He had numerous commercial relations with Egypt. According to Leo Africanus, there were still Christians in this kingdom as well as nearby Nubia.

**GASSA-KOUMBE.** Gassa-Koumbe, a young **Banda** Yanguéré of the Bounda clan, was captured at age 12 by the **Ngaoundéré Fulbé**. Regaining his liberty, he took charge with the young **Baya**-boupane leader **Bafio** of a popular revolt to drive the Fulbé from Upper Sangha about 1890.

**GAUD, FERNAND-LEOPOLD (1873–?).** Born in Puymeras (Vaucluse) on 16 October 1873. After studying pharmacy, he began his colonial career as a third-class inspector in the civil guard in the Congo, then he became commander of the **Bangui** region between 1900 and 1901. Dismissed in September 1901 for budgetary reasons, he was employed in Upper Shari in December 1902. He served as Administrator **Georges Toqué**'s assistant at the head of the Fort **Crampel** circle during the **Mandjia** insurrection of 1903–1904. Gaud directed the spectacular execution by dynamite on 14 July 1903 of the **Pakpa** guide who had been arrested for treason after the battle with the Mbres. News of this event reached High Commissioner **Emile Gentil** and became the object of considerable political debate in France. The following year the ministers arrested the providential scapegoats, Gaud and Toqué, in a spectacular fashion. Their trial had as its real goal the elimination of the exploitation and oppression that was so prevalent in the colonial system in **Ubangui**. Gaud is the author of ethnographic works on the Mandjia. The 500 pages of this study are still quite authoritative.

**GAULLE, GENERAL CHARLES DE.** On many occasions, General de Gaulle expressed his sympathy for the **Ubangui-Shari** territory, which rallied to **Free France** as early as August 1940. Far removed from power, he came to **Bangui** on 17 March 1953 and refused to support the violent political intrigues directed by the Ubangui Rassemblement du Peuple Français (**RPF**; French People's Party) sections against **Barthélémy Boganda** and his partisans. In Paris in July 1958 he received Boganda, who was presiding over the Grand

Council of French Equatorial Africa and who was demanding immediate independence for the Federation. Boganda received General de Gaulle the following month in Brazzaville. The discussions in Brazzaville, at which Boganda's demands for the right to independence were accepted, led to the successful "Yes" vote in the 22 September 1958 referendum throughout all of French Equatorial Africa.

**GAZA. Administrative post** founded in Upper Sangha by the administrator **Alphonse Goujon**, under **Pierre Brazza**'s order in 1893.

**GBAGUIDI, DR. ROBERT.** Dahomean doctor chosen by **Barthélémy Boganda** in 1957 to participate in the first **Ubanguian** government presided over by Dr. **Abel Goumba**.

**GBAGUILI, POLYCARPE.** Close to Colonel **Alexandre Banza**, Gbaguili was arrested after the execution of the latter in April 1969. He was not released until 22 September 1979, after over 10 years of imprisonment without trial. Endowed with a strong moral fiber, he assisted many people sentenced to death by Emperor **Bokassa I**. His incredibly good memory proved him to be a methodical and precise witness to the crimes of the ex-emperor.

**GBANDI (or BOENDI).** Son of **Bilinga**, **Bandia** King of the **Nzakara** and grandfather of **Bangassou**, Gbandi waged war on the **Banda** Togbo of the Bakouma region. He was killed around 1860 in a battle against the Banda-Bougbou.

**GBEZARA-BRIA, MICHEL.** Several times ambassador under the **David Dacko** and then Emperor **Bokassa** regimes, foreign minister to General **André Kolingba**, he became the cabinet director for **Ange Patassé** before being **Jean-Paul Ngoupandé**'s foreign minister. Chosen as prime minister he opted on 11 February 1997 for a Gouvernement d'Action pour la Défense de la Démocratie (GADD; Government of Action for the Defense of Democracy), which included ministers from the opposition.

**GENTIL, EMILE (1861–1914).** Born on 4 April 1861 in Volmunster (Moselle), he died on 30 March 1914. **Pierre Brazza** had a ship's ensign, Emile Gentil from Lorraine, enrolled in the colonial administrative corps. In 1890 Gentil refused to go along with his compatriot **Paul Crampel** when he contested the liberal methods of command. In 1892 he was called to Upper Sangha by Brazza to replace Captain Decoeur. In 1895, while in Paris, Administrator Gentil let it be known to Minister Delcasse that he would volunteer to lead an expedition to Chad. Upon his arrival in Brazzaville on 23 October Gentil had not yet established the itinerary for his mission. He opted for the same one that was followed by **Jean Dybowski** and by **Casimir Maistre**, which would allow him to reach, after the **Ubangui**, the **Gribingui**, one of the tributaries of the **Shari** River. Frustrated in obtaining supplies because of the priority given to Captain **Jean-Baptiste Marchand**'s Congo-Nile mission, the expedition was immobilized for long months on the **Mandjia** plateau. Gentil founded the post of Fort Crampel at the foot of the **Kaga Bandero** on 17 June 1897. Aided by the Mandjia population, who disassembled and carried his steamboat (the *Léon Blot*), Gentil penetrated in **Baguirmi**. Its sultan, Gaourang, reduced to vassalage by **Rabih**, asked for a French protectorate. Similarly, as-**Sanusi**, Sultan of **Dar-al-Kuti**, threatened with reprisals by the **Wadaï** after Rabih's departure, solicited the same favor. The *Léon Blot* reached Lake Chad on 1 November 1897, Rabih having given the order to let the French pass.

Upon his return to France in 1898, accompanied by Baguirmi and Kuti dignitaries, Gentil obtained the organization of a military expedition to protect these areas against Rabih. After the defeat of **Henri-Etienne Bretonnet** and Gaourang, Emile Gentil was obliged to lead a campaign against Rabih's army. The Sultan of Bornu was defeated near Kousseri in April 1900, a little after the Gentil mission joined forces with two other French columns coming from North and West Africa. Crampel's plan for a single unified French Africa from the Mediterranean and the Atlantic to the Congo was thus realized. Emile Gentil, called to serve as the head of the French Congo in 1903, ran into problems with an inspection team sent out to investigate the extortions committed in the colony. He was recalled and finished his career as a **tax** collector near Bordeaux.

**GEORGES, PRINCE.** **Jean-Bedel Bokassa**'s oldest son, married to a Frenchwoman, Prince Georges was appointed by his father in 1977 as councilor to the Imperial Court in charge of national defense with the rank of minister. As his father's rival in a number of commercial deals, he was arrested on 19 September 1978, expelled on 6 October, and disinherited, along with his descendants, of his title and Central African nationality.

**GESSI, ROMOLO (A.K.A. GESSI PASHA) (1831–1881).** Born in Constantinople in 1831, he died in Suez on 30 April 1881. The Khedive of Egypt's governor of Bahr-el-Ghazal, the Italian Romolo Gessi used the former companions of **Zubayr** to organize the frontier regions of the Upper **Ubangui** as early as 1876. He then acted as representative for the **Zandé** sultan in the main town of **Mofio** in the Kordofali district, with allegiance to **Oufterrah**. Likewise, between the **Chinko** and **Vovodo** streams, he created the Katambour district, with its headquarters at Zemongo. His Egyptian troops, commanded by **Gnawi-Bey**, with the concurrence of Alikobo and of Abdalla and the banner chiefs **Rafaï-Aga** and **Printzi**, then carried out warfare against the **Bandia**. A post was built on the **Mbomou**, a little before the Chinko. Gessi Pasha obtained the Zandé Sultan Zemio's support by reinforcing the sultan's small army.

**GIDE, ANDRE (1869–1947).** French author most famous for his novels, such as *Les Nourritures terrestres* (Fruits of the Earth) or *Les Faux-monnayeurs* (The Counterfeiters), in 1909 he helped found the prestigious literary review *La Nouvelle Revue Française* with Jacques Copeau, Jean Schlumberger, and André Ruyters. Along with his prolific career as a novelist, he was known in the early decades of the 20th century for his audacity and courage in political and social criticism. From his travels in the Congo, Chad, and French Equatorial Africa, he brought back the controversial *Voyage au Congo* (Travels in the Congo) and *Le retour du Tchad* (Back from Chad), which, in 1928, were instrumental in the growing French awareness of the crimes of colonization, and specifically the **Botembélé massacre**. As early as 1914 in *Souvenirs de la cour d'assise* (Memories from the Criminal Court), he had also expressed his criticism of the justice system, as he would later be a voice for homosexual protest in 1924 with his book *Corydon*. A strong supporter of communism, he made his great disappointment known when in 1936, after having experienced life in Russia, he wrote *Retour de l'U.R.S.S.* (Returning from the U.S.S.R.). He was also known as a translator of William Shakespeare, William Blake, Walt Whitman, and Joseph Conrad. He was awarded the Nobel Prize for literature in 1947. *See also* LAMBLIN, AUGUSTE; SAMBA-NGOTTO.

**GILLET-THAON.** In 1949, at the request of the French colonial administration, the four private companies holding the monopoly of **cotton** marketing in **Ubangui-Shari** approached Gillet-Thaon, a French company, to create at Baoli a small spinning and weaving mill with secondhand material. This first cotton **industry** soon had to call for support from the territorial budget.

**GISCARD D'ESTAING, VALÉRY (1926– ).** Born in Coblence (Germany) on 2 February 1926, earlier France's Finance Minister, due to his passion for hunting he went on safaris in Central Africa several times as early as 1972, in the estate of Jean Laboureur, in the Kombala, east of **Ndélé**. His trophies allowed him to be a registered member of the Rowland-Ward. On 1 December 1974 Emperor **Bokassa** awarded him the title of honorary citizen of the Central African Republic. While president of the French Republic, he was the first French head of state to set foot on Central African soil during an official visit on 5 March 1974. In **Bangui** he presided over the meeting of French-speaking African leaders and addressed dictator Bokassa as "dear relative." On several occasions he helped the Central African Republic to obtain more credits. He made numerous hunting trips to the CAR, in particular one in August 1976 on a 70,000-hectare estate in the Upper Mbomou region that was given to his cousin François Giscard d'Estaing. In May 1979 he proposed to the African leaders gathered in Kigali to support a commission of inquiry into the accusations made against Bokassa regarding the repression of the demonstrations of students and pupils. The commission's report was damning for the emperor. In July 1979, after cancelling his hunting tour in Central Africa, the French president decided in favor of operation Barracuda intended to remove the embarrassing dictator. The fallen emperor sought revenge and confirmed the gifts he had made of **diamonds**, which sparked a fierce press campaign in France and was one of the causes of Giscard d'Estaing's failure in the 1981 presidential elections. In his memoirs the former French president dealt extensively with Central Africa and Bokassa. In 1983 he won a lawsuit against a slanderous book by Bokassa, written by **Roger Holeindre**, an assistant to the *Front National* (National Front/far-right) candidate Jean-Marie Le Pen.

**GNAWI-BEY.** Commander of the Egyptian troops from Bahr-el-Ghazal who, under the government of **Gessi Pasha**, occupied the eastern part of the present-day Central African Republic right up to **Mbomou**. In January 1876 Gnawi-Bey welcomed **Panegiotes Potagos**, a Greek who was the first European explorer to penetrate the region.

**GOLD.** Gold mining began in 1930–1931 in **Ubangui-Shari** (Roandji trading post near Ippy and Pouloubou trading post near Alindao). From 246 kilos in 1931, production rose to 906 kilos in 1934. But output remained between 600 and 700 kilos for the following years and fell below 200 kilos in 1951. At Maboma near **Mbaïki** the largest nugget in Black Africa was discovered (more than 8 kilos). Today, production is practically down to zero.

**GONEN, GENERAL SAMUEL.** An Israeli general who was relieved of his command right in the middle of the Yom Kippur War. He was Emperor **Bokassa I**'s military adviser and instructor of the imperial guard. For this he received a 30,000-square-kilometer grant for **diamond** prospecting. On 1 February 1981 he was placed under house arrest. He died in Milan in 1994.

**GONGORO.** Name given by the **Baya** and the **Banda** Yanguéré to the French administrator **Alphonse Goujon**, who became their war leader against the **Fulbé** occupants of Upper **Sangha**.

**GONO.** A **Banda Ngao** war leader, Gono set up his capital at **Ara** to the east of **Ndélé**. On a number of occasions he tested the strength of **Dar-al-Kuti**, but was finally vanquished by as-**Sanusi**. He became a French ally and protégé in 1897, but was ultimately killed by as-Sanusi and Ara was destroyed.

**GOTOAS, NICOLAS.** Headmaster at the *Lycée Boganda*, he was arrested on 9 March 1969.

**GOUANDJIA, MAURICE.** A militant unionist he became Emperor **Bokassa**'s Minister of Justice. Accused of sorcery, he was arrested on 13 September 1971, and pardoned on 7 December 1976. He again was then appointed Minister of Justice.

**GOUJON, ALPHONSE.** In November 1894 **Pierre Brazza** left the **Sangha**, where he had just spent two years. He had labored to reach a reconciliation with the *lamido* **Abo of Ngaoundéré**, in order to assure the northern advance of the French. The Franco-German treaty signed on 15 March 1894, in spite of Brazza's protests, had placed the *lamidat* in the German zone of influence. **François Clozel** was thus forced to search further east for a way to penetrate toward Chad (**Carnot** region). This treaty was renounced in January 1895. Brazza's assistant, Alphonse Goujon, who was appointed principal administrator of the Sangha, urgently requested help to defend the country against the **Fulbé** forces that were attempting to reoccupy the area. The *lamido*'s representative had had the French **flag** cut down at the **Koundé** post and the incidents increased. **Slave** hunting began again. From February to April several thousand **Baya** and **Banda** Yanguéré gathered and called upon Goujon (called Gongoro) to place himself at their head to expel the Fulbé. After several battles Goujon and this popular army finally defeated the *lamido*'s army at Baboua on 30 June 1896. **Abo** then let it be known that he accepted the Lom as the boundary between his states and the French Sangha. He forbade **slave** hunting.

The news of this campaign, brought belatedly to the awareness of Paris by Brazza, frightened the French government. Recalled to France, Brazza advocated the abandonment of the whole region. Ministers Hanotaux and Lebon still came out for maintaining a French presence in order to ensure the advance toward Chad. Disparaged by a French newspaper (which denounced "the King of Sangha's escapades"), Goujon was replaced by **Blom**.

**GOULA.** Important and ancient population of the northern part of the Central African Republic and southern Chad, this region probably constituted the famous **Dar Koula** cited by the Scotch traveler **Walter George Browne** at the end of the 18th century. A distinction is made between the red, or Hamr, Goula and the black Goula. It is notable that the Goula language preceded Arabic as the commercial **language** of the whole region. **Rabih** and as-**Sanusi** exterminated the very numerous representatives of this population. One can still find a few groups of Goula Koumra and Goula Mede in the prefecture of **Ndélé**.

**GOUMBA, DR. ABEL (1926–).** Abel Goumba, son of a **Banziri** interpreter for the French colonial administration, was born on 18 September 1926 at Grimari (**Ouaka**). After his secondary studies and military service in the French army he was appointed an African paramedic (*medecin Africain de 3ème classe*) and assigned to the small medical posts of the forest region of the northern Middle Congo. In May 1957 **Barthélémy Boganda** had been appointed vice president of the **Ubangui-Shari** Government Council (the French governor was still the president of this organization), but he stepped down to offer this office to Goumba. He disagreed with **Roger Guerillot**, his Minister of Administrative and Economic affairs.

Guerillot was a French colonist of the First College who had rallied to **MESAN**. At the end of 1958 Goumba removed Guerillot by giving him the position of assistant delegate in Paris. At the time of the proclamation of the Central African Republic on 1 December 1958 Boganda himself took the position of head of government. Abel Goumba retained his portfolio as Minister of Finance and Planning. **David Dacko** received Guerillot's position. At Boganda's death on 29 March 1959, Dr. Goumba received the interim presidency. But, the following May, victim of a plot uniting the president of the **Chamber of Commerce**, the French high commissioner, and Boganda's widow, he was removed in favor of Dacko. In July 1959 Dacko excluded Goumba from his government, thus provoking an important split among the deputies. With the disposition of censure motion, Dacko secured the Assembly with the help of his European friends. In July 1960 Goumba and his friends founded the Mouvement pour l'évolution démocratique de l'Afrique centrale (**MEDAC**; Movement for the Democratic Evolution of Central Africa), which claimed to be the true depository of Boganda's political thought. The events in the neighboring Belgian Congo pushed the Central African Europeans to support Dacko. With the proclamation of independence on 13 August 1960, after a sham negotiation, Dacko, the head of the government, took over the functions of president of the Republic. In November a MEDAC demonstration was forbidden and a series of laws were passed restraining civil liberties. In December Goumba, hoping to avoid a confrontation, took his differences with Dacko before the heads of state of former French Black Africa meeting in **Brazzaville**.

On Christmas Eve, Goumba was arrested and imprisoned at the request of a French magistrate in cooperative service with the Central African government. His parliamentary immunity was removed. The French ambassador **Roger Barberot** asked France to support Dacko. Dacko, who rapidly instituted a single-party regime, managed meanwhile to delay under many pretexts the trial of Goumba and his friends. In January 1962, and in an appeal in June of the same year, the judges finally rendered a moderate judgment. A little later Goumba obtained authorization to go to France to continue his studies. As a medical doctor with advanced training, Goumba wanted to dedicate himself from then on to his career. As a doctor with the World Health Organization, he was sent to Rwanda. After Dacko's fall at the time of the **Saint-Sylvestre coup d'etat**, **Jean-Bedel Bokassa** firmly opposed the return of Goumba, a man remembered for his integrity, profound democratic ideas, and total devotion to his country.

During the Bokassa years, Abel Goumba remained abroad and founded the clandestine Front Patriotique Oubanguien (FPO; Ubanguian Patriotic Front), which organized the internal resistance against the dictatorship. At the time of the **Bangui Children's Massacre** he was in Cotonou. Thereafter he acted as the leader of a common front consisting of various opposition movements. In this role, on 18 August 1979, he launched an appeal to Central Africans asking them "to work together for the coming of a Second Central African Republic, a free and democratic one."

The day after the installation in **Bangui** of David Dacko by French troops Goumba protested the colonial character of the operation and demanded the organization of legislative and presidential elections in six months. At the beginning of March 1981, he returned to Bangui to run for president in the 15 March elections. He denounced the organized fraud. In July 1981 he went to Europe to finish his business with the World Health Organization. In his absence, and following the 14 July movie theater bombing, Dacko accused Goumba and the FPO of subversion. An international arrest warrant was issued against

Goumba. Returning to Bangui after Dacko's resignation, Abel Goumba was appointed Rector of the University of Bangui on 4 January 1982.

Arrested in his office on 22 August 1982, Goumba was accused of plotting by General **André Kolingba** and condemned to five years in prison by a special court on 21 April 1983. He was pardoned and released on 1 September 1983, along with 64 other political prisoners, only to be rearrested on 26 January 1984, and placed under house arrest, first in the eastern part of the country and then in Bangui. He was appointed professor in the faculty of medicine at the University of Bangui in October 1988.

Goumba was arrested again in September 1990 by General Kolingba along with many other opponents of the general. Upon his release from prison in March 1991 he established himself as a leader among the opposition. After he restored the multiparty system, Kolingba called for a great "national debate" that was boycotted by every party. On 19 September 1993 Abel Goumba ran as candidate for the presidential election lost to **Ange Patassé**, with 45.6 percent against 55 percent for Patassé. Abel Goumba, who was elected as deputy in his home region of Kouango, was Patassé's contender in several subsequent ballots but never won. Elected president of the opposition forces, General **François Bozizé** chose him for prime minister and Finance and Economic Minister on 23 March 2003. General Bozizé, after dismissing him as prime minister because he had protested the execution of two men denied a trial, entrusted Goumba with the newly re-created function of vice president of the Republic.

**GOUNDI.** A people that resided in Upper **Sangha** and played an important role in the precolonial trade of this region with the **Bobangui**. Only a few small groups of this population remain today.

**GOUNGA.** Son of Balouka, oldest son of the **Bandia** sultan, Bali of the **Nzakara** (and father of **Bangassou**), Gounga considered his uncle—Bangassou—a usurper. It was to protect themselves against him that Bali and his son Bangassou accepted some *bazinguers* of the Khedive's administration in 1883 and then in 1889 accepted the installation of some of King **Leopold**'s agents.

**GOURAUD, LIEUTENANT-COLONEL.** With Commander Emmanuel **Largeau**, Lieutenant-Colonel Gouraud tried to convince the French government to abandon Chad and order a withdrawal south of the 10th parallel, as advocated by the Minister of Colonies, in order to save the French Congo from imminent financial bankruptcy.

**GOYBINA.** Taking refuge on the sacred Pana mountain, the leader Goybina stubbornly held out against the Germans, to whom the French had ceded the region on 11 November 1911. On 23 April 1919, he was killed during a French military operation carried out in the same **Yadé** highlands.

**GPOBENGUE.** This great **Bandia** leader, with his three sons, Louzian, **Ndounga**, and **Kassanga**, achieved the organization of a Bandia state, which was already strong when the **Zandé** conqueror Ngoura invaded the region at the beginning of the 19th century.

**GRAND DESIGNS.** Before the independence, many "grand designs" had been thought of but never carried out: a railway linking **Bangui** to Chad, Bangui being connected to the Trans-Cameroon railway; the dredging of the **Ubangui** and **Sangha** tributary rivers, called the "great collectors" for the collection of **diamonds**; and a great **road** had also been envisaged, called the "fourth parallel road," from Bangui to Cameroon, part of a great Central African transportation system from Lagos to Mombassa. More recently, there was talk of a possible connection with the Trans-Sudan railways, now realized as far as Nyala. In 2002 President **Ange Patassé** mentioned the possible construction of a dam on the Ubangui River at Palambo, with the double purpose of diverting the waters of the High Ubangui River into Chad and redirecting the stream of the Lower Ubangui toward the Congo. These projects would require absolutely huge investments and remained nothing more than "grand designs."

**GRANDIN, MONSIGNOR MARCEL.** Born on 16 September 1885 in Beaulandais (Orne), he died on 4 August 1947 in **Bangui**. He was appointed Apostolic Prefect of **Ubangui** in 1928 and presided over the ordination of **Barthélémy Boganda** on 27 March 1938. Grandin suggested to Boganda that he run for office in the November 1946 legislative elections.

**GRATRY.** This industrialist from Lille was the president of "La **Mpoko**," the **concessionary company** on whose territory very bad incidents occurred at the beginning of the century.

**GRELOMBE, CHRISTOPHE (1942–1996).** Born in **Bangassou** in 1942, an officer in the gendarmerie, he was deported by Emperor **Bokassa** to **Ouadda**. Much later he helped General **André Kolingba** rise to power on 1 September 1981. In March 1982 he replaced General **François Bozizé** as Minister of Information. After serving as ambassador to Taiwan he became an all-powerful Minister of the Interior. On 5 December 1996, after the death of the gendarme killed during the attempted arrest of Captain Anicet Saulet on 15 November 1996, Grelombé and his son Martin were arrested, savagely tortured, and executed by the presidential guard. This action was strongly condemned by **Jean-Paul Ngoupandé**, the prime minister who was dismissed in February 1997.

**GRENFELL, GEORGE.** The English pastor Grenfell, of the Baptist **Missionary** Church, was on the banks of Stanley Pool as early as 1884. Financed by Arthington, a rich philanthropist of Leeds, he planned to expand throughout the whole Congo basin. He had greater resources at his disposal than either the French or King **Leopold**'s agents in the region. Thus he was the first to set forth on the **Ubangui** with his steamboat, *Peace*, in July 1884. He reached 1°25' north latitude on 13 October. Grenfell's information permitted Leopold II to organize his campaign to claim the whole Congo basin.

**GRESHOFF, ANTOINE.** This Dutch citizen was the first European trader to ascend the Congo to the falls. He directed the commercial section of the Nieuwe Afrikanische Handelsvermootschap, better known under the name *Maison Hollandaise* (Holland House). He maintained very good relations with the authorities of both Brazzaville and Kinshasa. The local population gave him the name Foumou Ntangou (Prince Sun). In 1892 he clashed with King **Leopold**'s authorities, who were attempting to gain a monopoly of trade in the Upper **Ubangui** for themselves. The French decorated him with the Legion of Honour at **Pierre Brazza**'s suggestion.

**GRIBINDJI.** Headquarters of **Rabih**'s army established in 1885 not far from the headwaters of the **Gribingui** in the center of the Central African Republic. Today the region is deserted.

**GRIBINGUI.** A tributary of the **Bamingui** River, the Grimbingui was long wrongly considered to be the **Shari**'s upper stream. This river was used by the French as means of access to Chad.

**GRIMALD, AIME (1983–2000).** Born in Villefranche-sur-Saône (Rhône) on 31 March 1903, he died in Paris in May 2000. The governor of Overseas France, Aimé Grimald, after having been secretary general of French Equatorial Africa, became the territorial head of **Ubangui-Shari** in 1952 and 1953. In 1955 he was the cabinet director for Jean-Jacques Juglas, French Overseas Minister, then in 1956 he became high commissioner in the Pacific.

**GROSS DOMESTIC PRODUCT (GDP).** The GDP of the Central African Republic was about 1.25 billion euros in 2001. On the chart of the United Nation's Development Program (UNDP), the CAR has recently slipped from 146th place to 166th. The primary sector is evaluated to 52 percent of GDP and occupies 60 percent of the population. The secondary sector represents 15 percent of GDP and includes 3 percent of the population, and the tertiary sector 26 percent for 22 percent of the population. The national debt has gone from 800 million euros in 1990 to 1,025 million in 1999; in 2001 it accounted for 25.7 percent of exports.

**GRÜNFELDER, LIEUTENANT.** An officer of the colonial army, Grünfelder received orders from Captain **Jean Modat** on 12 January 1911 to proceed to the **Ndélé** post and arrest sultan as-**Sanusi**, the largest part of whose army was then occupied in a war against the Youlou. The sultan and his son, supported by 300 fighters, seemed to have been forewarned. The lieutenant came upon them just as they were bringing out their guns. Grünfelder was seriously injured in the combat that followed between the post's riflemen and the sultan's soldiers. In 1912, Grünfelder was placed in charge of a police operation against the Langouassi and Togbo insurgents that took place between the Tomi and Kandjia Rivers.

**GUERET, FRANÇOIS.** Chosen by **David Dacko** in September 1979 as Minister of Justice, he resigned on 22 March 1980. He founded the Mouvement pour la Démocratie et l'Indépendance (MDI; Movement for Democracy and Independence) on 9 January 1981. Suspected of plotting, he was arrested by General **André Kolingba** upon his return from Paris on 13 February 1985. He spent more than a year in prison.

**GUERILLOT, ROGER (1904–1972).** Born on 12 November 1904, he was a Michelin technician from 1928 to 1935 posted to French Equatorial Africa as a river steamboat mechanic. Employed by Du Jardin, SEFI, and UNIROUTE in turn, he became an administrator of these companies. As a territorial adviser, he joined **Barthélémy Boganda** in 1953 and became secretary general of the Intergroup Libéral Oubanguien (ILO; **Ubangui** Liberal Intergroup). After serving as Minister of Economics and Administrative Affairs in the first Ubanguian government of 14 May 1957, Boganda took him out of administrative affairs and sent him to Paris on 23 August 1958 as assistant delegate of Ubangui to France. After Boganda's death, **David Dacko** appointed him economic adviser and ambassador to Paris, then to Brussels. He was confirmed in this later post by **Jean-Bedel Bokassa** in 1966.

**GUERLORGET, SERGEANT-MAJOR.** The arrival of European traders in **Yakoma** country, notably at the Setema post on the **Ubangui**, had ruined the traditional trade of the Yakoma leader Dangouta. A group of malcontents set fire to the **administrative post** on 21 September 1894, and assassinated Sergeant-Major Guerlorget, head of the post. Guerlorget's name was given to the Setema post. The leader who was held responsible for Guerlorget's death was captured on 17 August 1900, taken to **Mbaye**, and publicly executed on 29 August in the presence of **Henri Bobichon** and the Yakoma and **Sango** leaders who had been summoned to attend the punishment.

**GUIBET, GASTON (1881–1973).** Born in Amiens (Somme) on 6 October 1881, he died in Nice (Alpes Maritimes) on 30 March 1973.

Colonial administrator of the Bangui Division, Guibet denounced in December 1906, and again on 9 April 1907, the numerous crimes committed by the agents of the **concessionary company** "La **Mpoko**." Administrator Guibet later served in Gabon and Cameroon. During World War I he took part in the defense of Gabon, which came under German attack.

**GUIGONIS, COLONEL GEORGES.** Last head of the colonial Eaux et Forêts (**Water** and **Forests**) Service of **Ubangui-Shari**, then councilor to the Central African government, Colonel Guigonis made a systematic inventory of the Central African forest and drew up plans for its use.

**GUIMALI, ANTOINE (1928–).** Born in the village of Yetomane (Ippy), he was a cabinet clerk in the 1939 government, clerk recorder in 1947, and then head recorder of the Brazzaville Court of Appeal. After serving as Minister of Justice, Emperor **Bokassa** chose him as Minister of Foreign Affairs.

**GUINZA.** Before colonization, this term designated an iron money made by the **Yakoma**, one of the most powerful commercial peoples of the **Ubangui**. In the **Sango** lingua franca, the term now means money. Work is called *kwa ti guinza*.

– H –

**HADIA.** Born in 1863, Hadia was the daughter of **Muhammad as-Sanusi**, Sultan of **Dar-al-Kuti**. He gave her in marriage to **Fad al Allah**, the oldest son of **Rabih** in 1890. Taken by the French after the defeat of Fad al Allah, she was returned to her father by Lieutenant-Colonel **Georges Destenave**.

**HAKOUMA.** The term was used at the end of the 19th century in the western Sudan and Upper **Ubangui** for the khedival administration.

**HANOLET, CAPTAIN LEON (1854–1908).** Born in Mehaigne-Eghezee (Belgium) on 25 September 1859, he died on 1 December

1908. A Belgian officer in the service of the Congo Free State, he was in contact with the French explorer **Paul Crampel** in 1889. He later played an important role in the occupation of the region north of the **Mbomou** by King **Leopold**'s agents. On 23 April 1893, he replaced Commander Balat as Leopold's post head at **Bangassou**. In 1894 Leopold directed him to proceed toward the Kuti and conclude an agreement with **Rabih**. In 1894 Hanolet sent a message to as-**Sanusi** from the **Kreich** market of **Mbelle**, where he had established a post for Leopold. Hanolet asked as-Sanusi for authorization to cross his states but he received no response. When the Franco-Leopoldian agreement of 24 August 1894 was made known, Hanolet, like all of the other heads of Leopold's posts in the region, had to return to the south bank of the Mbomou. Shortly after Hanolet's departure as-Sanusi's cavalry totally destroyed the locality of Mbelle. Hanolet participated in the **Vangele** Mission and founded the Zongo post just opposite **Bangui** on 25 June 1889. His Zanzibarite militia introduced the traditional *pirogue* (dugout canoe) commerce on the **Ubangui**.

**HANSSENS, CAPTAIN EDMUND.** In the Steamer *En Avant*, King **Leopold**'s Captain Hanssens went up the **Ubangui** River, which Pastor **George Grenfell** had just discovered, and on 25 April 1884 took possession of both banks in the name of King Leopold's Congo Free State. On 11 May 1884 he drafted a report for **Sir François Walter de Winton**, who had just replaced **Henry Morton Stanley**. Recalled to Belgium by King Leopold, Hanssens left Kinshasa on 6 November 1884. He died on 28 December before leaving Africa. Since Leopold kept these discoveries secret, **Michel Dolisie** set up a French post on the north bank of the Ubangui.

**HASSEIN.** This officer of **Rabih**'s troops was of **Banda Tambago** origin. He was one of Rabih's best banner chiefs. He was gravely wounded in the battle of **Kaga Bandero** against the **Mandjia** in 1885. In 1890 he attacked the Ngapou group of the Banda **Ngao**, who had given **Paul Crampel** a friendly reception. The combat lasted six days without halt and provoked the dispersion, not only of the Ngao but also of the Ka, the Mbi, and the Ungourra, who belonged to the same Banda group.

**HASSEN, CLÉMENT (1930–1982).** Clément Hassen, whose mother was **Fulbé**, was born in Moundon (Chad) on 23 November 1930; he died in Paris on 4 December 1982. He was one of the first **Ubanguian civil servants** to become an administrator after a course of instruction at the National French Overseas School. After serving as secretary general of the presidency of the Republic and president of the Economic and Social Council, he became President **David Dacko**'s confidential adviser. Imprisoned for five years by Emperor **Bokassa**, along with his wife and three children, he was released on 5 June 1971 and asked, given his membership in the French civil service, to continue his administrative career in Paris as civil administrator to the French Overseas Territories Ministry. He died of wounds suffered in prison.

**HEALTH.** In 1956 health service personnel in **Ubangui-Shari** from doctors to nurse's aides numbered only 367 persons. Noticeable progress was made between 1956 and 1959; the number of consultations went from 600,000 to 1 million. In 1967, at the urging of **Barthélémy Boganda**'s Minister of Health, Captain **André Magale**, the Central African government made an exceptional budgetary effort in favor of public health. In spite of aid from the French government, the World Health Organization, and religious **missions**, the health situation in the country has remained very precarious. Life expectancy in the Central African Republic is no more than 40 years, and the number of doctors remains very low. Still, this situation is not at all comparable to that from 1905 to 1909. During this period, entire villages disappeared due to **sleeping sickness**, yellow fever, and **smallpox**, aggravated by malnutrition, forced labor, and **portage**.

**HENRY.** Administrator in Upper **Ubangui**, he was remarkable for his diplomacy. In 1898 he avoided a confrontation between **Bangassou** and the dissident leader Sate-Rato. In 1899 he was appointed government commissioner in Ubangui. He died at work in December 1899. His successor, **Henri Bobichon**, carried only the title of Delegate of the Commissioner General in Ubangui.

**HERMES.** Successor of **Boul** as head of the **Nana** post during the **Mandjia** insurrection, the agent Hermes died of jaundice at Fort **Crampel** in 1902.

**HERRIAU, REVEREND FATHER GABRIEL (1885–1965).** Born in Bourgneuf le Forêt (53) on 9 April 1885, he died in Saint-Denis (Réunion) on 7 May 1965. A Holy Ghost **missionary**, he encountered the 12-year-old **Barthélémy Boganda** in 1922 at the small **Mbaïki** military post school. He sent Boganda to the Betou missionary **school** on the **Ubangui**.

**HETMAN.** Son of the **Bandia** Sultan **Rafaï**, Hetman succeeded the sultan after his unexpected death on 15 June 1900. Speaking and writing French, Hetman was a faithful collaborator with the French authorities. When he died, the sultanate was replaced by simple canton heads.

**HEUGLIN, VON.** Austrian consul and traveler during the years 1862–1864. He alerted European public opinion to the **slave** trade carried on by the merchant lords of the Upper Nile with the complicity of European commercial houses of the Sudan.

**HEYMANS, CAPTAIN FLORENT.** One of King **Leopold**'s officers, Heymans was head of the **Yakoma** post. In August 1892, he had the leader Gremboui—who had attempted to seek refuge in the French zone—beheaded.

**HIYAZI, ALI.** A businessman from Libya, Hiyazi settled in the Central African Republic in 1972. He was soon on friendly terms with Emperor **Bokassa**, who introduced him as his "adoptive son." In September 1979 he accompanied Bokassa to Tripoli, during which trip Bokassa learned of his fall. A quarrel opposed Hiyazi to **François Giscard d'Estaing**, president of the French Export Commercial Bank, about a so-called theft of **diamonds** in Switzerland. Ali Hiyazi was reemployed by **Ange Patassé**.

**HOLEINDRE, ROGER (1929–).** Born in Corrano (Corsica) on 21 March 1929. A former soldier in Indochina and an active member of the Organisation de l'armée secrète (OAS; Secret Army Organization) in Algeria, he was vice president of Jean-Marie Le Pen's Front National (National Front). He was introduced as a photo-reporter for *Paris-Match* magazine to Emperor **Bokassa** in 1977 on the eve of the latter's coronation. He got on friendly terms with the Emperor and took his side when the latter was defeated. In June 1985 he recruited Bokassa as a member of the Cercle Natinal des Combattants (National Veterans Circle), a group close to the National Front. Bokassa first rented to him and then sold him his castle of Neuvy-sur-Barengeon in the Sologne region, which became a school for the National Front's cadres. On 9 May 1985 Bokassa published in France a book of memoirs entitled *Ma vérité* (My truth). In fact, this book was written by Roger Holeindre, who admitted in an article in *Le Monde* to having been Bokassa's ghost writer. Upon a lawsuit filed by President **Valéry Giscard d'Estaing** and upon the request of the Côte d'Ivoire President Houphouët-Boigny and his wife, the 1,000 copies of the book already printed (out of the 43,000 planned) were seized by warrant from the president of the Paris High Court on 13 May 1985. The ex-emperor watched them be destroyed on 27 June. After becoming a National Front deputy in Seine-Saint-Denis, Roger Holeindre was accused of having planned the attempted return of Bokassa to power in October 1986, during which the ex-emperor was arrested upon arrival at the **Bangui**-Mpoko airport.

**HOMET, MARCEL.** Small-time French trader who clashed in 1932 with the Lobaye **concessionary companies** and the administration. He was arrested and sentenced to a six-month deferred sentence in 1932 for insulting the attorney general and the lieutenant governor in a broadside called *Don Quixote*, which he published in Brazzaville. In Paris in March 1934, he published *Congo, terre de souffrance* (Congo, Land of suffering), a book denouncing the atrocities committed against the Lobaye populations. This book impressed young **Barthélémy Boganda** very much.

**HOSSINGER, CAPTAIN.** The officer of the colonial army found himself under **Victor Liotard**'s orders in Upper **Ubangui**. He crossed the **Mbomou**-Bahr-el-Ghazal watershed in January 1896 and persuaded the **Zandé** Sultan Tamboura, threatened by Mahdist forces, to place himself under a French protectorate.

**HOUNDA. Yakoma** leader who accepted French authority in 1893.

**HUNTZBUCHLER, ERNEST (1854–1898).** Born in Belfort on 23 June 1854, he died in Brazzaville on 2 December 1898. **Emile Gentil**'s assistant in September 1896, Huntzbuchler was able to gain the confidence of both the **Banda** and the **Mandjia**. He was the main cause of the mission's success. A legionnaire in the Flatters Mission, he later accompanied **Lieutenant Louis Mizon** to Benouein 1891.

**HUOT, DR. LOUIS VICTOR.** French medical doctor and explorer who was the first to link Fort **Crampel** to Fort **Carnot** (20 October to 2 December 1900). Crossing the Upper Lobaye (or **Bafi**), he nonetheless confused this river with the Congolese river Likouala-aux-herbes.

**HUSSON, CAPTAIN FRANÇOIS.** In April 1891, with **Gaston Gaillard**, he was the first Frenchman to arrive at the **Bania** rapids on the Upper **Sangha**. He returned with Gaillard in 1892 to Upper **Ubangui**, where he died in the **Mobaye** rapids while trying to disengage the steamer *Le Ballay*.

**HUTIN, COLONEL NICOLAS.** In August 1914, Colonel Hutin commanded the French column that retook first the Lobaye and then Upper **Sangha** from the Germans.

**HYDROGRAPHY.** A third of the land (203,400 kilometers) is part of the Chad basin that stretches over 2.5 million square kilometers, of which only 600,000 square kilometers (the **Shari**-Logane basin) flow into Lake Chad, whose level is sinking. The other two-thirds of the Central African territory covers 344,400 square kilometers for the first part and 69,500 square kilometers for the second, within the huge Congo basin (3.7 million square kilometers.) The average flow of the **Ubangui** River is seven and a half times superior to that of the Ouham-Shari. Yves Boulvert has revealed two geographical errors reproduced in map after map by the colonial cartographers. North of Ovadda, the Bongos mountain land is only a small rocky slope, and the river that flows into the Shari upstream is not the **Bamingui** nor the **Aouk** but the Bahr-Sara. In 2003 President **Ange Patassé** wanted to divert the Ubangui River into the Shari, a project that was deemed utterly utopian and impossible.

– I –

**IAECK, ADMINISTRATOR ALPHONSE.** Permanent delegate of the commissioner general, Iaeck, at the instructions of **Emile Gentil**, he conducted an inquiry into the affair of the **Bangui hostages** discovered by Dr. **Fulconis** on 30 June 1904.

**ICCA (INDUSTRIE COTONNIERE CENTRAFRICAINE: CENTRAL AFRICAN COTTON INDUSTRY).** In January 1965, irritated by the **Gillet-Thaon** company's refusal to increase the size of its **textile** plant at **Boali**, President **David Dacko** founded the ICCA with the Willot Brothers. This company, in which the Central African government kept a financial interest thanks to the Fond d'Aide et de Coopération (FAC; Aid and Cooperation Fund) support, built a modern factory in record time in **Bangui**. The ICCA soon absorbed the Industrie Cotonnière de l'Oubangi (ICOT; Ubangui Cotton Industry), which ran the Boali factory. In January 1976, the ICCA was nationalized by Emperor **Bokassa**. Its activities were transferred to a state company, the Industrie Centrafricaine du Textile (ICAT; Central African Textile Industry).

**IDDI LALA, RODOLPHE.** Holding a doctorate in sociology, he became the director of the Ecole Nationale Centrafricaine d'Administration (Central African National School of Administration). He then returned to Brazzaville to teach at the university. As secretary general of the Front Patriotique Oubanguien-Parti du Travail (FPO-PT; Ubanguian Patriotic Front/Labor Party), he participated in the 1980 "round table" conference organized by President **David Dacko**. Excluded from the FPO-PT in September of the same year, he founded a group called the Mouvement Centrafricain de Libération Nationale (MCLN; Central African National Liberation Movement), linked to Libya. In Lagos he claimed responsibility for the movie theater bombing in **Bangui** on 14 July 1981.

**INDEPENDENCE. General Charles de Gaulle**, in the proposed 1958 **Constitution**, had laid down the principle that territories that become independent could not stay in the French Community. The Constitution was modified in 1960 to permit both independence and membership in the community. After the demands for accession to international sovereignty by the Mali Federation and Madagascar, the other territories were invited to open negotiations to achieve this accession. The territories making up French Equatorial Africa preferred, under colonist pressure, to negotiate their independence separately, and not as a group.

Independence for the Central African Republic was proclaimed in **Bangui** on 13 August 1960 by the French Minister André Malraux. "France bequeaths to you," he declared, "the administration, because there is no state without administration."

**INDEPENDENTS.** This term curiously designated the councilors of the **Territorial Assembly** favorable to the colonizers and hostile to **Barthélémy Boganda**'s Mouvement pour l'évolution sociale de l'Afrique noire (**MESAN**; Movement for the Social Evolution of Black Africa). The "independents" systematically joined their votes to those of the European councilors of the first college, thus thrusting MESAN into the role of opposition. The formation of a single college in 1956 caused the rapid disappearance of these so-called independents.

**INDIGÉNAT.** The term *indigénat* applied to the rules of a French police administration organized over the indigenous African population by the decree of 31 May 1910, and largely expanded by the decree of 31 December 1925. Imprisonment could be imposed by administrative authorities for minor faults, sometimes for such simple acts as refusing to salute the flag. In fact, this system procured free labor for the administration. Article 22 of the decree of 1925 provided for very heavy punishment, up to internment for 10 years and the confiscation of goods. Article 23 even provided for collective sanctions, in general, fines that were payable in money or in days of work levied against collectivities. Some exceptions were provided for in the case of local rulers, veterans, holders of decorations, license holders, **civil servants**, and so on. This arbitrary and unjust system persisted until the end of World War II.

**INDUSTRIALIZATION.** The distance from the sea and the absence of communication routes other than rivers toward the exterior have constituted a major obstacle to industrialization in the Central African regions. However, a first effort was made by the colonial authorities in

1953: the installation of a **hydroelectric** plant at **Boali**, a spinning and weaving plant, and a brewery. A second effort was made beginning in 1962 by President **David Dacko**'s government, which was able to set up a number of factories using Central African raw materials (**textile** investment, which was more in keeping with the production of the country and the needs of the population; roselle spinning and weaving; jute substitutes; oil-mills; brickyards; and **diamond cutting** workshops) as well as various small assembly factories, intended to reduce the very high price of imported merchandise. This industrial investment remained concentrated in or near **Bangui**.

Presently, industrialization has not gone beyond the level of small enterprise (workshops, really), which operate with limited capital and technology. The two major obstacles are foreign investment, which is mainly directed toward luxury consumer goods for a small privileged class and the limited national market. Any "take-off" is linked to an increase in **agricultural** and mining output and the increase of size of the market.

The industrial sector now only accounts for 15 percent of the **gross domestic product (GDP)**. It revolves around four companies: MOCAT Breweries, SOCACIG (Cigarettes), SOGESCA (Sugar), and CENTRAPALM (Palm Oil).

**ISKANDERY, MUHAMMAD BEN AL.** Algerian teacher placed in charge of the **Koundé** post by **Pierre Savorgnan de Brazza**. On 15 January 1895 Iskandery journeyed to the *lamido* of **Ngaoundéré**. On his return, he witnessed a **slave** column bringing more than 11,000 slaves captured among the **Laka**. At Ngaoundéré he gathered information on **Rabih** and his **Fulbé** ally, Ayatou. Iskandery's report caused **Alphonse Goujon** to decide to help the **Baya** and the Yanguéré in their revolt against the Fulbé.

**ISRAEL.** From **independence** on, Israel, which was an important buyer of Central African **diamonds**, offered its cooperation to the new state. It was to Israel in 1962 that President **David Dacko** made his first foreign visit, just before going to Paris. Dacko used Israeli experts to organize the National Young Pioneers as well as a number of **rural** development projects and to set up certain **industrial** workshops. In spite of his affirmed sympathies with the Arab League (which went as far as his short-lived conversion to Islam), Emperor **Bokassa** maintained ties with the Israelis.

**IVORY.** At the end of the 19th century and the beginning of the 20th, both the French and King **Leopold**'s agents purchased, often at absurdly low prices, large quantities of ivory from Congolese and **Ubanguian** leaders who traditionally had monopolies on this **trade**. Later professional hunters established themselves in Upper Ubangui, provoking a veritable massacre of the elephant herds. The most famous of these hunters was Fredon, a Frenchman who had been debarred from the administration for having killed a guard, and an American, **Cherry**, a former mechanic on the steamboats of the Congo Free State. Between 1892 and 1895, Leopold set up a state monopoly on ivory buying in all of Upper Ubangui to which his officers paid close attention. With the destruction of the elephants, ivory production fell off very rapidly. After World War II, the French authorities severely regulated hunting.

Since **independence**, with the strong rise in ivory prices, there has been an elephant slaughtered every year. Ivory has become the object of a clandestine trade that disturbs local authorities as well as world animal preservation organizations. The Central African elephant herds may well be wiped out soon.

**IZAMO, COMMANDER JEAN-HENRI.** With what seemed to him to be support from the French embassy, Commander Izamo, head of the gendarmerie, had by the end of December 1965 formulated a project to seize power from President **David Dacko**, who was allowing power to slip into his hands anyway. Colonel **Jean-Bedel Bokassa**, the **Army** Chief of Staff, knowing of this project, called Izamo to his camp under an administrative pretext on 31 December 1965. No one ever saw Izamo alive again. During the night of 31 December to 1 January, Bokassa had the army intervene in the **Saint-Sylvestre coup d'etat**. After an exchange of fire with **Jean Mounoumbaye**'s security people—then in charge of the presidential palace—Bokassa took the presidential palace, which Dacko had abandoned. Bokassa claimed that Izamo had worked out an agreement with the People's Republic of China and hatched a plot that, according to Bokassa, had as its first objective his own assassination. Wounded and thrown in the headquarter's house at camp

**Roux**, Izamo died in his cell at **Ngaragba** Prison on 22 February 1966, according to **Maurice Adama-Tamboux**'s testimony, which reports having seen him thin and hardly recognizable. His body, like that of so many other political prisoners, was never found.

## – J –

**JACQUIER, CAPTAIN JULES.** Head of the Upper **Ubangui** division with a residence at **Mbaye**, Jacquier conducted operations against the **Banda** leader **Baram-Bakie** in 1909. Defeating him on 10 May 1909, Jacquier took possession of his fortress, Mdahaye, near Motto. In 1912 Jacquier went to Bria to organize the fight against **Baram-Baria**, Baram-Bakie's principal lieutenant. On 18 April 1912 he created the **Mouka** subdivision north of Bria. This new post served as the point of departure for military columns, which, passing through **Ouadda**, laid siege to the **Ouanda-Djallé** rock, on which as-**Sanusi**'s son **Kamoun** had entrenched himself with the remnants of the **Dar-al-Kuti armies**. After the combat of 17 December 1912, Jacquier organized an Upper Kotto division, then a Dar-al-Kuti division. Jacquier also acted against the **concessionary company** of Kotto, which was causing the ruin of the country already severely damaged by as-Sanusi's **slave** raids.

**JACQUINOT, LOUIS.** As Minister of Overseas France, Louis Jacquinot came to **Bangui** in 1952. He was the first French minister to visit this colony, which had been particularly neglected by the metropole.

**JAFFRELOT, LIEUTENANT LOUIS.** Jaffrelot replaced Lieutenant Arnould as the head of the Bria post in 1912. On Jacquiers' orders, he occupied **Mouka** and **Ouadda** the next year.

**JAMOT, DR. EUGENE.** Doctor for the colonial troops, he participated in 1914 in the military operations against the Germans in Upper **Sangha**. In 1916, trying to control **sleeping sickness** in **Ubangui-Shari**, he launched the first prophylactic campaign in the colony. Until 1931 he devoted all of his energies to the organization of the struggle against this sickness, which had tens of thousands of victims.

**JOREZ, URBAIN and ADOLPHE.** Director of the **concessionary company** called "La **Mobaye**," the Belgian Urbain Jorez took up his duties on 17 October 1900. A few months later, with his brother, Adolphe, he was arrested by **Henri Bobichon** for "armed looting in villages."

**JOURNIAC, RENE (1921–1980).** Born on 11 May 1921, he was a French Overseas magistrate, and adviser to President **Valéry Giscard d'Estaing** for African and Malagasy affairs. In August 1979 he met Emperor **Bokassa I** in Gabon and unsuccessfully asked him to abdicate. Journiac died in an airplane accident on 6 February 1980 in northern Cameroon. The president of the Republic replaced him with his colleague, Martin Kirsch.

**JULIEN, LIEUTENANT (then CAPTAIN) EMILE.** This French officer came from a family that had spent a long time in Egypt and the Sudan. He was chosen by the Duke d'Uzes to command the Algerian Rifles, which the Duke had recruited for his private mission—the refief of Khartoum, then occupied by Mahdist forces. D'Uzes's mission never left Upper **Ubangui**. **Victor Liotard** used Julien and his riflemen, after **Léon Masredon de Poumeyrac**'s death, in reprisals against the Bougbou and tried to occupy **Bangassou**, which was held by King **Leopold**'s forces. Julien then participated in the march toward Chad. He was chosen as resident at **Dar al-Kuti** and published some well-documented articles on the as-**Sanusi** states.

**JUNKER, DR. WILHELM (1840–1892).** This Russian doctor was born in Moscow and died in St. Petersburg. He completed his medical studies in Prussia and was the first European explorer to spend time in Central Africa and describe the country and its inhabitants. His first trip was to Bahr-el-Ghazal and Equatoria (1876–1878), then into the **Zandé** sultanates (1880–1883). He founded the Egyptian government station of Lacrima for **Emin Pasha** at Sultan Ndorouma's headquarters. Then he set himself up on the **Mbomou** with Zemio, the young son and successor of **Tikima**. He visited **Alikobo**'s *zeriba*, a few days march west of **Yakoma**. His minute account of travels in Zandé country is a valuable source for Central

African history. Written in German, then translated into English, it has never been translated into French and remains little known to Central Africans.

## – K –

**KABYLO, ETIENNE (1918–).** Born 21 October 1918, in Mbandjifaro (Upper Sangha). He was a private **school** teacher and became Territorial councilor and a member of the Grand Council of French Equatorial Africa at the end of the colonial era. He was a member of **MESAN**.

**KADHAFI, COLONEL MOUAMMAR (1942–).** As head of the state of Libya, he wanted his country to be a leader among countries south of the Sahara. He tried to turn Central Africa into an offensive base against Chad. He met with Emperor **Bokassa** in Tripoli from 1 September to 4 September 1976. He managed Bokassa's conversion to Islam as well as that of his prime minister, **Ange Patassé**. But Bokassa returned to Catholicism in January 1977. Kadhafi still pursued his military cooperation with Central Africa. On 20 September 1979, during operation **Barracuda**, French soldiers captured 27 Libyan soldiers and confiscated an arms depot. The Libyan soldiers were sent back to Tripoli a few days later. A friend of Patassé who sends his children to him for holidays, Kadhafi provided a military group in charge of his protection from 2001 to 2003.

**KAGA.** Granite peaks that rise up in the middle of the Central African plateau. These summits have served as citadels throughout Central African history. There are caves in these mountains that are still unexplored and that offer a field of investigation of great interest for archaeological research. *See also* KAZAMBA.

**KAKA.** This important **Baya** group established in Upper **Sangha** and Cameroon was created in the 19th century after the absorption of indigenous Bantu-speaking populations.

**KALAK.** A title, of Nilotic origin, borne by the Kings of **Wadaï**.

**KALLOT, JOSEPH (?–1969).** The Bangui city police commissioner, and close to Colonel **Alexandre Banza**, he was arrested shortly after the latter on 10 April 1969. Brought to Emperor **Bokassa**, Kallot jumped on him despite his handcuffs, insulted him, and tried to strangle him. Stopped by General **Timothee Malendoma**, Kallot was thrown in prison, where he was tortured at length. He died of his injuries in his cell at **Ngaragba** on 30 June 1969. His family was also arrested by Bokassa.

**KAMACH, ICHARME (1942–).** Born in Syria, Kamach arrived in **Bangui** in 1946. He worked for Cattin and Co. successively as an orderly, then unskilled worker, then supervisor. About 20 years later, Kamach bought several companies left behind by their European owners, namely Davum-Métallurgie-Centrafrique in 1973, owned by Pont à Mousson—Saint Gobain, SACD, then the Société Centrafricaine d'agriculture et de déroulage, in 1985. The Kamach holdings, which also bought various commercial firms in trouble, include a food supplies network, several movie theaters, and a golf course.

**KAMOUN.** For almost two years after the death of his father, **as-Sanusi**, Kamoun, who had been proclaimed Sultan of **Dar-al-Kuti**, remained entrenched on the heights of **Ouanda-Djallé** defying the French authorities. He was even able to send several convoys of **slaves** to Am Timan and also sought an alliance with Ali Dinar, the Sultan of **Darfur**. One of his slave-hunting columns crossed the **Dji** in December 1911 and burned the French trading post among the **Vidris**. Arriving too late, Lieutenant Bissey and his detachment of **Bangassou** caught up with the column of the Dji on 6 January 1912. The column soundly defeated Bissey's forces. The **Yalinga** post was created on 29 April 1912 to protect the **Banda** population. The French detachment from **Ndélé** under the command of Captain Souclier took Ouanda-Djallé on 17 December 1912.

**KARA.** A people that had for a very long time been established in Upper Kotto and the territory of Chad, they were dispersed by the **slaving** operations of the 19th century. A Kara group is still present at **Birao** and maintains the ancient traditions of this people.

**KARAMALLAH.** One of the Mahdi's lieutenants, Karamallah undertook the conquest of Bahr-el-Ghazal after having defeated **Frank Lupton**, the Khedive's English governor of **Dem Ziber** province (1884). Karamallah, even with the assistance of several **Banda** groups, was not able to penetrate into **Zandé** country. His taking of Dem Ziber was probably the reason why **Rabih** was forced to leave Upper **Ubangui** and try to find a more westward route.

**KARNOU (or KARINOU) (?–1928).** This charismatic leader was born Barka Ngainoumbey in Seri-Poumba between **Bouar** and Baboua. He preached resistance to the colonizers in his village of Nahing in 1927. Advocating nonviolence, he instigated a boycott of European merchandise and announced the union of all the blacks and the departure of the whites. His predictions rapidly resurrected the old war leagues among all of the **Baya** peoples. The Baya insurrection, called the Kongo Wara (War of the Hoe Handle), spread to neighboring groups. It lasted almost three years after the death of Karnou, who was killed on 11 December 1928 by a rifle patrol.

**KASSALA.** Clan head of the **Carnot** region, he was executed on 6 November 1894, at the orders of **François Clozel**, following the murder of a son of the leader Tendira and an Arabized merchant.

**KASSANGA.** Founder of the **Bandia** kingdom of **Chinko** at the beginning of the 19th century, Kassanga was the great-grandfather of Sultan **Rafaï**. He fought two battles with the **Kreich**.

**KAZAMBA (KAGA).** The heights of the **Mandjia** country between Fafa and **Gribingui**, Kazamba is one of the most important strategic sites of **Ubangui-Shari**. **Rabih** failed to take the stronghold in 1885. The Mandjia thus hindered his western movement (toward **Yola**). In 1901 Administrator **Georges Toqué**, aided by **Banda** Mbagga partisans of the **Ngao** group, took possession of the celebrated mountain after five days of furious combat.

**KERKHOVEN, CAPTAIN VAN.** Head of King **Leopold**'s expedition, the Belgian Captain van Kerkhoven was able, after heavy fighting and thanks to the assistance of some of Sultan Zemio's warriors, to force a passage to the Nile in 1892.

**KHADAFY, MU'AMMAR.** *See* KADHAFI, COLONEL MOUAM-MAR.

**KOBUR.** In 1874 Kobur, Sultan of **Dar-al-Kuti**, was faced with attacks by the lieutenants of **Zubayr**, Ma Ati, and Kheir Alla, who took his capital, **Cha**. In 1875 he was attacked by the **Banda Ngao** leader **Gono**, who was assisted by numerous **Kreich**. This attack was soundly repelled. In 1880 **Rabih** spared Dar-al-Kuti in exchange for the right of passage toward Lake Iro and the freedom to raid the Banda. Kobur remained more or less loyal to his sovereign, the Sultan of **Wadaï**. He warned the Sultan of Rabih's intrigues with the **Rounga**. Defeated by the **Mandjia** in 1885, Rabih was invited by Khalif Abdullah, the Mahdi's successor, to return to the Sudan. In 1887 Mahdist envoys approached both Kobur and Rabih, even though Wadaï took offense at the alliance concluded between Rabih and the **Salamat** Arabs. In 1890 Rabih came to Cha. He had Kobur chained and proclaimed Kobur's nephew, **Muhammad as-Sanusi**, as the new leader, with the title of Sheikh.

**KOLEGNAKO, COLONEL BASILE (?–1973).** A former student at Saint-Cyr, this officer was the first victim of a repression led by Emperor **Bokassa** after the discovery of a conspiracy attributed to **Mbongo** in 1973. Accused of hiding weapons near his villa, this man, a former director of penal establishments, was incarcerated at **Ngaragba**. Deprived of food and quickly sick, he was beaten to death with chains in his cell on 23 December 1973.

**KOLINGBA, ANDRE (1935–).** General and then President, Kolingba was a member of the **Yakoma** tribe. On **independence**, he transferred from the French Army to the **Central African Army** and became a general in 1973. He served as ambassador to Canada—replacing **Sylvestre Bangui**—and later to West Germany. In July 1981 President **David Dacko** appointed him chief of staff of the armed forces. In September 1981 Kolingba displaced Dacko in a bloodless coup and became president, an office he still holds today. The **constitution** was suspended, relations with France were improved, and a full military regime was established under a Committee for National Recovery. In May 1986 he announced the creation of a single party, the Rassemblement Démocratique Centrafricain (RDC; Central African Democratic Party). A referendum in November 1986 gave him a further six-year term as head of state.

Internal pressures have forced Kolingba to adopt a more democratic approach. In March 1991 he agreed to share his powers by appointing **Edouard Franck** as prime minister. He also set up a commission to revise the constitution with a view to adopting pluralism. Presidential elections took place in September 1994, which Kolingba lost in the first round with 12 percent of the votes against **Ange Patassé**'s 37 percent. In September 1999, he ran for president again when President Ange Patassé was reelected.

In 2001 Kolingba claimed responsibility for the attempted coup against Ange Patassé. He left the country to escape arrest and was soon sentenced to death. After living in Uganda, he came back to the Central African Republic in 2003, now a sick man, following General **François Bozizé**'s coup.

**KOMBET, JEAN-PIERRE.** Teacher and then inspector of teachers, President **David Dacko** appointed him ambassador to **Israel**, then to Rome. Emperor **Bokassa** made him ambassador to the United States. Arrested by Bokassa on 13 July 1971, he was released on 22 September 1979.

**KOMBOT-NAGUEMON, NESTOR (1934–).** Born on 14 November 1934 in **Yaounde**. Although secretary general of President **David Dacko**'s government, Kombot-Naguemon was maintained in this post by **Jean-Bedel Bokassa** after the 31 December 1965 coup d'etat.

**KOUDOUKOU, LIEUTENANT GEORGES-ALBERT (1894–1942).** Born in Fort **Crampel** in 1894. He volunteered on 20 June 1916 and joined the Third **Ubangui-Shari** battalion, and served again as Corporal in 1919. He fought in Morocco in a Senegalese infantry division and was awarded the military medal. Warrant officer in August 1940 at the Kassaï base in **Bangui**, he joined the **Free French** Forces. He was promoted to second lieutenant by 27 December 1941 after fighting the Vichy troops in Syria with the BM2. In January 1942 he fought in Egypt and was among the defenders of **Bir-Hakeim** under German siege. Badly wounded and with a leg amputated, he was evacuated to an Alexandrian hospital. A 9 September 1942 decree of **General Charles de Gaulle** awarded him the Liberation Cross posthumously. A large avenue in Bangui bears his name.

**KOUNDÉ.** Trading stop founded by the **Fulbé** on the route from **Ngaoundéré** to Sangha. At **Pierre Brazza**'s insistence, Koundé was placed in the French zone by the Franco-German convention of 15 May 1894. The *lamido* of Ngaoundéré did not recognize this situation until after the defeat inflicted on him by **Alphonse Goujon**'s **Baya** and the **Banda Yanguéré** forces.

**KOYAMBA, ALPHONSE.** One of **Jean-Bedel Bokassa**'s most faithful collaborators, Koyamba, who refused to follow him into exile, was chosen on 27 September 1979 to be vice prime minister in charge of Finance and the Economy by President **David Dacko**. Dacko broke with him in 1981.

**KOYAMGBOUNOU, GABRIEL (1947–).** Born in 1947, a customs officer, he was then assigned to the Ministry of Finance. He joined the Mouvement de libération du peuple centrafricain (MLPC; Movement for the Liberation of the Central African People) of **Ange Patassé**. Chosen for prime minister on 20 April 1995, he took the place of **Jean-Luc Mandaba**.

**KRÉDEDJÉ.** A village in **Banda** country. **Emile Gentil** founded the post he called Fort **Sibut** near Krédedjé.

**KREICH.** The name of this great people came from the deformation of the word *kirdi* (heathen), which they were called by the **Darfur** caravaners. This people seemed to have settled in Upper Kotto between **Goula** and **Sabanga** country about the 16th century. They were more or less supressed by the **Banda**, then decimated by **slave** raids. The Kreich, of which there remain some residual groups in the Central African Republic and the Bahr-el-Ghazal, called themselves Kpalla.

**KRIKRI.** Head of the **Kaka** region in **Zandé** country, he rose against the French in 1916. He was defeated and made a prisoner in 1917.

**KROUMA.** Leader of the **Banda** Togbo in the area of Kemo, Krouma signed a treaty with the explorer **Jean Dybowski** on 1 March 1892 by which he accepted a French protectorate over his country.

**KWA TI KODRO.** Name given by President **David Dacko** to an attempted renovation of **rural** enterprise in 1965. Literally, it means "village work."

## – L –

**LAKA.** The Laka, a people somewhat related to the Sara, neighbors of the **Mboum** in Upper Logone, suffered particularly from **Fulbé slaving** attacks, which lasted right up to the beginning of the 20th century.

**LAKOUÉ, ENOCH DERANT (1945–).** Lakoué belongs to the Baya ethnic group from Bossangoa. After graduating in economics, he served as minister under **Jean-Bedel Bokassa** from 1970 to 1972. Then he became the director-general of the Banque de développement des Etats de l'Afrique centrale (BDEAC; Bank for the Development of Central Africa) in Brazzaville until 1982. He continued his career in France as a consultant for various financial institutions, including the World Bank, the United Nations Development Program (UNDP), and the United Nations Educational, Scientific and Cultural Organization (UNESCO). When he returned to the Central African Republic, he joined **Ange Patassé**'s party, the Mouvement pour la libération du peuple centrafricain (MLPC; Movement for the Liberation of the Central African People), but left when faced with limited prospects of promotion. Lakoué then founded the Parti Social Démocrate (PSD; Social Democratic Party), which won a few seats at the National Assembly. He was active among the Concertation des forces sociales (Social Forces Alliance), a movement that grouped several parties opposed to President **André Kolingba**, founded and presided by **Abel Goumba**. He was a candidate against André Kolingba in the 1992 presidential elections that were canceled and postponed to 1993. André Kolingba subsequently appointed him to the Conseil national politique (CNP; National Political Council), which also included Ange Patassé and **David Dacko**, and was in charge of replacing the **National Assembly** and presenting the president with legislative projects.

Appointed prime minister by President Kolingba on 26 February 1993, Lakoué remained in power until 28 October 1993, during which time he was again an unlucky candidate in the presidential election on 22 August, when Ange Patassé was elected. Lakoué consequently took an active part in organizing the opposition parties, and it was he who drew up the united opposition parties' program in 1996. In 1999 he unsuccessfully ran for president again. Late in 2003, after General **François Bozizé**'s coup, Lakoué was appointed to the Banque des Etats de l'Afrique Centrale (BEAC; Central African States Bank).

**LAMBLIN, AUGUSTE (1870–1946).** Born in Besançon on 3 September 1870, he died in Paris on 8 April 1946. Auguste Lamblin directed the colony of **Ubangui-Shari** for more than 10 years (1919–1929). He worked harder by far than any other governor for the development of the territory. To him is owed the actual salvation of a country and a people drained by forced labor as **porters** and as wild **rubber** gatherers. He brought about the restoration of villages, the creation of large food crop farms, and a **road** network—all with very limited resources. In 1925 he received the writer **André Gide**, who remarked on the contrast that existed between the situation of **Ubangui-Shari** at that time and that which reigned in the Upper **Sangha** and Lobaye regions, which were then part of the Middle Congo colony.

**LAMIDO (*pl.* LAMIBÉ).** Title carried by the **Fulbé** leaders established in Cameroon. *Lamidat* refers to the territory under the authority of a *lamido*.

**LAMOTHE, HENRI DE.** Born in Metz on 8 August 1843, this journalist became the governor of Senegal in 1890. In 1898 de Lamothe followed **Pierre Brazza** as commissioner general of the French Congo. He went to **Bangui** in December 1899.

**LANCRENON, LIEUTENANT PIERRE.** A French officer who was given the mission in 1905 of finding access to Chad from **Koundé** on the Cameroon border, Lancrenon reached Baibokoum and then Lai. He brought to light two insurmountable obstacles to the use of this route: the very mountainous relief of the country and the absolute refusal of the **Baya** to act as **porters**. Lancrenon discovered the Ngou falls on this trek. These falls, which are among the biggest in Africa, are now named after him.

**LAND.** The Central African territory begins at 325 meters at the point where the **Ubangui** River crosses into Congolese territory and reaches 1,410 meters at mount Ngaoui on the border with Cameroon. With an average altitude of 600 meters, the CAR separates the Congolese basin from the Chad and Nile basins. The relief that rises beyond 1,000 meters (in the **Yadé** region in the northwest and in Dar Chala in the northeast) represents only 2 percent of the land. The plains (between 300 and 400 meters) cover 6 percent only, which makes plateaus predominant.

**LANESSAN, DE.** One-time governor general of Indochina and Minister of the Navy, de Lanessan presided over the parliamentary commission to which all of the documents of the **Pierre Brazza** mission were remitted in 1905. Following the government's wishes, de Lanessan drew up **concessions** that were "compatible with the interests of the concessioners and the honor of France."

**LANGUAGE.** The official languages of the Central African Republic are French and, since 1991, **Sango**. Sango was at first the language of **trade** used along the **Ubangui** River and spread by the colonists throughout the land, and as far as Chad and in Brazzaville.

**LANTEIGNE.** Agent of the **concessionary** company "La Kotto," Lanteigne was arrested 8 March 1901 by **Captain Victor Mahieu**, head of the Upper **Ubangui** region, and charged with homicide, armed robbery, and arson.

**LARGEAU, VICTOR.** Appointed head of the Middle **Ubangui** region, this experienced administrator arrived in **Bangui** with **Victor**

**Liotard** in January 1892. The Bangui **administrative post** was extended for the first time under his administration. Victor Largeau was the father of General Emmanuel Largeau.

**LARMINAT, COLONEL (then GENERAL) RENE EDGAR DE.** Born in Arles (Gard) on 29 November 1895. Colonel de Larminat was sent by **General Charles de Gaulle** and arrived in Leopoldville on 17 August 1940 by way of Cairo. He took power in Brazzaville on 28 August and came to **Bangui** on 4 September to receive the surrender of **Henri Cammas**. He served as high commissioner of **Free French** Africa from 12 November 1940 to 1 July 1941. Larminat fought in Libya, Syria, Italy, and Provence, and on the Atlantic front. Later president of the high military tribunal, he committed suicide after refusing to condemn to death General Salan.

**LAUZIERE, MAURICE (?–1891). Paul Crampel**'s companion who accompanied him as far as as-**Sanusi**'s capital, **Cha**. Crampel sent him to the rear to bring up the mission's troops. But Lauzibre died of sickness in the **Banda** Ngao village of **Mpoko** in March 1891.

**LEBOUDER, JEAN PIERRE (1944–).** Born in Sibut, he received his diploma at the National Advanced School of Agronomy at Toulouse in 1971. In 1972 he directed the Office of Studies at the Union commerciale cotonnière centrafricaine (UCCA; Central African Cotton Association) and became the Minister of **Agriculture** in **Ange Patassé**'s 1976 cabinet. In **Bernard Ayandho**'s 1980 cabinet, he was Minister of Planning and Cooperation and succeeded Ayandho as prime minister on 1 September 1980. At present, he works for the World Bank.

**LE BRIZ.** A Navy quartermaster, Le Briz accompanied **Albert Dolisie** during the foundation of **Nkoundjia**, the first **Ubangui** post, on 16 May 1885. He died shortly after.

**LEDOT, JEAN GAUTHIN.** Born in **Bangui** in 1932, he was a youth leader and became director of President **David Dacko**'s cabinet in 1961. He served as secretary of state in 1964 and was arrested by **Jean-Bedel Bokassa** on 1 January 1966.

**LEGISLATIVE ASSEMBLY.** *See* ASSEMBLY, LEGISLATIVE and NATIONAL.

**LE MARINEL, LIEUTENANT GEORGES.** One of King **Leopold**'s officers who, in violation of the 29 April 1887 convention, went back up the Kouango in November 1889.

**LENFANT, COMMANDER (1865–1923).** Born in Melun (Seine et Marne) on 11 April 1865, he died in Paris on 21 March 1923. Entrusted with a mission to the **Baya** and **Mboum** areas in 1906, Commander Lenfant confirmed **Pierre Lancrenon**'s observations on the difficulty of organizing an access route to Chad in this area. Cavalry Marshal Ernest Psichari took part in this mission. Lenfant was a colonel in Indochina from 1910 to 1912. He was promoted to general and military commander of Chad, but could not accept the assignment for health reasons.

**LEO AFRICANUS.** The Moroccan diplomat El-Ahssan Ibn Wezaz traveled widely in black Africa. Returning by sea from Egypt in North Africa, he was captured near Djerba by Christian corsairs. He was presented to the Medici Pope Leo X, who baptized him and gave the name John Leo. As a professor of Arabic at Bologna, Leo Africanus wrote his celebrated *The History and Description of Africa*, published in 1550 by Ramusio. This book mentioned a powerful central African state, **Gaoga**, between Bornu and Egypt.

**LEOPOLD II (1835–1909).** King of the Belgians, sovereign of the Congo Free State, Leopold II was a major historical figure for the African continent. In fact, he precipitated the "scramble for Africa" and its partition among the European colonial powers (1875–1885). He played a determining role in the history of the **Ubanguian** regions from 1885 to 1895. Leopold signed agreements with France on 29 April 1887, and again on 24 August 1894, that recognized French possession of the north bank of the Ubangui and the **Mbomou** Rivers.

**LEOPOLDIAN POSTS OF UPPER UBANGUI.** The Franco-Leopoldian convention of 24 August 1894 provided that the Congo Free State posts, which had for several years been located north of the

**Mbomou**, were to be turned over to French authorities. It became apparent that all the other posts, presented as such by Leopold's diplomats during the course of the negotiations, were in reality only camp sites with neither installations nor permanent agents in residence.

**LEROUX, LEOPOLD (1904–1972).** Born in Lesneven (Finistère) on 14 April 1904, he died in Brest (Finistère) on 16 November 1972. As administrator of Upper **Sangha**, Leroux minimized the **Baya** insurrection in August 1928. Within a few weeks, all of the region's posts were threatened. He was obliged to retire for reasons of disability.

**LESSE. Ubangui** tributary not mentioned in the partition of the Lobaye and **Mpoko** regions among the **concessionary companies**. The Lesse basin attracted greedy merchants. Concessionary extortions reached their climax in this sector.

**LHUILLIER, JEAN.** The agricultural engineer Jean Lhuillier introduced **coffee** growing in **Ubangui** in 1931. He participated in the **Free French** battles and was elected councilor in the French Union after the war.

**LIBABA, CASIMIR (?–1970).** The father of Colonel **Alexandre Banza**, he was arrested and tortured before being deported to **Biaro**, where he starved to death on 22 April 1970.

**LINGOUPOU, MARTIN (1936–1973).** Born in Sibut in 1936, **Jean-Bedel Bokassa** appointed him head of gendarmes in 1966. He was made lieutenant in 1967 and directed the **Baya** country repression at the death of **Banza** in 1969. Promoted to general in 1973, he was soon accused of being a subversive menace by Bokassa and thrown into prison. He died there on 8 October 1973.

**LIOTARD, VICTOR.** As a Navy pharmacist working in the colonial health service, Victor Liotard was entrusted with a botanical mission by the Minister of Public Education and Fine Arts after a term in Gabon. He left Bordeaux on 10 July 1891. At Loango, he received **Pierre Brazza**'s instructions asking him to go to the **Abiras** post in Upper **Ubangui** among the **Yakoma**. Brazza charged Liotard with preparing the population for the establishment of French influence and to make possible further progression toward the Upper Nile. Brazza delegated to him part of his own duties with the title of Director of Upper Ubangui. Liotard had to confront the **Banda** Boubou, then in 1893 he clashed with the Belgians set up at **Bangassou**. His sangfroid permitted French diplomacy to obtain the withdrawal of King **Leopold**'s forces from the **Mbomou**'s north bank in the following year and enabled the French advance toward the Upper Nile.

Liotard was appointed governor of Upper Ubangui in 1894. He spread his personnel from **Bangui** to the Mbomou headwaters over more than 1,300 kilometers, and established the seat of the Ubangui administration at **Mobaye**. Liotard penetrated to Bahr-el-Ghazal in 1896. A 19 July 1896 decree placed **Captain Jean-Baptiste Marchand** under Governor Liotard's orders. Liotard was the main cause of this mission's success. Hostile to the systematic exploitation by French and Belgian companies of a region already afflicted by the misdeeds of the soldiers of the Marchand mission, Liotard was relieved of his duties in 1898. He was replaced at the head of the colony by **Dr. Aldolphe Cureau**.

**LIRANGA.** A French post established on the Middle **Ubangui** in 1887, Liranga served as a base for an advance toward the north. The commercial companies NAHV (called *Maison Hollandaise*) and Daumas were established here, as was the first Catholic **mission** in Ubangui under Monsignor Carrie and Reverend **Father Prosper Augouard**.

**LISSONGO.** The precolonial history of the Lobaye was marked by the rivalry between the two neighboring groups, the Mbaka and the Lissongo.

**LIVESTOCK RAISING.** Some Central African peoples raised livestock before their arrival on the **Ubanguian** plateau (the **Baya** at the beginning of the 19th century). Until 1926, the tsetse fly was an obstacle to all stock raising in the region. In the next 10 years, thanks to the activity of French veterinarians (**René Malbrant** and Bayrou, both of whom became members of parliament), **Fulbé** pastoralists (**Bororo**) from Cameroon were settled in the present **prefectures** of **Nana**-Mambéré, **Ouaka**, and Lower Kotto. A well-structured livestock service was established, and slaughterhouses were constructed in **Bangui**. By 1960 the Bororo herds reached more than 500,000 heads, kept in good health with aid from the veterinary services. After 1960, thanks to the efforts of Dr. Desratour and the financial aid of the **Fonds Européen de développement** (FED; European Development Fund), some tens of thousands of Baoule cattle were imported from the Côte d'Ivoire and distributed to sharecroppers, who were instructed by the livestock service. A small milk and cheese industry was established at **Bouar**.

At the end of the 20th century, Central African livestock raising developed spectacularly. It involved about 20,000 families, that is, around 300,000 people and 2.8 million heads of cattle, although due to a more sedentary society the average size of the herds has been declining. It is evolving toward a type of **agricultural** stockbreeding, due to the increasing poverty of some of the breeders. Meat production was estimated in 1999 at around 40,000 tons. The number of chicken farms is approximately 300, about 30 farms are involved with laying hens, and there are about 60 pig farms. There were also 2.5 million goats, 0.5 million sheep, and 0.5 million pigs.

**LONDRES, ALBERT.** In his book *Terre d'Ebène* (Ebony Land), journalist Albert Londres brought to public attention the treatment inflicted upon the construction workers on the **Congo-Ocean** railroad, who were recruited from **Ubangui** and Chad (1928). "The desolation of their state," he wrote, "appears nameless to me. They drag themselves along the line like nostalgic phantoms. Curses and blows do not bring them around. One would believe that, dreaming of their far away Ubangui, they are groping their way toward the entrance of a cemetery."

**LUND, OLAF.** A Swedish citizen, and principal agent of the **concessionary company** "La **Mpoko**," Lund was responsible for the death of numerous **rubber** gatherers. He poisoned himself on 1 August 1907 in order to avoid an investigation carried out by the administrator **Joseph Butel**.

**LUPTON, FRANK.** Born in Ilford (Sussex) in 1835. Governor of Bahr-el-Ghazal for the Khedive, this English officer was the first European to reach the Kotto River near **Bria** during a reconnaissance in 1883. Upon his return, he found **Dem Ziber** threatened by the Mahdists. On 3 November 1883 Lupton called his friends, the **Zandé** Sultans of the **Mbomou**, to his aid. **Rafaï** and **Sassa**, relatives of Zemio, responded. Zemio was held up on the Mbomou by sickness. On 28 April 1884 Lupton surrendered to his former sergeant, **Karmallah**, who sent him to the Mahdi's camp in chains. Lupton died there of typhus on 8 May 1888.

## – M –

**MAANICUS, MONSIGNOR ANTOINE-MARIE (1924–1999).** A **missionary** from the Netherlands, he was appointed the first Bishop of **Bangassou** on 10 February 1964.

**MAGALE, ANDRE (1929–1980).** Born on 24 May 1929 in Bangui. A strong supporter of **Ubanguian** scouting in 1953, he continued his career in the gendarmerie. Minister of public health in **Jean-Bedel Bokassa**'s government in 1966, he was promoted by Bokassa to general. André Magale became vice prime minister of the Central African Empire. Wrongly accused of plotting by Bokassa, he was chained to the ground at the Maboké investigation station near **Mbaïki** in 1980. After being brought back by Bokassa to Kolongo villa in **Bangui**, he was executed.

**MAHAMADI.** One of the close supporters of as-**Sanusi**, Sultan of **Dar-al-Kuti**, Mahamadi was a Sara. An expert in the making of eunuchs about 1890, he was given the command of the Wadda region, where he proceeded to exterminate or sell almost the whole population.

**MAHIEU, CAPTAIN VICTOR.** Head of the Upper **Ubangui** region in 1900, this officer fought against the abuses of the **concessionary companies**. He brought to justice several European agents accused of murder, looting, and armed attacks.

**MAÏDOU, CHRISTOPHE (1936–).** Born on 14 February 1936 in **Bangui**. This Central African diplomat began his career in 1962 as

First councilor at the embassy of the Central African Republic in Paris. In 1979 he was promoted to secretary general in the Ministry of Foreign Affairs and then appointed ambassador to the United States. Maïdou is currently with the Central African Republic embassy in Paris.

**MAÏDOU, HENRI (1936–).** Born 14 February 1936 in Bangui and the twin brother of **Christophe Maïdou**. This geography professor succeeded **Ange Patassé** as prime minister of the Central African Empire in July 1978. On 4 September 1979, he sent a letter on behalf of the government calling for French assistance in ending Emperor **Bokassa**'s tyranny. As early as 21 September 1979, President **David Dacko** appointed him vice president of the Republic. Removed from office by Dacko at the end of 1980, he founded the Parti Républicain du Progres (PRP; Republican Party of Progress) on 27 December 1980. He then worked as head of a bank before he was chosen by **General André Kolingba** to be his special adviser on 12 January 2004.

**MAÏDOU, MAURICE.** Father of **Christophe** and **Henri Maïdou**. After a long career in the colonial health services, Maurice Maïdou became, under **David Dacko**'s presidency, a member of the governing committee of **MESAN**.

**MAISTRE, CASIMIR.** In 1892, at the age of 23, Casimir Maistre was chosen by the French African Committee to relieve the sick **Jean Dybowski**. Accompanied by Brunache, Briquez, **Ferdinand de Behagle**, and **Bonnel de Mezieres**, Maistre went up the Kemo and then the Tomi. He made treaties with the **Banda** leaders Azangouanda and Amazaga. On 18 July 1892 he penetrated **Mandjia** country and concluded a treaty with the leader Kandia. The protectorate treaty was ratified on 20 May 1893 by decree of the president of the Republic, **Sadi Carnot**. In September, Maistre reached the **Gribingui** and Sara country, where he made treaties with the leaders Dakamba and Mandjiatezze. He then turned west and reached Gako on the Bahr Sara (the lesser branch of the Ouham). From there, he was able to reach **Yola** on the Benue without difficulty. Then he embarked on a Royal Niger Company steamboat for Lagos. This important expedition permitted France to make good its claims to Banda, Mandjia, and Sara country while blocking English and German attempts to penetrate the **Ubangui**. The expedition also opened an access route to Lake Chad, the shores of which had been reached in 1892 by Colonel **Parfait Monteil** coming from Senegal.

**MAKOUROU.** Head of the Bougoumi branch of the **Mandjia** in the **Kaga** Bandero region, he was an informer for **Emile Gentil** and **Fernand-Leopold Gaud**. Makourou passed down some information to them in about 1893 on the Mandjia living north of the **Ubangui** and also on the dispersal of the **Sabanga**. Gentil appointed Majourou superior "chief" of the Mandjia in 1903. His son, Matifara, was the first Mandjia interpreter.

**MALBRANT, RENÉ (1903–?).** Born on 8 March 1903 in Dange. As a colonial veterinarian, in 1927 René Malbrant organized the coming to **Ubangui** of **Bororo** (**Fulbé**) herds. After World War II, he was the main leader of the reactionary current, opposing the various liberalization measures. Elected deputy of the First College for Chad and Ubangui-Shari, Malbrant organized the **Etats Généraux de la Colonisation** (States General of Colonization) in Paris in July 1946. This action resulted in, among other things, the introduction into the October 1946 constitutional draft of arrangements for the overseas territories that marked a definite retreat from those adopted by the French Parliament in April 1946. In Ubangui, Malbrant conducted a hate campaign against Deputy **Barthélémy Boganda**.

**MALENDOMA, CAPTAIN TIMOTHEE (1935–).** Born in Dekou, Timothee Malendoma entered the French army in 1953. Malendoma fought in Indochina; then he was admitted to the Frejus School and the military administration school in Montpellier. Chosen by **Jean-Bedel Bokassa** as Minister of the National Economy in January 1966, he did very well in his task and cleaned up the **diamond**-purchasing field. The following year, the smugglers obtained his removal from this post and finally his disgrace. He was appointed Minister of State in the government formed by President **David Dacko** on 27 September 1979. A militant Christian, General Malendoma presides over the Church of Christ and started a political party, the

Forum Démocratique (Democratic Forum) when the multiparty system was restored in 1990.

**MALEOMBHO, PIERRE-FAUSTIN.** A clerk at Fort Lamy, he was called to **Bangui** by **Barthélémy Boganda** who made him Minister of Civil Engineering, Transport and Mines on 8 December 1958. Chosen by Boganda to fill the position, he was elected president of the Central African **Legislative Assembly** in April 1959. After Boganda's death, Pierre Maleombho came out in favor of **Abel Goumba** and joined the ranks of the Mouvement pour l'évolution démocratique de l'Afrique Centrale (**MEDAC**; Movement for the Democratic Evolution of Central Africa). On 9 May 1960, he was ousted from the presidency of the Assembly by **Michel Adama-Tamboux**, a loyal follower of **David Dacko**. After Dacko's fall, **Jean-Bedel Bokassa** appointed him as attorney general in 1966. One of the first witnesses of Bokassa's crimes, Maleombho helped organize the resistance movement. Following the attempt on Bokassa's life on 3 February 1976, the police found the files of this movement at his home. He was executed with several dozen others.

**MAMADOU, JOSEPH-GILBERT (?–1980).** An official in the financial and administrative services, Mamadou was part of the first Government Council, created on 14 May 1957, as Minister of Social Affairs, Health and Public Education. He left the government on 8 December 1958, and was appointed the Central African Republic's ambassador to France in 1962. Then, a little before the **Saint-Sylvestre coup** of 1965, he was ambassador to Beijing. In 1967 he returned to Paris. In 1980 he became the cabinet director of Prime Minister **Bernard-Christian Ayandho**.

**MANDABA, JEAN CLAUDE (?–1979).** Promoted to general by Emperor **Bokassa**, he was appointed ambassador to Romania. Under suspicion of organizing a coup, he was imprisoned on 8 May 1976 at **Ngaragba**. Condemned to 20 years detention by a military tribunal on 17 May 1976, he was killed in prison on 10 June 1979.

**MANDABA, JEAN LUC.** Upon his return from France where he was a hospital doctor, he becomes prime minister under **Ange Patassé** on 25 October 1993.

**MANDÉ, COLONEL (?–1974).** Former Saint-Cyr student, Mandé is a cousin of **Basile Kolegnako**, and was implicated in the **Mbongo** coup d'etat in 1973. He was arrested and imprisoned at **Ngaragba**. He was allegedly executed without trial on 24 January 1974.

**MANDJIA. Baya** subgroup that coalesced under this name during a stay on the south branch of the **Ubangui** River. During the 19th century, the Mandjia took over the central Ubanguian plateau. They settled on the watershed between the Shari (**Gribingui**) and the Ubangui (Kemo). In 1885 they blocked the way to **Adamawa** for **Rabih**'s army. In 1892 the Mandjia accepted the French protectorate proposed by the explorer **Casimir Maistre**, and in 1896 they assured the success of **Emile Gentil**'s expedition. Forced first to serve as **porters** to supply the Chadian army and then for commercial and administrative needs, they were decimated by disease, **famine**, and poor treatment. Finally in 1903 they staged a mass uprising. The French conducted a veritable war of repression against them.

**MANGIN, CAPTAIN (then GENERAL) CHARLES** (1867–?). Born in Sarrebourg in 1867, he was **Jean-Baptiste Marchand**'s companion at Fashoda in 1898. The future General Mangin, creator of the "Black Army," was called upon between 1905 and 1908 to look into the exactions committed by the **concessionary companies**. "As samples of our race," he wrote on the subject of the European agents of these companies, "they are very badly chosen and lead to all the abuses, all the vengeance, which makes and remakes the history of this unhappy colony, as long as the regime is not changed."

**MANGIN, CAPTAIN GEORGES (?–1908).** Brother of General **Charles Mangin**, Captain Georges Mangin of the marine infantry, after having participated in West African operations against Samory, was injured in 1903 in **Ubangui** during operations against the **Mandjia**. He was killed in Mauritania in 1908.

**MANIOC (CASSAVA).** Following a number of **famines**, the colonial administration substituted the growing of manioc for that of millet in numerous regions of the **Ubanguian** plateau. If famine was abolished, it was only at the expense of a gross imbalance in village diets. Manioc is presently the staple food of Central

Africans. It is also distilled. The alcohol obtained (*argui*) is particularly unhealthy.

Manioc is cultivated throughout the land. In the northern and eastern regions, it has replaced millet. Manioc crops cover over 40 percent of cultivated land. With very variable yields, the average production reaches 660,000 tons a year. Families sell between 40 and 50 percent of the output. The Food and Agriculture Organization (FAO) financed a pilot operation involved in multiplying and distributing healthy cuttings. *See also* AGRICULTURE.

**MANTION, GENERAL JEAN CLAUDE.** A former airborne lieutenant at **Bouar** in the 1960s, Lieutenant Colonel Mantion arrived in **Bangui** on operation **Barracuda**. In charge of President **David Dacko**'s safety, the latter put him in charge of forming his presidential guard. Mantion gradually fit into the administrative and political life of the country, monitoring the comings and goings inside and outside the country, searching for opposition members, and being present while political prisoners were interrogated. He had a firm grasp on all the police activity in the land. In 1981, without informing Paris, he mounted the coup d'etat that overthrew Dacko, who was replaced by the latter's chief of staff, **General André Kolingba**. Mantion then became the new ruler's special adviser. Nicknamed "the Viceroy" or "Clint Eastwood," he rapidly acted as the president-general's right-hand man, deciding on the agenda of the Ministerial Council, interfering in the president's meetings with foreign leaders. He instigated all the arrests of the country's political leaders, in particular **François Gueret** and **Abel Goumba**. In 1982 his personal intervention prevented the attempted coup planned by Generals Mbaikoua and **François Bozizé**, which intended to put **Ange Patassé** in power. On 23 October 1986, informed that former Emperor **Bokassa**'s plane was due to land at Bangui-Mpoko airport, he arrested him and led him to the prison at camp **Roux**. He was his jailor there and also confident, and he helped him in preparing for his trial. In 1993 as Colonel Mantion, taken ill, waited for his contract to expire, he was brought back to France for health reasons in July. This evacuation coincided with his being called back to Paris by the government, which recalled the French ambassador as well, with whom he had had a falling out. This double departure favored the return of democracy to

Central Africa. After his recovery, Mantion was assigned to New Caledonia. Patassé accused him of secretly corresponding with Kolingba, who lost the election. Mantion was promoted to brigadier general on 1 August 1997.

**MANVILLE, MARCEL.** A French lawyer of Antilles origin, Manville was chosen as lawyer by **Abel Goumba**. While traveling to **Bangui** to defend his client, he was forcibly removed from his ship by the French police at Marseille on 23 January 1962.

**MARADAS-NADO.** An influential member of the governing committee of the Mouvement pour l'évolution sociale de l'Afrique noire (**MESAN**; Movement for the Social Evolution of Black Africa) created by **David Dacko** in 1962.

**MARALI.** In December 1904, the Bidigri rose up and attacked the factories of this western locality and massacred 12 foreign African agents working for the **concessionary companies**.

**MARAN, RENE.** Of West Indian origin, Rene Maran rejoined his father at **Bangui** in 1909. He entered the colonial administration. His most famous novel recounted the life of Batouala, a leader in the **Banda** country. This novel earned him the Goncourt Prize in 1921. Leopold Sedar Senghor considered Rene Maran the "precursor of *Négritude*."

**MARCHAND, CAPTAIN (then GENERAL) JEAN-BAPTISTE.** In October 1894 **Governor Victor Liotard** met this colonial infantry officer at Grand Bassam. The march toward the Nile had been made possible by the Franco-**Leopoldian** agreement of 24 August 1894, and Marchand multiplied his approaches to all the ministers and an incalculable number of members of parliament, to obtain the dispatch of a military column from Loango on the Atlantic to Fashoda on the Nile. After having engaged in multiple battles between the ocean and the Congo, Marchand arrived on 5 April 1897 at **Zinga**, to the south of **Bangui**. The whole Upper **Ubangui** colony was mobilized to ensure the success of this mission, which ended with the taking possession of Fashoda on 10 July 1898. This well-known Franco-Britannic incident risked the unleashing of a war between the two colonial powers and ended in the convention of 21 March 1899. The French had to evacuate all of the Bahr-el-Ghazal, thus depriving Upper Ubangui of its natural outlet. The failure of the Marchand mission caused the French to turn all their efforts toward the conquest of the Chad region.

**MARKOUNDA.** A Central African locality on the Chad border taken by armed commandos supporting **Ange Patassé** in the night of 9 November 1984. When it was retaken by the Central African army, several villages were burned including that of General Mbaikoua.

**MARTIN, DR. GUSTAVE.** The mission of Drs. Martin and Lebeuf in 1907 and 1908 took them all over the Central African area ravaged by **sleeping sickness**. In 1909 a sleeping sickness surveillance service was created with the concurrence of the Pasteur Institute.

**MARTINE (THE TWO "MARTINES").** **Jean-Bedel Bokassa,** who already had two children, Jean-Charles and Saint-Cyr, born from a Vietnamese concubine, learned in 1970 that a young half-breed woman from Saigon, Martine Thi Ba'i, claimed to be his daughter. After he had her come to **Bangui**, a Saigon newspaper, the *Trang Dan*, stated that he had been cheated and that she was not his daughter. It reported that another Martine had gone to the French embassy with her mother and had brought various pieces of evidence showing she was born 30 January 1953 and was in fact the daughter of Bokassa and his then concubine Mrs. Nguyen Thi Than. On 22 February 1971 Bokassa, in a show of generosity, said he would recognize both as his daughters on his birthday. On 30 January 1973, he gave one of them in marriage to Dr. **Jean-Bruno Dedeavode** and the other to Chief of Battalion **Fidèle Obrou**, during a luxurious ceremony.

The two sons-in-law of Bokassa were to meet tragic ends. Fidèle Obrou, accused of having plotted against the president, was sentenced to death and shot on 23 February 1976. On the same day, at the Bangui hospital, Dr. Dedeavode murdered, using an injection, the newborn baby of Fidèle Obrou. Tried for this crime, he was sentenced to death and shot on 24 January 1981. After her husband died,

Fidèle Obrou's widow had taken refuge with Catherine, Bokassa's wife. Bokassa pretended he had sent her back to Vietnam. Several witnesses testified that she was strangled in a quarry near Bangui airport. The Central African people nicknamed the first "Martine" to arrive *Kota* (the big one) because she was taller than the other, whom they called *Ketté* (meaning the small one).

**MARTINEAU, ALFRED.** Acting commissioner general, Martineau unsuccessfully sought the end of the **Mpoko concessionary company**, on the lands of which numerous crimes had been committed by the company's agents.

**MASSI, CHARLES (1952–).** A former mining minister and founder of the international **Bangui diamond** exchange, Massi was taken hostage by the **rebel** soldiers in 1996. Accused of having caused the diamond purchase offices not to pay their fines, in 1997 he formed an opposition party, the Forum Démocratique pour la Modernité (FO-DEM; Democratic Forum for Modernity). Dismissed on 17 December 1997 from his post of Minister of Agriculture and Livestock, he was placed under house arrest until 21 September 1998. He proved an unsuccessful candidate in the presidential and legislative elections of 1998–1999. After founding the Front Uni pour la Restauration de l'Unité Nationale et de la Démocratie en Centrafrique (FRUD; United Front for the Restoration of National Unity and Democracy in Central Africa) on 25 March 2002, Massi was stricken from the armed forces register.

**MASSIEPA.** In 1895 the Upper **Sangha** leader, Massiepa, submitted to the French administrator **Goujon** and placed at his disposition 800 riflemen for use against the **Fulbé**. Massiepa's father had been executed by the *lamido* of **Ngaoundéré**, Issa.

**MATHIEU, LIEUTENANT EMILE.** The Belgian officer commanding the detachment of 300 Zanzibari riflemen at King **Leopold**'s **Bangassou** post who was involved with the French director of Upper **Ubangui**, **Victor Liotard**, in a confrontation on 16 March 1893. Liotard landed with 36 Senegalese and Algerian riflemen, and Mathieu withdrew when faced with Liotard's cool courage.

**MAYNARD, LIEUTENANT DE.** In May 1909, under **Captain Jules Jacquier**'s orders, Maynard built an **administrative post** at the village of the **Banda** leader Bambari, on the **Ouaka**, the principal branch of the Kouango River. This post was the origin of the present-day **prefecture**.

**MAYOMOKALA, GENERAL JOSYHAT.** Second-in-command to Emperor **Bokassa**'s chief of staff, he commanded the troops assigned to the bloody repression of the demonstrators in **Bangui** in April 1979. Sentenced to death, he was shot on 24 January 1981.

**MBAÏKI.** Military post created in 1906 to contain the insurrection of the population against the agents of the **concessionary companies**. This locality is today the **prefecture** of the Lobaye region.

**MBAKA (or NGBAKA).** This group of clans of Bantu-speaking origin settled in Lobaye after having fled from the banks of the Congo. They played a major role in the colony's history. They were one of the groups to enter into contact with the French at the **Bangui** post in 1890. **Barthélémy Boganda**, **David Dacko**, and **Jean-Bedel Bokassa**, as well as numerous Central African ministers and civil servants, belong to this ethnic group.

**MBAKA-MANDJIA.** Ethnic group created through a **Mandjia** contribution to the local **Mbaka** population.

**MBANG.** The Kings of Banguirmi and some Sara leaders gave themselves the title of *mbang*, meaning "the sun."

**MBARI-DABA (1932–).** Born on 20 December 1932, he was a teacher and the director of a primary **school**. In 1966 **Jean-Bedel Bokassa** made him Minister of National Education.

**MBARI-RENGO (or MBALI-LENGO).** Nephew of Sultan **Bangassou**, Mbari-Rengo attacked a **Dar-al-Kuti** caravan in 1902. This attack resulted in the death of 30 people and the confiscation of the caravan's **slaves**, **ivory**, and guns. In order to avoid a war between as-**Sanusi** and Bangassou, the commissioner general obliged Mbari to pay 300 silver thalers as an indemnity.

**MBAYE, LIEUTENANT.** Captain Anicet Saulet's second-in-command, and leader of the 1997 **army rebellions**, he joined **General François Bozizé** in 2002 and became his spokesman.

**MBELLE. Kreich** trading town established between **Ndélé** and **Mouka**. The inhabitants of Mbelle had accepted the suzerainty of **Wadaï**. The Belgians set up an **administrative post** there in 1894. The town was razed by as-**Sanusi** in 1897, and most of its inhabitants were sold as **slaves**. Its ruins were seen in passing by the explorer **Auguste Chevalier** in 1903.

**MBEMBE.** A village that became the present Kolonge quarter of **Bangui**. On 26 June 1889 its leader entered into a "blood brotherhood" with **Michel Dolisie**, the founder of the French **administrative post** in Bangui.

**MBIMOU.** The Upper **Sangha** (Nola) Bantu-speaking group that was most affected by **sleeping sickness** from 1908 on.

**MBOKASSA.** Official spelling of the name of **Jean-Bedel Bokassa** when he was in the French **army**.

**MBOMOU.** Many books state that the Mbomou River, along with the **Ouellé**, form the **Ubangui**. This geographic fiction was conceived by King **Leopold** in order to keep the region situated north of the Ouellé, the major branch of the Ubangui, from being claimed by France.

**MBONGO, AUGUSTE (?–1974).** Taken into the French army in 1955, he completed training at the Frejus School. An engineering officer, he was promoted to general by Emperor **Bokassa** and put in charge of the gendarmerie. From 1967 to 1972, he was Minister of Civil Engineering. Under suspicion of plotting, he was incarcerated at the **Mbaïki** prison. Transferred to **Ngaragba** Prison on 26 February 1974, he died shortly after under torture.

**MBOUM.** Very ancient people settled in northern Cameroon and the western Central African Republic. They were for centuries the lords of part of **Adamawa**. **Ngaoundéré** came from this group. The **Fulbé**

waged innumerable **slave** wars against them. The Mboum resisted both French and German colonization.

**MBOUNDJOU-VOKO.** Literally "white-black." **Barthélémy Boganda** used this deprecatory term for **Ubanguians**, said to be *evolués*, who had adopted the European lifestyle and rejected their ancestral customs.

**MECKASSOUA, KARIM.** A brilliant economist, he was working in France when he was asked by Prime Minister **Jean-Paul Ngoupandé** to become his cabinet director in June 1996. Meckassoua was to play a key role in bringing peace to the chaos of the military **rebellions**. On 19 January 1997 **Ange Patassé** had him arrested after a meeting at the presidential palace, along with General **Amadou Toumani Touré**, who was there as a negotiator—a meeting during which the military side of the **Bangui agreement** was examined. In March 2003, **Abel Goumba** appointed him foreign minister.

**MEDAC (MOUVEMENT POUR L'EVOLUTION DEMOCRATIQUE DE L'AFRIQUE CENTRALE; MOVEMENT FOR THE DEMOCRATIC EVOLUTION OF CENTRAL AFRICA).** After President **David Dacko**'s monopolization of the Mouvement pour l'évolution sociale de l'Afrique noire (**MESAN**; Movement for the Social Evolution of Black Africa), Dr. **Abel Goumba** and a few members of the movement founded MEDAC, which claimed to be the only heir to **Barthélémy Boganda**'s political thought. Goumba achieved some success in **Bangui** and the north and center of the country, provoking Dacko's accusation that it was a tribal movement. In December 1960 MEDAC was dissolved by Dacko, who established a single-party regime.

**MERCURI, TOUSSAINT.** A trader who acted as the unpaid French resident in **Dar-al-Kuti** in 1889. He gained the sultan's friendship and organized the solemn reception for as-**Sanusi** and his army at the Fort **Crampel** post in 1901. He died almost unnoticed at **Ndélé**.

**MEREKE.** Important leader in the now-deserted areas of the Upper Kotto basin. In 1900 he was accused by the **Kreich** Sultan Said Baldas of having caused the witchcraft death of Baldas's father. Mereke fled into the Sudan, and his village rapidly disappeared.

**MERLIN, MARTIAL.** Secretary general of the Congo in 1902, he was appointed governor general of the French Congo on 26 June 1908. He maintained a policy of cooperation with **concessionary companies** and firmness toward local peoples. He continued the practice of forced **portage** and prescribed a fiscal census to ensure the collection of the head **tax**, which he extended to women. Multiplying posts, he unsuccessfully advocated a new phase of colonial penetration, which he called "the active occupation of the country." The country was divided into divisions and subdivisions placed under the control, depending on the case, of officers or administrators, assisted by a rifle detachment or regional guards. In 1909 there was a general uprising of the population. Merlin occupied, valley by valley, all of the **Ubanguian** territory. According to the officers who kept the combat accounts from 1909 to 1912, a veritable "war of conquest" took place.

**MERWART, EMILE (1869–1960).** Born in Lemberg (Austria-Hungary) on 4 June 1869, he died in Paris on 7 September 1960. He was the first of his class throughout his studies at the Colonial School. He was appointed governor of the new **Ubangui-Shari-Chad** territory on 10 January 1906. To bring an end to the **slaving** activities of as-**Sanusi**, Merwart sent **Jean Modat** to make contact with the English authorities in the Sudan. He then decided to arrest the Sultan. Wishing to restore the authority of the **Zandé** and **Bandia** sultans, he ran into opposition with the **concessionary company** of the sultans. Brazzaville disavowed him. He next served as governor of Dahomey, then of Guadeloupe, before becoming director of the Treasury Department of Dahomey, then that of Réunion.

**MESAN (MOUVEMENT POUR L'EVOLUTION SOCIALE DE L'AFRIQUE NOIRE; MOVEMENT FOR THE SOCIAL EVOLUTION OF BLACK AFRICA).** Political party founded in Bangui on 28 September 1949 by **Barthélémy Boganda**, who wanted it to be open to "all the Blacks of the world." The statutes were registered in April 1950. Branches were created throughout **Ubangui** as well as at Fort Lamy and Brazzaville. The creation of MESAN provoked a hostile reaction on the part of the administration and Europeans. The Europeans set up branches of the Rassemblement du peuple français (**RPF**; French People's Party) to oppose the MESAN branches. Boganda also saw, on the other hand, a menace for his movement in the launching of the Rassemblement démocratique Africain (**RDA**; African Democratic Rally) in the three other territories of French Equatorial Africa. With the proclamation of the Central African Republic on 1 December 1958, MESAN limited itself to the former Ubangui-Shari. Boganda authorized other parties, reduced to tiny groups, but after his death **David Dacko** took over the party, threw out his political rivals, and in 1960 forged a single party. In 1963 MESAN became a sort of party of the state. With his accession to power in January 1966, **Jean-Bedel Bokassa**, after having imprisoned the majority of the members of the party's governing committee, proclaimed himself president of MESAN and assimilated the state and the party even more closely, creating a cult of Boganda as founder of both state and party.

**MESSAGERIES FLUVIALES DU CONGO. Transportation** company founded in 1899 in the Sangha region to meet administrative and company transportation needs.

**MICHEL, REVEREND FATHER (1911–1976).** Born on 4 September 1911 in Rennes, he died on 29 March 1976 in Chevilly-Larue. A Holy Ghost **missionary** and chaplain of the **Free French** troops at **Bir-Hakeim**, Father Michel was elected to the First College of the Territorial Council in 1947.

**MILZ, LIEUTENANT JULES.** One of King **Leopold**'s officers in Upper **Ubangui**, Milz negotiated a treaty in 1892 with the **Zandé** Sultan Zemio that placed part of Zemio's army at the disposal of the Belgians for their advance through the **Ouellé** basin toward the Nile.

**MINURCA (MISSION DES NATIONS UNIES EN REPUBLIQUE CENTRAFRICAINE; UNITED NATIONS MISSION IN THE CENTRAL AFRICAN REPUBLIC).** After the relative failures of the Mission d'Interposition et de Surveillance des Accords de Bangui (**MISAB**; Peacekeeping and Supervision Mission of the **Bangui**

**Agreement**), which had operated under a separate agreement between the CAR and friendly African countries, the United Nations finally realized that greater efforts and a stronger force were needed. This was decided by the Security Council, which passed Resolution 1159 on 27 March 1998. Under MINURCA, a multinational force of 1,350 military as well as policemen and civilian personnel were dispatched to the CAR to restore law and order. MINURCA's mandate was later expanded to include help with the organization and monitoring of the legislative and presidential elections. The mission was originally intended to last three months, but had to be extended several times and was only concluded in 2000 at a cost of $100 million to the United Nations.

**MIRAMBEAU, SERGEANT.** In 1909 Sergeant Mirambeau attempted to set up a post south of present-day **Yalinga**. He was attacked and killed by the **Vidri** leader, Maghacco. In 1912 Lieutenant Bissey proposed giving the name of Fort-Mirambeau to the post he had founded at Yalinga.

**MISAB (MISSION D'INTERPOSITION ET DE SURVEILLANCE DES ACCORDS DE BANGUI; PEACEKEEPING AND SUPERVISION MISSION OF THE BANGUI AGREEMENT).** After a period of strikes and demonstrations by civil servants and others for back pay that resulted in relative chaos in the capital, the Central African government sought aid from friendly African countries, which signed the **Bangui Agreement** on 25 January 1997. Under it a 750-man force was dispatched, including soldiers from Burkina Faso, Gabon, Mali, Senegal, Chad, and Togo, who were later joined by the command and logistic unit of the 9th DIMA (French Infantry and Navy Division). France also funded the operation, and it was eventually approved by the United Nations. MISAB carried out joint patrols along with the Forces Armées Centrafricaines (**FACA**; Central African Armed Forces) and restored law and order to some extent, disarming many of the demonstrators and others. But the crisis dragged on and stronger actions were required under the Mission des Nations Unies en République Centrafricaine (**MINURCA**; United Nations Mission in the Central African Republic).

**MISSIONS, CATHOLIC.** Coming from **Liranga** in Lower **Ubangui**, Monsignor **Prosper Augouard** of the congregation of Holy Ghost Fathers founded the mission of **Saint Paul de Rapides** near **Bangui** in January 1892. In September 1892 the Reverends Moreau and Rémy established a second mission near the confluence of the Kemo (Holy Family Mission). The start was very difficult. Many missionaries died of disease. Moreover, the excesses of forced **portage** and the **concessionary companies** did not favor evangelization. After the Holy Family Mission, the missionaries founded Saint Joseph Mission 70 kilometers from **Mobaye**. Fathers **Charles Tisserant** and **Joseph Daigre** then penetrated into the **Banda** homelands. It was not until about 1920 that the Holy Ghost Fathers could really progress inland. About 1935 the Capuchins arrived to back up the Holy Ghost Fathers. In 1937 the Apostolic Vicarate of Bangui was created. In 1955 Bangui became the seat of an archdiocese made up of the dioceses of Bangui, **Berberati**, and Fort Lamy and the apostolic prefectures of Moundou and **Bangassou**. Bangassou and Berberati in turn became bishoprics. In 1970 Bambari and in 1980 **Bouar** became bishoprics as well.

In 1909 Ubangui had only 761 Catholics. By 1924 there were 2,800; in 1928, 3,500; in 1937, 16,635; and in 1946, 31,686. Presently more than 470,000 Catholics live in the CAR. From 1938 to 1988 the number of Central African priests rose from one to 45. At present there are 203 expatriate priests in the country, as well as 89 lay missionaries. Since 1911 missionaries have been helped by monks and nuns who today number 261, including 22 Central Africans. A minor seminary was begun in Sibut in 1947.

**MISSIONS, PROTESTANT.** Protestant missionaries arrived in **Ubangui** about a decade later than their Catholic colleagues. It was not until after World War I that seven American, one Swedish, and one Swiss Protestant missions were established. The French colonial administration was not at all favorable to their work. In 1921 the Baptist Mission Society's Mid-Africa Mission was set up in **Bangui**. It was then established at Fort Sibut, Bambari, **Bria**, Ippy, Kembe, and **Bangassou**. At about the same time the Evangelical Mission of Ubangui-Shari, emanating from the Foreign Missionary Society of the Brethren Church of Long Beach, California, was established in the west at **Bossangoa**, Bouca, Bozoum, Bassai, Yaloke, and **Mbaïki**. The Grace Brethren Foreign Missions (formerly known as the Foreign Missionary Society of the Grace Brethren Church) began working in what is today the Central African Republic in 1918 under the leadership of James Gribble. There are now 588 churches with 138,519 members. The Grace Brethren operate two 110-bed hospitals at Yaloke and Boguila. They also run the Brethren Biblical Seminary at Bata with about 26 students.

A little later, the African Inland Mission of New York was established in **Zandé** country with posts at Obo and Zemio. The Swedish Baptist Mission was established in Upper **Sangha** (Carnot and Nola) and in the region of **Bouar**. The others limited their action to one district: the Home Office Missions—Mishiwara at **Ndélé**, the Lutheran Sudan Mission at Baboua, the Central African Pioneer Mission at Carnot, and the Swiss Elam Mission at Alindao. The colonial government encouraged the creation in Bangui of a French Protestant coordinating level for the various foreign missions. The number of private Protestant schools remained throughout, very much less than the number of private Catholic **schools**. Well-equipped medical centers, notably in Ippy, Carnot, and Yaloke, favor evangelization. Like the Catholic missionaries, the Protestant missionaries developed the **Sango** language as a means of communication. *See also* MISSIONS, CATHOLIC.

**MITIKO.** A term derived from the Arab *mitkal* (shield), this word was used in the precolonial era for the copper bars that served as money on the Congo and the **Ubangui**.

**MITTEL-AFRIKA.** Under this name, Pan-Germanists dreamed of creating a vast German Central Africa from Douala to Rwanda and from Namibia to Chad. This plan was developed by Otto Richard Tannenberg in *The Largest Germany, the Work of the Twentieth Century*. France's cession of part of **Ubangui** and the Middle Congo in November 1911 was the first step in this plan. The Germans proceeded to make studies for a Douala-Bangui railroad. The arrival point was fixed not far from Mongoumba on a peninsula baptized "German Point." A plan for the conquest of the Belgian Congo was also worked out.

**MIZON, LOUIS.** The lieutenant of the vessel *Mizon*, who found his mission in contradiction with the Franco-Britannic convention of 1890, was able in 1892 to cross **Adamawa** to Sangha with a weak escort without firing a shot. He sealed good relations with the **Fulbé** Emirs of **Yola** and **Ngaoundéré**.

**MOBAYE.** The **administrative post**, founded in 1892 by Administrator **Gaston Gaillard**, was until 1900 the capital of the Upper **Ubangui** territory.

**MODAT, CAPTAIN JEAN.** The French resident at as-**Sanusi**'s court, Modat traveled to the Sudan in 1910 to meet the Englishman Captain Stoney, who was upset by the **slave** traffic that as-**Sanusi** was carrying on toward **Darfur**. Captain Modat organized as-Sanusi's arrest in January 1911, during which the sultan and his son were killed.

**MODIBO. Fulbé** leaders gave their secretaries or educated collaborators this name.

**MODZAKA.** Before **Bangui**'s founding, Modzaka was the northernmost French post in the **Ubangui**. In April 1888 the head of the Modzaka **administrative post**, Veistrofer, scouted out a place for the Bangui post, which was founded the next year.

**MOFIO (also called *MOPOI-MOKROU*).** The oldest son of **Nounga**, who was himself the son of Mabengue and younger brother of Ngoura (the founder of the **Zandé** people), Mofio established his capital in the Beti valley to the east of the Upper **Chinko**. With his brother Zangabirou, he obtained the submission of the Dinga or Diga peoples about 1850, but this led to violent combat with his brothers Eliwa, Bamvourougba, and Senango. His kingdom was torn apart soon after his death by internal dissensions among his sons, in which the merchant lord of the Upper Nile soon intervened.

**MOKOA, CAPTAIN JOSEPH (?–1981).** He led the military detachment guarding prisoners at **Ngaragba** Prison and answered directly to Emperor **Bokassa**. The executions ordered by Bokassa were carried out in his presence, often using chains and hammers. Accused specifically of the murder of children in 1979, Mokoa was sentenced to death, then shot on 24 January 1981 along with two of his fellow accused.

**MONEY (PRECOLONIAL).** A number of types of money were utilized by the Central Africans for their traditional commerce. They include copper money, in wire or bars, iron money (called *gulnza* by the **Yakoma** who made it), cowries, bands of locally woven **cotton**, pearls called *baiaka*, as well as merchandise like salt. The silver thaler (or *talari*) with Marie-Therese's effigy had wide use in Upper **Ubangui** (*pata* in **Sango**, a word then applied to the five-franc bill or coin).

**MONTEIL, COLONEL PARFAIT.** Commander Monteil, who had forged links from Chad to St. Louis, Senegal, by establishing good relations with the Sultans of Sokoto and Bornu, had attracted the attention of Delcasse. The latter took Monteil to the president of the Republic, **Sadi Carnot**, on 4 May 1893. President Carnot wished to persuade Monteil to take command of a Fashoda expedition. On 30 May, Delcasse, following the Franco-Leopoldian incident at **Bangassou**, ordered Monteil to take charge of a small expeditionary force intended to reinforce the French positions in Upper **Ubangui**. Upon his arrival at Loango, Monteil was requested to go to the Côte d'Ivoire. Negotiations had begun with King **Leopold** with a view of reaching an agreement on the Ubangui.

**MONTROSIER, RAYMOND COLRAT DE.** Member of the **Bonnel** Mission to Mezieres (1898–1900), he was the author of an account of the mission entitled *Deux ans chez les anthropophages et les Sultans du Centre Afrique* (Two Years among the Cannibals and Sultans in Central Africa).

**MOPOI-INGUIZIMO.** **Zandé** sultan established between the **Mbomou** and the **Ouellé** in the Belgian Congo. Attacked in 1911 by the Congo public force, Mopoi-Inguizimo sought refuge with the French authorities. They decided to place a military post near the village constructed by the sultan's men. Bothered by Mopoi's attention to the local population, which he incited to resist the exactions of the **concessionary company** of the sultanates of the Upper **Ubangui**, the French decided to arrest him. A rifle platoon from the Mopo was routed by the sultan's *bazinguers* on 11 February 1916. Captain Lebouc asked for the cooperation of Major White, an Englishman at the Sudanese post of Tamboura, and Major Fredriksen of the Belgian post of Bongoro. This made an army of nearly 500 guns, which on 17 March attacked the village of the last heir of the great Zandé conquerer, Ngoura. Fleeing, Mopoi was caught by a patrol on 15 April.

**MORISSON, LOUIS.** This high French officer and military commander of **Ubangui** carried out an attack on the German post at Lobaye on 15 August 1914. The post fell without resistance. He then ordered his troops to proceed toward the Sangha.

**MOUKA.** This old **Banda-Tambago** leader received the French Lieutenant **Bos** on 28 February 1901. Bos promised Mouka his support against **as-Sanusi**. But it was not until 1911 that a military post was established, and by then the extermination of the Banda-Tambago by as-Sanusi had already been accomplished.

**MOUKTAR.** Son of the **Zandé** Sultan Zemio, Mouktar was elected territorial councilor in 1952. The administration supported him against the **MESAN** candidate.

**MOUNOUMBAYE, JEAN.** A soldier of Sara origin, Mounoumbaye was President **David Dacko**'s confidante. He was made head of the security service by David Dacko. For this purpose, he recruited about 60 men entirely devoted to Dacko. Taking part in the fighting during the **Saint-Sylvestre coup d'etat** in 1965, he was arrested a few weeks later in the forests of the Lobaye by Lieutenant Colonel Banga. Returned to **Bangui** and tortured, he was executed in an atrocious manner at **Jean-Bedel Bokassa**'s orders.

**MPOKO (CONCESSIONARY COMPANY OF).** It was on the territory granted this company not far from **Bangui** that the criminal incidents of 1908 took place. These happenings created the greatest scandal of the colonial period in French Equatorial Africa.

**MSA (MOUVEMENT SOCIALISTE AFRICAIN; SOCIALIST AFRICAN MOVEMENT).** This party had a small following in

**Ubangui** in the 1950s. Its local leader, Bandji-Kobakassy, founded the Bloc Démocratique Oubanguien (Ubanguian Democratic Block) in 1951. This party had a small number of members in the urban centers of **Bangui** and **Bossangoa**. It was dissolved in November 1962 by President **David Dacko**, who instituted the single-party regimen to the benefit of **MESAN**.

**MUSY, MAURICE.** On 15 September 1889 this former noncommissioned officer, who had served in Tonkin, came to help **Michel Dolisie** set up the new **Bangui** post. On 23 September he replaced Dolisie, who returned home for health reasons. In January 1890 Musy was drawn into an intervention against the Salanga by the villages of Yakouli and Botambi, who accused the Salanga of stealing from their farms and carrying off their women. Musy and his small escort were massacred in an ambush. In November the explorer **Paul Crampel** entered into negotiations with the Salanga, who agreed to return the arms they had taken and Musy's skull, displayed as a war trophy according to **Bouaka** custom.

## – N –

**NACHTIGAL, GUSTAV (1839–1885).** Born on 22 February 1839 in Eichstedt-Stendal (Germany), he died in Las Palmas on 20 April 1885. In 1873 this celebrated German explorer decided to return to Europe, no longer by the Sahara as planned, but through **Wadaï** and **Darfur**. The *kalak* Ali of Wadaï was then attempting to extend the limits of his kingdom to the south of the vassal principality of **Dar-al-Kuti**. Immobilized at Abecher, Nachtigal gathered, especially from a Bornu merchant, interesting information about **Goula** and **Banda** country.

**NANA A.** French post founded in 1896 by **Emile Gentil** on the Nana River, a tributary of the **Gribingui**, in the heart of **Mandjia** country.

**NANA B.** Second French post on the Nana created by **Emile Gentil** on 21 September 1896, at the point where this river becomes navigable; the post lies astride the rapids that Gentil named the **Huntzbuchler** Rapids.

**NATIONAL ASSEMBLY.** *See* ASSEMBLY, LEGISLATIVE and NATIONAL.

**NATIVE RESERVES.** The 8 February 1899 decree on **concession- ary companies** specified that the concession grants did not include land reserved for necessary food production by local people. **Emile Gentil's** 9 October 1903 order estimated that one could compute 6 percent as the share of the crops considered to have come from zones regarded as native reserves. The reserves were never delim- ited. The 9 October 1903 order permitted most of the crops har- vested by the "natives" without the concessionary company's knowledge to be considered as "stolen" from the concessionary company.

**NAUD, RENE (1907–?).** Born on 9 April 1907 in Chatellerault (Vi- enna). president of the **Chamber of Commerce** and territorial councilor of the First College, René Naud, hoping to become mayor of **Bangui**, joined forces with **Barthélémy Boganda** in 1956. The latter, elected mayor of Bangui, chose him as first deputy. Naud be- came an ardent promoter of the Bangui-Chad railroad project, which after a series of cost studies was abandoned by **David Dacko** in 1962.

**NDAKO, LIEUTENANT COLONEL.** Chief of the gendarmerie un- der Emperor **Bokassa**, he was chosen to replace Colonel Ngbabé, as- signed to **Bouar**.

**NDAKRI.** A leader in the Bambari area, Ndakri took over the leader- ship of a group of insurgents from various ethnic groups in 1910. The insurgents were able to isolate the new French post of Bambari. On 10 January 1911, surprised by Lieutenant Duval's detachment, Ndakri fell after a heroic resistance.

**NDAYEN, MONSIGNOR JOACHIM (1934–).** Born on 2 December 1934 in Loko (Lobaye), he was ordained a priest on 22 July 1961, and appointed Co-Adjunct Bishop of Bangui on 5 September 1968. He became Archbishop of Bangui on 16 September 1970.

**NDAYO.** On 8 April 1900, Ndayo, with a group of Dendi, attacked and plundered a Dutch commercial company's (NAHV) arms and munitions depot at Ouango. **Bangassou** and his men destroyed the villages of those who took part in this operation. Retreating to an island on the **Ubangui**, Ndayo put up a lively resistance to the attack launched against him by Lieutenant **Gailliard**.

**NDÉLÉ.** 1. In 1897 as-**Sanusi** transferred his capital from **Cha** on the **Banda** plateau to a place called Ndélé, which he fortified. After the death of as-Sanusi in 1911 Ndélé became the principal center of the **Dar-al-Kuti** division, then seat of an independent district. Today Ndélé is the seat of the **Bamingui-Bangoran prefecture** in the center of a region highly regarded for its big-game tourism. 2. The name Ndélé is also carried by a once-important **Banda** Yanguéré village located on the Bondegue in the Lobaye basin at the border with the Democratic Republic of Congo. In 1907 Ndélé was an important center of resistance to the **concessionary companies**.

**NDJADDER, FRANÇOIS.** A young officer close to **Jean-Bedel Bokassa**, he later became a general. **Ange Patassé**, his relative, placed him at the head of his presidential guard. He was killed during the attempted coup d'etat of May 2001.

**NDOUNGA.** Son of **Gpobengue** and brother of Louzian and **Kassanga**, Ndounga was one of the founders of the **Bandia** nation at the beginning of the 19th century, more especially the Kingdom of **Nzakara**, after the elimination of the **Voukpata**, the ruling clan of these people. He was **Bangassou**'s ancestor.

**NDRE.** Name of a **Banda** group settled in the **Bangui** region even before the foundation of the **administrative post**. An important district north of the capital is named "The Ndres."

**NEU-KAMERUN.** Name given by the Germans in November 1911 to part of French Equatorial Africa ceded to them by the French. This zone was subjected to a special regime by the new occupants. The head **tax** was suppressed, and stores were well stocked with merchandise.

Neu-Kamerun (New Cameroon) was reconquered by French troops at the beginning of World War I.

**NGAKOLA.** Mythical ancestor venerated by the **Banda** and the **Mandjia**. His name was given to initiation societies, which were literally a traditional education system. Ngakola was perhaps a strong king who had reigned over the Banda kingdom before the great dispersal over the **Ubanguian** plateau.

**NGALE (or GARE).** Among the Banou, **Baya**, **Bouaka**, **Mandjia**, and so on, Ngale (or Gare) is the name of the supreme being.

**NGAO.** An important **Banda** group that many times successfully resisted the Sultans of **Dar-al-Kuti** and waged numerous wars against the **Mandjia**. Thanks to arms furnished by the French, as-**Sanusi** was able to gain a decisive victory over the Ngao in 1897. They also suffered heavy losses to **Rabih**'s attacks. In 1901 Captain **Paulin Thomasset** of Fort **Crampel** carried out a campaign of destruction against the remnants of this people. In December the group's leader, Ouaganda—the successor to Djamo, who had been killed by Rabih—fell while defending the village of Ngaka against Thomasset's riflemen.

**NGAOUNDÉRÉ.** Capital of the **Fulbé** Emirate founded in the center of **Mboum** country by the **Adama**'s **companies** in the beginning of the 19th century. This town was the point of departure for numerous **slave** raids against the populations of Chad and Central Africa.

**NGARAGBA.** Name of a neighborhood on the bank of the **Ubangui** River in an eastern suburb of **Bangui**. The French built a walled prison there, measuring 100 by 100 meters. It was in this prison that Emperor **Bokassa** locked up numerous political prisoners without due process and under terrible conditions. Many died under torture. In 1979 numerous adolescents were arrested during demonstrations and thrown into cells at Ngaragba. A number of them suffocated or died from beatings by guards.

**NGARO, SIMON-BEDAYA.** A graduate medicine professor, then minister to the Imperial Court of **Berengo**, and later Foreign Minister of **Ange-Félix Patassé**, to whom he was close. The latter then chose him to be his diplomatic adviser.

**NGBONGO.** A lieutenant-colonel, and Emperor **Bokassa**'s military aid, he followed him during his exile in Abidjan.

**NGOKO-SANGHA.** A regrouping of **concessionary companies** running a deficit, in 1907, animated by the shady dealer Mestayer, it mounted an immense blackmail operation at the expense of the French government under the pretext of damages caused by the proximity of the dynamic German society, Sud-Kamerun. Since Mestayer and his accomplice André Tardieu (the future president of the council, then a lawyer) were aware of Germany's Congo ambitions, they could easily take advantage of the situation. The legal difficulties continued until World War II, when Ngoko-Sangha obtained a comfortable and scandalous indemnity.

**NGOTTO.** A post established on the Lobaye in **Boffi** country. It was at Ngotto that the leader **Samba-Ngotto** revealed to **André Gide** in 1925 the atrocities committed in the region.

**NGOUMBA.** Name of the spirit of fighting among the **Zandé**.

**NGOUNIO, ETIENNE (1920–).** Born on 19 August 1920 in Kembe (Lower Kotto), and elected senator of **Ubangui-Shari** in 1958, Etienne Ngounio, a private school teacher, after the death of **Boganda** in 1959, became mayor of **Bangui** and president of the Mouvement pour l'évolution sociale de l'Afrique Noire (**MESAN**; Movement for the Social Evolution of Black Africa). He was eliminated from the party in 1960 by the coup of **David Dacko**.

**NGOUPANDE, JEAN-PAUL.** Former Central African ambassador in Abidjan, then in Paris, he was called back to **Bangui** in June 1996 to help organize the Gouvernement d'Unité Nationale (GUN; Government of National Unity), facing the **army rebellion**. He succeeded in calming the situation as well as keeping the rebels free from charges, but after the murder of **Christophe Grelombe** and his son by the presidential guard, he was brutally sacked on 30 January 1997 by

**Ange Patassé** and for a time placed under house arrest in Bangui. He published for L'Harmattan Editions in Paris the very objective *Chronicle of the 1996–1997 Central African Crisis* in September 1997. An unsuccessful candidate in the presidential elections, he was nevertheless elected deputy in the **Mandjia** region and set up a political party that emphasizes national reconciliation.

**NIAM-NIAM.** Name given in the 19th century by the Arab caravaners and the European explorers to the people making up the **Zandé** nation.

**NILE, LAW OF THE.** Rules governing the fortified commercial posts of the "merchant lords of the Upper Nile" in the Sudano-**Ubanguian** confines (1854–1864). The theoretician of this system was the Frenchman Alphonse de Malzac.

**NKOUNDJIA, AGREEMENT OF.** A conference between French agents and King **Leopold**'s agents was held from 26 January to 26 February 1886 in this first French post in Lower **Ubangui**, founded by **Albert Dolisie** in May 1885. These agents reached an agreement fixing the point of departure toward the north of an arbitrary frontier between the two possessions running 400 meters from the village of Pombo on the Congo, below the mouth of the Ubangui and just a little below the Equator. This agreement, which left the whole Ubangui basin to the French, aroused King Leopold's wrath—he disavowed his representatives on 23 March 1886.

**NOGUES, ROGER.** One of the most active directors of the **concessionary companies** in the French Congo, Nogues achieved a merger of several bankrupt companies into the Upper **Sangha** Company with the support of the Minister of Colonies. In 1907 he placed a credit of 100,000 francs at the government's disposal to underwrite the **Lenfant** mission, which was entrusted with a reconnaissance of the unexplored regions between the Sangha and the Lobaye.

**NORO-ANGARA.** A Sudanese **slaver**, and **Zubayr**'s lieutenant, nicknamed Yambassa by the **Banda**, Noro-Angara located the center of his operations at Yato, to the east of **Ouanda-Djallé**. In the 1870s he undertook extermination operations against the Youlou, the **Kara**, and the Banda. He joined with General Charles Gordon in 1874, who appointed him *moundir* (governor) of the province of Suga el Areba.

**NOUNGA.** Younger brother of the **Zandé** conquerer Ngoura, and son of Mabengue, Nounga was also called Ngoura II. About 1830, he imposed his domination over the greater part of Zandé country between the **Chinko** and the **Ouellé** River. He allowed the **Bandia** to organize themselves in the west. Nounga's youngest son, Sultan Zemio, made treaties with the **Leopoldians** and then the French at the end of the century.

**NSARA-ABIED (WHITE CHRISTIANS).** Nickname given to the French by the inhabitants of **Dar-al-Kuti** at the end of the 19th century.

**NZABAKOMADA-YAKOMA, RAPHAEL (1944–1985).** Born in Baboua, he died in **Bangui**. He was the author of a remarkable history thesis on the Gbaya uprising of 1928 (known as the *Kongo-Wara War*). In 1980 he became Dean of the Faculty of Letters at the University of Bangui, but died prematurely of ill health.

**NZAKARA.** The residual group of a once-powerful **Sabanga** group that had numbered some 30,000 persons and held power on the **Ubanguian** plateau. This group constituted a kingdom directed by the **Bandia** at the end of the 19th century.

**NZALA, JEAN CHRISTOPHE.** Young head of President **David Dacko**'s political cabinet, he organized the National Young Pioneers. Arrested on 1 January 1966 and imprisoned at **Ngaragba**, he died a few days later from the beatings he had received.

**NZAPA.** Name of the supreme being among the **Sango**, this term is now used for God in the Sango lingua franca.

**NZILAVO, BARNABE.** Born on 15 September 1915 in Yabimbo. A colonial administration clerk, Nzilavo was one of the founders of Mouvement pour l'évolution sociale de l'Afrique Noire (**MESAN**;

Movement for the Social Evolution of Black Africa) with **Barthélémy Boganda** in 1949.

## – O –

**OBROU, FIDÈLE (1943–1976).** Born on 3 January 1943 in Brazzaville, he was the son of a military man from Ippy. Battalion leader Fidèle Obrou became Emperor **Bokassa**'s son-in-law on 30 January 1973. The organizer of a failed coup d'etat on 3 February 1976, he fled to Zaire the night of the attack. Arrested at Gemena, Zaire, a few days later, he was returned to Bokassa by General Mobutu. Condemned to death on 13 February 1976, he was immediately executed. His son, who was born on 19 February, was killed—at the orders of the head of state—on 24 February by Dr. **Jean-Bruno Dedeavode**, another of Bokassa's son-in-laws.

**OCCUPATION ACTIVE, POLITIQUE D' (ACTIVE OCCUPATION, POLICY OF).** This euphemism was used to designate the military conquest that Governor General **Martial Merlin** ordered for almost all of present-day Central Africa from 1902 to 1912.

**OLEAGINOUS PRODUCTION.** Central Africa is ecologically favored for the production of a series of oleaginous plants, but this production has never achieved a level sufficient for export. Peanuts and sesame are of good quality. **Cotton**seed is also particularly used for oil.

**OMAR (?–1922).** Oldest son of Sultan **Kobur** of **Dar-al-Kuti**, deposed in 1890 by **Rabih**, Omar achieved a reconciliation with **as-Sanusi** in 1893 and renounced his succession rights. A loyal collaborator of the French, Omar died in **Ndélé** in 1922.

**OMBANGA.** Name given to the post created about 1872 by the Sudanese administration in the **Mofio** states. The post was given to **Rabih** in 1873. The district called Kordofali organized around this post in the Upper **Chinko** and Ouarra valleys is now unpopulated because of the ravages of **slavery**.

**OMBELLA.** Northern tributary of the **Ubangui**, this river was an old artery of commercial penetration.

**ONDOMAT, CHARLES.** Director of President **David Dacko**'s cabinet in 1962, Ondomat was one of the 19 members of the **MESAN** direction committee appointed by the Bambari Congress in 1962, at Dacko's suggestion. Imprisoned on 1 January 1966 by **Jean-Bedel Bokassa**, he was tried on 13 August 1973.

**OPANGAULT, JACQUES.** In October 1958 Opangault, president of the Middle Congo Governing Council, seconded **Barthélémy Boganda**'s greater Central African Republic project and signed an agreement for its realization with him. The French high commissioner's intervention caused the project to fail and made inevitable the proclamation of separate autonomy for each territory of the French Equatorial African Federation. Opangault was replaced not long after by Father Fulbert Youlou.

**OTTO, ACHILLE.** Former Belgian noncommissioned officer, he became assistant director of the **Concessionary Company** of the Sultanates of Upper **Ubangui**. In 1901 Achille Otto signed a convention with Sultan **Bangassou** the terms of which gave the company "the total monopoly, exclusive and absolute, of all **trade** by barter or money throughout **Nzakara** country for all vegetable and animal products" as well as "a monopoly of all transport by bearers or paddlers." Bangassou gave full power to the company to "pursue, in his name, delinquent accomplices or receivers of stolen goods." This convention was disavowed by the French Minister of Colonies, but Otto nonetheless exercised a de facto dictatorship over all of Nzakara country.

**OUADDA.** On 30 April 1913, the French military post of **Mouka** was transferred to Ouadda by Lieutenant Arnould. He built the post on the ruins of a fort that had belonged to **Mahamadi, as-Sanusi**'s officer, who had undertaken the quasi extermination of the population for the Sultan of **Dar-al-Kuti**. The French helped the local leader, Bandassa, reassemble the survivors. In view of the small population of the Ouadda subdivision (about 3,000 inhabitants), it was most often joined to that of **Yalinga** for administrative purposes.

**OUAGANDI.** Leader of the **Banda** Ojoungourou, chosen by the **Ngao** to replace their leader Zama, who had been beheaded by **as-Sanusi** in 1890. In 1892 Ouagandi defeated the **Dar-al-Kuti** troops commanded by **Allah Djabou**.

**OUAKA. Banda** name for the major branch of the Kouango River, the northern tributary of the **Ubangui**. It serves to delineate the region as well as the **prefecture** of Bambari.

**OUAKA, CAMPAIGN OF THE.** Violent combat undertaken in 1910 by the French military against the **Ouaka** populations armed by the **concessionary companies**.

**OUANDA-DJALLÉ.** Rock fortress of the Youlou, Ouanda-Djallé was defended in 1910 by the leader **Djellab** against Kuti troops commanded by **Allah Djabou**. Allah Djabou took control of it in December. After the death of as-**Sanusi** on 12 January 1911, and the French defeat of Allah Djabou on 7 February 1911, as-Sanusi's son **Kamoun** found refuge here with his last troops. On 17 December 1912, the French captain Souclier took over the fortress.

**OUARNAK (or WARNAK).** Title carried by **Wadaïan** officers.

**OUARRA-BANDA.** One of the most brilliant **Banda** officers in the army of **as-Sanusi**, Sultan of **Dar-al-Kuti**.

**OUBANGUI.** *See* UBANGUI.

**OUBANGUI-CHARI.** *See* UBANGUI-SHARI.

**OUDAI.** *See* WADAÏ.

**OUELLÉ (or UELE).** Major branch of the **Ubangui** River that was "discovered" in 1876 by **Georg Schweinfurth**, who thought that this stream was the major branch of the **Shari**. In order to annex Upper Ubangui and the regions between the **Mbomou** and the Ouellé, from 1890 on King **Leopold II** held that the Ubangui stopped at the Ubangui-Kourangui confluence rather than at the Mbomou-Ouellé confluence.

**OUESSO.** Colonial post established on the **Sangha** from which **Pierre Brazza** undertook the occupation of Upper Sangha in 1892.

**OUESSO, DISASTER OF.** On 21 August 1914 a group of French civilians, agents of the Upper Sangha Forestry Company, accompanied by regional guards of the **Ouesso** post and numerous villagers, attacked and burned the little German post of Mbirou. The German steamer *Bonga*, seeing the fire's glow, attacked the French colonists gathered on the steamer *Bougou*. All the passengers were killed, and the French post of Ouesso was occupied the next day by the Germans. Evacuated by the Germans on 31 August, Ouesso was reoccupied a little later by the French. In October 1914 the French garrison was reinforced by a company of the Belgian Congo *force publique*. Ouesso served as a take-off place for the French attack against the German Cameroons in December 1914.

**OUFTERRAH.** Head of the Sudanese district of Kordofali before **Rabih**'s arrival at **Ombanga** in 1873.

– P –

**PAKOUROU (or KPAKOULOU).** Youngest son of Balouka, eldest brother of Sultan Bali and father of **Bangassou**, Pakourou reproached Bali for having profited from the **Rabist** invasion in 1883 by appropriating the majority of Balouka's soldiers and arms. Pakourou's alliance with Bali's other two living brothers, **Ganda** and Moda Boendi, pushed Bangassou to accept a protectorate treaty with King **Leopold**'s officer, **Alphonse Vangele**, in June 1890.

**PAKPA.** Imprisoned at Fort **Crampel** for having led a French column into an ambush, the **Mandjia** guide Pakpa was executed with dynamite in July 1903 by **Fernand-Leopold Gaud**.

**PAMBIA.** Residual population in the Sudan-**Ubangui** area that disappeared in the wars waged by the **Zandé** sultans and **Zubayr**'s **slavers**.

**PANDE.** A once-numerous ethnic group today reduced to a few villages in the Lobaye and Upper **Sangha** basins (notably around Bambio).

**PANGA-PANGA.** Surname of the Arab leader of the area around the falls in the Upper Congo who launched his bands into the **Zandé** country of the **Ouellé** in 1888. Panga-Panga made an alliance with the **Bandia** Sultan **Djabir** to attack **Rafaï**, who was himself allied with another Arab **slaver**, Lembe-Lembe. The Belgian Jerome Becker welcomed Panga-Panga to King **Leopold**'s post at Basoko.

**PAOURA.** The **Banda-Vidri** leader of the **Yalinga** region, Paoura, after having been attacked by **Rafaï**'s son **Hetman**, then by **Bangassou**, designated his Zanzibari adviser, **Muhammad Said**, to administer the Vidri country. Paoura allied himself with the **Nzakara** leader Bazouma to attack the French post of Fouroumbala in Lower Kotto.

**PARTI DU REGROUPEMENT AFRICAN (PRA; AFRICAN RE-GROUPING PARTY).** In 1958 **Barthélémy Boganda** approached Leopold Sedar Senghor's Parti du Regroupement Africain. In July 1958, the Mouvement pour l'évolution sociale de l'Afrique Noire (**MESAN**; Movement for the Social Evolution of Black Africa) was represented by a delegation composed of **Abel Goumba**, **David Dacko**, and **Albert Fayama** at the Cotonou Congress organized by the PRA. At the close of the Congress, Boganda, hostile like Senghor to a "balkanization" of Africa, decided to link MESAN with the PRA.

**PATASSÉ, ANGE (1937–).** Born in January 1937 in Paoua (Ouham-Pende), Ange Patassé completed his **agricultural** studies in France and rapidly advanced to become the director of the Central African Republic's agricultural services. In 1966 **Jean-Bedel Bokassa** appointed him Minister of Rural Development. In 1976 he became prime minister of a government called the Conseil de la Revolution (Council of the Revolution). In December 1976 Bokassa conferred the presidency of the first imperial government on Patassé. Patassé, who planned to relegate Bokassa to the Imperial Court of **Berengo**, was soon disappointed. The emperor continued to exercise, without any delegation of authority, all of the real power. Discord grew, and in July 1978 Bokassa replaced Ange Patassé with **Henri Maïdou**.

As president-director general of the Société Centrafricaine d'Agriculture (Central African Agriculture Association) in semiexile in Paris, Patassé became the head of a Front de Libération du Peuple

Centrafricain (FLPC; Front for the Liberation of the Central African People). In June 1979 he launched an appeal for insurrection from Paris. Together with **Sylvestre Bangui**'s Front de Liberation des Oubanguiens (FLO; Ubangui People's Liberation Front), the Association Nationale des Etudiants Centrafricains (ANECA; National Association of Central African Students), and Dr. **Abel Goumba**'s Front Patriotique Oubanguie (FPO; Ubanguian Patriotic Front), he accepted the creation of a common action front to overthrow Bokassa. This movement was focused around the former president of the first Ubanguian government. Prevented from returning directly to Bangui after Bokassa's overthrow, Patassé went to Tripoli.

Arriving in Bangui from Libya on 24 October 1979, he was arrested at the airport. Imprisoned at **Ngaragba**, he was not released until 27 November 1980, after a nonsuit ordinance. In spite of the presence of several of his supporters in the Dacko government, he kept his FLPC party in opposition and ran for president in the 15 March 1981 election. Riots broke out when it was announced that he had won the majority of the votes in the city of Bangui. When Dacko resigned on 1 September 1981, Patassé fled to Paris. On 27 February 1982 he returned to Bangui planning to seize power. On 3 March 1982 his attempted coup failed due to the intervention of the presidential guard commanded by the French officer, Colonel **Jean-Claude Mantion**. Patassé, calling on the support of the first secretary of the French Socialist Party, took refuge in the French embassy. General **André Kolingba** unsuccessfully demanded that Patassé be turned over to him for judgment. After mediation by Guy Penne, President François Mitterrand's adviser, a French military plane took Ange Patassé to Togo, where he had obtained political asylum. Involved in agricultural and commercial operations in that country, Patassé returned to Central Africa, after 13 years in exile, when the multiparty system was restored.

He was the Mouvement pour la Libération du Peuple Centrafricain (MLPC; Movement for the Liberation of the Central African People) candidate for the presidential elections of September 1993 and was elected in the second round with 52.5 percent of the votes, more than Abel Goumba (45.6 percent). Former Presidents Dacko and Kolingba had also been present in the first round but were eliminated. Before his mandate expired, Ange Patassé was confronted by three **army rebellions**. During each of those uprisings, the rebels asked Patassé to resign; he had to call upon his ambassador in Paris, **Jean-Paul Ngoupandé**, to help him put together a Gouvernement d'Unité Nationale (GUN; Government of National Unity). Contrary to rumors, Patassé was reelected on 19 September 1999 as president of the Republic in the first round, well ahead of his contenders. In March 2003, as he returned from an African conference, he learned in Yaoundé that General **François Bozizé** had taken power. He took refuge in Lomé, where President Eyadema granted him asylum. Patassé was accused by Human Rights Watch of crimes against humanity. Guilty of many illegal doings, he is widely held responsible for his country's ruin.

**PATRI (or KPATILI).** A cluster of peoples in Lower **Mbomou** and Lower Kotto before the creation of the **Bandia** and **Zandé** states.

**PAYAO, ALBERT.** Chosen by President **David Dacko** on 1 May 1959 as Minister of Finance, Economy and Commerce. As Minister of **Agriculture** four years later, he carried out the structural reform of the **cotton** sector.

**PAYSANNATS (PEASANT SETTLEMENTS).** The name given to the pilot experiments carried out in the rural milieu by the French colonial administration (governor general of French Equatorial Africa's memo of 20 October 1952). These experiments were inspired by operations carried out by the Belgians in the Congo.

**PEDRON, REVEREND FATHER MARC (1877–1936).** Born in Surzur (Morbihan) on 22 March 1877, he died there on 25 September 1936. Father Pedron was the founder of the **Berberati** Mission in 1923 and the author of a **Baya** (Gbaya) language catechism.

**PEHOUA, FRANÇOIS.** Treasury inspector, director of the Banque des Etats de l'Afrique Centrale (BEAC; Central African States Bank) first in **Bangui** and later in Yaounde. In 1979 he founded an opposition group.

**PENDE.** With the Mberd, the Pende, in the west of the Central African Republic forms the Logone River. Its name is joined to the Ouham, name of the major branch of the Bahr-Sara, itself a branch of the **Shari**, to designate one of the most highly populated **prefectures** of the country.

**PERRIN.** Agent of the Kotto company in March 1901, he was arrested by **Captain Victor Mahieu** for homicide, armed looting, and theft.

**PETHERICK, JOHN.** Welsh engineer hired by **Abou Mouri Ali** to search for coalmines in the Sudan. He was a trader at El Obeid and an English Vice Consul. Petherick founded Mechra-el-Reck in 1853. A few years later, he was suspected of having participated in the Bahr-el-Ghazal **slave** traffic.

**PETITS BLANCS (LITTLE WHITES).** The expression designated the French employees and lower-level officials who opposed all African promotion during the colonial period. The **Brazzaville Conference** in February 1944 had to recommend a strict control of Europeans coming to settle in the colony. It advocated that certain "moral conditions, health and professional knowledge" as well as "a certain culture and a good education" be required.

**PETROCA (SOCIETE DES PETROLES DE CENTRAFRIQUE; CENTRAL AFRICAN OIL COMPANY).** This national **company** holds a monopoly on the storing and distribution of oil products in Central Africa. An 18 September 1998 law decree regarding the liberalization of the oil industry transformed this company into a mixed-capital company that includes the Central African state (75 percent) and the Shell, Fina-France, Agip, Total, and Mobil companies (25 percent). Although it only held 7 percent of the shares, Total was designated as technical partner.

**PIERRE, CHARLES.** Director of the **concessionary company** of the Upper **Ubangui** sultanates, Pierre brought about the **Rafaï-Ndélé** connection in 1899, which the Belgians of the Upper Ubangui had failed to do a few years before.

**POLITICAL PARTIES.** The multiparty system was established in 1992. At present, the Mouvement pour la Libération du Peuple

Centrafricain (MLPC; Movement for the Liberation of the Central African People), led by President **Ange Patassé** since the party congress in November 1995, is only supported by the Parti Libéral Démocrate (PLD; Liberal Democratic Party), which has seven elected deputies; the Convention Nationale (National Convention, four elected deputies), and the **MESAN** (one elected deputy). The Conseil Démocratique des Partis d'Opposition (CODEPO; Democratic Council for the Opposition Parties) includes the Alliance pour la Démocratie et le Progrès (ADP; Alliance for Democracy and Progress, six elected deputies), the Forum Civique (Civil Forum, one elected deputy), the Front Patriotique pour le Progrès (FPP; Patriotic Front for Progress, seven elected deputies), the Mouvement pour la Démocratie et la Renaissance en Centrafrique (MDREC; Movement for Democracy and the Rebirth of Central Africa, one elected deputy), the Parti Social Démocrate (PSD; Social-Democratic Party, three elected deputies), and the Union pour le Développement et la Renaissance Centrafricaine (Union for the Central African Development and Rebirth, a nonparliamentary group).

**POLITIQUE INDIGÈNE (COLONIAL MEMORANDA).** The evolution of the *politique indigène* of the French colonial authorities appears clearly in reading two large memoranda, that of Minister **Etienne Clementel** (letter of instructions published in the *Journal Officiel de la République Française*, 14 February 1906, pp. 983–987) and Governor General **Félix Eboué**'s memorandum of 8 November 1941, published by the *Journal Officiel de l'AEF* (1 December 1941, pp. 687–699). The first, which betrayed a spectacular regression of **Pierre Brazza**'s African policies, held that the African population was a population "in infancy" and that it would be necessary to prevent "the Blacks" from contracting "new vices" from contact with the new civilization. It would be necessary to help these "primitive populations, little by little," to evolve toward "a higher ideal." The ministerial instructions reflected the contempt with which the traditional African societies were still considered. For the second, after almost 40 years of colonization, a similar attitude and the disorderly exploitation of which the colonizers were found guilty made the colony run the risk of collapsing. It tardily recognized the need to search out traditional leaders who embodied the group and were recognized by custom. It took notice of indigenous **civil servants**, "slackers in the brush," who had no brakes but "the fear of prison."

The Felix Eboué memorandum was one of the documents upon which the imperial **Brazzaville Conference** was based. This conference opened on 30 January 1944 and was presided over by **General Charles de Gaulle**. Governor General **Paul Chauvet**'s memorandum of 4 April 1955 (*Circulaires de base* 1952–1956 of the high commissioner of the French Republic in French Equatorial Africa, Official Printing Office, Brazzaville) verified the impossibility of a return to ancient social structures. It recommended developing the political **education** of the population to create rural communities in place of administrative townships. It was these policies that gave **Barthélémy Boganda** and his successors the idea of trying to reconstitute a rural society after the colonial test.

**POMBEIROS.** Name given to the Congolese or *métis* (half-breed) who in the 19th century served as intermediaries for the Portuguese **slave** buyers or their coastal intermediaries. The name *pombeiros* was given them because their establishments were found precisely on the Mpoumbou (Stanley Pool), from whence numerous slaves flowed, notably from the **Sangha** and **Ubangui** basins.

**PONCET, AMBROISE and JULES.** French traders who carved out a considerable territory in the Sudano-**Ubanguian** area in association with the Upper Nile **slavers**. In 1867, after the scandal provoked by the revelations of their activities, the Poncet brothers were obliged to sell off their domain to a "djobel **company**" directed by Captain Ghattas. The establishments (*zeriba*) then fell to **Zubayr**, who gave himself the title of sheik, and strove to found a vast merchant state resembling the ancient Tekrourian states of the north.

**PONEL, EDMOND.** Zone leader who arrived in Bangui on 9 August 1890. Assisted by the post leader, **Alphonse Fondere**, Ponel had a hard time maintaining the post without men, ammunition, or supplies. The help of the **Paul Crampel** mission, though, permitted Ponel to save the post. In March 1892, Ponel accompanied **Pierre Brazza** to Upper **Sangha**.

**PORTAGE.** For many years, human portage was accomplished by the use of dugout canoes, the only means of transport utilized for the exportation of products and the importation of merchandise, arms, and equipment. The recruitment of porters, especially to cross the divide between the **Ubangui** and the **Shari**, provoked an uprising among the population. Already in 1900, the explorer **Alfred Fourneau** noted the ravages caused by portage among the **Mandjia** population. The military operations necessitated by the conquest of Chad made portage still more oppressive. Villages were required to supply not only carriers but also their food. **Pierre Brazza**'s 1905 inspection in the region made the disastrous consequences of such a system evident.

A press campaign by the *Journal* in July 1912 again revealed the scandal of bearer recruitment between the Ubangui and the Shari. The wives of bearers were held as hostages during their husbands' entire term of forced labor. In 1920 Governor General Angoulvant announced the abandonment of the direct railroad project between Bangui and Fort Crampel, and he let it be known that it "was difficult to foresee for a long time the suppression of human portage." The commercial companies considered portage as "the only means of transport adapted to the degree of the country's development." The construction, by Governor **Auguste Lamblin** in 1924–1925, of a network of tracks passable by automobile, which were built practically without credit but with the help of villagers, finally permitted this plague to be stopped. Portage had struck a very hard blow on the Mandjia and **Banda** populations in the center of the old **Ubangui-Shari** colony.

**POTAGOS, PANEGIOTES.** This Peloponnesian Greek traveler had traveled throughout Europe and Asia before establishing himself in Cairo. There, in 1876, he met **Georg Schweinfurth**, who told Potagos about his interest in exploring the unknown area between the **Rounga**, reached by **Gustav Nachtigal**, and the **Ouellé**, known to Schweinfurth himself. Thus, from June 1876 to March 1877 Panegiotes Potagos traveled throughout the **Mbomou** basin. His travel account, translated into French in 1885, is little more than a banal travel notebook that accumulates errors and confusion. For example, the Ouellé is presented as a branch of the Ogoué! As imperfect as it was, however, this account does provide some useful information on the situation of the **Bandia** sultanates in 1876.

**POUMEYRAC, LEON MASREDON DE.** The **Nzakara** leader **Ganda** persuaded Poumeyrac, **Victor Liotard**'s adjunct director of Upper **Ubangui**, that his villages were threatened by the **Banda** Bougbou, their hereditary enemies. Poumeyrac burned two Bougbou villages, but on 17 May his small troop was encircled. He fell with his throat cut by a throwing knife. Among the dead were five of Ganda's sons, a son of Labassou, 35 Nzakara, and 12 **Yakoma**. In France, Poumeyrac's death was mistakenly blamed on Belgian intrigue. The arrival of the Duke d'Uzes's mission permitted Liotard to attack the Bougbou in February 1893. He forced them to make peace and restore the skulls of Poumeyrac and his companions.

**PREFECTS, SUBPREFECTS.** In 1960 the districts and the regions of the former colonial territory of **Ubangui-Shari** were maintained by the Central African state both in their boundaries and their structures. They were simply renamed prefectures and subprefectures. The French administrators were rapidly replaced by Central African subprefects and prefects. However, these replacements rapidly became suspect in the eyes of their government, as much due to their political unreliability as for the frequency of their embezzlement of public funds. A few of them were brought to justice. A 6 November 1964 decree went so far as creating a "vigilance committee" in each prefecture to regulate the numerous differences between the prefectural administration and the party representatives. Later on, posts of prefectural secretary-general were created. But the Central African administration never had a sufficient number of **civil servants** of a good level to fill the many assignments that had formerly been the responsibility of the colonial administrators.

**PRINS, PIERRE.** A companion of **Emile Gentil**, Prins was appointed colonial administrator and sent in November 1897 to as-**Sanusi**, who was then at **Ara**. Prins obtained as-Sanusi's neutrality, and in return as-Sanusi was not bothered about **Paul Crampel**'s murder. Then transferred to **Rafaï**, on 31 December 1900, Prins received a call to aid the **Kreich** Sultan, **Said Baldas**, and the Koursi, Abba, who represented the King of **Wadaï** in Upper Kotto. On 11 March, Prins signed a protectorate treaty with the Kreich leader and obtained Wadaï's renunciation of control over the region. Upon his return to

Rafaï, Prins was not supported by his superiors. All the territory he had covered had been conceded to the **concessionary company** of Sultanates of the Upper **Ubangui**, and the government did not intend to invest another man or franc on the occupation of **Banda** or Kreich country. These were abandoned to more than 10 years of as-Sanusi's raids. The text of Prins's treaty and his report of the mission constitute a precious document on an area that is uninhabited today.

**PRINTZI.** One of **Zubayr**'s principal lieutenants and **slave** suppliers in **Mbomou** in 1876.

**PROKOS, CAPTAIN GEORGES.** Captain Prokos directed the 1907 to 1909 "pacification" operations carried out by the French in the Lobaye and Ibenga regions, which were revolting against the **concessionary companies**.

**PROTESTANT MISSIONS.** *See* MISSIONS, PROTESTANT.

**PSIMHIS, JEAN LOUIS.** He was the CAR ambassador to Paris in 1967 and served as minister a number of times. He was Minister of National Education in 1979 at the time of the student uprising. He served as foreign minister under **André Kolingba**.

## – R –

**RABIH (or RABI, RABAH) (1845–1900).** Born about 1845 in the province of Khartoum, Rabih, after having served in the Egyptian army, entered the service of **Zubayr** for whom he became the main lieutenant in 1872. Like all the former lieutenants of merchant lords, he became a Sudanese civil servant and commanded a post in the **Chinko** region. In 1878 he supported Souleiman ben Zubayr in his insurrection, but in 1879 he refused to follow his submission. From 1879 to 1890, Rabih's action was limited to the Central African area. He waged many wars against the **Banda**, the **Kreich**, and other ethnic groups in the north, east, and center of the country. It was in Central Africa that Rabih put together his strong army. Nevertheless, in 1883 he failed against the **Nzakara** in the south and in 1885 against the **Mandjia** in the west. Rabih refused to join the Mahdist army in spite of the invitations made to him. In 1890 he removed **Kobur** as Sultan of **Dar-al-Kuti** and replaced him with **as-Sanusi**, who broke with the King of **Wadaï**, suzerain of the country.

In 1891–1892, Rabih ravaged Sara country. Then, in less than two years, due to his army's superiority, he made himself master of the **Baguirmi** kingdom, conquered the Bornu empire, and threatened the **Fulbé** Sokoto empire. In 1897 Rabih allowed **Emile Gentil** to make his way to the banks of Lake Chad. In 1899 the French, under the protectorate that they had placed over the Baguirmi and Dar-al-Kuti, went to battle with Rabih's army. The April 1900 coming together in Chad of three French missions that had left from Algeria, Senegal, and Bangui brought about Rabih's defeat and death under the walls of Kousseri.

**RABIH, OFFICERS OF.** Numerous Central Africans in Rabih's army were promoted to important positions. Among Rabih's most celebrated officers can be cited his assistants **Hassein** and Mbringui, both **Banda** Tombago. The officers Mangavella and Guerimbassa were also Banda, as were **Fad al Mola**, Ngomo, and the banner leader **Capsul**. The latter particularly appreciated by Rabih. He was killed at Kousseri.

**RAFAÏ.** Son of the **Bandia** leader, Bangoye or **Bangui**, the young Rafaï was noticed by the Sudanese merchant Bilinza, who had him taken to **Zubayr**. There Rafaï rejoined his cousin **Bacpayo**, who had adopted the name **Djabir**. After Zubayr's imprisonment in Cairo, Rafaï and Djabir were taken to Bandia country by **Rafaï-Aga**.

**RAFAÏ-AGA.** Natural son of the merchant Al Arbad, Rafaï-Aga was **Zubayr**'s friend and administered the Bandia zone for him in 1876.

**RAMEDANE, JEROME (1936–1981).** Central African naïve painter, author of many watercolors of the Central African country and of major historical events in the land. His work has been publicized in Europe by René Deverdun, an engineer in a **cotton** factory, himself a painter.

**RATO (SATE-LATO or SATE-RATO). Bandia** sultan, great-grandson of Gbelou and son of Dounga. His lineage never admitted the predominance of Bari and his son, **Bangassou**, in **Nzakara** country. In April 1893, Rato's independence was so apparent that the Belgian Lieutenant **Léon Hanolet** concluded a protectorate treaty with him. Sate-Rato's army carried out a campaign against the **Banda-Vidri** in 1897. Administrator **Henry** avoided a war between Bangassou and Rato in 1898. However, in 1900 Bangassou's son, Mbari, attacked Rato with 900 men. His territory was lost but, Rato was able to find refuge with **Rafaï**.

**RDA (RASSEMBLEMENT DEMOCRATIQUE AFRICAIN; AFRICAN DEMOCRATIC RALLY).** This large party, with branches all over French West Africa and French Equatorial Africa, included a section in **Ubangui-Shari** in 1951 that **Antoine Darlan** joined. But this section never gained a large audience due to competition from the Mouvement pour l'évolution sociale de l'Afrique Noire (**MESAN**; Movement for the Social Evolution of Black Africa). The RDA, like all political parties other than MESAN, was forbidden by **David Dacko** in 1962.

**REBELS, REBELLION.** *See* ARMY.

**REFERENDUM.** On 13 July 1958, **Barthélémy Boganda** took a stand for the immediate **independence** of **Ubangui-Shari** within a broad Franco-African Confederated Republic. He obtained from **General Charles de Gaulle** the inclusion of the right to independence in the projected **constitution**. On 7 September, he made it known that he was advising a "yes" vote in the 28 September constitutional referendum.

**REMY, REVEREND FATHER JULES (1863–1942).** Born on 15 June 1863 in Chaource, he died 11 January 1942 in Langonnet. A Holy Ghost missionary, Father Remy arrived in **Bangui** on 9 February 1893, and on 15 February he chose the site of the future **Saint Paul Mission** at the village of the leader Souguebiou. In January 1894 the construction of the mission began. In September 1894 Father Remy and Father Joseph Moreau founded a second mission near the confluence of the Kemo and the **Ubangui** (Holy Family Mission).

**RENARD, CAPTAIN.** As secretary general of the French Congolese Union, a sort of pressure group created in 1901 that united the directors of the **concessionary companies**, Captain Renard spearheaded a very lively campaign against the colonial administration.

**RENARD, EDOUARD.** Prefect of the Seine, Edouard Renard was designated in 1934 to succeed the head of French Equatorial Africa, Governor General **Raphael Antonetti**, who left Brazzaville after a 10-year proconsulate. Edouard Renard, underestimating the importance of an administration distributed over all the territory, reorganized French Equatorial Africa, making of it a unified colony divided into four regions. The **Ubangui-Shari**, larger than the present Central African territory and making up half of French Equatorial Africa's population, was divided into six **departements**. An administrative school, called Ecole des Cadres and later Edouard Renard School, opened in Brazzaville. Its objective was to rapidly give each subdivision headquarters in French Equatorial Africa an indigenous monitor. These monitors were to be in charge of a school and act as a sort of town clerk. In March 1935 Governor General Renard, who had come to **Bangui**, disappeared in an airplane crash near Bolobo in the Belgian Congo.

**REQUIRED SERVICE.** To the head **tax**, which hit all men and women during the colonial period, was added a tax of required days of work organized by the decree of 9 April 1915. This text provided for four categories of work for which all able-bodied citizens could be used without pay. Among these, the care of **roads** and villages held a major place. This required service was suppressed in 1946.

**RESTE DE ROCCA, DIEUDONNE, FRANÇOIS-JOSEPH (1879–1976).** Governor General Reste was born in Pia (Pyrennées Orientales) on 22 May 1879, and died in Perthus (Pyrennées Orientales) on 15 March 1976. He left the Colonial School in 1900, and succeeded **Edouard Renard** at the head of French Equatorial Africa on 20 April 1935. He occupied this post until 2 May 1939, when he retired. Reste should be given credit for the restoration of a local administration compromised by the lack of personnel in the centralist reform of 1934, the reconstitution of an **economy** scourged by the depression, and certainly the softening of a coercive regime.

**REVOLUTIONARY COUNCIL.** *See* CONSEIL REVOLUTIONNAIRE.

**RIVIEREZ, HECTOR.** Recommended to **Barthélémy Boganda** by the League against anti-Semitism and Racism (LICA), this Parisian lawyer of Guyanese origin played an important role in **Ubanguian** political life from 1951 to 1959. He was successively elected senator, then president of the **Territorial Assembly**. After Boganda's death, President **David Dacko** appointed him president of the Supreme Court. Without ties in the country, Rivierez preferred to continue a political career in Guyana, where he was a deputy from 1967 on.

**ROADS.** The network of roads in the Central African Republic is in poor condition due to its lack of maintenance. At the end of the 20th century, there were 22,260 kilometers of roads suitable for vehicles — only 458 of which were asphalted.

**ROBERT, OLIVIER.** A French industrialist, Olivier Robert joined **Roger Guerillot, René Naud, René Chambellant**, and a small group of French in the private sector in 1954, within the Intergroup Libéral Oubanguien (ILO; **Ubanguian** Liberal Intergroup), in supporting **Barthélémy Boganda**. This group hoped to associate Boganda with their business ventures.

**ROUANET, GUSTAVE.** Socialist deputy from Paris, his intervention at the Chamber of Deputies on 19–21 February 1906, during the great parliamentary debate on the Congo, is considered one of the first and decisive offensives of French anticolonialism. Rouanet defended the Central African population, which was so savagely exploited by the **concessionary companies**.

**ROULET MISSION.** Leaving the **Ubangui**, Captain Roulet reached Gara-Chambe on the Nile with an escort of 40 riflemen on 20 March 1899.

**ROUNGA.** A cluster of peoples of **Banda** origin and Muslim religion settled in the Chad-Central African area. Dar Rounga, first subject to **Darfur**, fell under the suzerainty of the King of **Wadaï** in the 19th century. The coup d'etat provoked by **Rabih** in Kuti made **Muhammad as-Sanusi** the Sultan of **Dar-al-Kuti** and of Dar Rounga. As-Sanusi was never able, though, to make himself master of Dar Rounga.

**ROUX, BATTALION LEADER ROBERT DE.** Roux was the founder of the BM2, the **Ubanguian** fighting unit that participated in all of the military action of the **Free French** forces in the Middle East, then found fame at **Bir-Hakeim** in 1942.

**RPF (RASSEMBLEMENT DU PEUPLE FRANÇAIS; FRENCH PEOPLE'S UNION).** In 1950, the RPF had a large following among the French in **Ubangui** who were hostile to the reforms and the up-grading of status among the local population. The colonists created many RPF sections throughout the colony, and these were joined by leaders and civil servants hostile to **Barthélémy Boganda**. This action resulted, among other things, in making the term RPF a synonym for the colonial regime and, by extension, for forced labor and coercion in the **Sango** lingua franca. In 1953, during his stay in **Bangui**, **General Charles de Gaulle** severely judged the actions of the local RPF.

**RUBBER.** From the beginning of the 20th century, rubber gathered from vines and roots made up one of the principal export products from the Congo and **Ubangui**. This production offered an opportunity for the worst abuses. The market collapse in 1920–1922 forced the administration to look for new resources, but the rising prices in 1924 provoked new exactions on the part of the **concessionary companies**. These companies were sharply denounced by **André Gide**, and his book *Voyage au Congo* (Travels in the Congo) was distributed to the Bureau International du Travail (BIT; International Labor Bureau) in 1928 as a document on forced labor. About 1925 **cotton** was progressively introduced into Ubanguian villages to avoid the forced gathering of wild rubber. Plantings of millions of ceara rubber plants around these villages were soon overcome by the savannah, an apparent failure. During World War II, an attempt once again to force the gathering of wild rubber was very poorly received by the population. At the end of the hostilities, a Cameroonian society—the SAFA—established a large hevea rubber plantation in the Lobaye **forest**, which has an annual production of about 1,000 metric tons.

**RURAL HOUSING.** Around 1920, the colonial administration imposed an important change of rural housing. It ordered the replacement of the traditional round houses by large rectangular ones of clay brick with several rooms. The change was, in fact, a return to techniques used before the great insecurity of the **slave**-war period.

**RUTH-ROLLAND, JEANNE MARIE (A.K.A. THE "PASSIONARIA CENTRAFRICAINE") (1937–1995).** Born in 1937 of a French father, Jeanne Ruth was a supervisor for the national **education** system in 1956, then a teacher until 1964. She married a French armsdealer from **Bangui**, with whom she had five children. She joined the Central African **army** as a social worker, then headed the army social services. She left the army with the rank of battalion chief. In 1979 she becomes an adviser, then the Minister for the Promotion of Women's Status. As such she helped the street children of Bangui and was nicknamed "Aunt Ruth." She also headed the Central African Red Cross. In 1986 General-President **André Kolingba**, who did not want to hear her overly honest criticism, threw her in jail, where she remained for five years. In 1992 she was a candidate in the first multiparty elections and was triumphantly elected as deputy of Bakouma. But General Kolingba had the ballot annulled. In that same year, she was nevertheless appointed Social Affairs Minister, and she remained in the government until the presidential election of 22 August 1993 for which she was a candidate—the first woman candidate ever to run for president on the continent. She was again elected as deputy in Bakoume and ran a gold prospectors' consortium in the east of the country. She indulged in another of her passions, which was diamond collecting. Taken ill, she was evacuated to France and died in a Paris hospital on 4 June 1995.

– S –

**SAB (SOCIETE ANONYME BELGE DU HAUT-CONGO; BELGIAN COMPANY OF THE UPPER CONGO).** Founded in Brussels on 10 December 1888, this Belgian company, which was very active in the Congolese banks, was one of the first European companies to trade in **Ubangui**. As early as 1891, at the same time as its Dutch (NAHV) and French (DAUMAS) rivals, it opened a factory at the small French **administrative post** of **Bangui**.

**SABANGA.** This generic name was given by the **Banda** to the ethnic group that inhabited the **Ubanguian** plateau before them. It means, "Those who pull the jawbone" (implying their prisoners). The **Nzakara**, **Patri**, and Dokoa were part of this group. There are only three small groups of Sabanga now left in the middle of Central Africa. These have, for the most part, adopted the Banda language for several generations. The **Bandia** Sultans who laid claim to Sabanga origin recognize Bakia or Baza as their mythical ancestor. The Dabanga know him as a legendary leader who led their group from the Nile basin to the Ubangui basin.

**SABANGA RIVER.** In 1860 **Zubayr** gave this name to the Kotto, a tributary of the **Ubangui**.

**SACCAS, ATHANAISE MICHEL (1911–1985).** Born in Janina (Greece) on 10 May 1911, he died in Savoie (France) on 20 July 1985. He was a horticulture teacher in Patras from 1933 to 1938, an engineer in the French national **agriculture** school in Grignon in 1941, then an attaché to the Centre national pour la recherche scientifique (CNRS; National Center for Scientific Research), the National Museum of Natural History in Paris, and the Office de la Recherche Scientifique et Technique Outre-Mer (ORSTOM; Overseas Science and Technique Studies Center). As Research Director at the Boukoko Research Center in Central Africa, he ran this Center from 1958 to 1983. He developed new species of plants, several of which were **coffee** trees. He was involved in research on cryptogamic diseases that destroy many plantations. A close friend of the first leaders of the Central African Republic, he was awarded the highest rank of the Central African Order of Merit.

**SACHER, OTTO.** Born in Prague, he was a lieutenant in the Czechoslovakian army and joined the French Foreign Legion in 1940. He went to London and took part in the **Free French** combat in Egypt, Libya, and Syria. In 1944 he joined the Czech legion, which was integrated into the Red Army. He took part as a colonel in the liberation of his country. In 1948 he settled in the Lobaye to run a **coffee** plantation. In 1960 he was recruited by President **David Dacko** to be bailiff of **Ngaragba** Prison. He maintained this post during Emperor **Bokassa**'s regime and became a Central African citizen. On 14 July

1972, after a six-month sentence for the escape of a prisoner, he was replaced as director of the prison by Captain Edouard Mbongo, becoming the latter's technical adviser.

**SACOD (SOCIETE ANONYME DE COMMERCIALISATION DE L'OR ET DU DIAMANT; GOLD AND DIAMOND MARKETING COMPANY).** One of the three **diamond** purchasing bureaus approved in 1962. This company was part of a Dutch group. One of its Directors, the former French Minister Edmond Hubler, was drawn into an ambush and killed on 28 December 1965, near **Bangui**.

**SAFARIS.** In 1965 President **David Dacko**, striving to develop big-game hunt tourism, granted large areas to safari organizers for wealthy foreign hunters.

**SAID BALDAS.** A son of Baldas, the great **Kreich** leader whose authority stretched from **Ndélé** to **Zubayr**, young Said Baldas was taken to the Sudan by Zubayr. Upon his return to Upper Kotto, he accepted **Wadaï** suzerainty along with his **Dar-al-Kuti** neighbors and some of the **Banda** leaders. Threatened by **as-Sanusi**, the Dar-al-Kuti Sultan put in place by **Rabih** in 1890, Said Baldas successfully resisted. In 1900 he called for Wadaïan help, and they sent him a *koursi* (a sort of consul) but no help. He therefore sought help from the French at **Mbomou**. Administrator **Pierre Prins** granted him a protectorate treaty in 1901, but this was disavowed by the French government. Attacked by as-Sanusi, Said Baldas was forced to flee into the Sudan with his surviving followers. His capital and all of the Kreich localities were destroyed. His country became a desert.

**SAID (or SAIM) MUHAMMAD.** A Zanzibari noncommissioned officer and a deserter from the Public Force of the Congo Free State, he became **Bangassou**'s brother-in-law and also one of his principal war leaders. In 1901 he attacked the **Vidri** for the Sultan, but was forced to retreat as **Rafaï**'s troops had already cleansed the area. In 1905, Said left his new Guita-Koulouba residence to occupy Bangassou's Vidri country. Then Said was chosen by the French as head of the canton created by them in 1912 at **Yalinga**. After 20 years of service, he was accused of squandering the sum total of the **tax** collected by his diligence, and he hanged himself.

**SAINT FAMILLE DES BANZIRIS.** This was the second **Catholic mission** in **Ubangui**. It was founded on 12 November 1894 in **Banziri** country by Fathers Moreau and Gourdy. It was closed in 1929.

**SAINT-MART, PIERRE DE (1885–1965).** Born in Verdun (Meuse) on 12 July 1885, he died in Paris on 16 September 1965. On 30 August 1940, the interim governor of **Ubangui-Shari**, Pierre de Saint-Mart, announced the territory's rallying to Colonel **René Edgar de Larminat**, who had come in **General Charles de Gaulle**'s name to take power in Brazzaville. He had to face Arms Commander **Henri Cammas** and his officers, who refused to join and remained holed up in the military camp until 3 September. Cammas was ultimately forced to surrender as the **Bouar**, Bambari, and **Bria** garrisons had not followed him. Governor de Saint-Mart was appointed governor general of Madagascar when that territory joined the **Free French**. He retired in 1947.

**SAINT PAUL DES RAPIDES.** First **Catholic mission** in **Ubangui**, it was founded on 17 April 1894 by Monsignor **Prosper Augounard** near the **Bangui administrative post**.

**SAINT-SYLVESTRE, COUP D'ETAT OF.** On 1 December 1965, President **David Dacko** appeared to the guests invited for the National Festival as morally and physically exhausted. **Adama-Tamboux**, the president of the **National Assembly**, openly conspired against him. Colonel **Jean-Bedel Bokassa**, the army chief of staff, who had been refused support for the gendarmerie by the Assembly, accused Dacko of giving the country away to the People's Republic of China. On 31 December Dacko, having destroyed his personal papers and dismissed his personnel, left the presidential palace. The next day the leader of the gendarmerie, Captain **Jean Izamo**—according to Bokassa's version of the facts to justify his actions—with what seemed to him to be the French ambassador's approval, took power without any bloodshed. During the night, alerted by members of Dacko's entourage and fearing arrest,

Colonel Bokassa decided to forestall the coup d'etat. Under the pretext of signing some administrative minutes for the end of the year, he called Izamo to Camp de Roux during the night. Bokassa seized Izamo and executed him on the parade ground. Captain **Alexander Banza** took over the administrative centers, where the ministers, diplomats, colonists, and high officials were celebrating the New Year.

The ministers were arrested. One of them, **Maurice Dejean**, was killed. The **army** captured the gendarmerie camp after a rapid exchange of fire. On 1 January Bokassa and Banza took possession of the presidential palace, which they found empty. Bokassa feared French intervention and was prepared to renounce, but he was threatened by Banza. Captain Banza occupied the airport, then arrested Dacko on the road to **Mbaïki** and brought him back to the presidential palace. At 5:30 a.m., the Central African president under threat signed his resignation and the transfer of all his powers to Colonel Bokassa. It was not until morning that the population of greater **Bangui**, which had heard shots without knowing what was happening, learned from the Central African Radio that the army had taken over and the government had resigned. Bokassa proclaimed: "The time for justice has come. The **bourgeoisie** is abolished and a new era of equality among all citizens is established."

In the days that followed, Bokassa dissolved the **Assembly** and appointed a Conseil Révolutionnaire (**Revolutionary Council**) made up of military and civilian personnel (three of whom were Dacko's ministers—**Jean-Arthur Bandio**, **François Gueret**, and **Antoine Guimali**). One of the French advisers drew up **constitutional** acts for him modeled after those taken by Marshal Petain after the overthrow of the French Third Republic. The announcement of the Bangui coup d'etat irritated **General Charles de Gaulle**, who waited several months before receiving a member of the new Central African government.

**SAINTOYANT, CAPTAIN JULES.** Born in Nemours in 1869, Captain Saintoyant was designated to accompany **Pierre Brazza** on his 1905 inspection mission. Upon his return to France, struck by lightning, he was forced into an unanticipated retirement, which allowed him to write a comprehensive history of French colonialism.

**SALAMAT.** In 1890 **Rabih** was encamped in **Dar-al-Kuti**, at the head of which he had placed **Muhammad as-Sanusi**. Here Rabih established relations with the Salamat Arabs settled in the Chad territory in the vicinity of Lake Iro, a caravan junction of the first importance. The Salamat alliance allowed Rabih to forward his **slave** convoys and receive arms. It permitted him to conquer the **Baguirmi** and then take over the empire of Bornu. The Salamat alliance, though, coming after the coup d'etat perpetrated by **Wadaï**'s vassal-state, Kouti, set off a permanent state of war between Rabih and Wadaï.

**SALUT ECONOMIQUE.** *See* COMMITTEE OF ECONOMIC SAFETY.

**SAMBA-NGOTTO.** In October 1925, during his journey to the Congo and **Ubangui**, the writer **André Gide** arrived at Boda in the official car of **Auguste Lamblin**, the governor of Ubangui. Samba-Gotto, leader of the **Boffis** of Poutem on the Lobaye, took him for an inspection of administrative affairs. This leader told Gide that during the night of 27–28 October 1925, the territorial guards had closed in and burned alive a number of women and children at **Botembélé**. He also told him about the atrocities committed by the agents of the Sangha-Ubangui **concessionary company** as well as the abuse of power committed by the Boda district head, Georges Pacha. Upon his return André Gide made a report to the governor general of French Equatorial Africa, who was also the governor of the Middle Congo Colony, to which the Lobaye region was then attached. In his book *Voyage au Congo* (Travels in the Congo), Gide denounced the exactions discovered. Samba-Ngotto was condemned to 10 years in prison for having spoken. But after the inquest, which proved the reality of these facts, he was released. Samba-Ngotto's courage gave him a great notoriety throughout the region. Tardily, at the proposal of the author of this dictionary, the French government invited him to Paris in 1955 and gave him the Legion of Honour the following year. Samba-Ngotto was also widely known in the region for the relations he maintained with the lions of the savannah.

**SANA, COLONEL FRANÇOIS SYLVESTRE.** In 1965 this officer was placed at the head of the first battalion based in **Bangui** at Camp

**Roux**. Lieutenant Colonel **Alexander Banza** replaced him during the **Saint-Sylvestre coup d'etat**. Sana was successively the CAR ambassador in Yugoslavia, Iraq, and Egypt.

**SANDJAK (or SANJAK).** Military term of Turkish origin used by **Zubayr** (Ziber) and **Rabih** for their assistants.

**SANGHA-LOBAYE, CAMPAIGN OF THE.** The name given to the military operations unleashed in 1904–1905 against the populations of the **Sangha**, Lobaye, and Ibenga valleys that had risen at the call of the religious leader of the Ibenga, **Berandjoko**. The regions of the Lobaye, the Ibenga, and the Motaba were united at that time in the vast military district of Middle Congo, entrusted to Captain Méchet.

**SANGO.** A riverine canoeing people of the **Ubangui** valley, the Sango belong to a Ubanguian branch that had pushed Bantu-speaking groups farther downstream. The Sango, before the French arrived, went up the many northern tributaries of the Ubangui River to carry on their **trade**. Their **language** was known in these various valleys. With the French occupation, this language became the lingua franca for all of the **Ubangui-Shari** territory, even spilling over into Chad and the Middle Congo. It is along with French, since **independence**, the official language of the Central African Republic.

**SANMARCO, LOUIS (1912–?).** Born in 1912 in Martigues. Following the serious incidents at **Berberati** on 30 April 1954 and faced with a possible insurrection of the Upper **Sangha** populations, Governor Louis Sanmarco arranged for Deputy **Barthélémy Boganda** to go with him to this village on 1 May. Boganda and Sanmarco were able to calm the population.

**SANUSI, MUHAMMAD AS- (c. 1850–1911).** Muhammad, born about 1850 in **Wadaï** and named Sanusi by his father in honor of the Senoussya force in this country, came to **Cha** when he was very young to join his uncle, **Kobur**, the Sultan of **Dar-al-Kuti**. The Kobur family, removed from the **Baguirmi**, ruled the Wadaï vassal state from 1830 on. **Rabih**'s campaigns on the **Ubanguian** plateau from 1879 to 1890 had deprived Dar-al-Kuti of the bulk of its hinterland. In 1890, no longer able to organize the **trade** routes to the south and then the west, Rabih abandoned the Ubanguian country to set himself up in Sara country. Upon his departure, he deposed Kobur and proclaimed Muhammad as-Sanusi as Sultan of Dar-al-Kuti and Dar **Rounga** with the title of Emir. Rabih compelled as-Sanusi to give his daughter in marriage to Rabih's oldest son, **Fad al Allah**. He then left the area, taking all the food, ammunition, and **slaves** he could. The following year, as-Sanusi had the **Paul Crampel** mission massacred and attempted to rejoin Rabih and lay hold of some of his arms and materials.

From 1891 to 1897, while Rabih was taking over Baguirmi and Bornu, Wadaï was conserving its independence and defying Rabih as well as the Mahdists. Since the French were also manifesting their intention of making Chad the crossroads of their African possessions, as-Sanusi had to play a dangerous game. In 1894 his country was invaded by the Wadaïans, but he successfully reconstituted his strength with the help of Sila and settled on the **Banda** plateau at **Ndélé**. In 1897 he requested and obtained a French protectorate. Right up to 1911, with well-planned stratagems, he was able to defeat the Banda, the Youlou, and the **Kreich** and dispose of his slaves in **Darfur**. In 1903 the French had imposed a new protectorate treaty on him.

But it was not until after 1909, when the French made themselves masters of Wadaï, that they decided to get rid of this cumbersome ally. On 11 January 1911 as-Sanusi and his son Adem were killed at the Ndélé post. The same day, and again on 7 February, his army was dispersed. His son **Kamoun** was still able to maintain an army at the **Ouanda-Djallé** rock fortress. Captain **Jean Modat**, the French resident at Ndélé, estimated that "as-Sanusi was more intelligent than Rabih and Zubayr and he would have surpassed them if circumstances had better served him." As-Sanusi, who possessed 600 wives, had numerous descendants. One of his grandsons was a territorial councilor and the deputy from Ndélé in the first Central African **Assembly**.

**SASSA.** The **Zandé** Sultan Sassa, Zemio's uncle and rival, and an ally of Mopoi-Benzogino, attacked the Belgian post of **Mbomou** in 1894.

**SATO, ALBERT.** This Central African minister who had taken Dr. **Abel Goumba**'s side was, like him, removed from the government by **David Dacko**'s coup in July 1959.

**SAUTOT, HENRI (1885–1963).** Born in Bourbonne les Bains (Haute-Marne) in 1885, he died in Noumea on 25 May 1963. Governor Sautot was replaced at the head of **Ubangui-Shari** in April 1946 by **Jean Chalvet**.

**SAYO.** Sultan **Bangassou**'s son, Sayo ran for the **Territorial Assembly** against **MESAN** in 1952 with the colonial administration's support.

**SCHOOL.** *See* EDUCATION.

**SCHOUVER (1936–).** Father Schouvert was a **missionary** in **Bangui** and in 1992 became Father Superior of the Holy Ghost Order.

**SCHWEINFURTH, DR. GEORG** (1858–1925). Born in Riga, Latvia, on 29 December 1858, he died in Berlin on 19 September 1925. The celebrated explorer of the Upper Nile in 1870 was the first European traveler to visit the **Zandé** of the **Ouellé**. He left an enthusiastic description of them. Schweinfurth drew attention to the presence of a people named **Bandia** several days to the west of Zandé country. He met the Akka ("Pygmy") in the Ouellé **forests**, which had been mentioned under the same name in Pharonic antiquity.

**SERRE, JACQUES (1925–).** Born in Châteauneuf de Gadagne (Vaucluse) on 29 August 1925. After a stay in Niger as administrator, Serre served in **Ubangui-Shari** as head of district in Nola, Bocaranga, and Grimari. In 1960 he became **Prefect** in Lobaye. He then worked as President **David Dacko**'s adviser, as secretary general to the Conseil économique et social (**Economic and Social Council**), and as head of department at the National Administration School in the CAR. In June 1966 he served in Côte d'Ivoire as the finance minister's adviser. Reinstated in the French administration, he was successively subprefect of Sartène (Corsica), secretary general of Guyana, and Sub-Prefect of Saverne (Bas Rhin). In 1979, after the fall of Emperor **Bokassa**, President Dacko chose him as secretary general to the presidency of the Central African Republic. Back in Paris, he became vice director at the Ministry of the Interior. In 1987 he was elected to the Académie Nationale des Sciences d'Outre-Mer (National Academy of Overseas Science).

Jacques Serre is a doctor in law and letters. He has written several books, most notably an economic and social history of the Grimari district in the CAR, a history of the CAR (originally a course given in 1965 at the Bangui ENA), and a study of Dahomey (1893–1894).

**SETO (or TO).** Divinity sent by **Ngale**, the supreme being. Seto, according to the **Mandjia**, gave cultivated plants and domestic animals to humanity. He is represented by the constellation Orion.

**SHARI.** *See* CHARI; UBANGUI.

**SIBUT, MEDICAL MAJOR.** Medical Major Sibut, a friend of **Emile Gentil**, died at Libreville on 10 April 1899, before he was able to join the mission. Gentil gave Sibut's name to the new **Krédedjé** post.

**SIMON, JEAN MARC (1947–).** Born on 9 May 1947, he became the French consul general in Beyrouth, then an adviser at the French embassy in Teheran before becoming second-director, then director of the Minister for Cooperation's cabinet in Paris. In 1996 he became the French ambassador for the Central African Republic. This diplomat played an important role in successfully helping with the negotiations during the several **army rebellions** that disrupted the country.

**SIP (SOCIETES INDIGENES DE PRÉVOYANCE; NATIVE PROVIDENCE SOCIETIES).** Compulsory administrative cooperatives to which all the inhabitants of a district were supposed to subscribe, the Sociétés indigènes (that is, African) de prévoyance promoted a number of rural development operations from 1937 to 1958.

**SISAL.** Climatic conditions are very satisfactory for sisal in the eastern part of Central Africa. After reaching 2,080 metric tons in 1953, production dropped because of the lack of plant-disease protection and insufficient administrative encouragement.

**SLAVES.** The main slave raids were carried out in the **Ubanguian** territories by the **Baguirmi**, **Wadaï**, and **Darfur** during the whole 19th century (especially according to the descriptions of **Muhammad al-Tounsy**). To this should be added after 1850 and in the west, the roving slavers of the **Fulbé** Emirs of **Ngaoundéré** (**Adamawa**) and, in the east, the merchant lords of the Upper Nile (or Bahara). Slave taking and exportation was, for more than 150 years, the essential **economic** activity of the Central African region. Men were the only merchandise that could be used for the acquisition of arms, and these arms were in turn used for the capture of more men. This vicious cycle lasted until 1912, the date of the fall of **Dar-al-Kuti**, the last slaving kingdom. The **Zandé** and **Bandia** sultans, **Rabih** and **as-Sanusi**, were only able to put together strong armies through slave trading.

Actual market price lists for slaves can be found in the accounts of al Tounsy and Dr. Louis Franck, published at the beginning of the 19th century. Many of these slaves were taken to Egypt; Turkey imported eunuchs. The Central African regions were long considered a supply area particularly favored by the caravan leaders. The resistance was nevertheless often fierce. The proliferation of arms in Africa coming chiefly from surpluses after the Crimean War and the American Civil War gave slaving in the center of the continent a genocidal character. Even before colonial exploration, the eastern half of the present-day Central African Republic was emptied of the majority of its inhabitants by the slavers.

**SLEEPING SICKNESS (or TRYPANOSOMIASIS).** By 1906 sleeping sickness had reached all the zones where Europeans were found, that is to say, the line of rest stops of the Upper Shari, **Ubangui**, and Sangha valleys and the principal penetration trails into the **concessions**. In spite of the six doctors sent after the alarming reports of the **Gustave Martin** mission, the share of those afflicted was still more than 50 percent in numerous regions in 1912. It was not until 1929, following the initiative of Medical Colonel **Eugène Jamot**, that general hygiene and prophylactic centers were created from which a more efficient fight could be undertaken. Some **forest** regions in the west and some valleys were nonetheless completely depopulated. The Nola region in Upper Sangha was the hardest hit.

**SMALLPOX (in French, VARIOLE).** Smallpox epidemics ravaged **Ubanguian** villages in addition to the damage caused by **sleeping sickness**, then yellow fever. From 1903 to 1905 all of the center, west, and east of the Central African countryside was devastated by smallpox. In **Nzakara** country, it killed a fifth of the population. The administration had logs cut in infected villages to burn the cadavers of the smallpox victims.

**SMDR (SOCIETES MUTUELLES DE DEVELOPPEMENT RURAL; MUTUAL SOCIETIES FOR RURAL DEVELOP-MENT).** Created in 1959 to replace the Sociétés indigènes de prévoyance (**SIP**; Native Providence Societies), the SMDR were dissolved in 1962 after facing serious administrative errors due to a total lack of competent personnel.

**SMI (SOCIETE MINIERE INTERCOLONIALE; INTERCOLO-NIAL MINING COMPANY).** Constituted in 1938 to manage **diamond** prospecting permits in Upper Sangha, the SMI contributed to the working of the rich deposits in this area along with the Compagnie Minière de l'Oubangui Oriental (CMOO; Eastern Ubangui Mining Company).

**SNEA (SOCIETE NATIONALE D'EXPLOITATION AGRI-COLE; NATIONAL AGRICULTURAL PRODUCTION COM-PANY).** Founded in 1963 to establish at Lobaye two vast national **rubber** and selected palm plantations, the SNEA was not able to carry out the project, and French financial aid was finally directed toward similar but more profitable projects in Côte d'Ivoire and Cameroon.

**SOCOULOLE (SOCIETE COOPERATIVE DE L'OUBANGUI-LOBAYE-LESSE; COOPERATIVE SOCIETY OF UBANGUI-LOBAYE-LESSE).** A rural cooperative created in Lobaye by **Barthélémy Boganda** in 1948 for the Yaka lands and the Loko in Lobaye, the SOCOULOLE had a brief existence. After a few months, it was liquidated.

**SONY-KOLÉ, THEOPHILE.** A union leader, periodically arrested and tortured by the authorities. As of 1995, he organized the total strikes (*ville-morte*, or "dead-city operations") in **Bangui** to protest the nonpayment of back wages.

**SOU (or SO).** Among the Sara, Sou, and among the **Baya**, So is the name of the creator god. So is materialized among the Baya by the cooking stones called *kouchi*.

**SOUTIKRA.** A **Yakoma** leader suspected of having burned the Cetema post in 1894, Soutikra was arrested on 27 August 1900 and publicly shot at Mobaye on 29 August in the presence of Administrator **Henri Bobichon** and 58 Yakoma and **Sango** leaders called to witness the punishment.

**STANLEY, HENRY MORTON (1841–1904).** The famous British traveler Stanley came across the confluence of the Congo and **Ubangui** Rivers as early as 1879 and mentioned it in his travel accounts. Stanley Pool is named after him.

**STATES GENERAL OF COLONIZATION.** *See* ETATS GENERAUX DE LA COLONISATION.

**STROOBANT, LIEUTENANT.** Belgian officer of the Congo Public Force, Stroobant was Lieutenant **Emile Mathieu**'s assistant. He confronted **Victor Liotard** at **Bangassou**. The Belgians next lent their support to **Rafaï** in his conquest projects. In carrying this out, Stroobant participated in various missions in **Banda** country.

**SUD-KAMERUN.** A German **concessionary company**, the Sud-Kamerun Gesellschaft (South-Cameroon Company), operated in the proximity of the French concessionary companies in Upper Sangha. Under the pretext of pretended incursions by German agents into the territory conceded to his company (the **Ngoko-Sangha**), Mestayer, aided by his lawyer, André Tardieu, attempted in 1908 to obtain indemnities. This campaign ended with the abandonment to Germany by France of a large part of the zones conceded in 1911.

**SULTANATS DU HAUT-OUBANGUI, COMPAGNIE DES (COMPANY OF THE UPPER UBANGUI SULTANATES).** Under this name, the most widespread of the **concessionary companies** was constituted in 1899. It received legal rights over all of present-day Central African territory, an area already sorely tried by **slaving** operations and wars between the sultans. The privileges given this company led to the rapid disappearance of the **Bandia** and **Zandé** sultanates.

– T –

**TAMBAGO.** Originally from Upper Kotto, the **Banda** Tambago put up a fierce resistance to **Rabih** and **as-Sanusi**'s attacks.

**TAXATION.** In order to lighten costs to the metropole, the French colonial authorities received instructions in 1901 to have the population of the French Congo pay all the administrative and equipment costs of the colony. This tax was at first fixed in kind. Each inhabitant was to supply a certain quantity of goods (essentially **rubber**), which was resold by the administration to commercial companies. The introduction of money was delayed for a long time because of the opposition of these companies. When **cotton** growing was introduced, it was to serve as legal tender to pay the people's taxes. The harvest price was regulated in a collective fashion by the village leader, who immediately turned over to the administration the taxes due from his area.

At present the "numerical tax," an actual direct personal tax (or "head tax"), still constitutes the main fiscal resource for the Central African state. Tied to memories of forced labor, this tax remains very unpopular. Shortly after his rise to power, and thus honoring one of his many electoral promises, President **Ange Patassé** canceled the "individual tax," a highly unpopular measure that encountered many difficulties in its application. The indirect taxes and other direct taxes did not, however, allow the state to cover its expenses. At the end of the 20th century, the **diamond** taxes, in spite of massive fraud, amounted to 3 billion CFA francs. The informal **trade** in various goods that are smuggled in still escapes any taxation.

**TELECOMMUNICATIONS.** Since 1998 the telecommunications companies present on the Central African market have been competing. Today, only two remain: SOCATEL, the public company that holds a monopoly on land phones; and TELECEL for mobile phones. Both encounter serious financial difficulties.

**TERRITORIAL ASSEMBLY OF UBANGUI-SHARI (ATOC; ASSEMBLEE TERRITORIALE DE L'OUBANGUI-CHARI).** Succeeding the Representative Council of Ubangui-Shari, the Territorial Assembly of Ubangui-Shari was provided by the decree of 4 February 1957, reorganizing French Equatorial Africa in conformity with the enabling legislation (Loi-cadre) of 23 June 1956. On 31 March 1957, Mouvement pour l'évolution sociale de l'Afrique noire (**MESAN**; Movement for the Social Evolution of Black Africa), with 347,000 out of 356,000 votes, won all the seats in the new assembly. This assembly chose Senator **Hector Rivierez** as its president. On 17 May the ATOC approved the list of ministers for the first **Ubanguian** government, presided over by Deputy **Barthélémy Boganda**. On 30 December, the ATOC adopted an **economic** plan that had been devised by Minister **Roger Guerillot** and that was to be very unsuccessful. On 13 July 1953 Boganda had the ATOC vote a motion demanding the **independence** of the territory. After the failure of the **constitution** calling for a single Central African Republic reuniting the four territories of former French Equatorial Africa, for which Boganda had pushed very hard, the ATOC was reduced to proclaiming, on 1 December 1958, a Central African Republic that was limited to the former Ubangui-Shari territory only. The Assembly chose to remain part of the French Community. It was this same Territorial Assembly that adopted the first constitution of the new Republic on 9 February 1959. *See also* ASSEMBLY, LEGISLATIVE and NATIONAL.

**TEXTILES.** *See* COTTON.

**THIRIET, ARISTIDE. Alfred Fourneau**'s companion, Thiriet was killed in the **Baya** village of Kuisso on 12 May 1894, in the attack on the mission by **Bafio**'s troops.

**THOMASSET, CAPTAIN PAULIN.** In 1901 Captain Thomasset carried out a campaign of destruction against the **Banda** Ngao villages of the Bantagofo region. The Banda Ngao were themselves at war with the **Mandjia** of Fort **Crampel**.

**TIANGAYE, NICOLAS (1956–).** Born on 13 September 1956 in Bocaranga, this **Bangui**-based lawyer agreed to defend **Jean-Bedel**

**Bokassa** in 1987, even though he politically opposed the emperor. In 1990 he defended the military personnel and civil servants who supported multipartyism. Legal actions were brought against him by **Ange Patassé**'s governments. But he was also the president of the Central African Human Rights Association and, on 15 June 2003, was elected president of the Conseil National de Transition (CNT; National Transition Council).

**TIKIMA.** The strong **Zanda** Voungara leader, Tikima, son of Zangabirou, entered into an alliance with **Zubayr** in 1868 to eliminate his uncle, **Mofio**. Zubayr married Tikima's daughter. Zubayr was surprised to discover that the palisade of Tikima's *zeriba* was made of 3,000 to 4,000 **ivory** tusks. Thanks to Tikima, Zubayr could travel freely in the area from the Kotto to the **Ouellé**. In 1872 Zubayr had a falling out with his father-in-law and hammered away at his states. Mofio's former *zeriba*, which had fallen into Tikima's hands, was transformed by Zubayr into a government post and named **Ombanga**. **Rabih**, Zubayr's favorite *sandjak* took command. Many members of Tikima's family were reduced to **slavery** by Zubayr. Only Zemio, Tikima's favorite son, was allowed a comfortable life at **Dem Ziber**.

**TISSERANT, REVEREND FATHER CHARLES.** Born on 14 October 1886 in Nancy, he died on 27 September 1962 in Paris. Father Charles Tisserant, a Holy Ghost **missionary** and the brother of Cardinal Eugene Tisserant, was one of the first at the beginning of the 20th century to evangelize the **Banda**. He was also the first to study their history and their customs. An eminent botanist, Father Tisserant carried out numerous studies on traditional plants and **agriculture**. He was the first director of the Boukoko Agronomy Research Center in Lobaye. He worked in Central Africa from 1911 to 1954. A well-known botanist, he was also a remarkable linguist and ethnologist.

**TOBACCO.** From 1948, the French tobacco office encouraged the growing of tobacco in **Ubangui-Shari**, notably in Upper Sangha and Lobaye (wrapping tobacco) and in the east (cut tobacco). In 1956 production was still low, scarcely more than 50 metric tons. In 1965 the Société d'Exploitation Industrielle du Tabac et des Allumettes (SEITA;

Industrial Tobacco and Match Production Company) formed with the Central African government the Société Franco-Centrafricaine du Tabac (French-Central African Tobacco Company). Production is now more than 2,000 metric tons, a large part of which is shipped to sweet cigar manufactures in France.

**TOKEUR, AL HAJJ.** As-**Sanusi**'s emissary to **Emile Gentil** at **Kaga** post, **Bandero** (Fort **Crampel**), in June 1897.

**TONNEAU, LIEUTENANT LEON.** The Belgian Lieutenant Tonneau received the order in December 1894, carrying out the Franco-**Leopoldian** convention of 24 August 1894, to turn the posts located to the north of the **Mbomou** over to the French. Possession was taken, one at a time, until June 1895.

**TOQUÉ, GEORGES (1879–1920).** Born on 3 February 1879, he was sentenced to death and shot in Vincennes on 15 May 1920. In 1902 the young colonial administrator Toqué was sent into a **Mandjia** country that was in the midst of an insurrection. In command of Fort **Crampel** he suffered, while returning from an operation against the **Ngao**, an attack of bilious hematuria. During his illness his assistant, **Fernand-Léopold Gaud**, proceeded on 14 July 1903 with the public execution by dynamite of a prisoner, the guide **Pakpa**, responsible for the Mbres ambush, which had cost the lives of several guards of the post. In 1904 Toqué and Captain **Charles Mangin** were severely injured at the head of a column sent to put down Mandjia insurgents. Returning on vacation in 1905, Toqué was questioned on the Pakpa affair.

On 14 February, on the point of leaving for the Congo, Toqué was arrested by virtue of a warrant signed by the Minister of Colonies. He was transferred to Brazzaville on 16 February, and the French daily *Le Matin* unleashed a violent campaign against him inspired by the Minister of Colonies. Faced with the scandal provoked by the extortions of the **concessionary companies**, the government then decided to recall **Pierre Brazza** to service and place him in charge of an inspection mission to the Congo. Toqué served as the providential scapegoat. His trial took place in Brazzaville. He was given light punishment in exchange for his silence on the numerous scandals of the colony. Later accused of having collaborated with a pro-German paper in the occupied zone during the World War I, Toqué was condemned to death in 1916 by a war tribunal and shot.

The Gaud-Toqué affair, following the scandal in France due to the revelation of the circumstances of the execution of Pakpa at Fort Crampel, has given rise to many fanciful tales. In 2001, in a very well-documented book, Jean Cantournet reestablished the historical truth concerning this tragic affair.

**TOUBA, THEOPHILE.** An opposition deputy, he was murdered on 1 June 2001.

**TOULOU (KAGA).** In this mountain in the **Ndélé** region is a cave that has served as a place of refuge for the populations of the region in many periods. As-**Sanusi** hid there for a little while in 1895 to escape the **Wadaï** troops.

**TRADE.** The import-export trade was long dominated by five large **concessionary companies** established during the colonial period. Import-export trade accounts for almost 40 percent of the annual budget, and it is estimated that 62 percent of the country's **economic** activity is tied to imports. Ninety percent of the exports are of four products: **cotton**, **coffee**, **diamonds**, and **wood**. Capital goods represent about one-fourth of the imports, and consumer goods more than one-third. The trade balance showed a deficit of 1,530 million CFA francs in 1960. Trade continued to show a high degree of fluctuation. From a surplus of 1,382 million CFA francs in 1972, it hit a record deficit in 1975 (4,503 million CFA francs) and again showed a surplus in 1976 (841 million CFA francs) thanks to the rise in raw-material prices. France remains the principal supplier of goods to the Central African Republic and the major purchaser of goods, followed by Italy, the Benelux countries, the United States, Chad, and Israel.

In 1960 the few large commercial companies belonged to Westerners. Their activity was largely in the hands of Portuguese or Greeks. Most of these companies were the descendants of the concessionary companies, which have since disappeared and were partly replaced by Haouassas, Libyans, or Syrians. Central African petty trade has become quite informal, without any way of accounting for it and thus without any possibility for the state to collect **taxes**. By

1998 imports had risen to $170 million, 42 percent of which came from the European Union.

There are no reliable statistics on Central African trade today, but the Banque des Etats de l'Afrique Centrale (BEAC; Central African States Bank) provides some estimates. One should also bear in mind the consequences of the 50 percent devaluation of the CFA franc that occurred in 1994, when attempting to make comparisons.

According to the available data, exports amounted to 89.8 billion CFA francs in 2002, imports reached 83.8 to 94.3 billion CFA francs in 2001, and the balance of trade deficit for the Central African Republic increased from 6.1 billion CFA francs in 1994 to 98.4 billion in 2001.

The main exports in 2001 consisted of wood, rising from 4.4 billion CFA francs in 1980–1984 to 23.1 billion in 1994 and 39.1 in 2001; diamond exports amounted to 44.6 billion CFA francs in 1994 and decreased to 41.2 in 2001; and, over the same period, cotton went from 5.7 to 7.5 billion; coffee exports decreased from 5.6 billion CFA francs to 2 billion; and tobacco—starting again from zero in 1994—increased to 0.2 billion in 2001. These numbers should be considered as mere indications. Nevertheless, it is possible to note a strong increase in wood exports, the collapse in coffee exports is due to the plantations being deserted and the low rates for coffee worldwide, and there is a small rebuilding of the tobacco industry after the destruction that occurred during the army rebellions. Concerning diamond exports, which could prove most profitable for the Central African Republic, the statistics have little value, as it is suspected that a third if not half of the most precious stones are exported illegally.

**TRADE, PRECOLONIAL.** The first result of colonization was the destruction of the precolonial interethnic trade. **Paul Crampel** noted in 1891 the existence of a market in iron at Bala, not far from **Bangui** on the opposite bank of the **Ubangui**. The **Bobangui** monopolized trade from Bonga at the juncture of the Sangha and the Ubangui, all along the Sangha and the Ubangui to the Bangui bend. The **Banziri**, **Bouraka**, **Sango**, and **Yakoma** held navigation and trade monopolies farther upstream, dividing the course of the Ubangui all the way to **Mbomou** into trading areas. In the north, center, and northwest, trade was in the hands of Muslim minorities generically designated as Hausas or Bornuans, whatever their country of origin.

**TRANSPORTATION.** The Central African Republic, as in colonial times, depends for its foreign **trade** on either Pointe Noire (1,850 kilometers) through the **Congo-Ocean** railway, on the Cameroon port Douala and the Matadi harbor by way of the Matadi-Kinshasa railway, or on the oil pipeline. The situation in Congo-Brazzaville and in the Democratic Republic of Congo may seriously disrupt the channels for the CAR's imports and exports. Moreover, there are fewer and fewer barges on the **Ubangui** and the Congo Rivers. There are no more beacons. The poor condition of the **roads** hinders trade with Cameroon, and toward the Sudan trade is almost nonexistent.

**TROUGOU (or TOROUGOU).** A **Sango** term, derived from the word *turk*, which designates, in the Central African countries, the soldiers, militia, guards, or armed auxiliaries of all armies of all countries. Its use goes back to **Zubayr**'s time.

**TRYPANOSOMIASIS.** *See* SLEEPING SICKNESS.

**TVIDES.** This scientific name, forged from the Bantu radical signifying "little," was given by the ethnologists Guslind and Schumacher to the "Pygmy" of Africa.

## – U –

**UBANGUI (or OUBANGUI).** The Ubangui derives its name from the **Boubangui**, the great trading people now settled in its lesser basin. Its major branch is the **Ouellé**, and the **Mbomou** is only one of its tributaries. The main northern tributary of the Congo, the Ubangui, given its length (1,850 km) is most often called a "river." The Ubangui as such remained unknown to Europeans until 1884, the date of its discovery by the English pastor **George Grenfell**.

**UBANGUIAN.** Under this title are grouped the riverine peoples (**Banziri**, **Bouraka**, **Sango**, and **Yakoma**) living along the **Ubangui** between the **Bangui** bend and the **Ouellé-Mbomou** juncture. These "Sudanic" populations left the Upper Nile regions in about the 16th century, pushing the Bantu-speaking commercial groups (notably Boubangui) downstream.

**UBANGUI-SHARI (or UBANGUI-SHARI-CHAD).** The French colonial territory of Ubangui-Shari, formed by the union of the region of Upper Ubangui and Upper Shari in the heart of the French Congo colony, and its dependencies, was created by the decree of 29 December 1903. The decree of February 1906 reorganizing the administration of the French Congo colony and its dependencies created Ubangui-Shari-Chad and placed it under the authority of a lieutenant governor, though the Chad territory maintained its budgetary autonomy. After the brief choice of Fort de Possel as administrative headquarters of Ubangui-Shari-Chad, the center was transferred on 11 December 1906 to **Bangui**. On 21 December 1907, the administrations of the Chad and Ubangui-Shari territories were once again separated. The regions of Upper **Sangha** and of Lobaye were again attached to the Middle Congo—German from 1911 to 1914 (**Neu-Kamerun**), and French again in 1919. They were reunited as Ubangui-Shari in 1934. At the same date, the Chadian regions of Logone and Shari-Bangoran were part of Ubangui-Shari. On 15 November 1934, Ubangui-Shari reached its largest geographic extension, making it the biggest territory of French Equatorial Africa by far. The vast territory was brought into the present-day Central African boundaries by the gubernatorial decision of 28 December 1936. On 1 December 1958, the territory of Ubangui-Shari abandoned this name for that of Central African Republic.

**UNIONS.** The Union des Travailleurs Centrafricains (USTC; Central African Workers Union), affiliated with the Confederation Internationale des Syndicats Libres (CISL; International Confederation of Free Trade Unions, or ICFTU), begun in 1995 to encourage new protests that were highly popular concerning the payment of back wages among **civil servants**. It includes unions from several sectors (health, education, various ministries). Total strikes, called operations *ville-morte* (literally, dead-city operations), are regularly carried out. Its leader, **Théophile Sony-Kolé**, has often been arrested and tortured.

**UNITED STATES.** About 1950, a Marshall Plan administrative mission visited the **diamond**-producing areas of **Ubangui-Shari**. In

1950 the Central African Empire offered assistance to two French companies (CMOO and SMI) in return for the promise of diamond deliveries to the U.S. government. In 1960, an American embassy was opened in **Bangui** and cooperative agreements were signed. In 1962 Assistant Secretary of State G. Mennen Williams visited Bangui. Following the arrest in 1977 of a correspondent with the Associated Press and a journalist from the *Washington Post*, relations between Emperor **Bokassa** and the United States became strained. On 6 December the State Department made it known that given the great sum expended on the Imperial Coronation, the United States did not foresee a continuation of aid. However the 1977 and 1978 commitments ($800,000 and $475,000, respectively) would be honored. Relations were normalized in 1978, only to be strained again over human rights violations in 1979. On 9 September 1979, the United States halted all aid to Bokassa.

**USMAN DAN FODIO (or OUSMAN DAN FODIO).** The wars of conquest of this **Fulbé** prophet at the beginning of the 19th century had direct consequences on the fate of populations in the western part of the present-day Central African Republic: the closing of the Bornuan **trade** routes toward the south, the installation of Fulbé **Adamawa** in the highlands of **Fombina** in Cameroon, the withdrawal of the **Baya** people in the direction of Lobaye and the **Ubanguian** plateau, and the occupation by the Fulbé of the northern part of the great **Sangha** trade route.

– V –

**VANGELE, ALPHONSE (1848–1939).** Born in Brussels on 25 April 1848, he died on 23 February 1939. Entering the service of the International African Association in 1881, the Belgian Lieutenant Vangele accompanied his compatriot **Captain Edmund Hanssens** up the **Ubangui**, which had just been discovered by the English pastor **George Grenfell** in 1889. Continuing his career in service, Vangele, after having been made to retreat before the **Yakoma** in 1888, was entrusted by **Leopold II** in January 1889 with the difficult task of establishing a whole series of fortified posts along the Ubangui up to the **Ouellé**. On

25 June, he founded Zongo just opposite the **Bangui** post created a few hours later by the French. In 1891 he got involved in a dispute with the French administrator **Gaston Gaillard**, but he nonetheless founded the Yakoma post not far from the Ouellé-**Mbomou** confluence. Farther upstream, the name Ubangui was no longer used by the river peoples. Given this fact, Vangele no longer felt bound by the 1887 convention recognizing the rights of France on the north bank of the Ubangui. Complying with the instructions of his king and sovereign, he occupied the region between **as-Sanusi**'s states and the Ouellé and organized the Leopoldian advance toward the Bahr-el-Ghazal.

**VAYSSIERE.** With **John Petherick** and the **Poncet** brothers, Ambroise and Jules, as early as 1858 Vayssiere was one of the principal associates of the Muslim **slavers**, with whom he established the infamous brotherhood of the Upper Nile "merchant lords."

**VEKIL.** The "merchant-lords" of the Upper Nile (1854–1864) gave the title of *vekil* to their assistants, to whom they entrusted the right of life and death over the inhabitants in a vast **trading** zone.

**VERGIAT, ANTONIN MARIUS-MARIE (1900-1983).** Born on 23 August 1900 in Villemontois (Loire), he died on 10 December 1983. He joined the colonial airforce in 1922 and specialized in aerial photography. After serving in Morocco and in Madagascar, in 1932 he became the section chief of the Division Aéronautique (Aeronautics Division) of French Equatorial Africa. He took the first aerial photographs mapping out the **Ubangui-Shari** territory. Passionate about ethnography, he jotted down many things about populations that had remained practically unknown. He was the author of two books published in 1936: *Rites secrets des primitifs de l'Oubangui-Chari* (Secret Rites of the Ubangui-Shari Primitives) and *Moeurs et Coutumes du Mandjias* (Manners and Customs of the Mandjias). These two works are very valuable documents on Central African history.

**VERMAUD-HETMAN.** This son of the **Zandé** sultan, **Hetman** was named Vermaud-Hetman in memory of French Lieutenant Vermot. Hetman was one of the first clerks of the colonial administration and financial service. In 1947 he became one of the first Territorial Councilors elected on a list supported by the administration against **Barthélémy Boganda**'s candidates.

**VIALE, JANE.** Franco-African daughter of a director of the **concessionary company** of the **Sultanates of Upper Ubangui**, Jane Viale was elected senator from Ubangui-Shari on the Overseas Independent ticket and on a program close to that of Deputy **Barthélémy Boganda**. She presided over the Woman's Association of the French Union and took part in numerous international meetings. She died on 9 February 1953 in an airplane accident in Bordeaux.

**VIDRI.** The Vidri were one of the most bellicose groups of the **Banda** nation. Set up in the **Yalinga** and Bria regions, the Vidri took an active part in the resistance to invaders of all origins (**slavers** from **Darfur** and **Wadaï**, **Rabih**'s and as-**Sanusi**'s armies, **Rafaï**'s troops and those of **Bangassou**, as well as French columns). **Baram-Bakie**, who took the lead of a vast insurrection against the French in 1909, was a Banda-Vidri.

**VILLAGES DE LIBERTE.** In the south of **Ubangui**, from 1894 on, the Holy Ghost Catholic **missionaries** bought **slaves** back, baptized them, and gathered them in villages they called *villages de liberté* (freedom villages). A few years later the missionaries had to give up this practice, which held up the evangelization of free people.

**VOUKPATA.** In the 19th century, **Bandia** clans in Lower Kotto and in Lower **Mbomou** overthrew the Pata caste or descendants of Pata (Voukpata), who had founded a state in **Nzakara** country.

**VOVODO.** The Vovodo valley, like that of the **Chinko**, was toward the middle of the 19th century the principal means of penetration by the "merchant lords" of the Upper Nile.

– W –

**WADAÏ (or OUADAI).** The strong Wadaï kingdom played an important role in Central African history. During the 18th and 19th centuries,

Wadaï **slave** raids overran a large part of the eastern territory of what is today the Central African Republic. In 1890 **Dar-al-Kuti**, Wadaï's southern border area, passed under the control of **Rabih**, who named as-**Sanusi** sultan. As-Sanusi broke all vassal ties between his principality and Wadaï. Until 1900 the Wadaïan authorities tried in vain to reestablish their suzerainty not only over Dar-al-Kuti, but also over certain Upper Kotto regions, where their political and commercial influence was strong. In 1900 Wadaï **traders** fell under suspicion of having poisoned **Rafaï**, the **Bandia** Sultan of **Mbomou**. Having successfully resisted Rabih, Wadaï did not lose its independence until 1909 (the taking of Abéche by French troops).

**WANDERER, BROTHER SEVERIN (1866–1898).** Born on 27 May 1866 in Buchofen (Bavaria), Brother Severin directed the construction of the **Saint Paul Mission** in **Bangui**. From 1893 on, he was able to establish a herd of cattle on the banks of the **Ubangui**. He was killed on 21 June 1898 by the **Bondjos** who had burned the neighboring Belgian post at Zongo.

**WATER.** *See* HYDROGRAPHY.

**WAUTERS, ALPHONSE.** In 1885 King **Leopold**'s geographer, Wauters, published various articles in the *Mouvement Géographique* supporting Leopold's claims to the **Ubangui** basin against those of the French. Wauters's well-made maps, sometimes faked, were handily used by King Leopold in the many negotiations with other countries to define the boundaries of the Congo Free State after the Congress of Berlin.

**WILDLIFE—FAUNA.** Once an animal paradise, the Central African Republic's animal wildlife has been drastically reduced in spite of the **reserves** created by the colonists and then by the government. The number of elephants has dropped from over 100,000 to less than 10,000, and the rhinoceroses have practically disappeared.

**WILDLIFE—FLORA.** The south of the Central African Republic is similar to the Guinea **forests**' climate, with a noticeable dry season. It is the region of dense semideciduous forests. Around these stretches a mosaic of savannah forests—thickets and high grass (sissango and imperata). In the middle of the country are the Sudanese and Guinean-type savannahs with a rainy season twice as long as the dry season, including in the west some burkéa savannahs, mostly on the Carnot sandstones. In the east are important traces of semihumid forests, while in the northwest some savannahs were damaged by overgrazing. In the northeast are vast savannahs that mark the transition with the Chad territory, with a dry season lasting longer than the rainy one.

**WINTON, SIR FRANÇOIS WALTER DE. Henry Morton Stanley**'s English successor as the leader of King **Leopold**'s Congo. De Winton opposed **Pierre Brazza** in 1885. He sent Ship's Lieutenant Massari into the Likouala-Massaka with Monsignor **Prosper Augouard**.

**WOMEN.** Polygamy, which was traditional among several tribes, has been made legal (up to four wives), but this practice meets with stronger and stronger resistance on the part of women. The law allows for divorce, and either spouse may file for it. The law, which differs from tradition, grants equal rights to both sexes in matters of inheritance and property. In May 1998, a new family code reinforced women's rights. The **schooling** rate for women in primary school is higher in the cities than in the country. In the universities, women only account for 20 percent of the students. A 1996 decree outlaws sexual mutilations on women (excision and infibulation), but the law meets with resistance in the country due to tradition. An estimated 40 to 50 percent of girls and women have endured these mutilations. The number of women in the political sphere is still very low. In 2000, only eight seats out of the 109 total were occupied by women. In 1999, for the first time, the government appointed five women as **prefects**.

**WOOD.** *See* FORESTRY.

– Y –

**YABOUROU. Victor Liotard** considered this **Yakoma** war leader, who in 1893 had held power among the Bougbou for many years, as the "**Bangassou**" of the Yakoma.

**YADÉ.** The Yadé plateau in Chad, Cameroon, and Central Africa acts as a sort of **water** tower for the whole region. It has played an important role as a fortress and refuge throughout Central African history.

**YAKOMA.** An already strong and commercially active subgroup of the so-called **Ubanguian** group established near the Kotto-Ubangui juncture, they opposed King **Leopold**'s agents in 1888. On 5 January 1888 the Yakoma attacked **Alphonse Vangele** and his companions, who were forced to fall back on 13 February 1888. The Belgians returned in 1891. Many Yakoma then took the French side against Leopold's forces.

**YALINGA.** After the 1911 attack on a French factory by the troops of **Kamoun**, **as-Sanusi**'s son, Lieutenant Bissey founded the Yalinga post not far from Kabou in 1912. Today, this is the **subprefecture** of Upper Kotto.

**YANGONGO, BARTHÉLÉMY.** **Barthélémy Boganda**'s nephew and godson, he studied law at the University of Kiev thanks to a Congolese government scholarship. As Emperor **Bokassa**'s Minister of Information, he struck up relations with the Front Patriotique Oubanguien (FPO; Ubangui Patriotic Front) refugees in Brazzaville. He was arrested on 1 March 1979 by Bokassa and, upon leaving prison, joined the FPO. Then, in 1981, turning Dr. **Abel Goumba** in to the authorities, he created another group in Brazzaville with the same name and initials.

**YANGONGO, GENERAL SYLVESTRE.** **Barthélémy Yangongo**'s brother, he was Minister of Justice under **André Kolingba**.

**YANGOU-MBILI.** Head of a **Banda** coalition, the Banda Ouassa leader Yangou-Mbili had, like **Rafaï** and Zemio, spent time with **Zubayr**, with whom he had learned a few rudiments of military tactics. Established near the **Dji**, Yangou-Mbili was the only **Ubanguian** leader to have manifested his sympathy for the Mahdists. He was in opposition to **as-Sanusi** as well as Rafaï by the end of the century. In 1899 Rafaï's troops captured his village, and Yangou-Mbili was taken to Rafaï as a captive.

**YETINA, JEAN-MARTIN.** A Catholic teaching monitor and Jeunesse Oubanguienne Catholique (JOC; Catholic Ubanguian Youth) militant, Yetina was one of **Barthélémy Boganda**'s first companions. With Ondomat, he founded a **Ubangui-Shari** Youth Council in 1951, which enrolled the future Central African Ministers **André Magale** and **Bernard-Christian Ayandho**.

**YOKADOUMA.** An Upper **Sangha** (Nola) territorial councilor, he was elected on the **MESAN** ticket.

**YOLA.** Navigation head of the Benué River. This locality was always one of Central Africa's strategic ports. Adama set up his capital there in 1835. His successors attempted to maintain suzerainty over the *lamibé* of all of **Adamawa**. The German explorer Heinrich Barth visited Yola in 1851. It was with the intention of ensuring access to Yola that **Rabih** unsuccessfully attacked the **Mandjia** in 1884. French Ship's lieutenant **Louis Mizon** attempted to establish a French protectorate at Yola in 1892 in spite of the Royal Niger Company's claims.

## – Z –

**ZANDÉ.** The origin of this term, used to designate a large group of people of Zaire, the Sudan, and the Central African Republic, is subject to some controversy. Ngoura, founder of the Zandé at the beginning of the 19th century, belonged to a clan with the name of Kogobili. The Kogobili migrated from the west toward their ancestral homeland on the Nile and settled as lords over the people living in the **Mbomou**, taking the historic name Zandé, which itself appears to derive from the ancient term Azania, which was applied to the people of the Nubian states of the Upper Nile. The term "Zandé" was, in turn, applied to the multiple peoples conquered by Ngoura and his descendants. The term "Zandéization" has been created to designate this remarkable process of ethnicity building. The conquering group's language was imposed as an ethnic cement, as was a remarkable politico-administrative structure.

**ZERIBA.** The merchant lords of the Upper Nile gave this name to the fortified (surrounded by palisades) trading posts in the Bahr-el-Ghazal and in Upper **Ubangui**.

**ZINGA.** Village of the Mongoumba sub**prefecture** in Lobaye, which at one time marked the end of regular navigation on the **Ubangui**. The Zinga limit was cleared of rocks in 1950 to permit boats to reach **Bangui** in all seasons.

**ZOUNGOULA, SISTER.** Along with her peer Sister Kalika, once a slave as she, she was bought back by Monsignor **Prosper Augouard** in the deep Central African–Congo **forest**. **Schooled** at the **Catholic Mission** in Brazzaville, they joined the Holy Ghost Order. These two sisters, whose biographies were written by Father **Ghislain de Banville**, dedicated their lives to the care of lepers. Themselves infected with leprosy, they died with the aura of saints. Their possible canonization was talked of in 1993 during the solemn celebration of the centennial anniversary of the Central African Church.

**ZUBAYR PASHA (ZOBEIR, ZIBER).** Leaving his employer, Bekir, the merchant lord of the Upper Nile, Zubayr took possession of the vast territories of the **Kreich** from 1858 on. He then attacked the Golo, enemies of the Azandé. He married the daughter of the Azandé sultan, **Tikima**. By 1863, settled in his capital Dem Zubayr (Dem Ziber) in Bahr-el-Ghazal, Zubayr had become a strong ruler. In 1867 he appointed himself sheik with an army of 11,000 men. In 1871, having defeated the Egyptian troops sent against him, Zubayr accepted being appointed by the Khedive governor of the vast territories he controlled. In 1872 he conquered **Darfur** for Egypt. Zubayr and his lieutenants then undertook numerous **slave** wars in Upper **Ubangui**, depopulating the country. Arriving in Cairo in August 1875, he was arrested by the Khedive. His son, Suleyman (Soleiman), took charge of a war against the Egyptian troops, then surrendered to them in 1879. Zubayr's most loyal lieutenant (*sandjak*), **Rabih**, refused to submit. In the eastern part of the Central African Republic, Zubayr's name is still remembered today.

# Heads of Government

## LIEUTENANT GOVERNORS OF UBANGUI-SHARI-CHAD

4 April 1906: Emile Merwart, 3rd Class Colonial Governor
28 February 1909: Lucien Fourneau, Chief Administrator (interim)
5 August 1910: Paul Adam, Chief Administrator (interim)
10 June 1911: Frederic Estebe, 3rd Class Colonial Governor
12 October 1916: Victor Merlet, 3rd Class Colonial Governor
17 July 1917: Auguste Lamblin, Chief Administrator (interim)
16 May 1919: Auguste Lamblin, 3rd Class Colonial Governor

## LIEUTENANT GOVERNORS OF UBANGUI-SHARI

31 August 1920: Alphonse Diret, Chief Administrator (interim)
December 1921: Auguste Lamblin, 2nd Class Colonial Governor (interim)
7 August 1923: Pierre Frangois, Chief Administrator (interim)
November 1924: Auguste Lamblin, 1st Class Colonial Governor
1 July 1926: Georges Prouteaux, Chief Administrator (interim)
July 1928: Auguste Lamblin, 1st Class Colonial Governor
22 October 1929: Georges Prouteaux, Chief Administrator (interim)
30 October 1930: Alphonse Deitte, 3rd Class Colonial Governor
8 March 1933: Pierre Bonnefont, Chief Administrator (interim)
February 1934: Alphonse Deitte, 2nd Class Colonial Governor

## GOVERNOR GENERAL'S DELEGATES IN BANGUI

17 August 1934: Alphonse Deitte, 2nd Class Colonial Governor
21 May 1935: Richard Brunot, 3rd Class Colonial Governor

30 May 1935: Pierre Bonnefont, Chief Administrator (interim)
24 October 1936: Max Masson de Saint-Felix, 3rd Class Colonial Governor

## HEADS OF UBANGUI-SHARI TERRITORY

28 March 1939: Pierre de Saint-Mart, Chief Administrator (interim)
15 July 1941: Pierre de Saint-Mart, 3rd Class Colonial Governor
30 May 1942: André Latrille, Chief Administrator (interim)
30 July 1942: Henri Sautot, 3rd Class Colonial Governor
3 April 1946: Jean Chalvet, 3rd Class Colonial Governor
24 May 1946: Henri Latour, Chief Administrator (interim)
October 1946: Jean Chalvet, 3rd Class Colonial Governor
25 April 1948: Jean Mauberna, 1st Class Administrator (interim)
1 December 1948: Auguste Even, 1st Class Administrator (interim)
27 January 1949: Pierre Delteil, 1st Class Governor of Overseas France
4 January 1950: August Even, 1st Class Administrator (interim)
1 March 1950: Ignace Colombani, 3rd Class Governor of Overseas France
9 July 1951: Pierre Raynier, Chief Administrator (interim)
19 October 1951: Aime Grimald, 3rd Class Governor of Overseas France
16 February 1954: Louis Sanmarco, Chief Administrator (interim)
23 March 1955: Louis Sanmarco, 3rd Class Governor of Overseas France
29 January 1958: Paul Bordier, 3rd Class Governor of Overseas France

## GOVERNMENT COUNCIL OF UBANGUI-SHARI

14 May 1957: Dr. Abel Goumba, Vice President, the French High Commissioner remaining President
26 July 1958: Dr. Abel Goumba, President

## GOVERNMENT OF THE CENTRAL AFRICAN REPUBLIC

1 December 1958: Barthélémy Boganda, President
30 March 1959: Dr. Abel Goumba, President
1 May 1959: David Dacko, President

## PRESIDENCY OF THE CENTRAL AFRICAN REPUBLIC

13 August 1960: David Dacko, Head of State and of Government

1 January 1966: Colonel Jean-Bedel Bokassa, Head of State and of Government, appointed General, then Marshal

4 March 1972: Marshal Bokassa appointed President for Life by a congress of the single party

2 January 1975: The President for Life appointed Prime Minister; Elisabeth Domitien, Vice President of the single party

8 June 1976: Government dissolved and a Council of the Revolution was designated, presided over by Ange Patassé

## CENTRAL AFRICAN EMPIRE

4 December 1976: President Bokassa had himself appointed Emperor under the name of Bokassa I by a congress of the single party. He crowned himself 4 December 1977

14 December 1976: Ange Patassé was appointed Prime Minister of the Central African Empire with broad powers (in theory)

17 July 1978: Henri Maïdou replaced Ange Patassé at the post of Prime Minister

## PRESIDENCY OF THE CENTRAL AFRICAN REPUBLIC

21 September 1979: David Dacko proclaims the downfall of Emperor Bokassa I and the restoration of the Republic, of which Dacko takes the presidency. Henri Maïdou is appointed Vice President of the Republic and Bernard Christian Ayandho Prime Minister.

15 March 1981: Election of David Dacko as President of the Republic

1 September 1981: David Dacko resigns and hands over his powers to General André Kolingba, who suspends the constitution and creates the *Comité militaire de redressement national* (CMRN; Military Committee of National Recovery), of which he is President.

21 November 1986: A new constitution is adopted by referendum and General Kolingba is elected as President of the Republic.

27 September 1993: Ange Patassé is elected as President of the Republic.

March 2003: General François Bozizé is self-proclaimed President of the Republic.

## VICE PRESIDENCY

27 September 1979: Henri Maïdou appointed Vice President; revoked 22 August 1980

12 December 2003: Abel Goumba designated by General François Bozizé as Vice President

## PRIME MINISTERS

This post, created anew in September 1979, was abolished in September 1981, then reinstated by General Kolingba on 1 January 1991.

27 September 1979: Bernard Christian Ayandho

19 November 1980: Jean-Pierre Lebouder

3 April 1981: Simon Bozanga

15 March 1991: Edouard Franck

4 December 1992: General Thimothée Malendoma

26 February 1993: Enoch-Derant Lakoué

25 October 1993: Jean-Luc Mandaba

20 April 1995: Gabriel Koyambounou

6 June 1996: Jean-Paul Ngoupandé

18 February 1997: Michel Gbezara-Bria

4 January 1999: Anicet Georges Doloquélé

1 April 2002: Martin Ziguélé

23 March 2003: Abel Goumba

# Bibliography

English-speaking people who wish to become acquainted with the Central African Republic face some linguistic difficulties, for even though this bibliography and this book are directed primarily to an English-language audience, it contains few citations in English. Not only is the author Francophone, but nearly everything that has been written about the Central African Republic has been written in French. Any scholar who deals with the published material relating to the Republic must have a reading knowledge of that language. To attempt serious scholarly research on any aspect of the Republic without this ability would be very difficult. For those who wish to begin in English, however, Thomas O'Toole's *The Central African Republic: The Continent's Hidden Heart* (Boulder, CO: Westview Press, 1986) is the best single source. Reference should also be made to Pierre Kalck's *Central African Republic* (London: Pall Mall; New York: Praeger, 1971). Other critical sources are Dennis D. Cordell's *The Savanna Belt of North Central Africa*, in *History of Central Africa*, volume 1, edited by David Birmingham and Phyllis M. Martin (London: Longman, 1983); Ralph Austen and Rita Headrick's *Equatorial Africa under Colonial Rule*, in *History of Central Africa*, volume 2, edited by David Birmingham and Phyllis M. Martin (London: Longman, 1983); and Brian Weinstein's *Eboué* (New York: Oxford University Press, 1972). Unfortunately, these books and many others in the bibliography are increasingly dated, so information on current events and developments over the past two decades must be sought in magazine and newspaper articles, or on websites such as www.sangotnet.com.

## CONTENTS

## I. GENERAL WORKS

Austen, Ralph A., and Headrick, Rita. "Equatorial Africa under Colonial Rule." In *History of Central Africa*, vol. 2, edited by David Birmingham and Phyllis M. Martin. London: Longman, 1983, 27–94.

Banville, R. P. Ghislain de. *Bibliographie Centrafricaine* [Central African Bibliography] (1750 entries). Bangui: Mission Saint-Charles, 1991, 102 pages.

Bruel, Georges. *L'Afrique équatoriale française, le pays, les habitants, la colonisation, les pouvoirs publics* [French Equatorial Africa, the country, its inhabitants, colonization, public services]. Paris: Larose, 1918.

Cantournet, Jean. *Inventaire cartographique de la République Centrafricaine* [The Mapping out of the Central African Republic]. Paris: Société d'Ethnographie, 1985.

Cordell, Dennis D. *A History of the Central African Republic*. Bangui: U.S. Peace Corps, Central African Republic (PSC/TR 676-75-019), 1975, mimeographed.

———. *Research Resources in Chad and the Central African Republic*, *History in Africa II*. (1975): 217–220.

———. "The Savanna Belt of North-Central Africa." In *History of Central Africa*, vol. 1, edited by David Birmingham and Phyllis M. Martin. London: Longman, 1983, 30–74.

Decraene, Philippe. *L'Afrique centrale* [Central Africa]. Paris: Centre des hautes études sur l'Afrique et l'Asie modernes, 2nd ed., 1993, 151 pages.

Denis, Vennetier et Wilmet. *L'Afrique centrale et orientale* [Central and Eastern Africa]. Paris: Presses Universitaires de France, 1971.

Donnet, N., Le Borgne, J. F., and Piermay, J. L. *La République Centrafricaine-Géographie* [Geography of the Central African Republic]. Paris: Hatier, 1967.

Eboué, Felix. *Les Peuples de l'Oubangui-Chari. Essai d'ethnographie, de linguistique et d'economie sociale* [People of the Ubangui-Shari: An Essay in Ethnography, Linguistics and Social Economy]. Paris: Comité de l'Afrique française, 1933.

Grillet, G., Mainguet, M., and Soumille, P. *La République Centrafricaine* [The Central African Republic]. Paris: Presses Universitaires de France, Collection Que Sais-je. No. 1943, 1982.

Institut Geographique National. *Atlas de la République Centrafricaine* [An Atlas of the Central African Republic]. Paris: Institut Geographique National, 1973.

Jean, Suzanne. *Bibliographie relative aux sciences humaines en RCA* [Bibliography of Social Sciences in the CAR]. Paris: Bureau pour le développement de la Production Agricole, 1961.

Kakoulingue, J. *L'inventaire du catholicisme à Bangui* [Inventory of Catholicism in Bangui]. Thesis, University of Bangui, n.d.

Kalck, Pierre. *Central African Republic*. World Bibliographical Series, volume 152. Santa Barbara, CA: Clio Press, 1993, 153 pages, 538 entries.

———. *Central African Republic, a Failure in Decolonization*. London: Pall Mall, 1971.

———. *Histoire Centrafricaine, bilan et perspectives* [Central African History, Situation and Prospects]. *Monde et Cultures* 42, no. 4 (1 October 1982): 813–829.

———. *Histoire centrafricaine des origines a nos jours* [Central African History from the origins until today]. Vol. 1: *Des origines a 1900 (passé précolonial et rivalités coloniales)* [From the origins to 1900 (precolonial history and colonial rivalries]; vol. 2: *De 1900 a nos jours (colonisation et décolonisation)* [From 1900 until today (colonization and decolonization)]. Doctoral diss. in letters, Paris: Sorbonne, 1970.

———. *Histoire de la République Centrafricaine des origines préhistorique à nos jours* [History of the Central African Republic from prehistoric times until now]. Paris: Berger Levrault, 1974.

———. *République Centrafricaine* [Central African Republic]. Paris: L'Harmattan, 1992.

Mestraud, Jean Louis. *Géologie et ressources minérales de la Republique Centrafricaine* [Geology and mineral resources of the Central African Republic]. Orleans: Editions du Bureau de Recherche Géologiques et Minières, 1982.

O'Toole, Thomas. *The Central African Republic*. Minneapolis: Lerner Publications, 1989.

———. *The Central African Republic: The Continent's Hidden Heart*. Boulder, CO: Westview Press, 1986.

Poutrin, G. *Esquisse ethnographique des principales populations d'AEF* [Ethnographic outline of the main peoples in French Equatorial Africa]. Paris: Masson, 1914.

*Recherches Centrafricaines (ouvrage collectif)*. *Problèmes et Perspectives de la Recherche historique* [Central African Researches (collective work). Problems and Prospects of Historical Research]. Colloque de Senanque 24–25 septembre 1981. Etudes et documents [Senanque Colloquium. Studies and Documents]. Institut d'Histoire des Pays d'Outre-Mer. University of Aix-en-Provence, no. 16, 1982.

*Recherches Centrafricaines (ouvrage collectif)*. *Problèmes et Perspectives de la Recherche historique* [Central African Researches (collective work). Problems and Perspectives of Historical Research]. Colloque de Paris [Paris Colloquium] ASOM, CHEAM, IPHOM, 29–30 septembre 1982. Institut d'Histoire des Pays d'Outre-Mer. University of Aix-en-Provence, no. 18, 1984.

Sanner, Pierre. *Bibliographie ethnographique de l'AEF* [Bibliography of French Equatorial Africa Ethnography]. 1914–1948. Paris: Imprimerie nationale, 1949.

Serre, Jacques. *Histoire de la Republique Centrafricaine (1890–1960)* [History of the Central African Republic (1890–1960)]. Bangui: Ecole Nationale d'Administration, 1964.

Sillans, Roger. *Les savanes de l'Afrique centrale* [The Central African Savannah]. Paris: Encyclopédie biologique LV Paul Le Chevalier, 1958.

Smith, Stephen. *Nécrologie, Pourquoi l'Afrique meurt?* [Necrology, Why is Africa dying?]. Paris: Calmann-Levy, 2003.

Teulieres, André. *L'Oubangui face à l'avenir* [The Ubangui and the Future]. Paris: Editions de l'Union Française, 1953.

Vansina, Jan. *Paths in the Rainforests: Toward a History of Political Tradition in Equatorial Africa*. Madison: University of Wisconsin Press, 1990.

Vennetier, P. (under the direction of). *Atlas de la Republique Centrafricaine* [Central African Republic Atlas]. Paris: Editions Jeune Afrique, 1984.

Villien, François, Soumille, Pierre, Vidal, Pierre, and Pirvano, Jean-Pierre. *Bangui, capitale d'un pays enclave d'Afrique Centrale: Etude historique et géographique* [Bangui, capital of a landlocked country in Central Africa: Historical and Geographical Study]. Bordeaux: Centre de Recherches sur les Espaces Tropicaux, 1990.

Zangato, Etienne. *Reflexion sur les sources d'histoire centrafricaine: traditions orales, culture materielle et archéologique* [Reflection upon the Sources of

Central African History: Oral Traditions, Material Culture and Archeology].
Thesis, University of Paris X, 1985 (typescript).

Ziegle, Henri. *Afrique équatoriale française* [French Equatorial Africa]. Paris:
Berger-Levrault, 1962.

Zoctizoum, Yarisse. *Histoire de la Centrafrique: Violence du développement,
domination et inégalités* [Central African History: A Violent Development,
supremacy and inequalities], vol. 1, 1879–1959. Paris: L'Harmattan, 1983.
Preface by Charles Bettelheim.

———. *Histoire de la Centrafrique: Violence du developpement, domination et
inegalites* [Central African History: A Violent Development, Supremacy and
Inequities], vol. 2, 1959–1979. Paris: L'Harmattan, 1983.

## II. PREHISTORY AND FIRST INHABITANTS

Bayle des Hermens, Roger de. "Recherches Préhistoriques en République Cen-
trafricaine" [Prehistoric Research in the Central African Republic].
*Recherches Oubanguiennes*, no. 3, Librairie Klinsieck, University of Paris
X-Nanterre, 1975.

Demesse Lucien. *A la recherche des premiers âges, Les Babinga* [In Search of
Primal Times, the Babingas]. Paris: P. Amiot, 1957.

Jacquot, A. "La langue des pygmées de la Sangha: Essai d'identification" [The
Language of the Sangha Pygmy: An Essay in Identification]. *Bulletin de l'Institut d'études centrafricaines* 17–18 (1959): 35–42.

Vidal, Pierre. *La civilisation mégalithique de Bouar: Prospection et fouilles*
[The Megalithic Civilisation of Bouar: Prospecting and Excavating]
1962–1966. Paris: Firmin-Didot, 1969.

## III. GAOGA, ALOA, ANZICA

Balandier, Georges. *La vie quotidienne au royaume de Kongo du XVIe au XVI-
IIe siècle* [Ordianry Life in the Kongo Kingdom from the 16th to the 18th
century]. Paris: Hachette, 1965.

Barth, Heinrich. *Reisen und Entdeckungen in Nord und Central Afrika in den
Jahren 1849 bis 1855* [Travels and Explorations in North and Central Africa
from the years 1849 to 1855], 5 vols. Gotha: 1857–1858; Paris: Bohne,
1860–1861, 4 vols.; London: F. Cass, 1969, 5 vols.

Carbou, Henri. *La région du Tchad et du Ouadaï* [The Chad and Wadaï re-
gions]. Paris: Leroux, 1912.

Confaliomeri. *Histoire du Congo* [Congo History]. Vatican Bibliography,
Codex, Vat. Lat. 12–16, fos. 103–125. Compilation de Lopez-Pigafetta et de

la relation des pères carmes Diego du Très Saint Sacrement et Diego de l'Incarnation [Documents Collected by Lopez-Pigafetta and Reports from Fathers Diego].

Cuvelier, J., and Jadin, L. *L'ancien Congo d'après les archives romaines (1518–1640)* [The Old Congo according to the Roman Archives (1518–1640)]. Brussels: Académie Royale des Sciences coloniales, memoires, vol. 36, 1954.

Kalck, Pierre. "Pour une localisation du royaume de Gaoga" [To Locate the Gaoga Kingdom]. *Journal of African History* 13 (1972): 529–548.

Modat, Capitaine. *Une tournée en pays Fertyt* [Rounds in the Fertyt Country]. Paris: Editions du Comité de l'Afrique française, 1912.

Palmer, H. R. "The Kingdom of Gaoga of Leo Africanus." *Journal of African History* 29 (1929–1930): 280–287, 357–369.

Pigafetta, Philippe, and Lopez, Duarte. *Description du Royaume du Congo et des contrées environnantes* [A Description of the Congo and Neighboring Regions]. Paris: Editions Nauwelaerts, 1963.

Walckenaer, C.-A. *Collection des relations de voyages par mer et par terre en différentes parties de l'Afrique depuis 1400 jusqu'à nos jours* [Collection of the Accounts of the Sea and Land Travels in Various Parts of Africa from 1400 until now]. Paris: n.p., 1842.

## IV. CENTRAL AFRICANS BEFORE 1900

### 1. East

Adoum-Pickanda. *L'enfant dans la sociéte traditionnelle banda* [The Child in Traditional Banda Society]. Thesis, University of Renne II, 1981 (typescript).

Bonnel de Mezieres, A. *Rapport sur le haut Oubangui, le Mbomou et le Bahr el Ghazal* [Report on the Upper-Ubangui, the Mbomou and the Bahr el Ghazal Countries]. Paris: Imprimerie Albouy, 1901.

Boulvert, Yves. *Bangui 1889–1989 à partir de cartes, plans, photos aériennes, images satellitaires* [Bangui 1889–1989 from maps, blueprints, aerial photographs and satellite pictures]. Paris: Institut geographique national, 1989.

——. *Bangui 1889–1989, Points de vues et temoignages* [Bangui 1889–1989, Points of View and Testimonies]. Paris: Editions Sepia, 1989.

——. *Bangui 1889–1989, un siècle de croissance de la ville, points de vue et témoignages* [Bangui 1889–1989, A Century of Growth for the City, Points of View and Testimonies]. Paris: Ministère de la Coopération, Editions Sepia, 1989.

Calonne-Beaufaict, A. *Les Azandé. Introduction à une ethnographie générale des bassins de l'Ubangui-Uélé et de l'Arnwimi* [The Azandé. Introduction to a General Ethnography of the Ubangui-Uele and Arnwimi basins]. Brussels: M. Lamertin, 1921.

Cantournet, J. "Points de vue nouveaux. Note sur les origines et la fondation de Bangui" [New Interpretations. Notes on the Origins and the Founding of Bangui]. *Revue française d'histoire d'Outre Mer* 73, no. 272 (1986): 347–357.

Comte, Paul. *Les Nsakkaras, leur pays, leurs moeurs, leurs croyances, etc* [The Nsakkaras, Their Country, Customs, Beliefs, etc]. Bar-le-Duc: Comte-Jacquet impr., 1895.

Dampierre, Eric de. "Des ennemis, des Arabes, des histoires." *Recherches oubanguiennes* [Enemies, Arabs and Other Stories], no. 8. Paris: Société d'ethnographie, University of Paris X-Nanterre, 1983.

Dampierre, Eric de. *Un ancien royaume bandia du haut Oubangui* [An ancient Bandia Kingdom in Upper-Ubangui]. Paris: Plon, 1967.

Evans-Pritchard, E. E. *The Azandé, History and Political Institutions*. Oxford: Clarendon Press, 1971.

Junker, Wilhelm. *Reisen in Afrika 1875–1886* [Travels in Africa 1875–1886], 3 vols. Vienna: Holzel, 1889, 1890, 1891. Translated by A. Keane. London: Chapman and Hall, 1890–1892.

Lagae, C. R., and Vanden Plas, V. H. *La langue des Zandé* [The Zandé Language], 3 vols. Ghant: Editions dominicaines Veritas, 1921–1925; vol. I: *Grammaire, exercices, légendes* [Grammar, exercises, legends]; vols. II–III: *Dictionnaire français-Zandé et Zandé-français* [French-Zandé and Zandé-French Dictionary].

Retel-Laurentin, A. *Infécondite et maladies chez les Nzakara (Republique Centrafricaine)* [Sterility and Diseases among the Nzakara people (Central African Republic]. Paris: Institut national de la statistique et des études économiques, 1975.

———. *Un pays à la derive. Une société en régression démographique. Les Nzakara de l'est centrafricain* [A Country Drifting. A Society in Demographic Decline. The Nzakara of Eastern Central African]. Paris: Jean-Pierre Delarge, 1979.

Samarin, William J. *The Black Man's Burden: African Colonial Labor on the Congo and Ubangi Rivers, 1880–1900*. Boulder, CO: Westview Press, 1989.

Santandrea, Stefano. *A Tribal History of the Western Bahr el Ghazal*. Verona: Editions Nigrizia, 1964.

Schweinfurth, Georg. *Im Herz von Afrika* [In the Heart of Africa], 2 vols. *Au coeur de l'Afrique (1868–1871). Voyages et decouvertes dans les régions inexplorées d'Afrique centrale* [Travels and Discoveries in the Unexplored Regions of Central Africa], 2 vols. Translated by H. Loreau. Paris: Hachette, 1875.

Tescaroli, Cirillo. *Azandé alla sbarra* [The Zandé borders]. Verona: Editions Nigrizia, 1962.

Thuriaux-Hennebert, Arlette. *Les Zandé dans l'histoire du Bahr el Ghazal et de l'Equatoria* [The Zandé People in the History of the Bahr, the Ghazal and the Equatoria]. Brussels: Institut de sociologie de l'Université libre, 1964.

## 2. Northeast

Browne, W. G. *Travels in Africa, Egypt and Syria from the Year 1792 to 1798*. London: T. Cadell Jr. and W. Davies, 1799.

El Tounsy, Cheikh Mohamed ibn Omar. *Voyage au Darfour* [Travels in Darfour]. Translated by Perron. Paris: Duprat, 1845.

——. *Voyage au Ouaday* [Travels in Wadaï]. Translated by Perron. Paris: Duprat, 1851.

Julien, Capitaine. "Mohamed es Senoussi et ses Etats" [Mohamed es Senoussi and his States]. *Bulletin de la Société de recherches congolaises* (Brazzaville) 7 (1925), 8 (1927), 9 (1928), 10 (1929): 104–177, 55–122, 49–96, 45–88.

Macmichael, Harold Alfred. *History of the Arabs in the Sudan and Some Account of the People Who Preceded Them and of the Tribes Inhabiting Darfur*, 2 vols. Cambridge: Cambridge University Press, 1922.

Magnant, J. P. *Terre et pouvoir dans les populations dite Sara du sud du Tchad* [Land and Power among the Peoples called the Sara in Southern Chad]. Ph.D. diss., University of Paris I, 1983.

Nachtigal, Gustave. "Voyage en Ouadai" [Travel in Uadai]. Translated by Joost van Vollenhoven. Paris: *Bulletin du Comité de l'Afrique française*, supplément, 1913.

Nougayrol, P. *Les parlers Gula, Centrafrique, Soudan, Tchad. Grammaire et Lexique* [The Gula, Central African, Sudan and Chad Speeches. Grammar and Lexicon]. Paris: CNRS, Collection Sciences du langage, 384 pages.

## 3. Center

Courseulles de Barbeville. *Essai sur la codification des coutumes banda* [An Essay in Writing down the Banda People's Customs and Codes]. Bangui: Archives de l'Oubangui-Chari, typescript.

Daigre. Les Banda de l'Oubangui-Chari [The Banda People in the Ubangui-Shari]. *Anthropos* 26 (1931), 27 (1932): 647, 151–181.

Gaud, F. *Les Mandjia (Congo français)* [The Mandjia People (French Congo)]. Brussels: de Wit, 1911.

Guillemin, R. *L'évolution de l'agriculture autochtone dans les savanes de l'Oubangui* [The Evolution of Native Agriculture in the Ubangui Savannah]. Nogent-sur-Marne: l'Inspection générale de l'agriculture de l'AEF, 1956.

Tisserant, Charles. "L'agriculture dans les savanes de l'Oubangui" [Agriculture in the Ubangui Savannah]. *Bulletin de l'Institut d'Etudes centrafricaines* (Brazzaville) 2 (1951): 73–102.

Toqué Georges. *Essai sur le peuple et la langue banda* [Essay on the Banda People and Language]. Paris: J. André, 1904.

Vergiat, A. M. *Moeurs et coutumes des Mandjia* [The Mandjia People's Traditions and Customs]. Paris: L'Harmattan, 1981.

———. *Les rites secrets des primitifs de l'Oubangui* [The Secret Rites of the Ubangui Primitive Peoples]. Paris: Payot, 1951.

## 4. South

Dolisie, Albert. "Notice sur les chefs batekes avant 1898" [Notes on the Batekes Chiefs before 1898]. *Bulletin de la Société de recherches congolaises* (Brazzaville) 8 (1927): 44–49.

Hutereau. *Histoire des peuples de l'Uéllé et de l'Ubangui* [History of the Uéllé and Ubangui Peoples]. Brussels: Goemare, 1922.

Leyder, J. "De l'origine des Bwaka (Ubangui)" [Of the Origin of the Bwaka People (Ubangui)]. *Bulletin de la Société royale belge de Géographie* (Brussels) 1 (1936): 49–71.

Sevy, Gabriel V. *Terre Ngbaka. Etudes de l'évolution de la culture matérielle d'une population forestière de RCA* [Ngbaja Land. A Study on the Evolution of the Material Culture of a Population living in the Forests of the CAR]. Paris: Société d'études linguistiques et anthropologiques de France, 1972.

Tanghe, Basile. "Pages d'histoire africaine: essai de reconstitution des liens de famille paternelle qui relient entre elles les populations soudanaises du Nord du Congo" [Pages of African History: An Essay in Reconstituting the Father-Son Relationships that Unite Sudanese Families from Northern Congo]. *Aequatoria* 6 (1943) and 7 (1944): 1–7 and 35–41.

Thomas, J. *Les Ngbaka de la Lobaye: le dépeuplement rural chez une population forestière de la RCA* [The Ngbaka of the Lobaye region: the rural depopulating among peoples from the Forests of the CAR]. Ph.D. diss., Paris-Sorbonne, 1963.

## 5. West

Faure, Henri. "Contribution à l'étude des races de la region de Carnot" [A Contribution to the Study of the Races of the Carnot Region]. *Bulletin de la Société de recherches congolaises* (Brazzaville) 2 (1935): 99–109.

Froehlich, J. C. "Le commandement et l'organisation sociale des Foulbe de l'Adamaoua" [The Chain of Power and Social Organization of the Foulbe People in Adamaoua]. *Etudes camerounaises* (Yaounde) 45–46 (1954): 3–39.

Guillaume, Henri. "Du miel au café, de l'ivoire à l'acajou. La colonisation de l'interfluve Sangha-Oubangui et l'évolution des rapports entre chasseurs-collecteurs Aka et agriculteurs (Centrafrique-Congo) 1880–1980" [From Honey to Coffee, from Ivory to Mahogany: The Colonizing of the Sangha-Ubangui River Exchange and the Evolution in the Relations between Aka Hunter-gatherers and the Farmers (Central Africa and Congo) 1880–1980]. In *Collection Langues et Cultures Africaines*, no. 27. SELAF, no. 393 éditions Peeters, Louvain, Paris, Sterling Virginia, 2001, 784 pages.

Lacroix, P. F. "Matériaux pour servir à l'histoire des Peuls de l'Adamaoua" [Documents for the History of the Adamaoua Peuls]. *Etudes camerounaises* (Yaounde) 5, nos. 37–38 (1952), and 6, nos. 39–40 (1953): 3–61 and 3–40.

*Marchés Tropicaux* [Tropical Markets], Paris, 15 March 2002, Spécial Centrafrique.

Nozati, F. *Les Pana: Une chefferie sacrée en République Centrafricaine* [The Pana People: A Sacred Chiefdom in the Central African Republic], University of Paris VIII, Saint-Denis, 15 May 1998, 2 vols.

Roulon-Doko, P. *Chasse, cueillette et culture chez les Gbaya de Centrafrique* [Hunting, Gathering and Farming of the Gbaya People of Central Africa] Paris: L'Harmattan, collection anthropologique, 1998.

Tessmann, Gunter. *Die Baja, ein Negerstamm in mittleren Sudan* [The Baja, A Negro Tribe in Central Sudan]. Ergebnisse der 1913 vom Reichs Kolonialamt ausgesandten völkerkundlichen Forschungs Reise nach Kamerun. Ergebnisse der Expedition zu den Baya 1913–1914, 2 vols. Stuttgart: Struker and Schroder, 1934–1937.

Vidal, Pierre. *La civilisation megalithique de Bouar* [The Bouar Megalithic Civilization]. Paris: University of Paris X, 1967.

———. "Garçons et Filles, Le passage à l'âge d'homme chez les Gbaya Kara" [Boys and Girls: The Transition to Adulthood among the Gbaya Kara]. In *Recherches Oubanguiennes*, no. 4. Paris: Laboratoire d'ethnologie et de sociologie comparative, University of Paris X-Nanterre, 1976.

———. *Tazunu, Nana, Mode, Toala.* Bangui: University of Bangui, 1982.

Zeltner, J. C. "Notes relatives à l'histoire du Nord-Cameroun" [Notes on Northern Cameroon History]. *Etudes camerounaises* (Yaoundé) 3536 (1952): 5–18.

## 6. Deportation

Berlioux, Etienne. *La traite orientale. Histoire des chasses à l'homme organisées en Afrique depuis 15 ans pour les marchés de l'Orient* [The Oriental

Slave Trade. A History of the Man-hunts organized in Africa for the Past 15 Years for the Oriental Markets]. Paris: Guillemin, 1870.

Cordell, Dennis D. "Blood Partnership in Theory and Practice: The Expansion of Muslim Power in Daral-Kuti." *Journal of African History* 20 (1979): 379–394.

———. *Dar-al-Kuti: A History of the Slave Trade and State Formation on the Islamic Frontier in Northern Equatorial Africa.* Ph.D. diss., University of Wisconsin, 1977.

———. *Dar-al-Kuti and the Last Years of the Transsaharan Slave Trade.* Madison: University of Wisconsin, 1985.

———. "The Delicate Balance of Force and Flight: The End of Slavery in Eastern Ubangi-Shari." In *The Ending of Slavery in Africa*, edited by Suzanne Miers and Richard Roberts. Madison: University of Wisconsin Press, 1988, 150–171.

———. "Eastern Libya, Wadaï, and the Sanuslya: A Tariqa and a Trade Route." *Journal of African History* 18 (1977): 21–36.

———. "Extracting People from Precapitalist Production: French Equatorial Africa from the 1880s to the 1930s." In *African Population and Capitalism: Historical Perspectives*, edited by Dennis D. Cordell and Joel W. Gregory. Boulder, CO: Westview Press, 1987, 137–152.

———. "The Labor of Violence: Dar-al-Kuti in the Nineteenth Century." In *The Workers of African Trade*," edited by Catherine Coquery-Vidrovitch and Paul E. Lovejoy. Beverly Hills, CA: Sage Series on African Modernization and Development, 1985, 169–192.

———. "Throwing Knives in Equatorial Africa: A Distribution Study." *BaShiru* 5 (1973): 94–104.

———. "Warlords and Enslavement: A Sample of Slave-Raiders from Eastern Ubangi-Shari, 1870–1920." In *Africans in Bondage: Essays presented to Philip D. Curtin on the occasion of the 25th anniversary of the African Studies Program*, edited by Paul E. Lovejoy. Madison: African Studies Program and the University of Wisconsin Press, 1986, 335–365.

Deschamps, Hubert. *Histoire de la traite des Noirs* [History of the Black Slave Trade]. Paris: Fayard, 1972.

Escayrac de Lauture, Comte de. *Mémoire sur le Soudan* [A Memoir on Sudan]. Paris: Société de géographie de Paris, 1855–1856.

Franck, Louis. *Mémoire sur le commerce des Nègres au Kaire et sur les maladies auxquelles ils sont sujet en arrivant* [Memoir on the Trading of Negros in Cairo and about the diseases to which they are afflicted with upon arrival]. Paris and Strasbourg: Armand Koenig, 1802.

Fresnel. "Notice historique et geographique sur le Ouadau et les relations de cet empire avec la côte septentrionale de l'Afrique" [Historical and Geographical Memorandum on the Ouadau and the Relationships of this Empire with the Northern African Coast]. *Bulletin de la Société de géographie de Paris* 11, 3rd series (January-February 1849): 5–75.

Samarin, William J. *The Black Man's Burden*. Boulder, CO: Westview Press, 1989.

## V. SCRAMBLE FOR AFRICA (1880–1900)

Alis, Harry. *Nos Africains* [Our Africans]. Paris: Hachette, 1894.

Alis, Hypolithe Perchet (alias Harry Alis). *A la conquête du Tchad* [The Conquest of Chad]. Paris: Hachette 1891.

Augouard, Prosper. *Vingt-huit ans au Congo* [Twenty-Eight Years in Congo], 2 vols. Poitiers: Oudin, 1905.

Autin, Jean. *Pierre Savorgnan de Brazza: Un prophète du Tiers-Monde* [Pierre Savorgnan de Brazza: A Prophet for the Third-World]. Paris: Libraire Académique Perrin, 1986.

Baratier, Lt. Colonel. *Au Congo, Souvenirs de la mission Marchand* [In Congo, Memories of the Marchand Mission], vol. II. Paris: Fayard, 1912.

Blanchard M. "Français et Belges sur l'Oubangui (1890–1896)" [French and the Belgian on the Ubangui (1890–1896)]. *Revue française d'histoire d'Outre-Mer* (Paris) 37 (1950): 1–36.

Boulvert, Yves. *Exploration, creation d'un pays nouveau, découverte scientifique: le cas du Centrafrique de 1880 à 1919—Milieux et paysages* [Exploration, Creation of a New Country, Scientific Discovery: The Case of Central Africa from 1880 to 1919—Environment and Landscapes]. Paris: Masson, 1986.

——. *Onze notes sur la découverte scientifique de la Centrafrique* [Eleven Notes on the Scientific Discovery of Central Africa]. Bondy: ORSTOM, 1983.

——. *Le problème de l'Oubangui-Ouellé ou comment fut exploré et reconstitué un réseau hydrographique à la fin du XIX siècle* [The Ubangui-Ouellé Problem, or How a Hydrographic System was Explored and Reconstructed at the End of the 19th Century]. Paris: Cahiers ORSTOM, 1985.

——. *Un problème historico-géographique, l'interfleuve Congo-Nil* [A Historic and Geographic Problem, the Congo-Nile Interfluve]. Bondy: Office de la Recherche Scientifique et Technique Outre-Mer (ORSTOM), 1982.

——. *Le site de Bangui-Zongo* [The Bangui-Zongo Site]. Bondy: ORSTOM, 1983.

Brunschwig, Henri. *Mythes et réalités de l'imperialisme colonial français* [Myths and Realities of French Colonial Imperial], 1871–1914. Paris: Armand Colin, 1960.

Chavannes, Charles. *Les origines de l'Afrique équatoriale française* [The Origins of French Equatorial Africa], vol. I, *Avec Brazza. Souvenirs de la mis-*

*sion de l'Ouest africain* (March 1883–January 1886) [With Brazza, Memories from the Western African Mission]. Paris: Plon, 1935. Vol. II, *Le Congo français. Ma collaboration avec Brazza (1886–1894). Nos relations jusqu'à sa mort, 1905* [French Congo. My Collaboration with Brazza (1886–1894). Our Relationship until His Death]. 1905. Paris: Plon, 1937.

Coquery-Vidrovitch, Catherine. *Brazza et la prise de possession du Congo. La mission de l'Ouest africain (1883–1885)* [Brazza and Taking Power over the Congo, the Western African Mission (1883–1885)]. Paris: Mouton, 1974.

Courcel, Geoffroi de. *L'influence de la conférence de Berlin de 1885 sur le droit colonial international* [The Influence of the 1885 Berlin Conference on International Colonial Law]. Paris: Les Editions Internationales, 1936.

Decorse, J. *Du Congo au lac Tchad, la brousse telle qu'elle est, les gens tels qu'ils sont (Mission Chari, lac Tchad, 1902–1904)* [From the Congo to the Chad Lake, the Savannah as it is, the People as They Are (Shari-Chad Lake Mission, 1902–1904)]. Paris: Asselin et Houzeau 1906.

Dehérain, Henri. "La province française du Bahr el Ghazal" [The French Province of Bahr el Ghazal]. *Bulletin section de géographie, Ministère de l'Education nationale* (Paris) 51 (1936): 41–51.

Dujarric, Gaston. *L'Etat mahdiste du Soudan* [The Mahdist Sudanese State]. Paris: Maisoneuves, 1901.

———. *La vie du Sultan Rabah. Les Français au Tchad* [The Life of Sultan Rabah. The French in Chad]. Paris: André, 1902.

Dybowski, Jean. *La route du Tchad. De Loango au Chari* [The Chad Route, from Loango to the Shari]. Paris: Firmin-Didot, 1893,

Emily, J. M. *Mission Marchand. Journal de route* [The Marchand Mission Logbook]. Paris: Hachette, 1913.

Etienne, Eugene. *Son œuvre coloniale, algérienne et politique (1881–1896). Discours et écrits divers* [His Colonial, Algerian and Political Work (1881–1896). Speeches and Various Writings], 2 vols. Paris: Ernest Flammarion, 1907.

Ferry, Jules. *Discours et opinions* [Speeches and Opinions], 7 vols. Paris: Armand Colin, 1893–1898.

Ganiage, Jean. *L'expansion coloniale de la France sous la IIIe République* [French Colonial Expansion during the 3rd Republic]. Paris: Payot 1969.

Generet, Marie-Jeanne. *La question de l'Oubangui-mémoire* [The Ubangui Question]. Diss. in Philosophy and Literature, Catholic University of Louvain, 1962, mimeographed.

Gentil, Emile. *La chute de l'empire de Rabah* [The Fall of Rabah's Empire]. Paris: Hachette, 1902.

Johnston, H. H. *The Life and Work of a Great Traveller: G. Grenfell and the Congo*, 2 vols. London: Hutchinson, 1902.

Kalck, Pierre. "Actualité de Crampel" [Crampel Today]. *Comptes Rendues de séances à l'Académie des Sciences d'Outre-Mer* [Proceedings from Lectures at the Overseas Science Academy] 31, no. 3. (November 1971): 483–498.

——. "La question internationale de l'Oubangui" [The International Ubangui Question]. *Aujourd'hui l'Afrique* (Paris), nos. 31–32 (1986): 22–28.

——. "Mohamed es Senoussi (1850–1911)." In *Hommes et Destins* [Of Fate and Men]. Paris: Académie des Sciences d'Outre-Mer, 1975, 569–571.

——. "Paul Crampel (1864–1891)." In *Hommes et Destins* [Of Fate and Men]. Paris: Académie des Sciences d'Outre-Mer, 1975, 165–167.

——. "Paul Crampel, 80 Ans Après" [Paul Crampel, 80 years Since]. *Revue française d'histoire d'Outre-Mer* (Paris) 59, no. 214 (1972).

——. "Paul Crampel, le Centrafricain" [Paul Crampel, the Central African]. *L'Afrique Littéraire et Artistique* 2 (1971): 60–63.

——. "Paul Crampel, le centrafricain (1864–1891)" [Paul Crampel, the Central African (1864–1891)]. Paris: 1970, typescript.

——. "Rabah (1845–1900)." In *Hommes et Destins* [Of Fate and Men]. Paris: Académie des Sciences d'Outre-Mer, 1975, 495–497.

——. *Un Explorateur du centre de l'Afrique, Paul Crampel (1864–1891)* [An Explorer of the Center of Africa, Paul Crampel (1864–1891), Paris: L'Harmattan, collection Racines du Présent, 1993.

Leroy-Beaulieu, Paul. *De la colonisation chez les peuples modernes* [About Colonization among Modern Peoples]. Paris: Guillaumon, 1902.

Lotar, L. *La Grande chronique de l'Oubangui* [The Great Chronicle of the Ubangui]. Brussels: Institut Royal Colonial Belge Memoires (Section Sciences morales et politiques) VII, 1937.

——. *La grande chronique du Bomu* [The Great Chronicle of the Bomu]. Brussels: Institut Royal Colonial Belge Mémoires (Section sciences morales et politiques), 9, 1937.

——. *La grande chronique de l'Uélé* [The Great Chronicle of the Uele]. Brussels: Institut Royal Colonial Belge Memoires ( Section Sciences morales et politiques), 14, 1964.

Magnant, Stanislas. "Le poste de Bangui entre 1891 et 1893" [Bangui Post between 1891 and 1893]. *Journal Officiel Oubangui-Chari-Tchad* (Brazzaville), September 15, 1907.

Mazenot, Georges. *La Likouala-Mossaka. Histoire de la pénétration du haut Congo* [The Likouala-Mossaka. History of Penetration of the Upper Congo]. Paris: Mouton, 1971.

Mazieres, Anne Claude de. "Liotard et Marchand" [Liotard and Marchand]. *Cahier d'Etudes Africaines* (Paris) 6, no. 22 (1966): 268–307.

——. *La marche au Nil de Victor Liotard, 1891–1897* [The March to the Nile of Victor Liotard, 1891–1897)]. Aix en Provence: University of Provence, 1982.

Menier, M. A. "La marche au Tchad de 1887 à 1891" [The March to Chad from 1887 to 1891]. *Bulletin de l'Institut d'études centrafricaines* (Brazzaville) 5 (1953).

Meynier, General O. *Les conquerants du Tchad* [The Conquerers of Chad]. Paris: Flammarion, 1923.

Michel, Marc. *La Mission Marchand* [The Marchand Mission]. Paris: Mouton, 1972.

Moniot, Henri. "Rabih, Emir d'un empire mobile aux confins soudanais" [Rabih, Emir of a mobile Empire in the Sudanese Backcountry]. *Les Africains* 4, edited by Charles-André Julien. Paris: Editions, J. A., 1977.

Monteil, Louis-Parfait. *Souvenirs vécus, quelques feuillets de l'histoire coloniale. Les rivalites internationales* [Memories from Life, a Few Pages of Colonial History. International Competition]. Paris: Sociéte d'Editions géographiques, maritimes et coloniales, 1924.

Musy, Maurice. "Correspondance de M. Musy, chef de poste a Bangui" [The Correspondance of M. Musy, Bangui Station Chief]. *Revue de geographie de Drapeyron* 27 (1890): 375–381, 455–457; 28 (1891): 64–68, 160–166, 210–214, 377, 454–455, 462–466.

Prioul, Christian. "Entre Oubanbui et Chari vers 1890" [Between Ubangui and Shari around 1890]. Paris: *Recherches Oubanguiennes* no. 6, Laboratoire d'ethnologie et de sociologie comparative, University of Paris X-Nanterre, 1981.

Serre, Jacques. "Louis Mizon." In *Hommes et Destins* [Of Fate and Men], vol. 8. Paris: Académie des Sciences d'Outre-Mer, 1975, 290–295.

Slatin-Pacha, R. *Fer et Feu au Soudan* [Iron and Fire in the Sudan], 2 vols. Translated by G. Bettex. Cairo: Diemer, 1898; Paris: Flammarion, 1898.

Stengers, J. "Aux origines de Fachoda: la mission Monteil" [At the Origins of Fachoda: the Monteil Mission]. *Revue belge de philosophie et d'histoire* 36, no. 2 (1958): 436–450; 37, nos. 2 and 4 (1960): 365–404, 1040–1065.

———. "Leopold II et la fixation des frontières du Congo" [Leopold II and the Defining of the Borders of the Congo]. *Revue belge des questions politiques et litteraires* (1963).

Uzes, Duchesse d'. *Le voyage de mon fils au Congo* [My Son's Journey to the Congo]. Paris: Plon, 1894.

Vangele, Alphonse. "L'Exploration de l'Oubangui-Doua-Koyou" [Exploring the Ubangui-Doua-Koyou]. *Bulletin de la Sociéte royale coloniale belge* 13 (1889): 5–36.

Vignes, Kenneth. "Etudes sur les rivalités entre les puissances en Afrique équatoriale et occidentale depuis l'acte géneral de Berlin jusqu'au seuil du XXe siècle" [Study of the Rivalries between the Powers in Equatorial and Western Africa from the General Act of Berlin to the Threshhold of the 20th Century]. *Revue française d'histoire d'Outre-Mer* 48 (1961): 5–95.

——. "Etude sur les relations diplomatiques franco-britanniques qui conduisirent a la convention du 14 juin 1898" [A Study on the French and British Diplomatic Relations that Led to the 14 June 1898 Convention]. *Revue française d'histoire d'Outre-Mer* 52, nos. 188–189 (1967): 352–403.

Zuylen, Baron P. van. *L'échiquier congolais ou le secret du roi* [The Congo Chessboard or the King's Secret]. Brussels: Dessart, 1959.

## VI. COLONIAL EXPLOITATION (1900–1940)

Allegret, Marc. *Carnets du Congo, Voyage avec Gide* [The Congo Notebooks, Travels with Gide]. Introduction and note by Daniel Durosay. Paris: Presses du Centre National de la Recherche Scientifique (CNRS), 1987.

Aymerich, General. *La conquête du Cameroun 1 aout 1914–20 fevrier 1916* [The Conquest of Cameroon, 1 August 1914–20 February 1916]. Paris: Payot, 1933.

Banville, Reverend Father Ghislain de. *Les débuts de l'Eglise catholique en RCA* [The Beginnings of the Catholic Church in the CAR]. Bangui: Maison St. Charles, 1988 (typescript).

——. *En son temps, le Père Joseph Daigre* [Father Joseph Daigre in his own Time]. Bangui: Maison St. Charles, 1988 (typescript).

——. *Itinéraire d'un missionnaire: Le Père Marc Pedron* [A Missionary's Path: Father Marc Pedron]. Bangui: Maison St. Charles, 1989.

——. *Ouaka 1900–1920, Documents d'histoire* [Ouaka 1900–1920, Historical Documents]. Bambari: Centre culturel St. Jean, 1982.

——. *Sainte Famille de Banziris* [The Banziris Sacred Family]. Bangui: Maison St. Charles, 1986 (typescript).

——. *Saint Paul des Rapides, Histoire d'une fondation 1893–1905* [Saint Paul des Rapides, the History of a Foundation, 1893–1905]. Bambari: Centre culturel St. Jean, 1989.

Bouche, Denise. *Les villages de liberté en Afrique noire française* [The Freedom Villages in French Black Africa]. Paris: Mouton 1968.

Bregeon, Jean-Noël. *Un rêve d'Afrique, Administrateurs en Oubangui-Chari, la Cendrillon de l'Empire* [An African Dream, the Administrators in Ubangui-Shari, the Empire's Cinderella]. Collection Destins Croisés. Paris: Denoël, 1998, 329 pages.

Cantournet. *L'axe de ravitaillement du Tcahd entre 1900 et 1905—Route de vie, route de mort* [The Supply Route for Chad between 1900–1905—A Road for Life, A Road for Death]. Paris: L'Harmattan, 2001, 693 pages.

——. *Des Affaires et des Hommes. Noirs et Blancs, commerçants et fonctionnaires dans l'Oubangui du début du siècle* [Of Business and Men. Blacks and Whites, Businessmen and Civils Servants in Early 20th Century Ubangui]. *Recherches Oubanguiennes*, no. 10, Paris: Société d'ethnologie, 1991.

——. *Les massacres du Congo et l'affaire Gaud-Toqué (1900–1906)* [The Congo Massacres and the Gaud-Toqué Case (1900–1906)], 2 vols. Paris: Académie des Sciences d'Outre-Mer, 1986, typescript.

Challaye, Felicien. *Le Congo français, la question internationale du Congo* [French Congo, the International Congo Question]. Paris: Alcan, 1909.

Chevalier, Auguste. *L'Afrique centrale française. Récit du voyage de la mission* [French Central Africa. The Story of the Mission's Trip]. Paris: A. Challamel 1907.

Coquery-Vidrovitch, Catherine. *Le Congo français au temps des grandes compagnies concessionnaires (1898–1930)* [French Congo in the days of the Great Concessionary Companies (1898–1930)]. Ph.D. diss., Paris, Sorbonne, 1970.

Daigre. *Oubangui-Chari. Témoignage sur son évolution 1900–1940* [Ubangui-Shari, A Testimony on its Evolution 1900–1940]. Issoudin: Dilhin, 1947.

Denis, Commandant M. *Histoire militaire de l'Afrique équatoriale française* [Military History of French Equatorial Africa]. Paris: Imprimerie nationale, 1931.

Dennis, John Alfred. *The René Maran Story: The Life and Times of a Black Frenchman, Colonial Administrator, Novelist and Social Critic, 1887–1960.* Ph.D. diss., Stanford University, 1987.

Deverdun, René. *Oubangui-Chari, la création du poste de Gribingui, port d'attache du vapeur Léon Blot* [Ubangui-Shari, the Creation of the Gribingui Post, Home Port of the Steamer *Léon Blot*]. Documents regroupés [Collected Documents], 1897, Nancy, 1995.

Egonu, Iheanacho Tobias-George. *L'œuvre africaine de René Maran* [The African Work of René Maran]. Ph.D. diss., University of Alberta, 1978.

Etat-Major des Troupes [Army Headquarters] (Brazzaville). *Une étape de la conquête de l'AEF 1908–1912* [A Step in the Conquest of French Equatorial Africa]. Paris: Imprimerie-Librairie militaire universelle C. Fournier, 1912.

Gide, André. *Voyage au Congo—Carnets de route* [Travels in the Congo—Notebooks]. Paris: Gallimard, 1927.

——. *Retour au Tchad* [Back in Chad]. Paris: Gallimard, 1929.

Godart, Reverend Father Louis. *De l'Esclavage à la liberté* [From Slavery to Freedom]. Bangui: Foyer de Charité, 1987 (typescript).

——. *Nos pères en la foi* [Our Fathers in the Faith]. Bangui: Foyer de Charite, 1987, typescript.

Headrick, Rita. *The Impact of Colonialism on Health in French Equatorial Africa, 1880–1934.* Ph.D. diss., University of Chicago, 1987.

Hochschild, Adam. *King Leopold's Ghost: A story of greed, terror and heroism in Colonial Africa.* Traduction française par Marie-Claude Elsin et Frank Straschitz. Paris: Belfond, 1998, 448 pages.

Kalck, Pierre. *Félix Eboué, administrateur de brousse* [Felix Eboué, Administrator of the Brush]. In *Actes du Colloque Félix Eboué* [Proceedings from the Felix Eboué Colloquium]. Paris: Ecole Militaire, 1985.

Lenfant, Commandant. *La découverte des grandes sources du centre de l'Afrique* [The Discovery of the Major Sources in Central Africa]. Paris: Hachette, 1909.

Marchal, Jules, E. D. *Morel contre Léopold II, l'histoire du Congo 1900–1910* [Morel Against Leopold II, Congolese History 1900–1910]. Paris: L'Harmattan, 2 volumes.

Mberio, Albert et Vidal, Pierre, sous la direction de. *Bangui a cent ans* [Bangui Is a Hundred Years Old]. CURDHACA, Bangui, 1992.

Mollion, Pierre. *Le portage en Oubangui Chari, 1890–1930* [Porterage in Ubangui-Shari 1890–1930]. Ph.D. diss., University of Provence, 1982.

Nzabakomada-Yakoma, Raphael. *L'Afrique centrale insurgée: La guerre du Kongo Wara, 1928–1931* [The Central African Uprising: The Kongo Wara War, 1928–1931]. Paris: L'Harmattan 1983.

O'Toole, Thomas. *Kongo Wara—The War of the Hoe Handle: A Central African Protest Movement, 1928–1931*. Paper presented at the annual Meeting of African Studies Association, Bloomington, Indiana, 1981, typescript.

———. "The 1928–1931 Gbaya Insurrection in Ubangui-Shari: Messianic Movement or Village Self-Defense?" *Canadian Journal of African Studies* 18, no. 7 (1984): 329–344.

Perraud, Reverend Father Isidore. "L'Eglise Catholique en Afrique Occidentale et Centrale—Répertoire des missions catholiques" [The Catholic Church in Western and Central Africa—A Catholic Missions Directory]. In *Catholic Church in West Africa* (English edition). Nantes: Editions missionaires, 1989.

Psichari, Ernest. *Terre de soleil et de sommeil (1907–1908)* [Land of Sun and Sleep]. Paris: Calmann-Levy, 1911.

Romeuf, Jean. *Vues sur l'économie de l'Oubangui-Chari* [Considerations on the Ubangui-Shari Economy]. Paris: Publications économiques et sociales, 1958.

Tardieu, André. *Le mystère d'Agadir* [The Agadir Mystery]. Paris: Calmann Levy, 1912.

Thomas, Jacqueline. *Les Ngbaka de la Lobaye. Le dépeuplement rural chez une population forèstiere de la République centrafricaine* [The Ngbaka People of Lobaya. The Rural Depopulation of a Forest People in the Central African Republic]. Paris: Editions Mouton, 1963.

Toqué, Georges. *Les massacres du Congo. La terre qui ment, la terre qui tue* [The Congo Massacres. The Land that Lies, the Land that Kills]. Paris: Librairie mondiale, 1907.

Toso, R. P. Carlo O. F. M. cap. *Centrafrique, un siècle d'évangélisation* [Central Africa, A Century of Evangelization]. Bangui: Conférence épiscopale centrafricaine, 1994, 589 pages.

Vidal, Pierre. "Bangui: histoire de l'origine et du developpement d'une ville" [Bangui: History of the Origin and Development of a City]. Wam Bessa: Revue d'histoire et d'archéologie centrafricaine [Central African History and Archeology Review]. Special centennial edition no.1. Bangui: University of Bangui, 1989, 12–28.

Violette, Maurice. *A la veille d'Agadir. La Ngoko-Sangha* [On the Eve of Agadir, the Ngoko-Sangha]. Paris: Larose, 1914.

Weinstein, Brian. *Eboué*. New York: Oxford University Press, 1972.

## VII. COLONIZATION AND DECOLONIZATION (1940–1960)

Adamby, Alpha Nationy Zentho. "Barthélémy Boganda ou l'abbé Gregoire de l'Afrique coloniale" [Barthélémy Boganda, or the Abbé Grégoire of Colonial Africa]. *Revue juridique et politique. Indépendance et coopération* [Political and Legal Review, Independence and Cooperation] 44 (January–March 1990): 60–65.

L'Ancre d'or-Bazeilles: *Bulletin de liaison des troupes de marine et des anciens d'Outre-Mer* [Liaison Bulletin of the Navy Forces and the Overseas Veterans], no. 247. Paris: French Ministry of Defense, 1988.

Anguile et David. *L'Afrique sans frontières* [Africa without Borders]. Monaco: Bory, 1965.

Ballard, J. A. "Four Equatorial States." In *National Unity and Regionalism in Eight African States*, edited by Gwendolyn Carter. Ithaca, NY: Cornell University Press, 1966, 231–235.

Decraene, Philippe. "Barthélémy Boganda, ou du projet d'Etat unitaire à celui d'Etats Unis de l'Afrique latine" [Barthélémy Boganda, or from the Project of one United State to that of the United States of Latin Africa]. *Relations Internationales* (Paris), no. 34 (1983).

———. "Les Etats Unis de l'Afrique latine" [The United States of Latin Africa]. In *L'Afrique et l'Asie moderne*, no. 161. Paris: CHEAM, 1989.

Dreux-Brézé, Joachim de. *Le problème du regroupement en Afrique équatoriale* [The Problem of Regrouping in Equatorial Africa]. Paris: Librairie générale de droit et de jurisprudence, 1968.

Gosselin, Gabriel. *Travail et changement social en pays gbeya (RCA)* [Work and Social Changes in Gbeya Country (CAR)]. Paris: C. Klincksieck, 1972.

Homet, Marcel. *Congo, terre de souffrances* [Congo, Land of Suffering]. Paris: Fernand Aubier, Montaigne, 1934.

Kalck, Pierre. *Barthélémy Boganda, élu de Dieu et des Centrafricains* [Barthélémy Boganda, Elected of God and of the Central African People]. Paris: Sepia, 1995, 219 pages.

——. *Barthélémy Boganda, le prêtre, le tribun, le père de la nation* [Barthélémy Boganda, the Priest, the Politician, the Nation's Founding Father]. Colloque du 30ème anniversaire de la mort de Boganda [Colloquium on the 30th anniversary of the death of Boganda], Paris, 1989

——. "Barthélémy Boganda, tribun et visionnaire de l'Afrique centrale" [Barthélémy Boganda, A Visionary Politician and Orator for Central Africa]. In *Les Africains*, edited by Charles André Julien et al. Paris: Editions Jeune Afrique, 1977, 105–137.

——. *Les possibilités du développement économique et social de l'Oubangui-Chari* [The Possibilities of Economic and Social Development of Ubangui-Shari]. Doctoral diss. in law, Faculté de droit et des sciences économiques de Paris, 1958.

——. *Réalités Oubanguiennes* [Ubangui Realities]. Preface by Barthélémy Boganda. Paris: Berger Levrault, 1959.

Kouroudoussou, Goukané. *La Justice indigène en Oubangui-Chari* [Native Justice in Ubangui-Shari]. Thesis, University of Aix-en-Provence, 1986.

Lebeuf, J. P. *Bangui (Oubangui-Chari, AEF)* [Bangui (Ubangui-Shari, French Equatorial Africa)]. Paris: Encyclopédie maritime et coloniale, 1951.

Lenormand, Jacques, and Jean-Pierre. *L'or et le diamant en France metropolitaine et dans l'union française* [Gold and Diamonds in Metropolitan France and in the French Union]. Paris: Société d'édition et de publicité, 1952.

L'Huillier Jean. *Le café dans la colonie française de l'Oubangui-Chari* [Coffee in the French Colony of Ubangui-Shari]. Paris: Imprimerie Humbert, 1933.

Londres Albert. *Terre d'ébène, la traite des noirs* [Ebony Land, Slave Trading]. Paris: Albin Michel, 1929.

Mangin General Charles. *Souvenirs d'Afrique* [African Memories]. Vol. 2: *Tournée d'inspection au Congo* [Congo Inspection Tour]. 1908. Paris: Denoel et Steel, 1936.

Maran, Rene. *Batouala*. Paris: Albin Michel, 1921.

Mbokolo, Elikia. "French Colonial Policy in Equatorial Africa in the 1940s and 1950s," in *The Transfer of Power in Africa*, edited by Prosser Gifford and W. Roger Louis. New Haven, CT: Yale University Press, 1971.

Michel, Marc. "Les débuts du soulèvement de la haute Sangha en 1928" [The Beginnings of the Uprising in Upper-Sangha in 1928]. *Annales du Centre d'enseignement supérieur de Brazzaville* 2 (1966): 33–49.

Mollion, Pierre, and Pierre Soumille. "Le ralliement de Bangui à la France Libre" [How Bangui Joined Free France]. *Ultramarines* (Aix-en-Provence) 3 (July 1991): 3–18.

Nzabakomada-Yakoma, Raphael. *La guerre du Kongo-Wara (1928–1931), un chapitre de la résistance anti-coloniale en Afrique équatoriale* [The Kongo-

Wara War (1928–1931), A Chapter in the Anti-Colonial Resistance in Equatorial Africa]. Doctoral diss. in history, University of Paris VII, 1974–1975, typescript.

——. "Karnou, prophète de l'indépendance en Afrique centrale" [Karnou, Prophet of the Independence of Central Africa]. *Jeune Afrique* 4, no. 48 (1977): 231–248.

O'Toole, Thomas. "Barthélémy Boganda." In *Biographical Dictionary of Modern Peace Leaders*, edited by Harold Josephson. Westport, CT: Greenwood Press, 1987, 90–92.

Pénel, Jean-Dominique. *Barthélémy Boganda: Ecrits et discours* [Barthélémy Boganda: Writings and Speeches], 5 vols. Bangui: University of Bangui, 1982, published by L'Harmattan, Paris, typescript.

Sanmarco, Louis. *Souvenirs et témoignages personnels sur Boganda* [Memories and Personal Testimonies on Boganda]. *Colloque du 30ème anniversaire de la mort de Boganda* [Colloquium on the 30th anniversary of the death of Boganda]. Paris, 1989.

Sautter, Gilles. *Un projet colonial sans lendemain: le chemin de fer Bangui-Tchad (AEF)* [An Unsuccessful Colonial Project: The Bangui-Chad Railway in French Equatorial Africa]. Report of 1959, published by Claude Arditi, with a preface, EHESS, Centre d'Etudes Africaines, Paris, 1999.

Serre, Jacques. "Le ralliement de l'Oubangui au général De Gaulle" [How the Ubangui Joined General de Gaulle]. *Mondes et Cultures Académie des Sciences d'Outre-Mer* (Paris) 2, 3, 4, (1989): 573–592.

Sicé, Medecin-general. *L'AEF et le Cameroun au service de la France* [French Equatorial Africa and Cameroon Serving France]. Paris: Masson, 1946.

Soriano, Raymond. *Histoire du bataillon de marche no. 2 de l'Oubangui-Chari* [The Story of the 2nd Infantry Battalion of Ubangui-Shari]. Beirut: Librairie catholique, 1942.

Soumille, Pierre. "De la fédération aéfienne à la naissance d'Etats-Nations en Afrique Centrale de 1940 à 1960 ou l'échec du projet unitaire de Boganda" [From the French Equatorial African Federation to the Birth of National States in Central Africa from 1940 to 1960, or the Failure of Boganda's Project of Unification]. In *Historiens et Géographes*. Paris: n.p., 1999, 225–238.

Terive J. D. "Analyse d'un coup d'état" [Analysis of a coup d'etat]. *France-Eurafrique* 171 (1966): 3–8.

Teulieres, Lt. Colonel André. "Oubangui et France libre" [Ubangui and Free France]. *Revue française d'Etudes politiques africaines*, no. 117 (September 1975).

Thiebaut, Jean Marie. *Mémorial du Souvenir français: Bangui 1889–1989* [A French Memorial: Bangui 1889–1989]. Bangui: 1989.

## VIII. CENTRAL AFRICAN REPUBLIC, CENTRAL AFRICAN EMPIRE, AND CENTRAL AFRICAN REPUBLIC (SINCE 1979)

Adolph, David Harold. *Agricultural Mechanization in the Central African Republic Using Renewable Fuels*. D.Sc. Dissertation, University of Washington, 1985.

Adoum-Pickanda, Fidel. *L'impact des relations franco-centrafricaines sur la politique extérieure à la Centrafrique. De l'independance à la chute de l'Empire (1960–1979)* [The Impact of French-Central African Relations on the Foreign Policy of Central Africa. From Independence to the Fall of the Empire (1960–1979)]. Ph.D. diss., University of Haute Bretagne, 1987, typescript.

Alexakis, Vassilis. *Les mots étrangers* [Foreign Words]. Paris: Plon, 2002.

Ammi-Oz, Moshe. "Le prononciamento du chef d'Etat centrafricain" [The Coup d'etat of the Central African Head of State]. *Revue française d'études politiques africaines* 149 (1978): 45–61.

Ato, Benoit-Faustin. *Péripéties des décisions en milieu rural centrafricain* [Difficulties in Decision-Making in Rural Central Africa]. Ph.D. diss., University of Poitiers, 1981, typescript.

Baccard André. *Les martyrs de Bokassa* [The Martyrs of Bokassa]. Paris: Le Seuil, 1987.

Barril, Paul. *Missions très spéciales* [Very Special Missions]. Paris: Presses de la Cité, 1984.

———. *Guerres secrètes de l'Elysée* [The Secret Wars in the Presidency]. Paris: Albin Michel, 1996.

Benot, Yves. *Idéologie des indépendances africaines* [Ideology of the African Independences], 2 vols. Paris: Maspero, 1969.

Biarnes, Pierre. "Centrafrique. Bokassa, empereur" [Central Africa. Bokassa, Emperor]. In *L'Afrique aux Africains* [Africa for the Africans], edited by Pierre Biarnes. Paris: Armand Colin, 1980, 329–397.

Bigo, Didier. *Approche pour une théorie du pouvoir personnel, un exemple privilégié: La Centrafrique* [An Approach to a Theory of Individual Power, a Special Example: Central Africa]. Paris: Etudes polémologiques, 1985.

———. *Forme d'exercice du pouvoir et obéissance en Centrafrique (1966–1979). Eléments pour une théorie du pouvoir personnel* [How One Rules and Obeys in Central Africa (1966–1979). Elements for a Theory of Individual Power]. Paris: UER de Sciences politiques, 1985.

———. *Le titre imperial comme légitimation d'une dictature. L'exemple centrafricain* [The Imperial Title as a Justification of Dictatorship. The Central African Example]. Diss. in Political Studies, University of Paris I, 1979, typescript.

———. *Power and obedience in Central Africa*. Paris: Karthala, 1980.

Boulvert, Yves. "Le Centrafrique au seuil du 3ème millénaire. Essai synthé-tique de géographie physique, économique et humaine" [Central Africa on the Eve of the 3rd Millennium. A Synthetic Essay in Physical, Economic and Social Geography]. In *La Géographie*, no. 1506 (no. 131). Paris: Société de Géographie, août 2002, 46–67.

———. "Centrafrique, l'horrible année" [Central Africa, the Horrible Year]. *Le Nouvel Afrique-Asie* (Paris), no. 148 (January 2002): 12–13.

———. "Centrafrique—Pourquoi Bozizé a joué son va-tout" [Central Africa—Why Did Bozizé Risk It All]. *Jeune Afrique L'Intelligent* (Paris), no. 2131 (13–18 November 2001).

Bouquiaux, Luc. *Dictionnaire Sango-Français, Bakari Sango Faranzi et Lex-ique Français-Sango*, *Kete Bakari, Faranzi Sango* [French-Sango Dictio-nary, Bakari Sango Faranzi and French-Sango Lexicon, *Kete Bakari, Faranzi Sango*. (Note: *Faranzi* is Sango for "French," *Bakari* means "dictionary," and *Kete Bakar*—literally, small dictionary—means "lexicon.")]. Paris: So-ciété d'Etudes linguistiques et anthropologiques de France, 1978.

Breton, Jean Marie. "L'acte constitutionnel du 21 septembre 1979 et l'organi-sation des pouvoirs publics en République Centrafricaine" [The 21st Sep-tember 1979 Constitution and the Organization of the Civil Service in Cen-tral African Republic]. *Revue juridique et politique. Independance et Coopération* 2 (1980): 555–563.

———. "La constitution du 1 fevrier 1981 et la tentative de rénovation des in-stitutions politiques en Republique Centrafricaine" [The 1st February 1981 Constitution and the Attempt at Renewing the Political Institutions in the Central African Republic]. *Revue juridique et politique. Indépendance et Coopération* 4 (October–December 1981): 867–882.

Bussieres, André. *La RCA sans Boganda* [The Central African Republic with-out Boganda]. Paris: Centre des hautes études sur l'Afrique et l'Asie mod-ernes, 1963, typescript.

Chapuis Jean-Louis. *Les mouvements de service civique en Afrique noire fran-cophone, l'exemple centrafricain. Armée, jeunesse et développement* [Civil Service Movements in French-Speaking Black Africa, the Central African Example. The Army, Youth and Development]. University of Paris I, Unité d'Etudes et de Recherches de Sciences politiques, 1972, typescript.

Chierici, M. *L'imperatore* [The Emperor]. Milan: Rizzoli, 1980.

Collectif Tiers Monde. *De l'Empire centrafricain à la République cen-trafricaine ou de Bokassa 1 à Dacko 2* [From the Central African Empire to the Central African Republic, or from Bokassa 1 to Dacko 2]. Poitiers, 2nd trimestre 1980.

"Constitution de la République Centrafricaine" [Central African Constitution]. *Afrique Contemporaine* (Paris), no. 175 (1995): 61–79.

Covi, Bernard. "Paranoïa à Bangui" [Paranoia in Bangui]. *Le Nouvel Afrique-Asie* (Paris), no. 137 (February 2001): 14–15.

Debato, Pierre. "Procès du Siècle: Coupable, Bokassa est condamné à mort et s'est pourvu en cassation" [The Trial of the century: Guilty, Bokassa is sentenced to death and files for an appeal]. *E Le Songo: Quotidien d'information* (Bangui), Numero spécial (1987).

Decalo, Samuel. "Jean-Bedel Bokassa, 'Emperor' of the Central African Republic." In *Psychoses of Power: African Dictatorships*. Boulder, CO: Westview Press, 1985, 129–178.

Delpey, Roger. *Affaires Centrafricaines* [Central African Business]. Paris: Jacques Grancher, 1987.

——. *La manipulation* [Manipulation]. Paris: Jacques Grancher, 1981.

——. *Prisonnier de Giscard* [Giscard's Prisoner]. Paris: Jacques Grancher, 1982.

Duchemin, Jacques. *L'empereur, récit* [The Emperor, a Story]. Paris: Albin Michel, 1981.

Dumont, René. *Le difficile développement agricole de la République Centrafricaine* [The Difficult Agricultural Development of the Central African Republic]. Paris: Annales de l'Institut National Agronomique, vol. 6, 1966.

Durieux, Evelyn. *Princesse aux pieds nus* [The Barefoot Princess]. Paris: Cerf-Michel Lafon, 1992.

——. *Le bonheur était ailleurs* [Happiness Was Elsewhere]. Paris: Michel Lafont, 1995.

*Empire Centrafricain. Congrès extraordinaire du MESAN tenu a Bangui du 10 novembre au 4 décembre 1976* [Central African Empire. Extraordinary Congress of the MESAN held in Bangui from 10 November to 4 December 1976]. Bangui: Imprimerie Centrafricaine, 1975.

*Empire Centrafricain. Ordonnances, décrets, arrêtés et décisions imperiaux* [Central African Empire. Edicts, Decrees, Rulings and Imperial Decisions]. Bangui: Imprimerie Centrafricaine, 1977.

Endjimoungou, Patrice. *Evolution psycho-sociologique de la femme centrafricaine: l'élite future?* [Psycho-sociological Evolution of the Central African Woman: A Future Elite?]. Ph.D. diss., Ecole Pratique des Hautes Etudes, Paris 1975.

Ettangondop, Mbu. *Regional Integration in Africa: A Case Study of the Central African Customs and Economic Union (UDEAC)*. Ph.D. diss., Howard University, 1985.

Faës, Géraldine. "Bokassa et son empire fantôme" [Bokassa and His Ghost Empire]. *Jeune Afrique*, no. 1734 (31 March–6 April 1996): 26–31.

Fédération Internationale des Droits de l'Homme [International Federation of Human Rights]. Rapport. Document Hors-Série de la Lettre Mensuelle de la F.I.D.H. *Droits de l'Homme en République Centrafricaine. Discours et Réal-*

*ités, un fossé béant* [Special Report on Human Rights in the Central African Republic. What Is Said and What Is Done, the Huge Gap]. Paris: Fédération Internationale des Droits de l'Homme, 2002.

Gallo, Thiery-Jaques. *N'Garagba, maison des morts—Un prisonnier sous Bokassa* [Ngaragba, the House of the Dead—A Prisoner under Bokassa]. Paris: L'Harmattan, Collection Mémoires Africaines, 1988.

Germain, Emmanuel. *La Centrafrique et Bokassa 1965–1979* [Central Africa and Bokassa]. Paris: L'Harmattan, collection Etudes Africaines, 2002, 286 pages.

"Giscard, la monarchie contrariée" [Giscard, a Monarchy Stymied]. In *Le Canard enchaîné/Dossiers du Canard*, Paris: 1981.

Goyemidé, Etienne. *Le silence de la forêt—Film documentaire sur les Pygmés de Centrafrique* [The Silence of the Forest—A Documentary Film about the Central African Pygmies]. Presented at the Cannes International Film Festival, 2003.

Gueret, Franpois. *La formation de l'unité nationale en Republique Centrafricaine* [Building National Unity in the Central African Republic]. Diss. in law and political studies, Paris, 1970, typescript.

Guille-Escuret, Georges. "Palmier à huile, vin de palme et transformation sociale en Lobaye (Forêt Centrafricaine)" [Oil Palms, Palm Wine and Social Transformations in Lobaye (Central African Forest)]. *Information sur les sciences sociales* 29 (1990): 327–353.

Hewlett, Barry Steven. *The Father-Infant Relationship among Aka Pygmy*. Ph.D. diss., University of California, Santa Barbara, 1987.

Hewlett, Barry Steven, et al. *Exploration Ranges of Aka Pygmy of the Central African Republic*. Man n.s. 17 (1983): 418–430.

Iddi Lala, Rodolphe. *Contribution à l'étude de l'évolution socio-politique en République Centrafricaine* [Contribution to the Study of the Social and Political Evolution in Central Africa]. Thesis in sociology, University of Paris X, 1971, mimeographed.

Kabylo, Jean Pierre. "Les droits de l'homme dans les entreprises centrafricaines" [Human Rights in Central African Companies]. *Revue juridique et politique. Indépendance et Coopération*, nos. 3–4 (July–October 1989): 414–425.

Kalck, Pierre. *République Centrafricaine, Encyclopédie politique et constitutionnelle* [Central African Republic, Political and Constitutional Encyclopedia]. Paris: Institut International d'Administration Publique and Berger Levrault, 1971.

———. "République Centrafricaine—Entre les décombres et le redressement" [Central African Republic, Between Ruble and Reconstruction]. In *Le Monde diplomatique*, August 1982.

———. "La sociéte centrafricaine après trois quarts de siècle de contacts avec l'Occident" [The Central African Society after Half a Century of Contact with the West]. *Revue juridique et politique. Indépendance et Coopération* 35, no. 2 (June 1981): 629–646.

———. "Triste histoire tropicale" [A Sad Tropical Story]. *Cultures et developpement* 15, no. 4 (1985): 727–742.

Keller, F. *L'administration publique centrafricaine* [Central African Public Administration]. Ph.D., University of Paris I, 1981, typescript.

Kpatindé, Francis. "Monsieur Propre est arrivé" [Mister Clean Has Arrived]. *Jeune Afrique—L'Intelligent* (Paris), no. 2203 (30 March–5 April 2003): 21–23.

Kromash, Neil. *Swimming Upstream, External Dependance and Political Change.* University of Washington, Independent Research Paper, May 4, 1998.

Laeba, Oscar. "La crise Centrafricaine de l'été 2001" [The Summer 2001 Central African Political Crisis]. *Politique Africaine* (Paris), no. 84, Editions Karthala (December 2001): 163–175.

Lafarge, M. *Enquête démographique en RCA* [Demographic Inquiry in the CAR]. Paris: Institut National de la Statistique et des Etudes Economiques (INSEE), 1960.

Leclerq, Claude. "La constitution de la République Centrafricaine du 21 novembre 1986" [The Central African Republic's Constitution of 21 November 1986]. *Revue juridique et politique. Indépendance et Coopération* (October–December 1987): 290–298.

Lemarchand, Rene. "Quelles indépendances?" [Which Independence?]. *Revue française d'Etudes politiques africaines* (February–March 1983).

*Ligue Centrafricaine des Droits de l'Homme. Centrafrique 1999. Situation des Droits de l'Homme. Rapport annuel 1999* [Central African Human Rights League. Central Africa 1999. Human Rights Situation. Annual Report 1999]. Bangui, 1999.

Liman, Zyad. "L'empereur et le journal" [The Emperor and the Newspaper]. *Jeune Afrique* (Paris), (31 March–5 April 1994): 31.

*Livre d'Or de la République Centrafricaine* [The Central African Republic's Visitor's Book]. Paris: Editions de l'Afrique nouvelle, 1969.

Loubat, Bernard. *L'ogre de Berengo* [The Berengo Ogre]. Paris: Hachette, 1980.

Mahlers, Andreas. *Central African Republic.* In *Elections in Africa—A Data Handbook*, edited by Dista Nothen, Michaël Krennerish, and Bornhard Thibaut. Oxford: Oxford University Press.

———. "Meuterei der Armes und Tribalisierung von Politik in der 'demokratisierten Neukolonie' Zentralafrikanisches Republik (ZAR)" [Army Mutinies and the Tribalization of Politics in the "Democratized Neocolony" of Central Africa]. In *Unvollendete Demokratisierung in Nichtmarktökonomien*, edited by H. Zinacker. Amsterdam: Facultas, 193–211.

——. "Präsidentschaft und Parlementswahlen in der Zentralafrikanisher Republik" [Presidencial and Legislative Elections in the Central African Republic] (2.8/19.9.1993). In *Wahlbeobachtung in Africa: Erfahrungen Deutschen Wahlbeobachten, Analysen und Lehren für die Zukunft* [Monitoring Elections in Africa: Experiences of German Elections Observers, Analysing and Learning for the Future] (Arbeiten aus IAK, Bd 90), edited by U. Engel, R. Hofmerer, D. Kohndert, and A. Mehler. Hamburg, Institut fur Afrika-Kunde, 195–209.

*Marchés Tropicaux et Méditerranéens.* Spécial Centrafrique, no. 2940 (15 March 2002): 554–590.

Martin, M. L. *L'armée et le pouvoir politique en Afrique noire* [The Army and Political Power in Black Africa]. Thesis, University of Bordeaux, 1972, typescript.

Mbeko, M. H. *Régimes issus des coups d'état militaires et transition démocratique en Afrique noire: le cas de la République Centrafricaine* [Regimes Springing from Military Coups d'Etats and Democratic Transitions in Black Africa: The Case of the Central African Republic]. Ph.D. diss., University of Laval, 1993.

Ndiaye, Rachid. "L'affaire Jean-Jacques Demafouth" [The Jean-Jacques Demafouth Case]. *Africa International*, no. 347 (October 2001): 18–21.

Ngoupandé, Jean-Paul. *Chronique de la crise Centrafricaine 1996–1997. Le syndrome Barracuda* [Chronicle of the 1996–1997 Central African Crisis. The Barracuda Syndrome]. Paris: L'Harmattan, 1999.

——. *L'Afrique face à l'Islam* [Africa and Islam]. Paris: Albin Michel, 2003.

Nozati, Françoise. *Les Pana de Centrafrique, une chefferie sacrée* [The Pana People in Central Africa: A Sacred Chiefdom]. Paris: L'Harmattan, collection Etudes Africaines, 2002, 334 pages.

Nwago, Jean-Baptiste. *L'économie Centrafricaine* [Central African Economy]. Paris: L'Harmattan, collection Etudes Africaines, 2002.

Onana, Charles. *Ascension et chute d'un empereur 1921–1996* [The Rise and Fall of an Emperor 1921–1996]. Paris: éditions Duboirris, novembre 1998, et Organisation panafricaine des journalistes indépendants, Paris: Lon Yes Production.

O'Toole, Thomas. "Jean-Bedel Bokassa: Neo-Napoleon or Traditional African Ruler?" In *The Cult of Power: Dictators in the Twentieth Century*, edited by Joseph Held. New York: Columbia University Press, 1983, 95–106.

——. "'Made in France': The Second Central African Republic." In *Proceedings of the Sixth and Seventh Annual Meetings of the French Colonial Historical Society 1980–1981*, edited by James J. Cooke. Washington, DC: University Press of America, 1982, 136–146.

——. "Shantytowns in Bangui, Central African Republic: A Cause for Despair or a Creative Possibility?" In *Slum and Squatter Settlement in Sub-Saharan*

*Africa: Toward a Planning Strategy*, edited by R. A. Obudho and C. C. Mhlanga. New York: Praeger, 1988, 123–132.

———. "Understanding Contemporary Central African Society." *Bulletin of the Southern Association of Africanists* 8 (June 1980): 11–17.

"Ange-Felix Patassé et Lansana Conté, deux calamités pour le plus grand malheur de leurs populations" [Ange-Felix Patassé and Lansana Conté, Two Disasters for the Greater Unhappyness of their Populations]. *L'Autre Afrique*, no. 8 (20 November 2001).

Paye, Denis. "Facteurs Socio-Economiques de l'insuffiance du développement en Afrique, l'exemple de la RCA" [Social and Economic Factors of Insufficient Development in Africa, the Example of the CAR]. *Revue française d'Etudes politiques africaines* (April–May 1985): 68–99.

Péan, Pierre. *Bokassa Ier* [Bokassa I]. Paris: Alain Moreau, 1977.

Peleket, Jean-Bosco. *Les Yakomas et la RCA, repères d'une histoire vraie* [The Central African Yakoma People, Guidelines to a True Story]. www.sangonet.com.

Perrin, Joseph. *Prêtre blanc en Afrique noire* [A White Priest in Black Africa]. Paris: Nouvelles editions Mame, 1980.

*Philosophie de l'opération Bokassa: Mythe et realité de l'opération Bokassa* [Philosophy of the Bokassa Operation: Myths and Truths of the Bokassa Operation], vol. 1. Paris: Firmin Didot, 1973.

*Philosophie de l'opération Bokassa: Opération Bokassa et développement* [Philosophy of the Bokassa Operation: The Bokassa Operation and the Development Issue], vol. 2. Paris: Firmin Didot, 1975.

Prioul, Christian. "L'industrie et le commerce en Republique Centrafricaine" [Industry and Trade in the Central African Republic]. *Les cahiers d'Outremer* 88 (October–December 1969): 408–429.

——— "Le Rôle des Relations Familiales entre Bangui et les Villages Centrafricains" [The Role of Family Relations between Bangui and the Central African Villages]. *Canadian Journal of African Studies* 5 (1971): 61–78.

"Le procès Bokassa devant le Cour Suprême Centrafricaine-Texte de l'arrêt de la Cour suprême, section judiciaire, rendu le 14 novembre 1987. Rapport du président de cette haute juridiction et conclusions de l'Avocat général" [The Bokassa Trial before the Central African Supreme Court—Text of the Supreme Court's Findings, Judiciary Section, Made Public on 14 november 1987. Including the Court's President and the Attorney General's Conclusions]. *Revue juridique et politique. Indépendance et Coopération* 42 (January-February 1988): 1–28.

*Profil République Centrafricaine. Courrier International* (Bruxelles), no. 177, (October–November 1999).

Raynal, Jean Jacques. "La Constitution Centrafricaine du 28 novembre 1986" [The Central African Constitution of 28 November 1986]. *Penant, Revue de droit des pays d'Outre-Mer* 798 (October–December 1988): 475–482.

——. *Les institutions politiques centrafricaines* [The Political Institutions of Central Africa]. Bangui: Ecole Nationale d'Administration et de la Magistrature, 1982, mimeographed.

"Retour à la dictature—Correspondance particulière de Bangui" [Back to Dictatorship—Letters from Bangui]. In *Afrique-Asie* (20 July–20 Aug., 1981), 27–28.

Rougeaux, Jean-Pierre. *Le parti unique en Republique Centrafricaine: le MESAN* [The One Party System in the Central African Republic, the MESAN]. Graduate paper, University of Paris, 1968, mimeographed.

Sammy-Macfoy, Pierre. *De l'Oubangui à la Rochelle, 18 juin 1940–18 juin 1945 ou le parcours d'un bataillon de marche* [From Ubangui to La Rochelle, 18 June 1940–18 June 1945, or the Journey of an Infantry Battalion], Paris: L'Harmattan, 2003.

——. *Mongou, fils de Bandia* [Mongou, Son of Bandia]. Paris: Armand Colin, 1970.

——. *L'odyssée de Mongou* [Mongou's Odyssey]. Paris: Hatier, ACTT, 1985.

——. *Les illusions de Mongou* [Mongou's Illusions]. Saint-Maur: Sépia, 2002.

Sanmarco, Louis. *Le colonisateur colonise. Souvenirs d'un gouverneur de la France d'Outre Mer* [The Colonizer Colonizes. Memories of a Governor in Overseas France]. Paris: P. M. Favre, 1983.

Sempéré, Jean-François. "ISTOM—Le Centrafrique, Un pays à la dérive" [Central Africa, A Country Adrift]. *Marchés Tropicaux et Méditerranéens* (22 June 2001): 1278–1281.

Serre, Jacques. "Six ans de gouvernement Dacko (1960–1966)" [Six Years of Dacko Government (1960–1966)]. *Revue française d'études politiques africaines* (Paris) 117 (1975): 73–104.

*Service international d'organisations pour un développement solidaire* [International Service for Solidarity in Development]. *Développement solidaire—Republique Centrafricaine* [Solidarity of Development in the Central African Republic]. *Cahier d'information du Centre International*. Le Rocheton. La Rochette: Melun, 1982, typescript.

Seurin, Jean-Louis. "Les régimes militaires" [Military Regimes]. *Pouvoirs* 25 (1983): 89–105.

Skard, Torild. "Rendons à Elisabeth (Domitien)" [Tribute to Elisabeth Domitien]. *Jeune Afrique—L'Intelligent*, no. 2108 (5–11 June).

Soudan, François. "Qui a voulu tuer Patassé?" [Who Tried to Kill Patassé?] *Jeune Afrique—L'Intelligent*, no. 2121 (4–10 September 2001).

Thompson, V., and Adloff, R. *The Emerging States of French Equatorial Africa*. Stanford, CA: Stanford University Press, 1960.

Thorin, Valérie. "La Chute de l'Ange" [The Fall of the Angel]. *Jeune Afrique—L'Intelligent*, no. 2202 (23–29 March 2003): 19–21.

Vidaud, Pierre. "Une condamnation du colonialisme et du gouvernement français" [Condemning Colonialism and the French Government]. *Cahiers du communisme* (November 11, 1979).

*Vie du Président M. Ange-Félix Patassé, Biographie officielle* [The Life of President Ange-Félix Patassé—Official Biography]. Bangui: SERAD (Webmaster: Franck Salvador), 2002.

Yangongo, Barthélémy. *La succession d'états en matiere de biens et dettes publics en Afrique equatoriale* [State Succession in Matters of Goods and Public Debts in Equatorial Africa]. Doctoral diss. in law, University Jean-Bedel Bokassa, Bangui, 1976.

Zanga, Antoine. "Quinze ans de destabilisation en Centrafrique. De l'action humanitaire au dangereux précédent" [Fifteen Years of Distabilization in Central Africa—From Humanitarian Action to Dangerous Precedents]. *Le Monde Diplomatique* (April 1980): 16.

Zecchini, Laurent. "Les militaires a l'épreuve de la rigueur" [The Military and Retrenchment]. *Le Monde*, November 30, 1984, special supplement, 13.

Zimmer, Klaus. "Zentralafrikanische Republik" [Central African Republic]. In *Die Wahl der Parlamente und anderer Staatsorgane* [Elections for Parliament and Other State Bodies], vol. II, *Afrika Politische Organisation und Reprasentation in Africa* [African Political Organization and African Representation], edited by Rainer Buren et al. Berlin: Walter de Gruyter, 1978, 2441–2474.

# About the Author

**Pierre Kalck** was born in Nancy on 19 December 1924. He studied at the Nancy University of Law and Lettres and then at the Louis le Grand Lycée in Paris. He joined the Free French and in the summer of 1944 took part in the liberation of the Lorraine region. A graduate administrator of the National French Overseas School, he was assigned to Maevatanana in Madagascar as head of district, then he was on assignment for the Finance Department of the Administration Services at Tananarive, from 1946 to 1948. Sent to Ubangui-Shari, he was at the head of the Yalinga-Ouadda district from 1949 to 1951. From 1951 to 1953, he worked for the Madagascar and Joint Territories Department of the French Ministry for Overseas Policy in Paris. Back in Ubangui-Shari in 1953, he was attached to the Social and Political Affairs Bureau in the colony, before he was assigned to Boda as head of district until 1956. From 1956 to 1958, he was the assistant of the Paris delegate at the High Commission of the Republic in French Equatorial Africa. In 1958, in Bangui, he was Dr. Abel Goumba's cabinet director when the latter was president of the Governing Council of Ubangui-Shari as well as finance and planning minister.

In February 1959, President Barthélémy Boganda chose him to be his representative to the president of the Community. After the death of Boganda, Kalck was assigned to the Industrial and Mining Bureau, then joined the civil courts as the French government's commissioner in Châlons-en-Champagne until 1962. At that time, he was assigned to the Central African Government as economic adviser at its Paris embassy, in which position he served until 1967. The Central African government chose him as its representative to the General Agreement on Tariffs and Trade (GATT) conference and the Economic and Social Council of the United Nations (ECOSOC) in Geneva. From 1967 to 1972 he was again on the staff of the civil court, as a government commissioner to the tribunals in Amiens, a city where he also taught civil law. In 1973, attached to the prefect of Lorraine, he was designated by the prime minister as director of the Regional Administration Institute of Metz, where civil servants are trained. He also taught for ten years the history of intertropical Africa at the Paris International Administration Institute, as well as civil law at the Metz University and at the Metz regional institutes and at Bastia. He presides over the boards of the Regional Administration Institutes of Strasbourg and Dijon, and taught at the Nancy Institute of Political Studies. In 1983 he was president of the civil court in Rouen, then in 1987 was section president of the civil court in Paris. As of 1990, he was section president at the Refugees High Commission's court of appeal. In February 1994, he was appointed international observer of the legislative elections in Togo by the minister for cooperation.

With a doctorate in Law, Economics, Letters and Social Sciences, Pierre Kalck was an officer of the Legion of Honour and held several foreign honorary distinctions, including the Grand Comore and the Mérite Centrafricain. He has received the Lucien de Reinach Award from the Political and Moral Sciences Academy for his book *Réalités Oubanguiennes*, and the Overseas Science Academy, of which he had been a member since 1973, gave him the George Bruel award for his book, *Histoire Centrafricaine des origines à nos jours*. He was also a member of the Metz National Academy. Pierre Kalck died on 12 February 2004, just before completion of the manuscript for this book.

# About the Translator

**Xavier-Samuel Kalck** was born on 23 August 1977. He is the grandson of the author of this book. He is French, and is currently involved in writing a thesis on contemporary American and English poetry at the Sorbonne University in Paris. He has previously worked on several other translations, and is in the process of editing a book of selected poems of a British poet. Along with this work, he is involved in independent filmmaking.

Working on this book gave him the opportunity to become much more familiar with the history and people of the country with which his family has always felt a close connection, and where his father spent his own childhood.

The history told here finds an adequate metaphor in the history of the manuscript for this book: it is not past but passed on.